A

MANUAL OF PHOTOGRAPHY.

A

MANUAL

OF

PHOTOGRAPHY:

INTENDED AS A

TEXT BOOK FOR BEGINNERS AND A BOOK OF REFERENCE
FOR ADVANCED PHOTOGRAPHERS.

BY

M. CAREY LEA.

PHILADELPHIA:
BENERMAN & WILSON.
1868.

PHILADELPHIA:
COLLINS, PRINTER, 705 JAYNE STREET.

PREFACE.

It is intended that this manual shall serve both as an introduction to Photography for the beginner, and afford a useful book of reference to those already versed in the subject.

Therefore, in the first part will be found brief and simple instructions, intended to enable the beginner to obtain a quick and thorough grasp of the subject. All those details which, although of great value to the already skilled photographer, would only confuse the student, have been thrown into the subsequent parts of the volume. The advantage of this arrangement seemed so great that it was deemed best to adopt it, although it was difficult to avoid occasional repetition in referring a second time to the subjects already treated of in the Introduction.

To compress all that it was desirable to say upon a subject now so extended into the compass assigned to this volume, was found extremely difficult. The writer hopes, however, that no serious deficiencies will be found.

CONTENTS.

PART I.

INTRODUCTION TO PHOTOGRAPHY.

PART II.

PHOTOGRAPHIC OPTICS AND THEORY OF PERSPECTIVE.

PART III.

PHOTOGRAPHIC MANIPULATIONS.

PART IV.

THEORETICAL CONSIDERATIONS.

PART V.

A MANUAL OF PHOTOGRAPHY.

PART I.

INTRODUCTION TO PHOTOGRAPHY.

CHAPTER I.

SELECTION OF MATERIALS.

§ 1.—Selection of Photographic Lenses.

THE first step of the beginner must be to provide himself with the necessary materials for his work; and the choice of his lenses will have much to do with his success. Unless he works with good lenses, his results can never be satisfactory. And further, they must not only be good, but must be such as are suited to the work which he intends to do.

Such a thing as a universal lens does not exist. One combination is best for one purpose, another for another.

For landscapes the *single view lens* is the best, that is, it gives more brilliant images than any other. But it has two defects. First, it includes but a small extent of view. This has been remedied by Dallmeyer in his wide angle view lenses, which include a considerable sweep. Secondly, the view lens gives curved lines, that is, lines that are straight in nature are rendered by the view lens slightly curved. So long as there are no architectural objects in the view, this is unimportant, but if such are to be included, then a doublet or triplet must be used. The triplet form of lens is an excellent one for many purposes. It cannot, however, be made to include as large an angle of view as the doublet.

The doublet lens exists in very many forms, a description of the most important of which will be found further on. Here may be cited, only very briefly, the Globe lens, the Zentmayer, the Dallmeyer ("rectilinear"), the Ross doublet, the Steinheil, &c.

Of these the globe has been a great favorite with many in this country and elsewhere. I have never shared this opinion, and cannot recommend the lens for any purpose except copying, which it does excellently. Zentmayer's lens gives admirable representations of architectural subjects. Some of the best architectural views made in this country have been executed with it. It works with too small a stop to be very useful for landscape work. Ross's doublets have been very highly spoken of by good judges, as also Dallmeyer's rectilinear lenses. Both of these include a very large angle, with perfectly straight lines. They are well suited for architectural work.

For landscape work, then, the photographer will prefer the single view lens and the Dallmeyer triplet, using, when he wants a wide angle, Dallmeyer's "wide-angle" lenses. It may be useful to remark that the additional angle which these last lenses include is accompanied with the disadvantage that (at least to the writer's experience) they curve the lines more than the common form of view lens. Jamin's (now Darlot's) view lenses are very good, and of extraordinary cheapness. The amateur of small means who wishes to take views cannot do better than begin with one or two of them.

For portraiture there is but the one form useful, the Petzval objective, commonly known as the "portrait combination," except when groups are wanted to be taken, and where the triplet is proper. Steinheil's new "aplanatic" may also be employed for groups. The portrait combination, though indispensable for portraits, has its utility limited to that one object. If applied to any other purpose whatever, it gives results inferior to those of the other lenses suited for that other work.

For copying engravings, plans, maps, &c., any form of lens may be used in which the stop is between the front and back lens, except the portrait combination.

To assist, as far as possible, those who may be desirous of accomplishing a variety of work with a limited stock of lenses, it may be said that the lens that comes nearest to being universal is a well-made triplet. It gives excellent views, takes architectural pictures, copies well, and does well for groups, but for portraits it is slow. And as in portraiture it is desirable to require the sitter to sit as little time as possible, this objection is serious.

Jamin makes portrait lenses of which one lens unscrews, and may be used as a single view lens. This is a good arrangement, and the lenses, though not always first-rate, can be well recommended, and are very inexpensive. The same maker now makes a so-called "universal" lens, in which a number of separate lenses can be variously combined.

The orthoscopic lens is a good deal used in Germany, and very good ones were at one time made by Harrison, in New York. This lens copies exceedingly well, and in Germany is much liked for views, but has never become popular elsewhere for that purpose, its pictures having generally a flat effect, and wanting relief. In this respect the large lenses of this sort are generally more objectionable than the small.

Further details will be found in Part II., Chap. V.

A few words of general advice may be usefully given here to the beginner.

Do not make the mistake of beginning with views too small or too large. The smaller the pictures are, the more easily they are taken in *every* respect; difficulty increases vastly with the dimensions. On the other hand, small prints are apt to be too trifling and insignificant to repay for the trouble expended upon them. Therefore the beginner will do well to start with "half size" plates, and go from that to whole size, after becoming perfectly familiar with all the manipulations. Eventually he will probably prefer to advance to 8 × 10 and perhaps larger work. Generally speaking, the most artistic effects are got with 8 × 10 and 10 × 12 plates. Larger prints are apt to be less pleasing, however technically perfect. It is no advantage whatever to have a lens embrace a very wide angle, except, indeed, where architectural objects have to be taken in positions where the photographer cannot recede beyond a certain point. An angle of 50° to 60° is generally best.

Lenses should be kept with the greatest care—never wiped with anything except clean soft chamois leather or soft old linen cambric, and even with these *only when necessary*. The exquisite polish on the surface is of the highest importance, and it is easily injured.

Do not begin by buying second-hand lenses, but go to responsible dealers and purchase the work of makers of reputation.

Always use as small a lens for views as will cover satisfactorily the plate. Do not make the mistake of buying, for example, a lens for whole size plates, when you expect to work principally half size, under the impression that the lens will do for occasional use on whole size plates, and for habitual work on half size. So it will; but it will not, for the most part, give as pleasing a picture on the half size plate as the lens made for that size of plate. This is especially to be observed with lenses that cover a small angle. There is less objection to using a wide angle lens for a smaller plate than that for which it is intended, than in the case of a common view lens or a triplet.

All makers, even the best, will occasionally, through inadvertence, send out bad lenses. And careless makers will now and then accidentally produce very good ones.

In choosing amongst a number of lenses by the same maker, view a piece of perfectly white paper through the lens, holding the latter close to it. If the appearance shows that the glass of which the lens is made has any color, especially if that color be brownish, the lens should be rejected: it may be expected to be slow. So, too, if, when carefully examined by reflected light, it shows any striæ, or hair-like lines. Very small bubbles, or white spots, if not exceeding one or two, are unimportant, and often occur in excellent lenses, though, of course, they are better absent.

These brief remarks are perhaps as much as the beginner can advantageously act upon. Other points will be explained later.

§ 2.—**Selection of Camera.**

Without a thoroughly good camera, or box, no first-rate work can be done, and the beginner cannot make a greater mistake than that of purchasing a cheap one. Any camera that is not thoroughly good is absolutely worthless.

A camera is to be tested as follows:—

1. Observe if all the wood-work is sharply cut and closely fitted.

2. Try the rack and pinion movement, to notice that it works easily and regularly, and not by jerks.

3. Rack the back forwards until all the bellows body is closed in; then continue to rack up till the back wood-work just comes into contact with the front. Observe attentively if this contact takes place everywhere at once—top, sides, and corners. If it does not, the camera is worthless, for the sensitive plate will in such a case not occupy a position perpendicular to the optical axis of the instrument.

4. These points having all been found satisfactory, it remains to ascertain whether the sensitive plate, when in place, occupies the exact position of the focussing screen of ground glass.

This is the most essential point of all, and is precisely that in which cameras, even of good makers, are apt to be defective. The fault, if it exists, is easily detected with a little attention.

Take a piece of plate glass of the size which the dark slide is intended to carry, set it in place, close the door, set the slide on the table, door undermost, and draw out the shutter. Lay across the middle of it a perfectly flat and rigid ruler, a draughtsman's straight edge, or a long, thick, narrow piece of plate glass. Take a piece of smooth hard card, rest one end of it on the plate glass, pressing the side close up to the ruler, and with a sharp hard pencil draw a hair-line where the card touches the ruler. Next repeat this exactly with the focussing slide, ground side of the glass uppermost. If the camera is well made, the two hair-lines will exactly coincide to make but one. If they do not, the camera will require to be fitted over again by the maker. Care and attention are necessary to make this trial effectual, but it is essential to make it with every new camera.

Fig. 1.

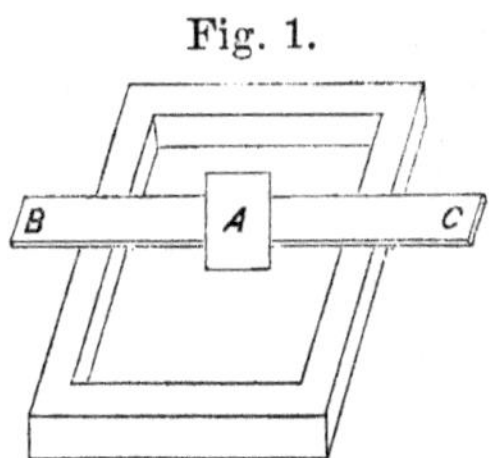

The bottom of the card *A* rests on the glass, the side rests against the ruler *B C*, and the pencil line is drawn where the edge *B C* touches the card *A*.

An absolute coincidence of the two lines must be insisted on. At the same time, the experimenter must be sure that he is doing the measuring correctly, and not producing an apparent discordance by careless manipulation.

§ 3.—Selection of Stand.

For out-door work, a folding tripod is employed. For in-door work many forms are in use. Those in which the table is supported by a single cylindrical stem are very objectionable, for want of steadiness. The most absolute steadiness is requisite, and a large proportion of the stands in the market fail to fulfil this requirement. A stand cannot be judged if almost unloaded. Place a heavy camera on it, strike it a gentle blow, and observe if any vibration follows.

§ 4.—**Selection of Chemicals.**

Few photographers have sufficient chemical knowledge to be able to apply tests of purity to their chemicals. Perhaps the very best advice that can be given to a beginner is to observe who amongst his friends is most regularly and completely successful, and then to obtain materials from the same place. In fact, the demands of photography are now so enormous, that good materials can be obtained almost anywhere. The substance most likely to give trouble, in the hands of a learner, is nitrate of silver. This last should always be purchased prepared expressly for photography—never from the druggist. Without the best and purest neutral nitrate, the negative bath cannot be expected to work well.

§ 5.—**Selection of Glass for Negatives.**

Of all matters connected with photography, this is that which is most habitually overlooked.

Plate glass has some evident advantages over blown. Its surface is a true plane; the material of which it is made is generally whiter, and it is free from blebs and other faults and irregularities. On the other hand, it has been asserted lately that the artificial surface of the plate glass, produced by polishing, does not hold the collodion and varnish so well after a lapse of years as the natural surface of the blown, and that with time the film is more apt to crack and suffer.

In consequence of the high price of plate glass in America, blown glass is almost exclusively used. But in this blown glass there is great variety of quality.

1. Some is much *greener* than other. A strong green color tends to considerably lengthen the time required for printing from the negative: this is always an objection.

2. Glass varies greatly in *thickness*. It is a great advantage

to have stout glass; the loss from breakage of negatives in the printing-frames is less, and the operator may venture to apply a strong pressure in his frames where his glass is strong: he thereby gets a sharper and cleaner print.

3. Blown glass varies extremely in *curvature.* Much of it is very flat; much, again, greatly curved. All that is not very nearly flat should be rejected.

To give some idea of the amount of curvature allowable, place a straight edge so that the two ends of the piece of glass shall touch it, and observe what distance the middle of the plate is from the straight edge. It may be said that where this distance exceeds $\frac{1}{16}$ of an inch in a plate of $6\frac{1}{2} \times 8\frac{1}{2}$, it should be rejected as unfit for photographic purposes. Because, first, the centre of the plate will not coincide with the position of the focussing screen. An error not exceeding $\frac{1}{16}$ of an inch is to some extent corrected by the pressure of the spring in the dark slide (the plate must *invariably* be collodionized on the concave or hollow face), and the error is thereby reduced. Secondly, glass that has any, but a very slight, curvature, runs a much greater risk of breaking in the printing-frame.

CHAPTER II.

MAKING THE NEGATIVE.

§ 1.—Absolute Cleanliness.

All photographic work depends upon the delicate turning of nicely-balanced affinities, which a slight alteration of the conditions may completely reverse. It is necessary, therefore, that the operator should not only follow closely the directions given, but that he should learn to constantly maintain a perfect cleanliness.

All the vessels which he uses must be irreproachably clean; and, as far as practicable, each should be restricted to some particular use, so that if slight vestiges of substances escape the attention, such may be less hurtful. The hands, especially, must be constantly washed; there is no way in which small portions of material are so readily transferred as by adhesion to the fingers.

In all these respects too much precaution cannot be taken, and many failures, perfectly unaccountable to the beginner, may be traced to trifling neglects of this sort.

§ 2.—Preparing the Glass.

Unless the glass be *perfectly* clean, a regular development cannot be hoped for. Perhaps the best method of cleaning glass is one introduced into photography by the writer a few years since, and which has since been extensively used.

Provide a large glass pan, into which make a mixture in the following proportions:—

Bichromate of potash	1 ounce.
Sulphuric acid	1 fluidounce.
Water	15 fluidounces.

Place the pieces of glass in the pan alternately, one at each end, so that their sides shall overlap a little, and allow the free passage of fluid between them. Pour on the above mixture. For new glass a day will be sufficient to destroy the greasiness. Old glass that has been used before, especially if it has been varnished, will require two to three days, or a mixture containing only half the above proportion of water.

So long as this bath is yellowish-brown, it is active. When it acquires a violet color, it is spent, and will want renewing.

After soaking in this bath the glasses will require no washing, but should be placed in a trough or other convenient vessel under a tap of water for ten or fifteen minutes. Then take them out one by one, *let the water run a few moments on each side*, and then rub dry with soft blotting-paper—*not* with cotton rags, as so universally directed. Cloths always leave fluff, which has to be carefully brushed away afterwards—paper does not.

It is necessary to roughen the edges of the glass with a coarse file. The film is less likely to slip off, and the hands are less apt to be cut. A coarse file is to be drawn two or three times along each edge; of course, it is only needful to do this on the edges of the concave or hollow side, as this is the one which invariably receives the collodion. The roughing should precede the cleaning. After cleaning the glass must be handled as little as possible; its face must *never* be touched by a finger, or there will probably be a finger mark developed on the negative. Clean glass should be rolled up in clean paper, and set in a box kept out of the reach of dust and vapors.

Nitric acid may be used for cleaning, or caustic alkali; but the above is not only the easiest and most economical, but is perhaps the only one with which an old picture never reappears on the development of a new one.

§ 3.—The Negative Bath.

Of all that the photographer works with, nothing exceeds in importance the negative bath. Its preparation is exceedingly easy, and, if thoroughly good nitrate of silver be used, it cannot fail to work well, if no mistake or oversight has been made in its preparation.

A vertical glass bath is to be procured; there is none other which is perfectly safe. In a porcelain bath, if there is the slightest flaw in the glazing inside, the solution will penetrate it, and gradually saturate the whole of the porous biscuit which makes the body of the vessel, between the inside and outside glazing. This not only involves a great loss of expensive silver solution, but after a time the outside glazing also probably cracks, and some day the operator finds his bath empty. In many cases porcelain baths last for years, but there is never a certainty about them, as there is with glass. The "photographic ware" has been much complained of in the same way.

A "whole-size" bath, for plates $6\frac{1}{2} \times 8\frac{1}{2}$, will be found a convenient one for the beginner, as, even if much smaller plates are worked with, it is not worth while to use a smaller bath—it holds too little solution and changes too rapidly. The "whole-size" baths require about 25 ounces of solution to charge them. This solution is to be made as follows:—

Dissolve 2 ounces of nitrate of silver in 25 ounces of water, which need not be distilled water. Leave the solution in a glass bottle in the sunlight for several hours, or in cloudy weather for a day or two near a southerly window. Separate this into two equal portions. Take 3 grains of iodide of potassium or iodide of ammonium, dissolve it in a few drops of water, and pour it into one of the halves; stir up well and let stand one-half an hour, or longer. Filter the *other half* into a clean bottle, and then filter into it the second half, that to which the iodide of potassium was added.

Observe: The two portions are not to be mixed until *after* they are filtered, and the portion to which the iodide was added is to be filtered *last*, if the same filter be used for both.

Next, take a clean six-ounce stoppered vial; place in it one fluidrachm of pure nitric acid, fill it up with water, and label it "Dilute nitric acid, ten minims to the ounce." To the twenty-five ounce bath add one fluidrachm of this dilute acid. This will probably be enough; but if the bath gives a foggy picture, you may add another fluidrachm, remembering, however, that *the less nitric acid added, the more sensitive your plates will be.* In summer more acid will be required than in winter to get clean plates and keep off fog.

The negative bath should always be kept covered to exclude dust and dirt. Constant care must be taken to let no extraneous matter get into it, and to place it in nothing, and nothing in it, that is not *perfectly* clean.

§ 4.—The Developer.

Make the developer as follows:—

Proto-sulphate of iron	450	grains.
Acetic acid, No. 8	1½	ounce.
Alcohol	1½	"
Water	20	ounces.

The developer, if kept corked, will keep for a couple of months. It is ready for use as soon as the solution of the sulphate of iron is complete and the whole has been filtered. As it grows older it becomes reddish, but so long as kept clear by filtration, the reddening is rather beneficial than otherwise.

§ 5.—Collodionizing the Plate.

Holding the clean glass plate by pressing a finger or two of each hand at the *edges* of the plate (the fingers must *never* touch the face), hold it up to the light, and look along the long edge to see which is the hollow or concave side, as that is invariably the one which is to receive the collodion. Next brush it off with a broad soft camel's hair brush, which must be kept clean and free from dust, and be used for no other purpose.

Hold the plate in your left hand, three fingers supporting it underneath, your thumb pressing on the corner, and the narrow end towards you. It is a good plan to fold up a piece of blotting paper, and put it between the bottom of the plate and the finger ends. For want of this there will occasionally appear curious mottled markings at the points where the fingers touch the under side.

Take the collodion bottle in your right hand, having previously removed the cork and wiped the lip to remove dust or fragments of dried collodion. (*Never* neglect this.)

Fig. 2.

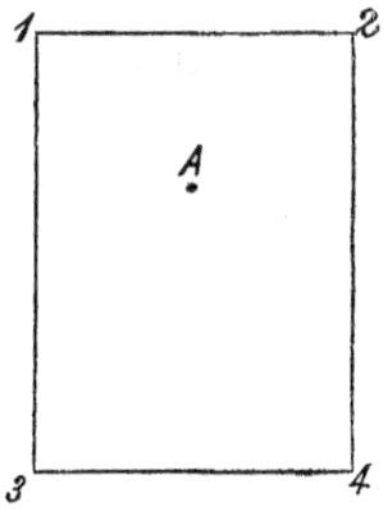

Hold at 3, pour on at *A*, and off at 4.

Pour the collodion slowly and steadily on, letting it come upon the plate at a spot a little further from you than the middle—say equidistant from the end and the two sides. Pour on till the pool covers rather less than half the plate.

Incline the plate so that the pool may extend itself to corner No. 1, then to corner No. 2, next to corner No. 3, where the thumb is, and then to No. 4, at which you pour off the excess.

This is all to be done quite coolly, and yet without loss of time. The collodion must go up *full* to the edge of the plate all round, and with a little practice this is accomplished with great ease and without spilling a drop.

It is best not to pour back the collodion into the bottle from which it came, but have a separate bottle ready, uncorked.

The operation of pouring off requires the operator's best attention. The plate must be slanted but very little, otherwise the collodion runs off too fast, and leaves too thin a film, especially at corner No. 1. At the same time the operator *rocks the plate*, that is, turns it backwards and forwards, one quarter round, without changing the inclination. If this be neglected, the film will be full of *crapy lines*. If the plate be properly rocked, it will dry as smooth as the glass itself.

I have endeavored here to give as clear a description of the method of collodionizing a plate as possible; at the same time it is unquestionably one of those manipulations which it is almost necessary to see done, in order to execute properly one's self.

I do not give here any formula for making collodion. I strenuously advise the beginner to introduce no unnecessary difficulty by such attempts, but to procure a reliable collodion from some professional photographer or trustworthy dealer. When he has mastered the manipulations, he may advantageously make his own collodion, for which a number of good formulas will be given further on. The nitrate bath, the developer, and the fixing solution, on the other hand, every one must learn to prepare for himself from the outset.

§ 6.—**Sensitizing.**

The collodion coating quickly sets—in half a minute or less in summer, whilst a minute may be necessary in winter. Its condition is commonly judged of by gently touching it near corner No. 4 with the tip of the finger; if the film does not wet the finger, but receives a slight depression from it, which remains after the finger is removed, it is called "tacky," and is now ready for immersion in the bath. Up to this time the rocking motion is to be steadily continued, pausing only for a second, if necessary, to ascertain the condition of the film. When this has attained the proper state of setting, the plate is to be rested upon the dipper firmly and steadily. The operator next lowers the dipper, carrying the plate with it, into the bath, by a gentle, continuous, and uninterrupted motion. For if he pauses for any fraction of time, however short, the part of the film which at that moment corresponded with the surface of the bath will show a distinct line, ruining the negative. No unnecessary delay should occur in putting the plate in the bath, or the risk of marbled stains is increased.

Dippers are made of porcelain, glass, and gutta-percha. If glass ones could be got of a right pattern, they would be preferable, but made of rods they are too fragile. The porcelain are good and the gutta-percha also, provided they are well made, and consist wholly of gutta-percha, without any metallic support in the centre. The porcelain dipper may rest in the bath when not in use; the gutta-percha dipper must never be left in the bath. The beginner is advised to use the porcelain.

The plate having been placed in the bath will be left quiet for a couple of minutes, and then must be moved up and down from time to time; and a side motion is also beneficial, especially if the plates show a tendency to form lines in the direction of the dip, a trouble of which much complaint has been made by some photographers, though it has never been experienced by the writer. Until the plate has been in some minutes it should not be raised in moving so as to be partly uncovered by the silver solution.

The *time* requisite for stay in the bath cannot be fixed in minutes with any positiveness, as it depends somewhat on the temperature, the nature of the collodion, and the condition of the bath. From three to five minutes is about the time. The plate is ready when, on withdrawing from the bath, no oily lines form on the surface, but the whole face presents a uniform moist film. The plate should never be left longer than necessary in the bath, as by so doing the film tends to dissolve, thus choking the bath with excess of iodide, and rendering the plate irregular. Worse still, there is a great tendency in such plates to give flat and dull images, at least in collodion containing bromides.

The plate is now to be removed from the bath and rested on several thicknesses of soft blotting-paper, changing its position every few seconds, until it no longer wets the paper. A thorough draining in this way is very important, and cannot be neglected without danger of streaks and other irregular action. At the same time the back of the plate is to be carefully wiped dry with soft paper. It is a very good plan to keep ready pieces of thick soft red blotting paper, half an inch smaller than the plate all round; and after it has been wiped clean to apply one of these pieces moist, but not too wet, to the back. This precaution, though recommendable, has not yet come into general employment. Its use is to diminish internal reflections, as will be more fully explained hereafter.

In all these operations the face of the plate must never be touched by the fingers, and with the same precaution the plate is to be lifted and gently set into its place in the dark slide, taking care that the shutter is in its place. The door is then closed.

From the time that the plate is lifted from the bath the same edge must carefully be kept undermost; that is, the side which went undermost into the bath must be kept undermost—must be that which rests on the blotting-paper—must be kept undermost in the transfer to the dark slide, and the slide with its plate in it must be carefully kept with that edge downwards, not only during exposure, but in carrying backwards and forwards and up to the moment of development. This *is essential;* neglect of it will almost certainly result in streaky lines and irregular deposits along the outside of the plate, running up in places some distance into the plate. If the small size of the bath renders it necessary to set the plate in *end* down, when the *side* is to be down in the slide, the plate must be turned *immediately* on taking it from the bath, and the draining and blotting done whilst it is in the same position which it is to have in the slide.

Particular descriptions of the dark room and glass room must be omitted for the present. Here it is sufficient to say that all the operations of sensitizing and developing must be performed by yellow light. A very simple way of converting an ordinary room into a dark room for photographic work consists in procuring some of the very thickest and stoutest brown paper made for envelopes, and pasting pieces of it over the panes of the window; a great deal of light will come through this, sufficient for all the operations, and yet, if the paper be good and thick and of fine grain and quality, there will be no danger of fogging. If, however, the sun shines directly, at times of the day, upon the window, it will be well to have a buff curtain on rollers inside the window, so that when the light is too strong it may be properly tempered.

If the room used as a dark room has two windows, it will be found preferable to cover the panes of one only, and to have closely fitting inside shutters to the other, over the joints of which black muslin must be pasted or tacked. In this way the room may be lighted at any moment, and may serve for other uses than merely as a dark room.

However the dark room be arranged, *provision must be made for its thorough ventilation*, the fumes of collodion being exceedingly depressing to the nervous system, and tending to undermine the health. This subject will be recurred to hereafter; it should never be lost sight of by the photographer who values his health.

§ 7.—**Focussing.**

If the photographer has not done his focussing beforehand, he may do it while his plate is in the bath, and should never, if possible, delay it until the plate is in the slide and waiting. As a general thing, the less time that elapses between the placing of the plate in the dark slide and the taking it out to develop, the greater will be the chance of a good negative.

Throwing an ample black cloth over the camera, and placing his head beneath it, the photographer proceeds to take his focus. Few persons have unassisted sight so sharp as to enable them to take a thoroughly good focus, although a delusion to the contrary is very wide-spread. It is always better to examine the image on the ground glass through a microscope, as a better focus can be got more quickly, and with less strain upon the eyes. The microscope should consist of two lenses in the same cylinder, *at least* an inch in diameter. The difference of fatigue to the eyes in using large and small lenses is enormous. A magnifier, with lenses of one and a half to two inches in diameter is the best; its expense is small, as it is not absolutely necessary that the lenses should be achromatized. The little doublets used by engravers are good, and larger ones can be got of any optician of the same pattern. The writer does not advise the system of focussing on clear glass with an adjusted eye-piece.

The operator is not to take his focus on any point of the picture indifferently, but according to the following rules:—

In taking a single portrait, focus on the face as the most important point.

In taking two heads equidistant from the centre, focus on either head, not on any more central object.

In taking a group, focus on one of the heads occupying a position midway between the centre and the extremity of the group.

In focussing a landscape, focus *on the foreground* at a point midway between the centre and the edge of the plate.

These directions are important, and cannot be disregarded with impunity. Careless focussing is almost the worst fault that a photographer can have, and will counteract every care or precaution that he can take in other parts of the process.

§ 8.—**Exposure.**

The time of exposure for a wet plate may vary from a fraction of a second to half an hour.

With a portrait combination, medium stop, and good light, from five to fifteen seconds, or even more, may be required. With landscapes, taken by a view or a triplet lens and medium stop, from ten seconds up to several minutes may be given, according to the light. With a bright light, and by having the chemicals in exact order, a picture may be got in a fraction of a second with a short focus lens, using a large stop. The operator, however, will do well to leave instantaneous photography until he succeeds regularly and without difficulty in ordinary exposures.

The slide should always be set into the camera steadily and gently, not with a jerk or snap, lest any dust be set in motion and settle on the sensitized plate, the result of which will be seen in *comets* or *pin-holes.*

§ 9.—Development and Redevelopment.

The operator brings back his dark slide, without loss of time, to the dark room, never forgetting for an instant to keep that part of the slide down which was lowest in the camera, and in all previous stages. Holding the slide with the left-hand edge in his left hand, he opens the door with his right, places his thumb on the upper edge of the plate with the fingers touching it lower down, and, by inclining the slide a little backwards, brings out the plate. This is now transferred to the left hand, always keeping the lower edge downwards. He now turns the plate up nearly to a horizontal position; a proper quantity of the developer (about an ounce for a whole-sized plate, or, for a beginner, a little more) has previously been placed in a suitable vessel—Fig. 3 represents a good shape; this the operator takes in his right hand, and, holding it a little inclined, and at the upper edge of the plate near the left hand, pours out the liquid, at the same time drawing the vessel towards the right, so that the liquid may spread rapidly and evenly over the whole surface of the plate. Some dexterity is required to do this, except with very small plates. Just as the developer spreads over the plate and reaches the lower edge, the plate is carried to a horizontal position, for it is an object not to let more than can be helped run over. The developer becomes mixed on the surface of the plate with the bath solution with which the film is impregnated, and this mixture provokes the development. If a portion is wasted by washing over the side, the image will come out less strong, and a redevelopment will be more likely to be necessary.

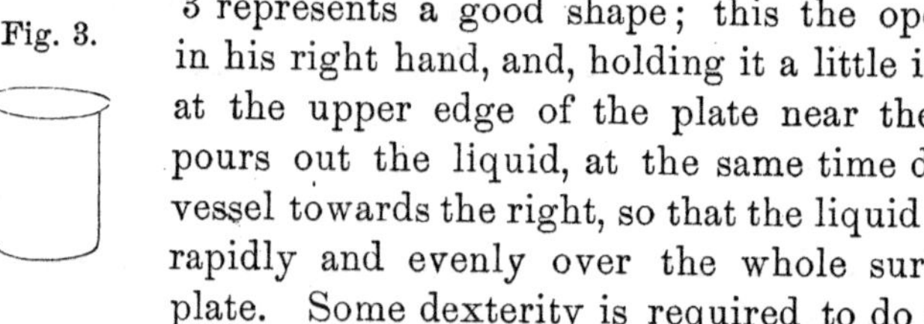
Fig. 3.

The rapidity of development under the action of the developer will depend on the exposure. If the picture flashes up instantly, the exposure has been too long, and the picture will want contrast. If the picture comes out slowly, reluctantly, so that after a minute or two only the strongest marked points of the subject are visible, the exposure has been too short, and the picture will probably be too full of contrast, wanting in detail, and hard and blocky. If the picture soon begins to show itself, and instead of flashing out suddenly, grows steadily and even rapidly in strength, a good result may be anticipated. As the development goes on the operator inclines the plate in different directions, so as to keep the developer in a state of constant motion, thereby rendering its action regular and even. When the plate has reached, or nearly reached the desired strength, the operator pours off the developer from one corner into its vessel again, and as he drains the last drop, he raises the plate perpendicularly between himself and the light, and judges of its strength and character. If these appear satisfactory, he stops the operation by washing off the plate; if not, he pours on the developer again (provided this last has remained active and clear), and keeps it on a few moments longer. But if it seems to have ceased its effects, and still more, if the slightest tendency to fog manifests itself, or if the developer looks in the least muddy, the operator quickly washes the plate, and if on a further careful inspection he finds that it still wants strength, he proceeds to redevelop.

Redevelopment may be done either before or after fixing, the difference is but very slight in the final result; as far as it goes, it may be stated as follows: If the contrasts are likely to be a little too great, or tend that way, redevelop before fixing; if the contrasts are scarcely sufficient, fix first and redevelop afterwards. Not much, however, in the way of a curative agency can be expected in this way, and pictures which are either too harsh or too uniform, are best wiped out at once and taken over.

The operator will always bear in mind, in deciding when his development or redevelopment is carried far enough, that the apparent strength of the picture, as he then sees it, will be considerably reduced in the operation of fixing, and for this he must make due allowance.

Negatives that come out of the right strength by the first development are the best. If under-exposed, they are apt to become hard and crude in the process of redevelopment; and if over-exposed, the evil is incurable. A brilliant print can only be got from a brilliant negative.

Redevelopment may be effected in various ways. The most usual is with pyrogallic acid, and that is the plan which I shall here describe.

To redevelop with pyrogallic acid, the operator keeps in a stoppered vial the following solution:—

Nitrate of silver	60 grains.
Citric acid	120 "
Water	6 ounces.

This mixture keeps for months. When the iron development has done what it can, and before any disposition to fog sets in, the plate is to be washed off. In a convenient developing vessel the operator puts water, about an ounce or a little less for a $6\frac{1}{2} \times 8\frac{1}{2}$ plate, and proportionately for other sizes. He next adds a little pyro, about two grains for the ounce of water, in which it immediately dissolves. He then adds a few drops, say fifteen or twenty, of the silver and citric acid solution to the ounce of water, and pours the mixture over the plate. The image immediately begins to grow in strength, and, by keeping the silver and pyro on, any desired degree of strength can be obtained. The redeveloper soon darkens to a wine color, and in that condition its action is still powerful. But if it becomes in the least muddy, it must be rapidly washed off the plate. So long as the solution remains transparent and bright, even if port-wine color, it is not easy to fog the picture. Still, even the pyrogallic developer is not to be trusted too far, or fog may set in in brown spots.

A pyrogallic development may be used in the first place instead of the iron. In this case the pyrogallic acid is simply dissolved in water, about a grain to the ounce, a little acetic acid is added, and the mixture is poured over the plate as it leaves the frame. This is a very easy development, and gives bright, strong pictures. But the preliminary development with iron is preferable, because softer pictures are got, and more full of detail.

Pyrogallic acid cannot be advantageously left in solution in water, as it spoils. If preferred, it may be kept dissolved in alcohol, sixty grains to the ounce, when ten or twelve drops will be equal to one grain of the crystallized acid.

The vessels used for developing must be kept scrupulously clean. If the remains of the developer be left in them a few minutes, it becomes turbid, and a gray-black precipitate of metallic silver collects round the sides and bottom. Any of this left in will tend to render the next lot of developer muddy, and therefore must be completely removed.

I am in the habit of keeping beside me the following solution in a beaker or wide-mouthed bottle:—

Concent. solution bichromate of potash . . .	1 fluidounce.
Sulphuric, or better, hydrochloric acid . . .	½ "
Water	3 fluidounces.

It is only necessary to pour this solution into the dirtiest developing vessel, and then immediately out again, when it will be found perfectly bright and clean. It is scarcely necessary to say that it must be well rinsed.

The same solution is very useful for removing silver stains from the fingers. If got into cuts or abrasions of the skin, it is to some violently irritating, to others quite indifferent, except a momentary smarting. It is much preferable to the use of cyanide of potassium, a most dangerous chemical, and the indiscreet use of which is injurious to health and may become destructive to life. *Perchloride of iron* may also be used for cleaning the fingers. Or they may be rubbed with strong tincture of iodine (alcohol 1 oz., iodine 40 grs.); and when the stain has become yellow (not before), it will dissolve in a strong solution of hyposulphite of soda.

Of these methods, the first will generally prove the most efficacious. All silver stains, however, should be attacked before they are *set* by exposure to light, otherwise the difficulty of getting rid of them is greatly increased.

§ 10.—**Fixing and Drying.**

The negative fixing-bath consists of a strong solution of hyposulphite of soda, in the proportion of five or six ounces to the pint of water. Some pour the solution over the plate until it is clear. But this involves a loss of time. It is better to keep the fixing-bath in a horizontal pan, and carefully to slide the negative into it. When the yellow opaque appearance of the iodide and bromide has completely disappeared, the plate is fixed. The same bath may be used for a number of negatives, but should not be kept too long.

The plate thus fixed is to be set under a tap and thoroughly washed by allowing a stream of water to fall upon it, whilst the plate is supported at such an angle that the ripple is seen to spread in all directions, and keep the water in continual motion over the whole surface of the plate. Ten to fifteen minutes is the right time for washing a negative, although much less is often given by hasty operators. It is almost as important to wash the *back* as the face, although the latter requires only simple rinsing off. If this be neglected, portions of the hyposulphite bath will remain there, and, when the plate is set up to dry, will run down to the edge, and thence be drawn up by capillary attraction into the film, preparing the way for spots and stains at some future time.

The plates are next allowed to dry, either reared up corner-wise in a drying-frame, or simply supported in a vertical position, resting on several thicknesses of blotting-paper.

From the time that the developer is thoroughly washed off, the plate may be exposed to the light without injury. But it is usually more convenient to fix in the dark room, though this is not really necessary.

If it is intended to redevelop the plate after instead of before fixing, the washing must be equally careful after the fixing solution is applied, or the application of the redeveloping solution will cause brown stains.

§ 11.—**Varnishing the Negative.**

To varnish a negative well will require both care and attention on the part of the beginner, until by habit and practice a complete control over the operation is obtained.

Choice of Varnish.—First as to the selection of varnish. The beginner should never attempt to make his own, but always procure a reliable commercial varnish. The experienced photographer should always make, never buy; not so much for economy, though the saving is material, but in order to be certain that he has exactly what he wants—a hard, tough varnish, made out of the very best materials. Suitable directions will be found in the latter part of this manual for preparing negative varnishes.

The commercial varnishes may be divided into two classes—the benzine and the spirit varnishes. The former will mostly dry clear, even if used cold; the latter always require the aid of heat. On the other hand, the benzine varnishes (so far as my experience goes) always reduce the strength of the negative considerably, whilst the spirit varnishes do not; and it is thought that the latter are more durable. A beginner can, perhaps, learn more easily on a benzine varnish, but the writer considers the spirit varnishes preferable on account of their acting less upon the density of the negative. The two different sorts can always be distinguished by the odor.

Applying the Varnish.—First dust off the plate, either *very* gently with a very soft, broad camel's-hair brush, or by blowing with a bellows. With plates developed with iron, or redeveloped, the latter is the better plan. To apply a spirit varnish, warm the plate either by a stove or over a Bunsen burner, or on a tin vessel filled with hot water. Try the temperature by holding it at one corner with the left hand, and moving the right hand under it and applying the side of the hand and back of thumb to various places to see if the heat be uniform. To be right, the temperature should just be pleasant, not feeling hot. If too hot, set aside a few minutes to cool. If used too hot, there is danger of getting *lines*, as will be presently described. If used too cool, the varnish will probably "dry dead." A benzine varnish requires no heat except in damp weather.

Pour on the varnish, holding the plate at the left corner, with the narrow side next you. Begin at the distance of an inch and a half to two inches (for a whole plate, proportionately for other sizes) from the far end, and midway between the corners. Whilst you are pouring, incline so as to get it down first to one corner, then to the other. Then having put on a liberal supply, slant the plate towards you and bring the pool of varnish towards you, *in a full, slow wave*, keep its border *as square as possible*, making it advance slowly and quietly; if one edge gets a little the advance, incline the plate the other way to bring it up. With too little varnish or too much tilt to the plate, long arms will start out, and whilst you are slanting the plate this way and that to get it covered on some part of the border, the wave will stop moving, and a *line* may result.

Having now got the whole plate covered, keep it quite level, or even tilt it backward, so as to send a returning wave clear up to far end of the plate. The varnish should rest on the whole plate five or six seconds before *beginning* to pour off, otherwise it will not soak in sufficiently, and so *dry dead.*

Having let it soak in sufficiently, incline it *very little*, so that it will run off at the right-hand near corner into the "pouring-off bottle" held there to receive it. After it has run slowly for three or four seconds, the plate being of course nearly level, *bring it suddenly up by a quick movement till it is vertical, and there hold it* perfectly still for half a minute or more that it may set. If moved at all short of this time, *ridges* may be expected.

Some varnishes require no more heat than the first application. Many, however, should be dried by heat, as well as be applied on a warm plate. If so, hold the plate exactly in the position that it drained off vertically, and bring it with its face within a couple of inches of a hot stove.

The main points are to get the corners covered immediately after you begin to pour, to put on enough, or to bring it down as above explained to a *full, slow, square* wave. The learner cannot pay too close an attention to these directions. By doing so he will get a smooth, even plate. Neglecting them, he will find:—

Ridges.—These start from some point at the edge of the plate and extend some distance over the face of, or even all across the negative. If strong enough to show in printing (they show less, of course, by printing in the shade than in sunlight), there is nothing but to remove the varnish and revarnish, a most disagreeable operation, and worse than half a dozen careful varnishings.

Lines result from a momentary stopping of the wave of varnish. The varnish dries a little on the hot plate during the pause, and the result is a line exactly marking the position it then had. The hotter the plate, the more apt lines will be to appear. If a line has been made and is seen before you begin to pour off, it may be lessened, and sometimes entirely removed, by keeping on the varnish a few seconds longer than usual before beginning to pour off.

Drying Dead.—This results in the production of a film looking like ground glass—sometimes fine, sometimes coarse. If fine, it may scarcely show in the printing; if coarse, it will. This may arise from several sources:—

From dampness of the Film.—After the film is surface dry, it takes a long time to dry through, and the drying must be *thorough* before the varnish is applied. So, too, the film is very absorbent of atmospheric moisture, and even after thorough drying and standing for weeks, may easily in damp weather absorb enough to affect the varnishing. It is therefore better, so far as convenient, to varnish in clear dry weather, or at least after the plate has remained some time in a warm dry room.

Too thin a varnish may also cause drying dead, or too little applied. If, as soon as the plate is covered, the varnish be poured off again, it will almost certainly dry dead, because the surface only was moistened; this presently soaks in and leaves the film only half saturated with varnish.

Breathing on the plate may at times, and under some circumstances, lead to spots of deadness.

A close attention to the above directions and a reasonable experience will enable the photographer to get through his varnishing with rapidity and certainty. But if the varnishing is defective, it must be removed and done over.

For this purpose the plate is to be laid in a flat pan, film side up, and covered with alcohol in the case of a spirit varnish, and benzine for a benzine varnish. Cover it up and leave for an hour or two, or till the varnish is pretty well dissolved. Wash off with clean alcohol, dry, and re-varnish. The operation is unsatisfactory, and generally as much trouble as taking a new plate.

The solution and removal of the varnish are rarely perfect, a whitish substance being left behind, which, however, mostly disappears by the new varnishing.

When it is intended to print a very large number of positives from one negative, two coats of varnish may be applied. Mr. G. W. Wilson, whose stereoscopic work is so remarkable, always gives two coats, touching out defects between the two. He also warms and dries his plates beside a fire in a grate even in midsummer.

It is a good plan, as soon as the face of the varnished plate is dry, to draw a piece of blotting-paper along the lower edge of the glass; this prevents the production of a thick ridge there, which would have a tendency to lift up the paper in printing, and prevent a close contact with the adjoining parts.

§ 12.—Ambrotypes and Ferrotypes.

The ambrotype is a thin negative taken on glass, the ferrotype on thin iron varnished. The exposure must be much shorter than for negatives, the bath a very little more acid, the collodion thoroughly ripe. Develop only till the details appear, and then wash immediately and fix in hyposulphite.

An ordinary negative collodion may be used if it is thoroughly ripe; if not, tincture of iodine may be added till it is sherry wine colored. (Tincture of iodine may be purchased, or may be made by dissolving iodine in alcohol. Forty grains of iodine to the ounce of alcohol is a convenient strength.)

Some photographers prefer a special collodion containing iodide of potassium, now never used in negative collodions. Mr. Thomas, of New York, uses the following proportions:—

Iodide of potassium	50 grains.
Bromide of potassium	30 "

Dissolve these salts in 3 ounces of alcohol. Take 60 grains of pyroxyline, dissolve it in 5 ounces of ether and 2 of alcohol. Then add the above.

The developer is to be the same as for negatives, taking care that it be sufficiently acidified, for which purpose one-half more acetic acid may be added than for negatives.

§ 13.—General Remarks.

Avoid doing anything which may cause dust in the dark room. Keep the dark slide clean and well wiped.

Notice the camera from time to time to assure yourself that the wood work is close and tight.

See that the focussing slide sits tight and close up. The springs that hold it to the body of the camera will sometimes get out of order and affect the two slides differently, so that one comes up more closely than the other. The result of this will be that the focussing surface no longer corresponds with the sensitive film, and no matter how carefully the focussing be done, the pictures will not be accurately sharp.

Make sure that the camera-stand is absolutely steady and not given to trembling.

See that the dark room is thoroughly ventilated, so that whilst at work you are not inhaling noxious vapors, and as little as possible of the fumes of collodion.

CHAPTER III.

MAKING THE POSITIVE.

§ 1.—Sensitizing and Printing.

We shall here only describe the proceeding with albumenized paper, now almost exclusively used. The process on plain paper will be described elsewhere.

Many excellent qualities of albumenized paper are to be found in the market. The sheets are to be cut up into convenient sizes, and one corner is to be folded backwards for half an inch or three-quarters. The piece is then held at its two ends, is folded into a loop by bringing the hands somewhat together so that the centre will be lowest, and the albumenized surface undermost. The centre of the sheet is made to touch the bath first, and then, by opening the hands and lowering them, the whole surface is regularly opened out on the bath. In this way air-bubbles are avoided. Should an air-bubble remain under the paper, its place will be marked by a white spot in the print.

Positive Bath.

Water	22 ounces.
Nitrate of silver	3 "

The paper remains on it about four minutes in winter, and two to three in summer. It is then lifted off by the corner turned up, and pinned to a rod or string to dry. A convenient method is to take a long strip of wood, and glue on it at spaces corks, into which to stick the pins.

When the bath turns dark, shake it up with half an ounce of kaolin, or add to it ten grains of citric acid dissolved in a little water. Let it stand some hours, with occasional shaking, and filter.

Examine the bath from time to time with red and blue litmus paper, and keep it as nearly neutral as possible. If the blue litmus turns red, the bath is too acid, and may be neutralized with a grain or two of bicarbonate of sodium. If red litmus paper turns blue, the bath is alkaline, and a little dilute nitric acid must be carefully added. It is best to have the solution an inch deep in the glass or porcelain bath. Too shallow a bath tends to irregular action.

See that the paper is thoroughly dry before printing it. A dense negative prints best in the sun, a thin one in the shade. That is, it is to be exposed at a window to a good light, but not to sunshine.

Print till the highest lights *just begin* to color. By this time the dark shadows ought to show the greenish, almost metallic, look known as "bronzing."

Examine the print from time to time, taking the frame to a darker part of the room, open the back gently, taking care not to shift the print, bend it back, and judge of the degree to which the printing has gone.

As fast as the exposure is finished, throw the prints into a dark drawer.

When all are ready, proceed to wash them by putting them *one by one* into a basin of water, where they lie ten minutes. This water is to be carefully added to the residues, as it is rich in silver. Change two or three times, then tone.

As the printing-bath will continually lose in strength, it should be kept up by adding crystals of nitrate of silver.

§ 2.—**Toning Bath.**

Water	16 ounces.
Chloride of gold	4 grains.
Acetate of sodium	1 ounce.

In five or six hours it will be ready for use. In very cold weather, a little more gold must be used; and the bath, except in hot weather, should be warmed till it is tepid.

Put in only a few prints at a time, and keep them constantly moving about. When they reach the shade you prefer, let them remain a little longer, as they will afterwards recede a little in color; then take them out, pass them through clean water, and proceed to fixing.

Prints that look blue when finished, have been *over-toned* by too long an immersion.

§ 3.—Fixing Bath.

Water	32 ounces.
Hyposulphite of sodium	4 "

Keep the prints moving about in this, and leave them in fifteen minutes. The above bath will suffice for two whole sheets, and must be increased in proportion if more are to be toned. *Never use on any subsequent day a bath that has had even only one single print fixed in it*, or the print so toned will surely fade.

§ 4.—Washing.

A very thorough washing is needed to prevent fading. Prints thrown into a tank into which a tolerable stream of moving water falls, will be sufficiently washed in six to ten hours, provided there are not too many of them. When the number is large, the tank must be continually emptied of water and refilled.

CHAPTER IV.

A FEW GENERAL RULES FOR BEGINNERS.

1. INVARIABLY wash the fingers under the tap immediately after they have been in *any* solution, but most particularly after hyposulphite. By neglecting this you will transfer portions of one solution to another, and lay the foundation of long series of failures, which may prove utterly distressing and perplexing.

2. Do not have the ambition to commence with difficult work. Point the camera out of the window, and take the view, such as it is, until you can do it with certainty and success. After that will be time enough to try portraiture—last of all, copying.

3. Begin with small plates, and do not try large ones until you have mastered the smaller. Half-size will be the largest proper to begin with.

4. Do not undertake to make collodion before you have learned how to use it. Be satisfied to purchase that which some experienced friend recommends.

5. Do not tend towards intensifying thin pictures by after

treatments. When photography was less understood this was oftener necessary. It is better to wash off and begin again, and generally less trouble to get a better result.

6. The quickest way to learn is this: take any simple object as above, a brick house for example, and try it again and again, varying the length of exposure and the length of development, until you get a negative that prints exactly right. This will teach more in a few mornings than as many weeks of random work.

7. Successes that come by chance are worthless, and prove nothing as to ability. Try to know exactly why you succeed and why you fail.

8. You may often succeed in getting the right exposure the first time, but you cannot be sure of it; yet a careful examination of the first trial ought to enable you to make sure of the second.

9. If the camera needs to be placed in the sunshine, throw the focussing cloth over it before the shutter is drawn out to make the exposure. The direct light of the sun may find its way through rents too small to admit diffused.

10. Once in a while wipe out the camera with a damp cloth to remove dust, which by settling on the plate may cause pin-holes or comets.

11. Treat the lenses with *the utmost* care. Never leave them about; never wipe them with anything but the softest old linen cambric, perfectly clean, or still better with soft chamois leather, and not even so except when needed.

12. Do not unscrew the tubes unnecessarily to wipe the inside surfaces of the lenses, or for any other purpose, and always do this in dry weather, or you will let in damp air, which will be apt later to leave a dew on the lenses. If any of the lenses are set loosely in the tube, be sure they are replaced with the same side front as before.

13. Do not let either the lenses or the camera stand in the sun, or you may expect warping and splitting of the wood, and discoloration of the lens.

14. Be sure that the camera stand is free from vibration. Uncover the lens very gently so as not to shake the camera in the least, or the definition will be impaired.

15. Unless the ground glass is of the best you cannot focus with

accuracy. Much of the ground glass in the cameras made for sale is very poor. The glass should, in fact, not be ground at all, but only "grayed," that is, have its surface removed by rubbing with fine emery powder. Focus a brick house 200 feet off with a short focus lens, and if you cannot see the white lines of the mortar either with the naked eye or with a magnifier, the glass is too coarsely ground; and it is to be expected that all the work done with it will be inferior.

16. Focussing with a microscope is less trying to the eyes, and gives sharper work. The larger the lens of the microscope used, the less the eye is strained. An engraver's glass set in horn is good, but a similar one, an inch and a half or two inches in diameter, tires the eyes still less.

17. Learn exactly how to make a negative bath, and then avoid doctoring. For the most part you will only injure it. Add a very little carbonate of soda, and sun it, if out of order, for some hours in direct sunlight, then filter and acidulate as directed for a new bath. Filter first, then acidulate.

18. Decaying organic matter, foul smells, sulphuretted hydrogen, and fumes of ammonia may be expected to produce fog.

19. Do not think it necessary to have the dark room too dark. There may be light enough to work with perfect comfort, and the strain on the eyes in going backwards and forwards will be so much the less: an important consideration.

20. Have nothing to do with cyanide of potassium. It is a substance of which the photographer has no real need. If used at all, it should be left to those who have learned their experience on less dangerous materials.

21. Remember that most chemicals are poisons, and that if the fingers are not washed immediately after being plunged in them, or if, even with this precaution, they are kept long in the solutions, mischief may ensue. What this mischief may be is of so gradual and insidious a nature, as to be ascribed to any other cause than the right one.

22. Remember also that most fumes are injurious. Vapors of ammonia disorganize and paralyze the blood corpuscles. Vapor of ether is very injurious to the nervous system, and depresses the whole tone of the body. Nitric acid is highly poisonous; its fumes, when inhaled, in even a moderately strong form, may cause death in a few hours.

23. Therefore make every provision for thorough and complete ventilation. And do not fancy (as many most unwisely do) that because your senses become habituated to such fumes, and cease to be inconvenienced by them, that the system is therefore not suffering.

24. Adopt invariably the maxim, that whatever is worth doing is worth doing well. Practice never makes perfect without care, and thoughtful and intelligent observation. Some will do a thing all their lives, and always badly.

25. Acquire the habit of rinsing out all the vessels as soon as emptied, and of not leaving the adhering portion to dry on the bottom and sides, when it will take five times the trouble to get it out.

26. Make it a rule to wash every vessel before you put it away, and again before you use it. Never trust to *anything* being clean, but make it so. If there is any one thing that is essential in photography, it is care of this sort. The delicate reactions on which photographic processes depend are sufficiently exacting, without further embarrassing the processes by introducing foreign matter of unknown nature.

27. Never forget that no vessel is rendered clean (even if what it has contained has been merely an aqueous solution) by simply pouring water in and throwing it out.

Hold therefore the vessel, whether beaker, bowl, bottle, or whatever it may be, under the tap, so that the water may run over *every* part, inside and out. Outside, because you can never be certain that a glass vessel is clean *inside* unless you have also made it so outside. Remember that if you hastily rinse out a vessel, you may leave drops of the old solution adhering to the sides above where you have washed, and that a single drop so left may spoil the following operation. This direction may be thought so much a matter of course as to be superfluous, but it *is not so.*

In all cases, except where the old contents are very easily removable by water, employ the bichromate cleaning solution, which for this purpose may be made of double or treble strength, so as to work more energetically.

28. Finally, the beginner in Landscape Photography is earnestly recommended to act upon a definite system. For example, let

him not run from one lens to another, but rather, having provided himself with one thoroughly good one, let him study out its capabilities and learn exactly how to use it. Different lenses work so differently, that, to the beginner, they are very confusing, and tend to conceal from him the sources of the mistakes and faults that he must necessarily make. Only in one way can he usefully employ himself with several lenses, and that is by using them in succession to take the same view, and observing and studying closely the differences in the results.

It has justly been observed by Mr. H. P. Robinson that there is no more effective way of learning than by selecting some one particular view, and working at it till a thoroughly good picture is obtained, regardless as to how numerous the attempts may need to be. One such piece of negative-making, worked thoroughly out, will teach as much as thrice the time spent in random view-taking. The student should bear steadily in mind that whilst a thoroughly good negative is very valuable, there is nothing more worthless than a tolerable one. A tolerable negative is not worth the trouble of printing, and is consequently worth nothing at all.

PART II.

PHOTOGRAPHIC OPTICS AND THEORY OF PERSPECTIVE.

A BRIEF exposition of those portions of elementary optics which are of special interest to the photographer seems indispensable to a manual like this; at the same time that it is evident that that only which is essential can be treated of. The subject will be divided into two heads—General, and Special Optics: to which will be added some remarks upon Perspective.

CHAPTER I.

GENERAL OPTICS.

§ 1.—Reflection and Refraction.

WHEN a ray of light (this expression will be more convenient, although wave of light would be more correct) falls upon any surface, a part is reflected and a part transmitted.

Let the ray *A O* (Fig. 4) pass from the rarer medium on one side of *E F* into the denser on the other; for example, out of air into glass. Part of the ray will be reflected and a part refracted. In order to study these phenomena, we draw a line perpendicular to the surface *E F* at the point of incidence *O*. This is the *normal*, and the angle *A O N* between the incident ray and the normal is the *angle of incidence.*

Fig. 4.

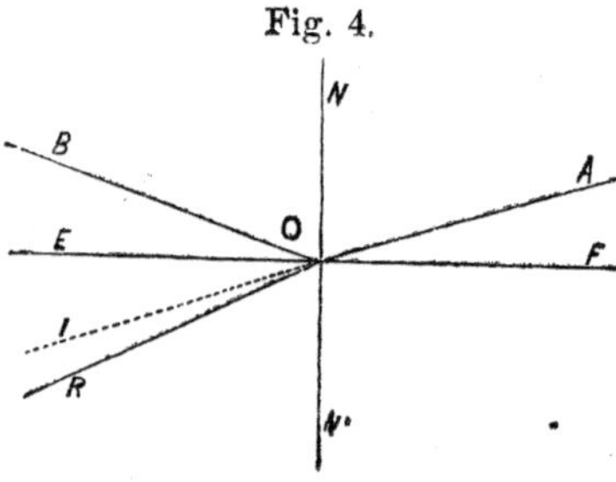

We find that the *reflected ray makes the angle of reflection B O N equal to the angle of incidence A O N.*

The refracted ray is bent out of its course *towards* the normal. In place of continuing on in the direction $O\ I$, it is deflected towards $O\ N'$, in the direction $O\ R$, and the quantity of deflection depends upon the character of the substance. The greater the deflection, the higher the refractive power is said to be.

In the foregoing we have considered the case of a ray passing from a rarer medium into a denser. In the converse case the converse result takes place. If in the above figure we suppose the directions to be reversed, and that the ray $R\ O$ passes at O from the denser medium into the rarer above it, then the ray $R\ O$ will be bent *away from the normal* to precisely the same extent, and will follow the path $O\ A$.

It therefore follows from this that when a ray passes from a rarer medium into a denser, and then through the denser again into the rarer, it will emerge in a direction *parallel to that in which it entered*, provided that the denser medium has parallel sides.

The ray $A\ D$ (Fig. 5), in passing through the denser medium, takes the course $D\ B$, being deflected towards the normal, and, on emerging, again assumes a direction $B\ C$ parallel to $A\ D$.

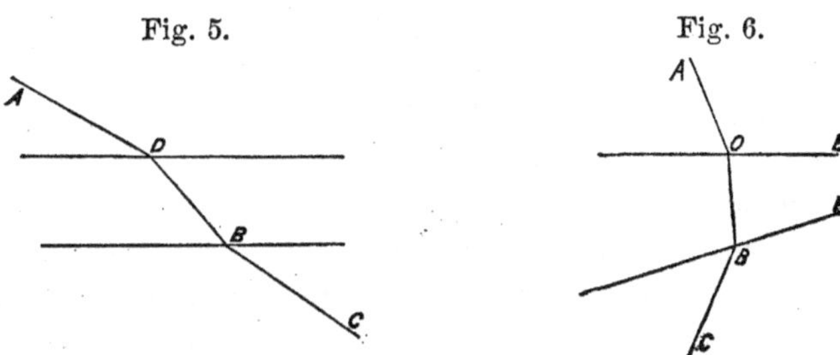

Fig. 5. Fig. 6.

But if the sides of the denser medium are not parallel, the ray will not emerge from the second surface parallel to the first direction. Thus the sides $O\ E$, $B\ F$ of the denser medium not being parallel, the ray $A\ O$, in passing through the surface $B\ F$, takes the direction $B\ C$. (Fig. 6.)

Different substances refract the rays of light very differently, and are therefore said to differ in refractive power.

We have a very convenient method of measuring refractive power, which is as follows:—

In Fig. 7 let $S'\ S''$ be the boundary line between an upper and rarer substance and a lower and denser one. Let any ray of light $R\ O$ pass at O out of the rarer into the denser, and let the line $O\ R'$ represent its deflected direction.

Fig. 7.

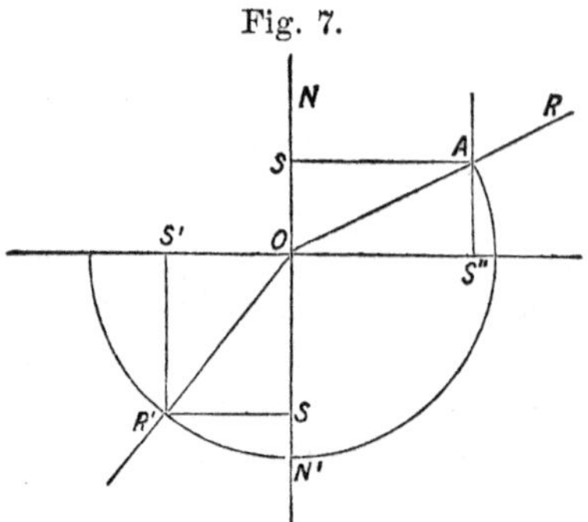

With any distance $O\ A$ as a radius, draw the curve $A\ N'\ R'$. Draw at the point O the normal $N\ N'$, and from the intersection A let drop the perpendicular $A\ S$, similarly from R' the perpendicular $R'\ S$.

$A\ S$ will be the sine of the angle of incidence and $R'\ S$ the sine of the angle of refraction. Each of these angles will be conveniently measured by its sine.

Now it is found that with any two given substances as the rarer and denser medium, the proportion between the lengths of $A\ S$ and $R'\ S$ is invariable. If the upper medium be air and the lower a certain quality of glass, the sine of refraction $R'\ S$ will always be exactly $\frac{2}{3}$ the sine of incidence $A\ S$, let the ray fall upon the dividing line $S'\ S''$ at what angle it may.

The ratio of the sines is then invariable for any given substance, and this ratio is called the *index of refraction.* In the case just mentioned $A\ S$ being to $R'\ S$ always as 3 to 2, the index of refraction of such glass is said to be $\frac{3}{2}$ or 1.5.

The construction of an angle of refraction is easily made as follows: Let the ray $R\ O$ pass out of air (or rather out of a vacuum, but the difference is unimportant here) into glass of refractive power 1.5. Draw the normal $N\ N'$ through the point of incidence and perpendicular to the surface. Set off any distance $O\ S'$, and taking this as unity make $O\ S''$ equal to the index of refraction. In this case $O\ S''$ will stand to $O\ S'$ in the proportion of 1.5 to 1. Draw the perpendiculars $S'\ R'$, $S''\ A$. Putting one leg of a compass at O and the other at A (the intersection of $S''\ A$ with $O\ R$) draw the curve $A\ R'$, the intersection of this curve with $S'\ R'$ when connected with O gives the path of the refracted ray.

§ 2.—**Dispersion.**

In the foregoing section we have reasoned as if light were homogeneous. But white light is made up of rays of very different refrangibility, so that when a ray of white light *A D* (fig. 8) passes at *D* into the denser medium bounded by the line *B C*, these

Fig. 8.

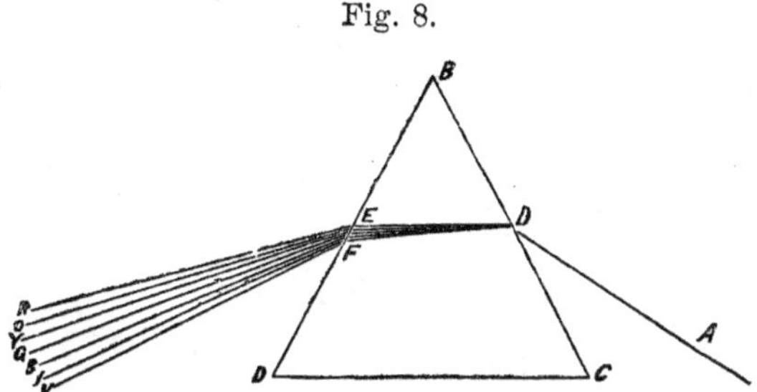

rays are differently affected. The more refrangible rays are bent more out of their course, following the direction *D F*; the less take the direction *D E*.

On reaching the second surface *B D*, if this surface is not parallel to the first, but is inclined to it, these different rays will have their divergence greatly increased, and will be spread out as there represented.

We find that a difference of color accompanies a difference of refrangibility, the most refrangible being violet, and so proceeding in the order, violet, indigo, blue, green, yellow, orange, and red. Under very favorable circumstances, and with well-exercised eyes, a commencing disposition to repeat this gamut, like octaves in musical sounds, is observable, for beyond the red a crimson tint has been seen, and beyond the violet, a lavender.

But, independently of these, the existence of non-luminous influences beyond the limits of the visible spectrum is easily detected. Beyond the red rays, rays of *dark heat* are made evident by the thermometer, and beyond the violet there exist rays also invisible, but having a powerful chemical and actinic effect, so that in a portion of space completely dark, sensitive paper is rapidly impressed.

Whilst rays, invisible to our eyes, are thus capable of exerting powerful actinic action, other rays, plainly and even brilliantly visible, exercise little or no actinic influence. The yellow and red rays, in which the chief illuminating power of light resides, scarcely act upon sensitive substances. The green rays exert an influence on some and not on others.

It is not a little remarkable that sulphate of quinine possesses the power of lowering the refrangibility of the rays beyond the violet, and thus rendering them visible to our eyes. If sulphate of quinine be dissolved in water acidulated by sulphuric acid, and the solution be placed in the dark rays beyond the violet, these become visibly blue.

CHAPTER II.

OF LENSES.

§ 1.—Nature of Lenses.

A LENS may be plane on one side and convex on the other—plano-convex. (Fig. 9.) Plane on one side and concave on the other—plano-concave. (Fig. 10.) Convex on both sides—double convex. (Fig. 11.) Concave on both sides—double concave.

Figs. 9. 10. 11. 12. 13. 14.

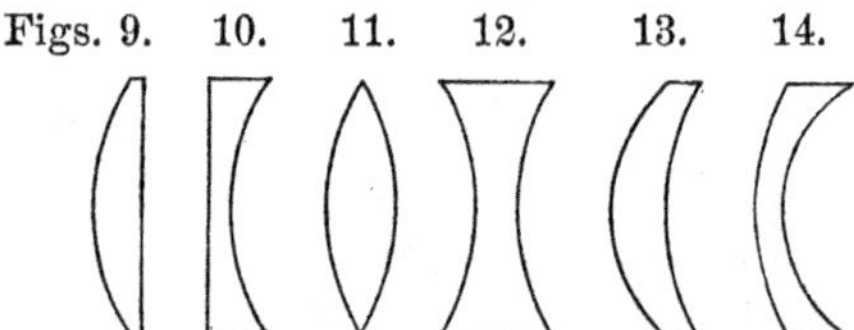

(Fig. 12.) Concave on one side and convex on the other—meniscus. The meniscus may be of two sorts. If the radius of the convex side is the shorter, the lens is thickest in the middle, and is called a positive meniscus. (Fig. 13.) If the concave curve has the shorter radius, the meniscus is thickest at the edges, and is termed a negative meniscus. (Fig. 14.)

To understand the action of a lens on rays of light, let us select a plano-convex lens and consider its properties.

Fig. 15.

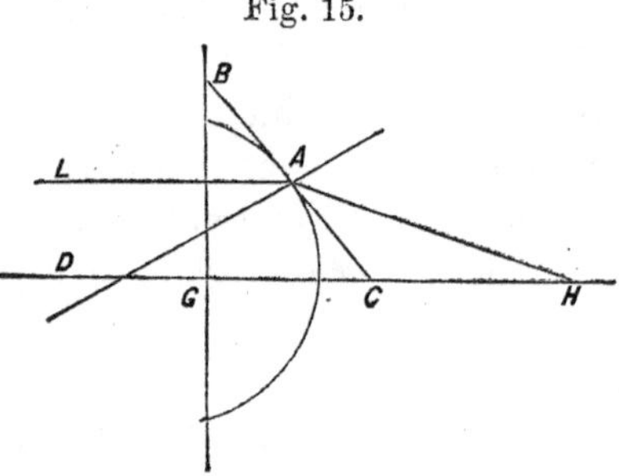

When a ray of light $L\,A$ falls upon any curved surface at any point A, we draw a tangent $B\,C$ at the point A, and we may then consider the solid body $A\,G$, as far as the ray $L\,A$ is considered, not as a body having a curved surface, but as a prism

B G C, for it will act towards the ray *L A* precisely as if it were such a prism. The ray *L A* passing out of it will be sent away from the normal in the direction *A H*, and will intersect the axis *D H* at the point *H*.

Fig. 16.

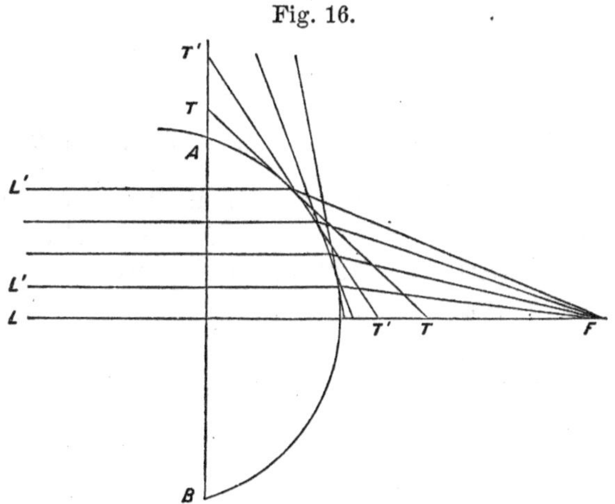

Let us now consider several rays of light *L*, *L'* &c. (Fig. 16). *L* strikes at the centre of the curve, where the tangent is parallel to the plane side *A B*, and is therefore influenced precisely as if it passed through a piece of plane glass, and emerges in the same right line. *L'* is bent on leaving the curved surface, and tends towards *F*. Other rays strike the curve still higher from the axis, where the tangents are still more inclined, and is therefore still more deflected. This greater deflection makes up for the fact that the original path of that ray was further from the central ray, and thus all the rays tend to gather together at a point F, called the focus.

What is true of the plano-convex lens, is true of all lenses that are thickest in the centre, of double convex, and of positive meniscus lenses. Those lenses which are thinnest at the centre are called negative. They do not collect parallel rays to a focal point, but cause them to diverge. They have no real focus, but only a virtual one. Such lenses taken alone would be of no use in photography, but they are often employed in connection with others.

If matters passed exactly in the manner above described, the construction of photographic objectives would be far more simple than it is. But the spherical lenses which we use are liable to faults, which will next be considered.

CHAPTER III.

FAULTS INCIDENT TO SPHERICAL LENSES.

THERE are five distinct sources of inaccuracy in the image formed by a spherical lens. These are, SPHERICAL ABERRATION, CHROMATIC ABERRATION, ASTIGMATION, CURVATURE OF THE FIELD, and DISTORTION.

§ 1.—Spherical Aberration and the Modes of Remedying it.

All lenses in use at the present day have their curves, parts of spheres; not because this is the best curve, but because it is the easiest to grind by very much.

Now it is a property of all spherical curves *A B*, Fig. 17, that they do not bring the rays exactly to a point at *F*. Just in proportion as the parallel ray *L′* is further from the central axis *L*, so is that ray, after passing through the lens, brought down to the central axis at a point nearer to the lens. The focal length of *F′* for the ray *L′* is shorter than the length of *F* for the ray *L*, and so on.

It will be seen, then, that for the lens *A B* there is no real focus, but a succession of foci all the way from *F* to *F′*, and although the fault is intentionally exaggerated in the figure, it is still so great as imperatively to require attention.

Fig. 17.

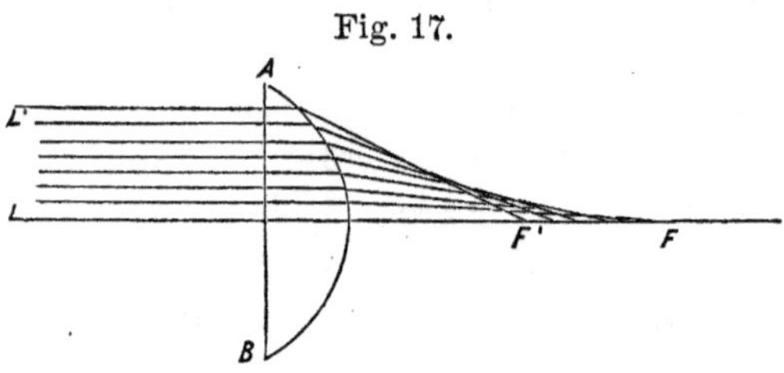

Spherical aberration may be destroyed, or at least diminished, in two ways. Either lenses may be so combined that their aberrations will be in opposite directions, and so compensate and destroy each other, or else diaphragms may be employed.

Correction by Diaphragms.—The ray $R'' A$ which would come to a focus at a point F' nearer to the lens than F (see Figs. 17 and 18) is cut off by the diaphragm $C D$. This point F lies in,

Fig. 18.

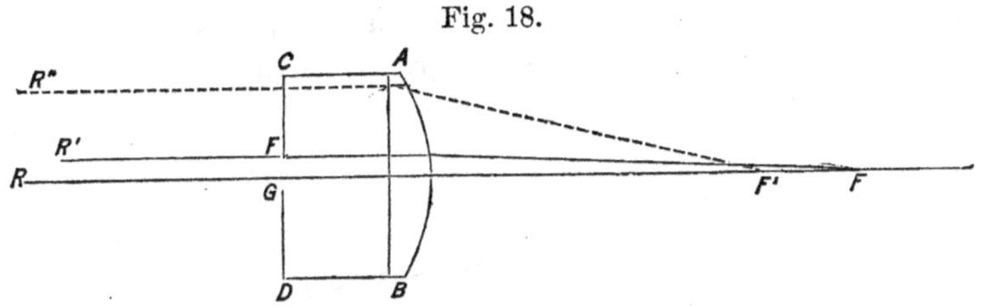

or nearly in, the same vertical plane as the focus of the oblique rays (see Fig. 28, page 61). We thus greatly increase the sharpness of definition by the use of a stop, though of course at a sacrifice of light.

This, then, is the theory of the correction of spherical aberration by the use of stops. The method has immense disadvantages, arising from its cutting off a great part of the light. Thus, if the lens is three inches in diameter, and the aperture of the diaphragm is a quarter of an inch, then, as the areas of circles are at the squares of their diameters, the loss of light is $\frac{143}{144}$, or only one one hundred and forty-fourth part of the whole light which would reach the sensitive film, if a full aperture could be employed, is left available.

Great as are these evils, the results gained much exceed them. The image, before dull and hazy, becomes at once sharp and crisp. Before, the lens seemed to have no true focus; now, for any given object, the focus can be found with exactitude.

§ 2.—**Chromatic Aberration and Mode of Correction.**

Spherical aberration is independent of the nature of the light employed, results wholly from the form of the lens, and occurs even with homogeneous light. We have next to consider a sort of aberration arising from the different indices of refraction of the different rays of which white light is composed.

When considering the subject of dispersion, we saw that when light fell upon a prism, it was spread out into a spectrum, in which its different constituents were arranged in the order of their refrangibility. And as a lens may be taken to represent a number of small prisms, it follows that the same spreading of the colors will there take place.

If, as in Fig. 19, a perpendicular ray of light strikes a plano-convex lens at A, it passes into it unchanged; but at B the dispersion of the rays takes place according to their refrangibility,

Fig. 19.

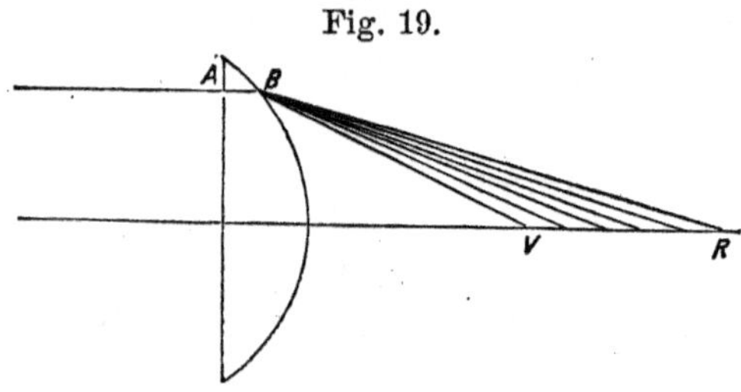

and the focus of the violet rays is nearer to the lens than that of the less refrangible rays at the red end of the spectrum. The distance between these two foci V and R is called the *chromatic aberration*, which in the figure is necessarily exaggerated for clearness.

This fact may be easily rendered visible by holding such a lens in the sunlight. The extreme rays of white light $L\ L$ (Fig. 20)

Fig. 20.

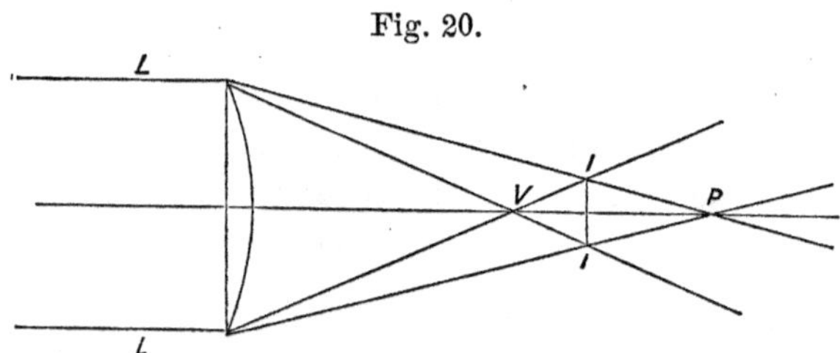

are divided, and the violet rays find their focus at V, the red at P. If a white screen be interposed anywhere between the lens and the point I, there will be a circular image of the sun with a red border; beyond I, where the violet rays cross the red and pass outside, the image will have a violet border. The distance along the axis between the foci of the red and violet is termed the *longitudinal aberration*, and that at *I I* the *lateral aberration*. *I I* is the place at which the least circle encloses the whole of the rays, it is therefore the best focus.

To understand clearly how the chromatic aberration is corrected, it is necessary to bear in mind that the *refractive* power of substances and their *dispersive* power are not proportionate to each other. For substances may exist of equal refractive power, and different dispersive, and conversely.

Let us, then, take two sorts of glass differing in these properties, and construct a double convex lens of one of them, and a double concave one of that which has the highest dispersive power, giving them such curves that the negative lens may exactly correct the dispersion of the positive. The power of the positive lens will be thereby largely diminished, but not extinguished, whilst its chromatic aberration is destroyed. Several modes of correction are shown in the figures; even lenses of three pieces are made, as will be seen further on.

Fig. 21. Fig. 22. Fig. 23.

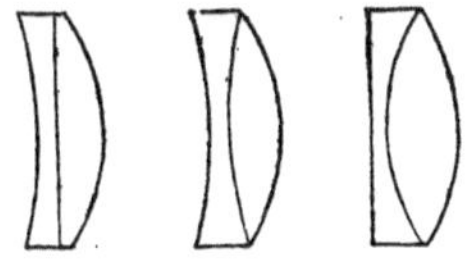

Of course the curves which it is necessary to give to the glass to effect this purpose, will depend entirely on the relations between the respective powers of the respective pieces of crown and flint glass of which the lens is composed. And glass varies so much, even when made according to any one formula, that it is only by actual experiment that the relative curvatures of the glass can be determined. This is one reason why the different lenses produced by the same makers vary so much in power and in excellence, especially when the comparison is made between those produced at different times and with various specimens of glass. And it will consequently happen that careless makers will occasionally produce good lenses, whilst the most attentive will occasionally make great failures. To purchase a lens untried is like putting into a lottery. Some of Mr. G. W. Wilson's finest work was done with a pair of the cheapest sort of French lenses, without even the name of the maker on them. And sometimes lenses for which extravagant prices have been paid, will turn out almost wholly worthless. It is understood that the celebrated makers are more careful in trying their lenses, and reject those of inferior quality. This is doubtless so, but they are not always very successful in their discrimination. Let no one who obtains a lens that works to his satisfaction, be easily persuaded to part with it. A first-rate lens is not to be easily met with.

§ 3.—Astigmation.

Astigmation is produced where pencils of light fall obliquely upon a lens.

Let *C D E F* represent the *face* of a lens, not a section as

Fig. 24.

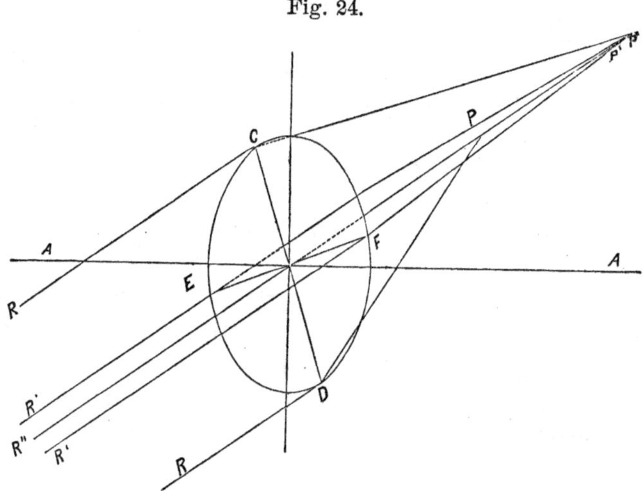

usually shown in the figures. Let *R R*, *R' R'*, *R''* be rays of light coming from an object so distant that they are parallel. Let the central ray *R''* pass through the optical centre of the lens; it will emerge parallel to its original direction; its prolongation in the direction *p* will constitute a secondary axis. Let *E F* be a diameter of the lens, perpendicular to the axial ray *R''*, and *C D* another diameter at right angles with the first. Now the rays *R' R'*, which reach the lens at *E* and *F*, strike it under absolutely the same circumstances. They will, therefore, undergo equal refraction, and will meet the secondary axis at some point *P'*.

This is not at all the case with the rays *R R*, which fall on the ends of the diameter $C D$. They will fall upon the lens under very unequal angles, and will be very differently refracted. $R D$ will reach the axis at some point P, $R C$ at some point p.[1]

But the use of a diaphragm cuts off $R D$ and the neighboring rays. Of the rays that are left, $R C$ and the neighboring rays have their focus at p, whilst $R' E$, $R' F$ have their focus at P'.

It follows, therefore, that oblique pencils have no true focus. For if P'' be taken as the focus, then the rays $R' E$, $R' F$ will have crossed at P', and at p they will have widened out again, and the image of the radiant point, instead of being a point, will be an ellipse, having its major diameter in the direction $E F$. Conversely, if P' be taken as the focus, $R C$ and the neighboring rays will not have converged to a focus, and their section on the focussing screen will form an ellipse, having its major diameter in the direction $C D$. In neither case will the point have its image as a point, hence the name astigmation (α, no, and στιγμὴ, point). The image of the point will appear as an ellipse, whose greatest diameter will change its direction according as the focussing screen is further or nearer to the lens.

Rays incident perpendicularly upon the lens, do not produce astigmation. If, then, we examine the case of a pair of lenses having convex surfaces outside, and a stop between them, we shall see that if this stop be placed at the centre of curvature of the outside surfaces, then only rays of incidence nearly perpendicular to the surfaces of the lenses will be permitted to pass through the stop. This is the case with the globe lens, which consequently is almost free from astigmation, when a very small stop is used. Other lenses, with central stops, will have more or less astigmation, according as their central stop corresponds more or less nearly with the centre of curvature.

In the single meniscus view lens, the astigmation will be less in proportion to the depth of concavity of the front surface. It will also be controlled by the position of the front stop. The nearer this is placed to the centre of curvature of the front concave surface, the more nearly will the incidences be perpendicular, and consequently the less the astigmation.

Coma.—Spherical aberration is much more easily removed for

[1] The unequal refraction of $R C$, $R D$ is the cause of *coma*, which will be presently treated of.

direct rays than for those that strike the lens in an oblique direction. Let the rays R R' R'' strike the plano-convex lens in an

Fig. 25.

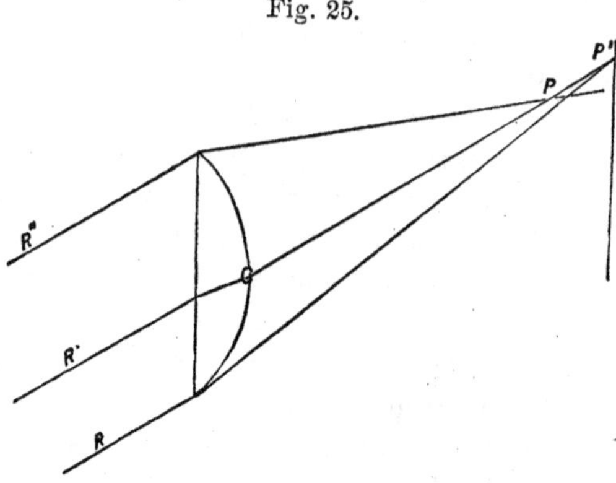

oblique direction. One ray, R', which, after refraction at the first surface of the lens, passes through the optic centre C, emerges in a direction parallel to that which it originally took. This line C P' is the axis of the refracted pencil. The ray R'' meets the axis at P, whereas the ray R meets it at P' farther on. Thus whilst the rays corresponding with R are gathered at the point P', those corresponding with R'' are spread out below it constituting *coma*. (Fig. 26.)

Fig. 26.

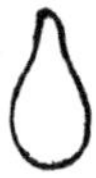

This incorrectness, like so many others, is kept within bounds by the use of the diaphragm, which in the above case would cut off the ray R, and permit only such to pass as would converge on the axis C P to a single point, P, or to a sufficiently near approximation.

§ 4.—Curvature of the Field.

If we suppose an object of some size placed before a lens, we shall find that its extremities do not come to focus on the same plane as its centre.

Fig. 27.

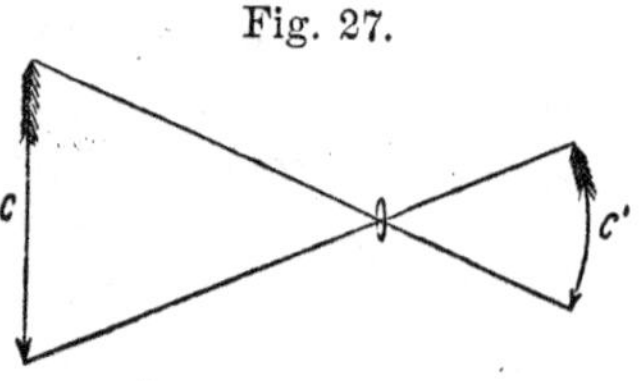

The arrow C is supposed to be so distant that its ends and centre may be regarded as equally far removed from the lens. Now if the centre of the arrow C has focus at C', its extremities will have their focus not in a plane perpendicular to the axis of the lens, but at points nearer to the lens. The whole image, therefore, will not fall upon a plane, but upon a concave surface. As it is necessary that it should be rendered flat, we shall consider the means of doing this by the conjoint operation of the diaphragm and the correction of the lens.

Diaphragms.—If a diaphragm or stop were placed immediately in contact with a lens, it would virtually reduce the lens to one the size of the diaphragm. But the diaphragm is always placed some distance away, and then every part of the lens concurs in forming the picture, but each part is only permitted to act upon those rays for which it is intended.

Fig. 28.

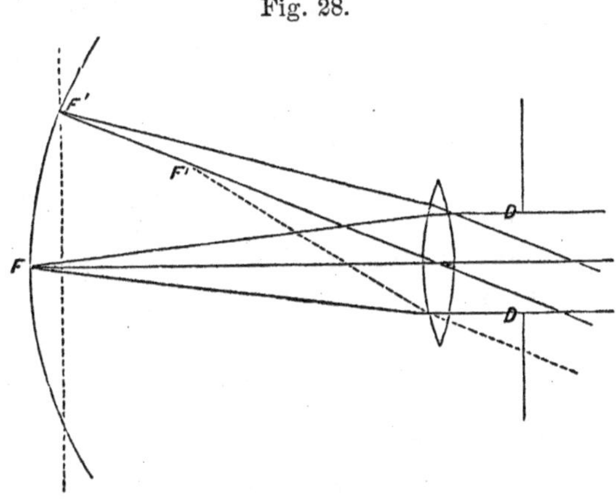

By the interposition of the diaphragm, the dotted oblique ray, for example, which would reach its focus at a much nearer point, is cut off, and only those rays are permitted to pass which meet at a focus as nearly as possible in the plane in which the central rays find their focus at *F*. Here is at once a valuable approximation towards a plane field.

Moreover, by virtue of the stop the rays which form the image meet with a very small angle, and it is evident that the focussing screen may be brought into such a position that all parts of the image will be very good focus at the same time.

This is *flattening the field by use of the diaphragm.*

Correction.—But the field may also be flattened in the same manner that the correction for chromatic aberration is applied.

Fig. 29.

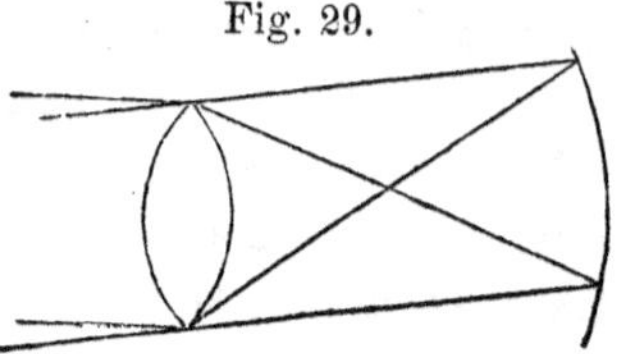

In the simple lens, as seen in Fig. 29, the field is very curved. If we now add the correcting negative lens to remove the color, we shall lengthen out the oblique pencils *more* than the central, as seen in Fig. 30. *This is flattening the field by correction of the lens.*

Fig. 30.[1]

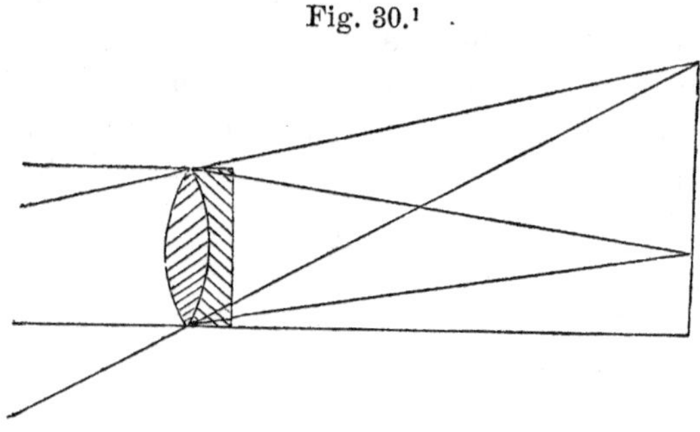

As this correction may be applied to any extent, it may even be carried so far as to bend the field backward, and throw the foci of *the oblique* pencils *beyond* the plane of the central ones.

§ 5.—Distortion.

The mathematical conception of a lens regards it as consisting merely of its bounding planes, and destitute of thickness. If lenses actually possessed this form, the images produced by them would correspond strictly with the principles already laid down. But all lenses necessarily possessing a definite thickness, the image is thereby deformed, unless special measures be taken to correct such distortion.

Every right line, no matter what be its inclination, if it be directly in front of the lens, so that the prolongation of the axis of the lens passes through it, is imaged on the screen as a right line, whether perpendicular, horizontal, or inclined, because of its symmetrical position with respect to the different parts of the lens.

But if the line be not symmetrically placed, that is, if the prolongation of the axis of the lens do not pass through it, then the

[1] By an error of the engraver the oblique rays of this figure have not been deflected at the lens.

image of such a right line will be curved, with its concavity turned toward the axis of the lens, and a square, for example, will be represented, as in Fig. 31.

Fig. 31.

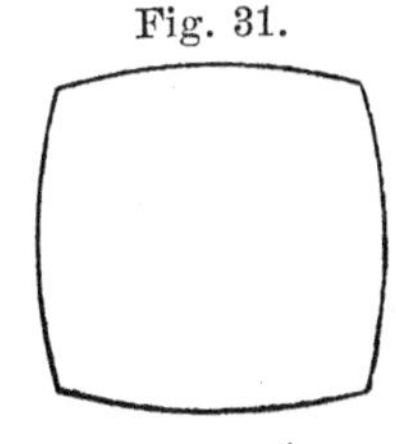

This is termed *barrel distortion*, and is seen in the single view lens.

The *position of the diaphragm* has necessarily a strong influence on distortion. When the diaphragm is in front of the lens, as in the case of the view lens, the crossing of the rays takes place in front of the lens, and the lower part of the lens receives the rays from the upper part of the object, and the distortion is barrel-shaped. If the diaphragm be placed behind the lens, the crossing of the rays takes place *behind* the lens, and the lower part of the lens receives the rays from the lower part of the object. If now we take the case of two lenses with a stop between, as in photographic doublets, the one compensates the other, and the distortion disappears completely if the lenses be exactly similar and the stop be placed equidistant from each.

CHAPTER IV.

FOCAL LENGTHS OF LENSES.

§ 1.—**Images of External Objects.**

NOTHING is more important to the photographer than to have a clear conception of the action of lenses in forming images of objects; and this the writer will endeavor to present in a manner as simple and as much divested of technicalities as possible.

If in the shutter of a dark room we make a small opening, images of external objects will be formed upon the opposite wall; and it is important to the student to remark that these images are formed without the interposition of any lens whatever.

If several small openings be made at irregular distances, several images of the whole external view will be formed upon the wall, irregularly superposed upon one another, and consequently producing complete confusion. If, now, these various openings be supposed to approach each other until they join, they will form one larger opening. The confusion spoken of before will now be materially diminished. Although each part of the opening produces its separate image, yet all these innumerable images will be more or less nearly superposed. External objects will be recognizable, but their borders will be indistinct and undefined. *The brightness* of the picture will increase exactly with the area of the opening, and diminish as it diminishes.

We thus find ourselves in the dilemma, that to obtain a well-defined image, the opening must be so diminished[1] that the illumination becomes utterly insufficient. On the other hand, where the opening is large enough to give a good illumination, the definition is totally destroyed.

It is here that the lens gives us its indispensable aid; and the manner in which this aid is given is exceedingly instructive. Let A be the opening in a shutter, the image $D\ E$ of any external object, $B\ C$ will be formed on the wall behind the opening.

Fig. 32.

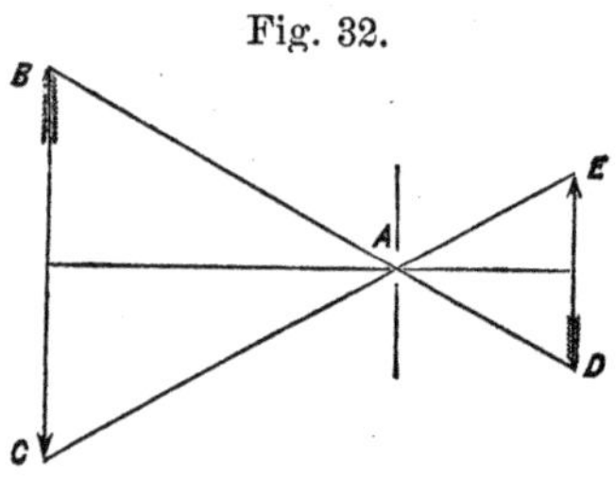

But the image of each point in the external object will be expanded over a considerable surface, and will overlap the images of the surrounding objects, as in Fig. 33, light from the point P, instead of being confined to the point P' of the image, reaches a surface $A'\ B'$. We have already seen that

Fig. 33.

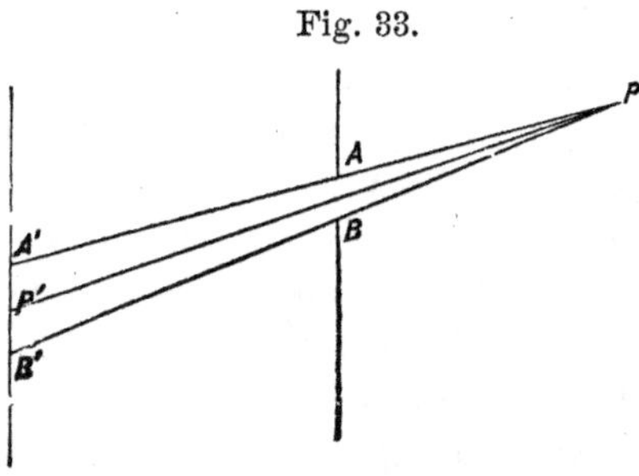

a lens has the property of bringing parallel rays to a focus. If, therefore, we place a lens at the opening, all the rays from a

[1] With an excessive diminution of the opening, another difficulty presents itself, that of diffraction. The lines of light are bent by the edges of the opening.

given point that reach that lens, are again brought to a point inside the room.

Thus, if *P*, Fig. 34, be any object exterior to a room, it is evident that if there were no shutter *A B* interposed, the parallel rays coming from any distant point *P* would fall upon every part of the opposite wall. If now we interpose a shutter with an opening *A B*, the light from *P* is restricted, and can only reach the part of the wall *A′ B′*. An indistinct image is therefore formed—indistinct because the rays from *P*, which, for a sharp picture, should have only reached *P′* at the centre of *A′ B′*, have spread all over it. If now we place a lens at *A B*, which will cause all the parallel rays from *P* to meet again at *P′*, we shall then obtain a sharp image.

Fig. 34.

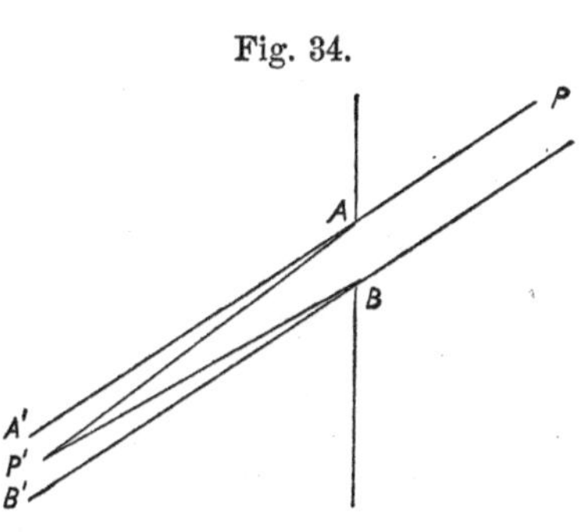

But now a new condition comes in with the lens *A B*. Images were formed though the wall were at any distance from the opening. But with the lens the surface that receives the image must be at a fixed distance from the lens. This distance is its focal length. Measured from the back surface of the lens, it is called the "back focus," an extremely rough and erroneous mode of measurement. Measured from the true point (the centre of emission, hereafter explained) it is the *absolute* focus, also called the principal focus or equivalent focus.

If rays from an external object fall upon the lens *L*, Fig. 35, and an image is formed at *F*, the focal length would be the distance from *F* to the lens at *L*, supposing the lens to have no thickness. But as all lenses have thickness, the question immediately arises, from what point or part of the lens or lenses is the measurement to be taken?

Fig. 35.

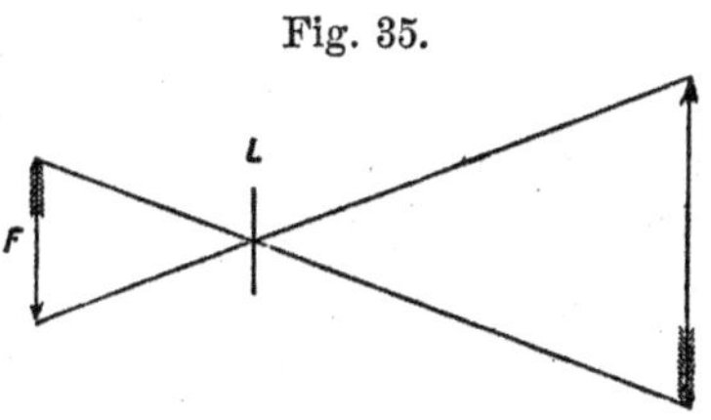

To answer this question it is necessary that we should get a clear idea of certain remarkable points belonging to lenses, single or compound.

§ 2.—Optical Centre.

All lenses have a remarkable point, to which the above name has been given. All lines that pass through the lens and also through this point, are termed *transversals*, and have the remarkable property that all rays which pass through the lens along their path, emerge from the lens parallel to the direction in which they entered it.

Fig. 36.

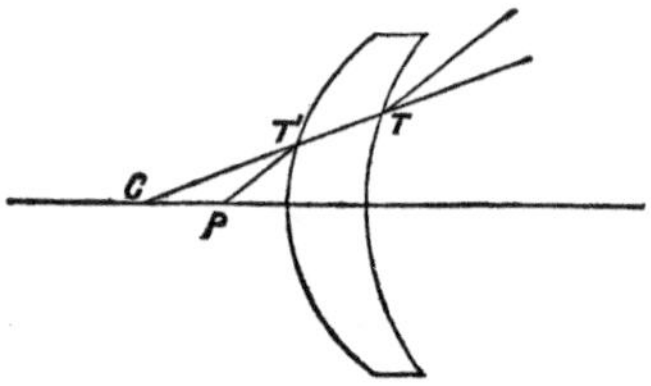

If C be the optic centre, any line $C\ T$ passing through it will be a transversal. If now a ray of light strike the lens at T at such an angle that it follows the path $T\ T'$, it will, on emerging at T', follow the direction $T'\ P$ parallel to its original course.

The optical centre of any lens is easily found. It is only necessary to draw parallel radii from the two centres of curvature, to connect the points at which these radii meet the curves, and to prolong this line till it intersects the axis.

From the centre C of the one curve draw any radius $C\ R$. From the centre C' of the other curve draw another radius $C'\ R'$,

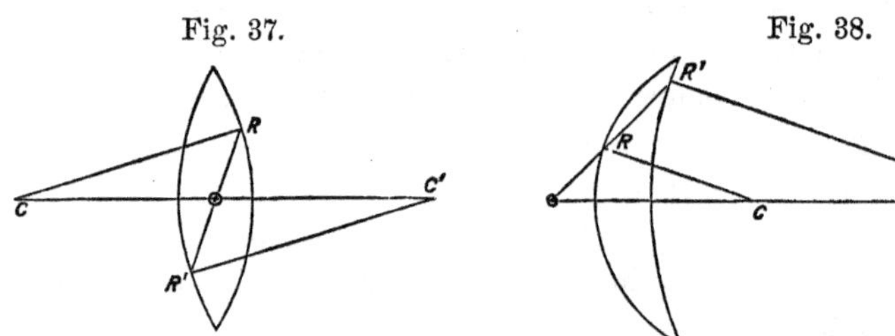

Fig. 37. Fig. 38.

parallel to the first. Connect the points $R\ R'$, prolonging, if necessary, the line of connection $R\ R'$, till it intersects the axis $C\ C'$. The point of intersection O will be the optical centre of the curve. In a double convex lens (Fig. 37) the optical centre falls inside the lens, in the meniscus (Fig. 38) outside of it. In a double convex lens, whose surfaces are of equal curvature, the optical centre will coincide with the centre of the lens.

§ 3.—Centres of Admission and Emission.

These centres play too important a part in photography to be here passed over.

Let O be the optical centre, as before, of a double convex lens; then any lines drawn through it, as $T\ T$, $T'\ T'$, are transversals, and any rays that strike the points $T\ T'$ at such angles of incidence as to follow the course of the transversals, will, as before explained, emerge at $T\ T'$, on the other side of the lens, and follow paths parallel to their original direction.

Fig. 39.

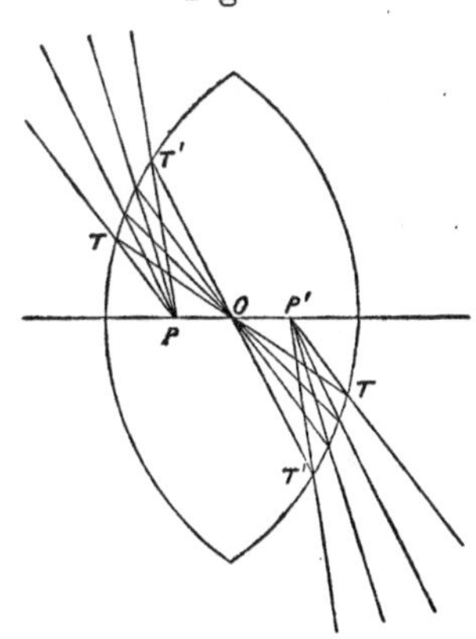

If, now, all the entering rays be prolonged in their original directions, they will converge to a point P on the axis of the lens. This is the *centre of admission*. If the emerging rays be likewise prolonged, they will meet at a point P'. This is the *centre of emission*.

This statement is rigorously true only for rays very nearly parallel with the axis, for others it is simply an approximation.

Now, if in Fig. 40 we have a biconvex lens, and $A\ B$ be an object before it, $C\ D$ its image, the focal length of that lens must be measured from P, its centre of emission, that being the point to which all the rays, $C\ P$, $F\ P$, $D\ P$, converge. And similarly, if we wish to take into account the distance of the object from the lens, it is to be computed neither from the exterior of the lens nor from its centre, but from the centre of admission P'. Consequently, when we speak of the conjugate foci belonging to the lens for an object $A\ B$, and its image $C\ D$, these focal lengths are the lines $F'\ P'$, $F\ P$.

Fig. 40.

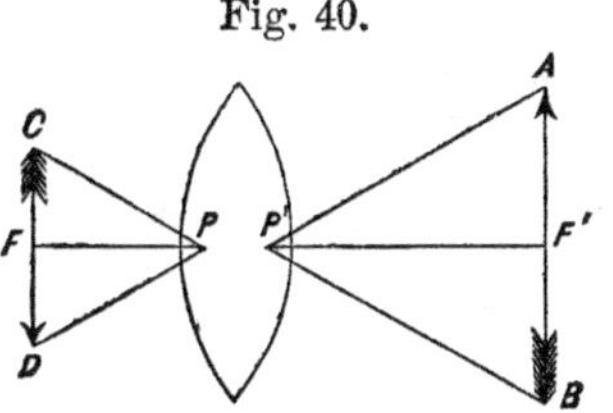

In the following figure of a meniscus lens, the transversals are seen centering at O, the optical centre of the lens. The respective rays $R\ R\ R\ R$ are those that undergoing refraction at the surface

A B, follow the courses of the transversals through the lens. Emerging they take directions *T R′*, &c., parallel to those which they originally had, and all cut the axis at *P*, the centre of emission.

Fig. 41.

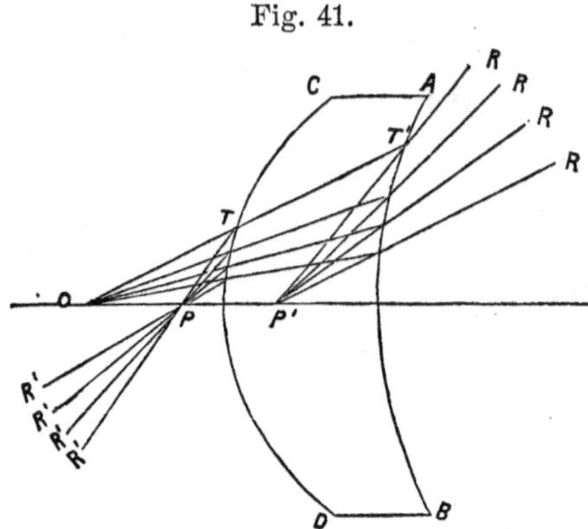

The focal distance of any object in front of this lens will therefore be measured to the centre of admission *P′*. And the focal distance of any image will be measured from that image to the centre of emission *P*.

If the first surface of the lens *A B* be plane, the lens becomes a plano-convex, and the points *O* and *P* both recede to the intersection of the curve *C D* with the axis *O P′*, where they coincide.

§ 4.—To Determine Focal Lengths by Actual Measurement.

This may be done without actually finding the points *P P′*, as follows:—

Suppose that in the accompanying figure *A B* is a distant object, and that with a given lens *L*, it is in correct focus at *F*. Let us substitute another lens, and let us say that thereupon we find the focus removed to any other point *F′*, nearer or further from the lens. Now it is evident that the respective triangles are similar, and therefore the two images are to each other in the same proportion as the lines *P′ F*, *P′ F′*, which are their respective focal lengths. It follows, then, that if we knew either of these focal lengths, we could find the other by measuring the sizes of the images. If we knew the focal length of the first, and found the second to give an image of twice the size, we should know that its focal length was precisely twice that of the other.

Fig. 42.

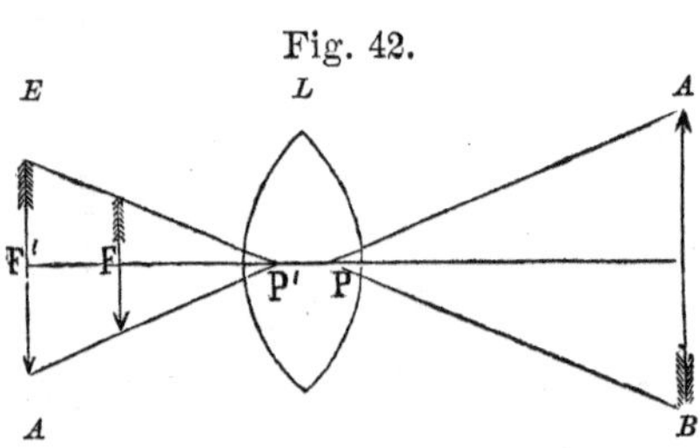

It consequently follows that if we know accurately the focal length of any one lens, we have an easy way to fix that of any other lenses or of any combination of lenses; and this is the method commonly employed by photographic opticians. A standard lens is kept, the focal length of which has been accurately measured. Some convenient distant object, as for example the distance between two distant houses, both far from the observer, is carefully focussed, and the size of the image measured. The known focal length is then divided by the size of the image. This gives a constant number, which, multiplied by the size of image given by any other lens, gives the focal length of that lens. For example, if the standard lens has a focal length of 12 inches, and the image given by it has a length of 4 inches, then $\frac{12}{4}$, that is, 3, is the constant number. If it is found that other lenses, single or compound, give the images respectively $2\frac{1}{2}$, 3, and 5 inches in length, then these lenses have their focal lengths respectively $7\frac{1}{2}$, 9, and 15 inches.

It is obvious that if (as here supposed) the camera is placed always in the same position, the standard lens is unnecessary after the first measurement. Thus, for example, having once ascertained that a given distant object is represented of a given size by a lens of known focal length, we can fix, in the easiest possible manner, the true focal length of any other lens, by measuring the size of the image of such object as rendered by it.

It remains to determine the focal length of a lens or combination without the aid of a comparison of lenses. The only lens which permits of a direct measurement of its focal length, is the plano-convex. If this be adjusted with its plane side to a distant object, the distance from the centre of its convex surface to the focussing screen is the true or absolute focal length.

A plano-convex lens is therefore especially well adapted for a standard of comparison, having, as here figured, its centre of emission at the intersection of its axis, with curved surface.

Fig. 43.

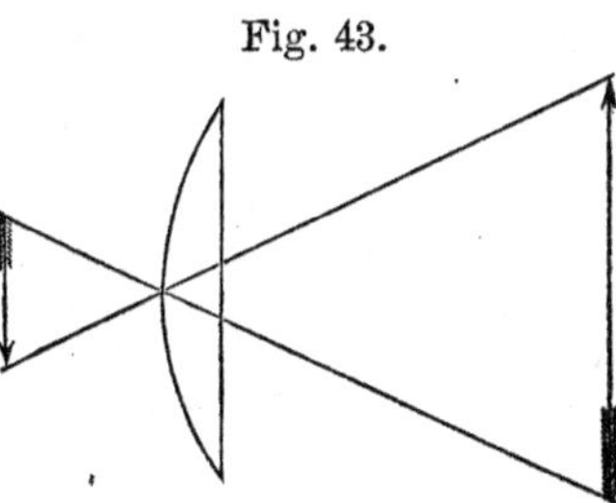

If the plane surface becomes convex, the centre of emission passes into the body of the lens, as seen in a previous figure. If it becomes concave, the centre of emission moves backward from the lens, so that the centre of emission of a meniscus is always outside of the lens (see Figs. 36 and 41). It will thus be seen how far from correct the mode of measuring the focal length from the back of the lens is, since with a meniscus the "back focus" so measured is longer than the true one, and with other forms of photographic objectives shorter.

Another practical method of determining the focal length of any form of photographic objective has been indicated by Mr. Grubb.

Mark the centre of the focussing screen by drawing diagonals from opposite corners. Set the camera on a large sheet of white paper; place the camera so that the images of two well-marked distant points shall be equally distant, one on each side of the centre. Measure the distance of these two points from each other on the screen. Now turn the camera so that one of these points shall fall exactly upon the centre. Having done this, run a pencil along the side of the camera, ruling a line on the paper underneath. Now turn the camera around again, till the other point falls on the centre of the focussing screen, and draw another line on the paper.

Fig. 44.

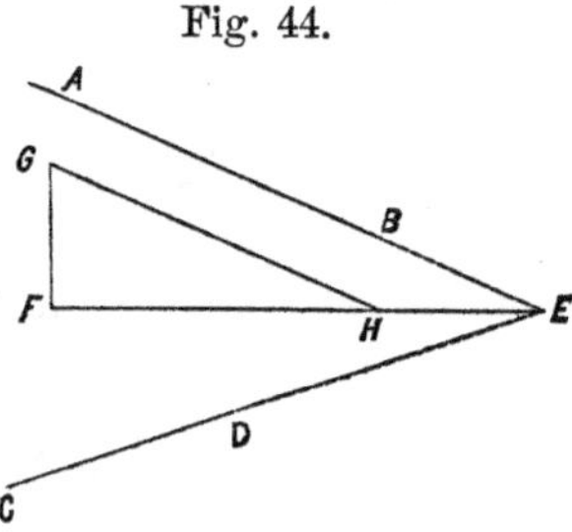

Let $A\ B$ and $C\ D$ be the lines so drawn; continue them till they meet at E. Bisect the angle $A\ E$ by the line $E\ F$. At any point F erect the perpendicular $F\ G$ equal to half the length of the space measured on the ground glass between the points. From G draw $G\ H$ parallel to $A\ B$. The distance of $F\ H$ of its intersection H from F will be the absolute focal length of the objective used.

This having been once correctly done for any one lens, it will serve as a standard for the easy determination of others by the method above described.[1]

[1] Another method is the following: Focus two objects, so that their images will fall upon the ground glass equally distant from the centre, as before described; then measure with a theodolite the angle which these objects subtend. Calling this angle α, and d the distance measured on the ground glass, the focal length will be found by the expression—

$$f = \frac{d}{2 \tan \frac{\alpha}{2}}$$

The method that has frequently been brought forward for finding focal lengths by focussing an object of its own size, and taking one fourth of the distance between the object and the image for the focal length, is essentially inaccurate. It furnishes a tolerable approximation only.

§ 5.—To Calculate the Focal Length of a Lens from its Dimensions.

In the following formulæ, it will be taken for granted that the lens is made of glass, having its refractive power equal to 1.5. The more general expressions will be given in foot-notes. The focus in all cases is determined for sunlight or parallel rays falling parallel with the axis of the lens, and the focal lengths are measured from the centre of the lenses.[1]

In the case of a *glass sphere* the focal length is $1\frac{1}{2}$ times the radius, measured from the centre of the sphere. It falls therefore beyond the sphere at the distance of half the radius from the surface.[2]

Double Convex Lens.[3]—If the curves on both sides are equal, the focal length will be equal to the radius.

If unequal, multiply the radii together, and divide by half their sum. If the radii are respectively 5 and 7 inches, the focal length will be $\frac{35}{6}$ inches or $5\frac{5}{6}$ inches.

Plano-convex Lens.—Where the plane side is exposed, the focus will be twice the radius, measured from the convex side. Where the rays fall on the convex surface, $\frac{2}{3}$ the thickness of the lens must be deducted from twice the radius, and this will be measured from the plane side.

Meniscus Lens.—Multiply the radii, and divide the result by half the difference of the radii. For example, a meniscus has its positive curve with a radius of 5 and its negative 7 inches, its focal length will be $\frac{35}{\frac{1}{2}(7-5)}$, or 35 inches.

[1] These calculations are all based (except when otherwise specified) according to custom, and for simplicity, upon the supposition that the lens has no thickness.

[2] The general expression is as follows: Let r equal index of refraction, R the radius, f the focal length, then $f = R\frac{r}{2(r-1)}$

[3] The general expression for the focal length of any lens in terms of its radii, is $\frac{2RR'}{R \pm R'}$, the positive sign belonging to the biconvex lens, the negative to the meniscus.

If the concave surface had a radius of 5 and the convex of 7, the focus would be the same, but it would be a *virtual focus*, an imaginary one in front of the lens.

Fig. 45.

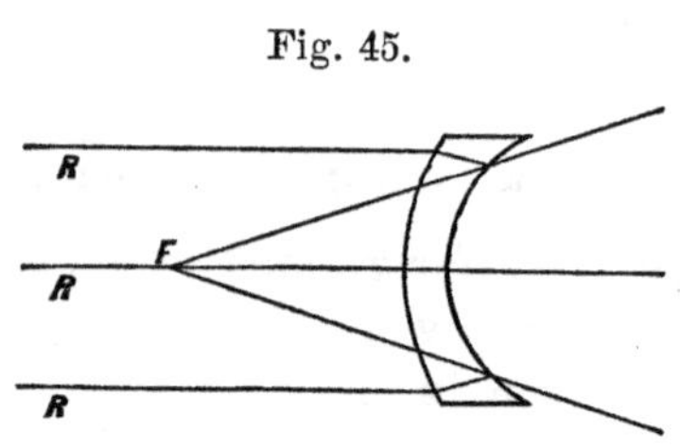

So in Fig. 45, the parallel rays *R R R* are spread out by the negative meniscus, so that if their direction were continued backwards, they would meet at *F*, the virtual focus.

Although this focus has only an imaginary existence, it becomes important in computing the effect of introducing a *negative lens*, as in several forms of photographic objectives.

§ 6.—Focal Lengths of Combined Lenses Computed from their Elements.

Where two lenses of known focal length are combined together, it is easy to determine the focal length of the combination. It becomes here necessary, however, to take into account the distance at which *the two lenses are separated*, as the focal length always increases as this separation increases.

Add the two focal lengths together, and subtract the distance of separation. Multiply the two focal lengths together, and divide this last quantity by the first, which gives the focal length.[1] This formula, which, like the preceding, proceeds on the supposition that glass with a refractive power of 1.5 to the material of the lenses, is the mode of calculation employed by opticians in their constructions.

Two lenses of 6 and 10 inches focal length respectively, separated one inch, will have their combined focal length $\frac{6 \times 10}{16-1}$, or 4 inches.

If these lenses when combined are to have a focal length of 5 inches, this can be effected by giving them a separation of 4 inches, because $\frac{6 \times 10}{16-4}$ is 5 inches.

[1] If f and f' are the respective focal lengths, and d the distance of separation, then the combined focus will be $\frac{f f'}{f+f'-d}$

§ 7.—Conjugate Foci.

Up to the present point we have considered parallel rays only. But when divergent or convergent rays fall upon a lens, its focal length is thereby necessarily altered.

Thus the lens A B having its focus at F for parallel rays, may have it at D for diverging, and at E for converging rays.

Fig. 46.

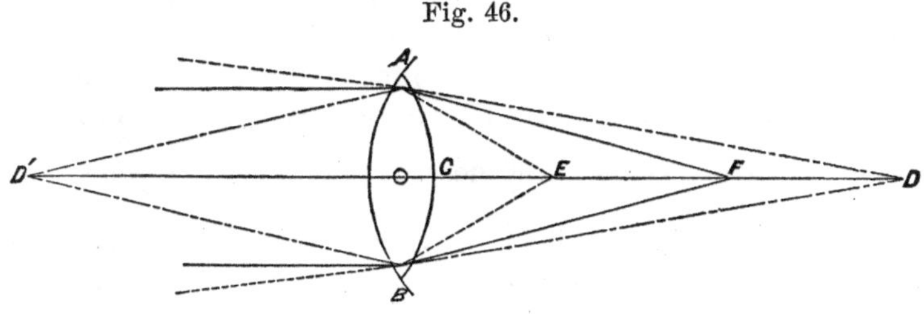

If D' be a point from which diverging rays emanate and these converge again after passing through the lens, at D, these two points D and D', are termed conjugate foci. If D' be an object, it will have its focus at D. These points are interchangeable, so that if the object be placed at D, its focus will be at D'.

Fig. 47.

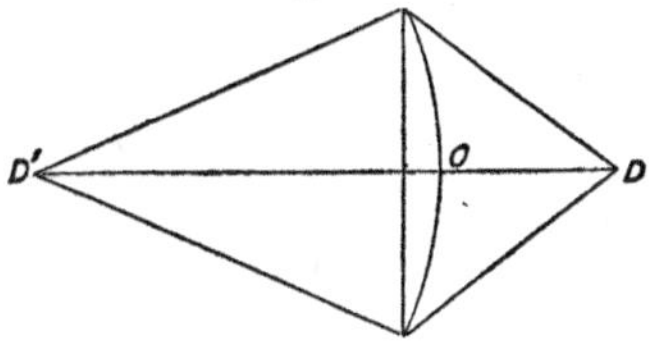

To observe this better, let us take a plano-convex lens, with its plane side to the object.

The object D' has its focus at D. If the principal focus (that for parallel rays) be called f, and the distance D' C, u and C D, v, then we shall have this relation :—

$$\frac{1}{f} = \frac{1}{u} + \frac{1}{v} \text{ or } v = \frac{fu}{u-f}$$

This equation will permit, if the principal focal length is known, to determine the position of the image D of any object situated at any point D.′ If, for example, the lens have a focus of 6 inches, and the object D' is 10 feet or 120 inches off, we shall have—

$$v = \frac{6 \times 120}{120-6} = \frac{720}{114} = 6.315.$$

The focus of the lens will, therefore, be a little over three-tenths of an inch longer for an object at the distance of 10 feet, than for a very distant object, that is to to say, for parallel rays.

It will be seen that this formula gives a very simple rule for calculating focal lengths. If the principal or absolute focal distance of a lens be known, and we place an object nearer to the lens, and require to know what will be the focal length of the lens for such an object, we have only to take these two quantities—the absolute focal length and the distance of the object. First multiply them and then subtract them, and divide the first number by the second, as in the example where 120 was multiplied by 6, and divided by 120 less six.

It is a very important point, and one that has been too often overlooked in treating the subject elementarily, that the formula $\frac{1}{f} = \frac{1}{u} + \frac{1}{v}$ neglects the thickness of the lens. In practice it is necessary either to introduce a correction for this quantity[1], or else to consider the various focal lengths as measured from the centres of admission and emission already described (p. 67). In the case of a plano-convex lens, these centres fall together at the centre of the convex curve, and the focal lengths are correctly measured from the point C in the figure.

CHAPTER V.

PHOTOGRAPHIC OBJECTIVES.

In this chapter will be briefly considered the various forms of photograpic objectives now chiefly used.

§ 1.—The View Lens.

By a view lens is understood a single achromatic combination, usually consisting of two pieces, forming a meniscus or a plano-convex lens, with the concave or plane face, as the case may be,

[1] The most general form of expression for conjugate foci is

$$v = \frac{u \left\{ n\, r\, r' - (n-1)\, t\, r' \right\} + t\, r\, r'}{u \left\{ n\,(n-1)\,(r + r') - (n-1)^2\, t \right\} + (n-1)\, t\, r - n\, r\, r'}$$

where t is the thickness of the lens, r r' the radii, and n the index of refraction.—*Secretan, Systèmes Optiques Convergents*, 54.

turned to the light. This form of lens is figured at page 57, Fig. 22. The combination of a double convex of crown and a double concave of flint glass is the usual method employed.

Latterly Dallmeyer has produced a wide angle view lens, constructed of three pieces, as shown in the margin (Fig. 48).

A flint negative meniscus is inclosed between two menisci of crown glass. In these two latter the crown glass is not of equal refractive power, the rear lens having a somewhat less index of refraction than the front.

Fig. 48.

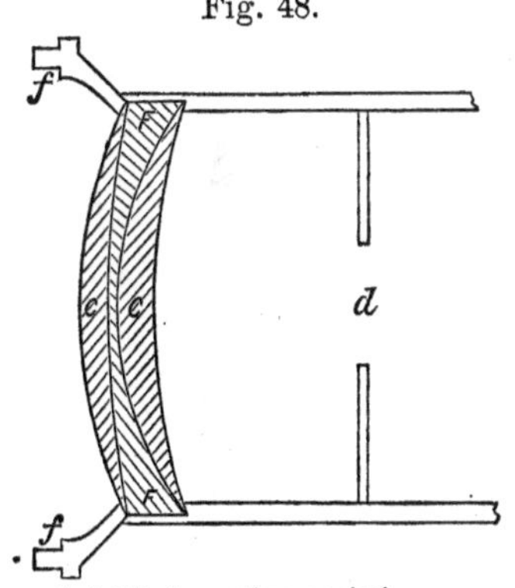

f, f. Flint negative menisci.
c, c. Two positive menisci of crown.
d. Diaphragm.

Grubb's aplanatic is another form of the single view lens. It is, moreover, arranged with a "portable mount," by which the position of the stop is altered. And when it is desired to include a larger angle than usual, the stop is pushed in until this angle is exactly attained. The arrangement is advantageous, and might well be used by others. This lens, and Dallmeyer's wide angle, are excellent lenses for landscapes, though, as in such lenses it is impossible to avoid distortion, they are quite unsuitable for architectural work; copying, also, they are quite unfit for. But atmospheric perspective, which is so desirable in all views of natural scenery, is better rendered by the view lens than by the more complex forms, which give straighter lines. In general, it may be affirmed in photography that each description of work has its appropriate form of lens, for which another can rarely be substituted without some disadvantage.

If a comparison be instituted between these two best forms of the single view lens, it will be found that the Dallmeyer lens embraces a considerably wider angle of view, so that a picture of the usual oblong shape can be obtained, whose greater dimension is equal to the focal length of the lens—that is, a lens of $8\frac{1}{2}$ inches focal length will cover a $\frac{4}{4}$ plate, a 10 inch focus lens an $\frac{8}{10}$ plate.

§ 2.—The Portrait Lens.

The form of objective represented at Fig. 49 is that at the present time exclusively used for portraiture. It was the result of

Fig. 49.

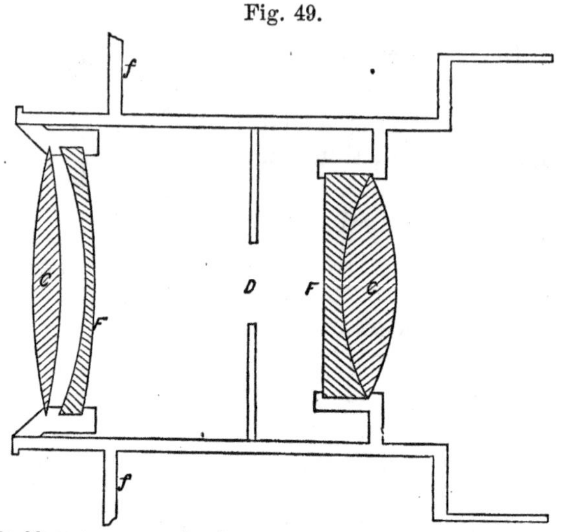

C, C. Double convex crown glass lenses.
F, F. Negative flint lenses; the front, plano-concave, the back, negative meniscus.
f, f. Flange.
D. Diaphragm.

the labors of Petzval, of Vienna, who calculated this combination, and by its immense improvement over the systems previously in use for portraiture gave a vast impetus to that branch of photographic art. A glance at the figure will at once explain the nature of the arrangement.

As the portrait is most natural and effective when the sitter has not been compelled for a length of time to retain his position, and as the chances of moving are greatly increased with the length of the exposure, the great object of the portrait combination is to throw as strong a body of light into the camera as possible. Considerations of depth of focus, correction for spherical aberration, &c., have been necessarily, to some extent, subordinated to the one great need.

It follows that, instead of having many planes in excellent focus simultaneously, as in the case of the view lens, the portrait lens is very restricted in this respect, and hence cannot be appropriately used except for the purpose for which it is intended.

Some portrait lenses, especially the Jamin Darlot lenses, are arranged to permit of the front portion, consisting of the double convex and plano-concave, to be unscrewed, and after reversing, be screwed into the same flange for use as a view lens. This is a very convenient system; it is, however, liable to the objection that the front surface of the view lens thus made is plane, instead of concave. Now, to get the best results, not only the front surface should be concave, but this concavity should be considerable. Such a view lens cannot, therefore, be expected to give strictly first-rate results, though it may do good work. It cannot be too clearly understood by the student, that the whole system of photographic objectives is a system of compromises between conflicting troubles; that these compromises can always be best adjusted for some definite end, and that consequently when one sort of objective is made to do another's work, such work is always done at a disadvantage.

Another maxim, familiar to experienced photographers, is *never to strain a lens.* Some who purchase a lens intended to cover a given size of plate, and who find that by using a very small stop, good definition can be got over a materially larger plate than that for which the lens was advertised, think they have made a useful discovery, and perhaps avail themselves of it habitually. The work so produced will never have the boldness, atmospheric effect, gradation of distance, and transparency of shadow given by a lens used with a larger opening.

On the other hand, it is a mistake to use a lens intended for larger views, in taking small ones. Lenses for large views are unavoidably slower, and the extent of angle included in a small view, taken by a longer focus lens, is too small. An exception to this is when a lens, like the triplet, is used for instantaneous effect, and where it is worked with a large stop, rejecting all but the centre of the image.

§ 3.—**The Triplet.**

The triplet lens consists of two large achromatized menisci, between which is placed a small negative lens as near as possible to the diaphragm. The length of the focus is thereby increased, but at the same time marginal definition is obtained.

The triplet is a lens which, although possessing great merits, has been somewhat over-praised. It is a useful lens undoubt-

Fig. 50.

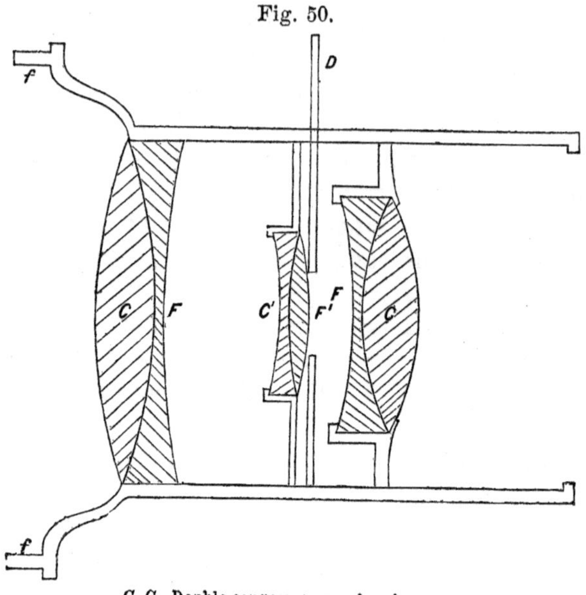

C, C. Double convex crown glass lenses.
F, F. Double concave flint.
C'. Double concave crown.
F'. Double convex flint.
D. Diaphragm with its opening at *F'*.
f, f. Flange.

edly, but since critically examining its power, the writer finds himself led to the following comparison:—

For architectural objects, it is surpassed by Zentmayer's lens, which gives lines equally straight, and includes a very much larger angle. Where angle is no object, where we have free open space to the desired direction about the architectural object, there only the triplet has an advantage in the larger diaphragm and quicker actions which it admits of.

For copying, it is surpassed by the same lens.

For views not embracing architectural objects, or where these are not near the margin, and are inconspicuous, it is undoubtedly surpassed by the view lens, especially by Dallmeyer's wide angle view lens.

For portraiture, it is inferior to the portrait lens, being much slower. By removing the central negative lens, however, its action is increased; but the centre of the image only is sharp enough for use, as in the case of portraits to be vignetted.

For groups it is the best lens that we have, unless it shall prove to be surpassed by Steinheil's new Aplanatic, and Dallmeyer's Rapid Rectilinear, as now seems possible.

The triplet may, therefore, be considered as a servant of all work, but (except in the case of groups) scarcely doing any of it as well as lens especially made for that specific work. For such amateurs as wish to do a variety of work, but feel that they can allow themselves but one lens, it will be an appropriate acquisition. It should be distinctly understood that a good triplet is capable of doing almost any photographic work well, that it is, in fact, the only approach we have to a universal lens. Some beautiful landscapes, by G. W. Wilson and other distinguished photographers, have been taken with it, and exquisite copying work. Perhaps my meaning will be more clear, if I say that some landscapes can be taken fully as artistically with the triplet as with the view lens, but others again cannot. Some engravings can be copied very well by the triplet, but in other cases of copying, particularly where extreme exactness is needed, it is surpassed by other lenses.

The triplet possesses one advantage, which must not be passed over. An extension of the size of the diaphragm, whilst it greatly impairs marginal definition, does not at the same time destroy that of the centre. Consequently, where rapid work is wanted, as in taking photographs of animals, instantaneous views, &c., it may advantageously be employed. Of course, the size of the plate to be covered must be proportionately diminished, or else want of definition at the margin must be submitted to.

It is evident, however, that if we can cover a half plate by using a whole plate lens with large diaphragm, and so greatly shorten the exposure, we have what, in many cases, is a very material advantage. And this we gain with the triplet.

The many surfaces of glass in the lenses composing the triplet is an objection to it, as tending to the introduction of diffuse light into the camera. Triplets made by different makers vary very much in their performances, especially in the size of stop with which they will work, and their value is always in proportion to the size of stop with which they can be satisfactorily used.

§ 4.—The Globe Lens.

The globe form of lens was devised in this country by Mr. Schnitzer, and was manufactured by him in connection with the late Mr. Harrison. Its characteristic feature lies in this, that the exterior curves, back and front, form part of one and the same sphere, the diaphragm being placed at the centre of that sphere. Consequently it follows that the incident ray R, Fig. 52, which passes through the centre, has a *nearly* perpendicular incidence upon the outside surface. It therefore undergoes but little deviation at either of the four surfaces, but necessarily encounters some, and is bent from its original direction $R\ P$ down to D.

Fig. 51.

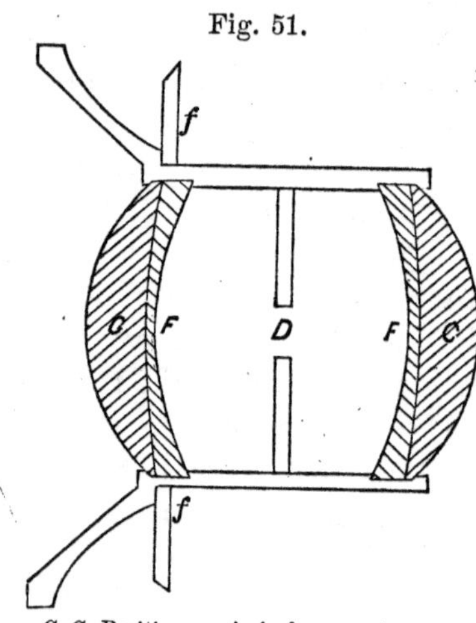

C, C. Positive menisci of crown glass.
F, F. Negative menisci of flint glass.
D. Diaphragm.
f, f. Flange.

More erroneous statements, both favorable and unfavorable, have been published in respect of this, than of any other lens that ever was invented. The inventors claimed too much for it, whilst some of its critics made unjustifiable misstatements respecting it. Its appearance unquestionably made an era in photography, by putting it into the power of the photographer to obtain pictures embracing an angle never before possible. This

Fig. 52.

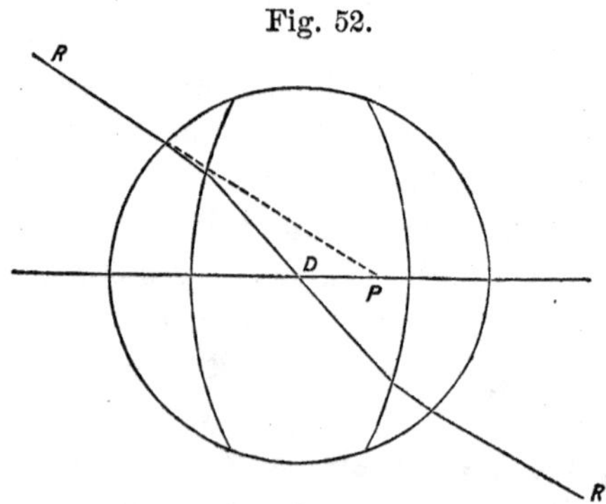

improvement was so well appreciated, that the lenses were strained to cover more than they properly could, an effect attainable only by using the very small stops. It resulted that flat and meaningless pictures were produced in great quantities, and the advance of landscape photography in America was materially retarded, for these lenses acquired a great popularity here, and for a time nearly superseded all others for landscape work. Great numbers were also exported. The form of lens was also largely imitated abroad, both by exact reproductions and by modified forms, depending upon the same idea.

This and another American lens, that of Mr. Zentmayer, are remarkable for the absolutely true perspective which they give. Where a great breadth of what is known to artists as "parallel perspective" is represented, the triplet gives a slight convergence, as the writer has convinced himself by actual measurement, whereas the globe preserves a perfect parallelism.

It is to be concluded, therefore, that when the globe is judiciously employed—that is, when the smallest stop, and, if practicable, the next to smallest is avoided, and it is not sought to cover too large a plate—it is capable of doing good work. It is in one respect like the triplet, that is, it is capable of being turned to a great variety of uses—landscape work, portraiture, architectural reproductions, and copying, in each of which—certainly at least in the first two, and probably in the others—it is surpassed by other lenses.

§ 5.—**The Zentmayer Lens.**

Mr. Joseph Zentmayer, of this city, has succeeded in making a photographic objective of a single sort of glass, his lenses being both uncorrected menisci. Nevertheless, in these objectives the chemical and visual foci are practically coincident. This single fact would be enough to invest the lens with interest, but its performances are sufficiently remarkable to indicate that this lens will be adopted for all those descriptions of work to which it is especially suited.

Fig. 53.

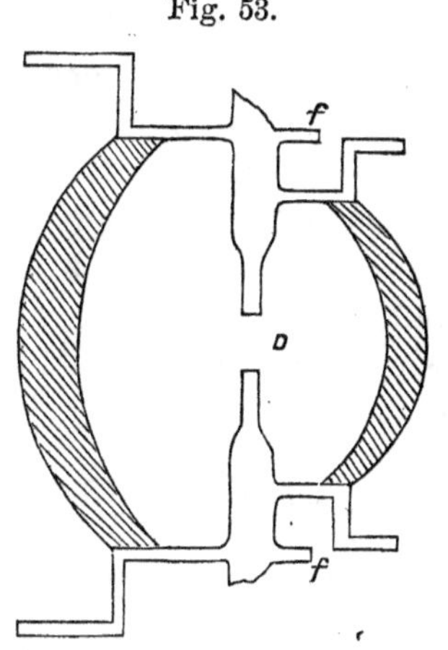

D. Diaphragm. *f, f.* Flange.

Fig. 53 will give a clear idea of the system of construction. The front and back curves of each lens stand to each other in the relation of 12 to 13, and the two lenses to each other in the ratio of 2 to 3. The stop is advanced a little nearer to the front lens than the centre of curvature of the exterior surface of the larger lens.

It is evident that by having a series of lenses of different sizes, the larger lens of one pair may serve as the smaller lens for the next larger pair. On this principle these lenses are manufactured. The complete sets embrace six lenses, capable of forming five pairs, having a great range of focal lengths. Smaller sets are made, in which four lenses form three pairs.

The revolving diaphragms are furnished with three holes. The larger of these is simply for focussing, and cannot be used for photography, the image so attained being quite destitute of definition. The middle stop is the most generally useful.

These lenses include a wonderful angle—fully as much as can ever be advantageously used, and much more than covered by the globe lens. The architectural effects attained are good, and bolder than would be expected from the small size of the stop that must be used. The reflecting surfaces which the ray meets in this lens are fewer than in any other centrally stopped objective, and this gives brilliancy as well as diminishes the proportion of light lost. For copying these lenses are at least as good as any, and perhaps better. As they are not achromatized, the cost of making is greatly diminished.

It is affirmed that these lenses give a circular field of very nearly double their focal length, and this computed by their true focal length, which, of course, is longer than the "back focus" often used to roughly indicate the focal length of lenses. In comparing different lenses, it is always necessary to bear this carefully in mind, otherwise injustice is done. The focal lengths by which Zentmayer's lenses are known, are always the true focal lengths. Those advertised to the globe lenses are the "back foci," than which the true focal lengths may be one-half longer, as, for example, a globe lens in my possession sold as a "3-inch," has, in fact, a focal length of 4½ inches when correctly measured.[1]

[1] Public opinion should compel all opticians to sell their lenses under the designations of their true, absolute, or "equivalent" foci. No other system does justice to the purchaser.

§ 6.—The Steinheil Lens.

The lens of Professor Steinheil, like the foregoing, consists of a pair of uncorrected menisci, but in this case of equal size. The visual and chemical foci do not here coincide, but require a correction. The focussing screen, after taking the usual focus, must be returned $\frac{1}{48}$ for very distant objects, and materially more for near ones. For example, if the object and the image be of equal size, the correction will be about $\frac{1}{12}$, and intermediate for intermediate distances.

Fig. 54.

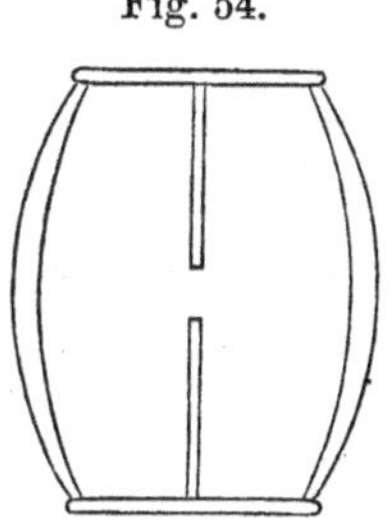

The inconvenience of this correction is a sufficient objection to the lens. It gives, however, a very remarkable angle; and it is wonderful to see how large a picture is produced by a very small lens of this description. As the diaphragm is small, the illumination is consequently faint, and the exposure prolonged. This lens is not the less a remarkable optical work, though less so than Zentmayer's, with which its discovery appears to have taken place at nearly the same time. Both forms are patented.

Steinheil has lately constructed an achromatized doublet, to which he gives the name of "aplanatic," which has proved itself to be a useful lens. Like the triplet and globe, it may be employed for taking groups, portraits, and views. Its sphere of utility corresponds nearly with that of a good triplet, whilst it includes a much larger angle. In using it the focus must invariably be taken with the largest stop, and then a smaller must be introduced to give the necessary sharpness. This evidently creates a difficulty in deciding how small a stop is needed in any particular case. Nevertheless, the instrument has been very highly spoken of by good judges.

§ 7.—Ross's Doublet.

Mr. Ross's form of doublet, Fig. 55, has been favorably spoken of. It is intended for views and architecture, of which last it preserves the straight lines, and for copying. A material convenience is afforded with this lens, an internal shutter, sliding across the opening of the diaphragm, instead of covering and un-

Fig. 55.

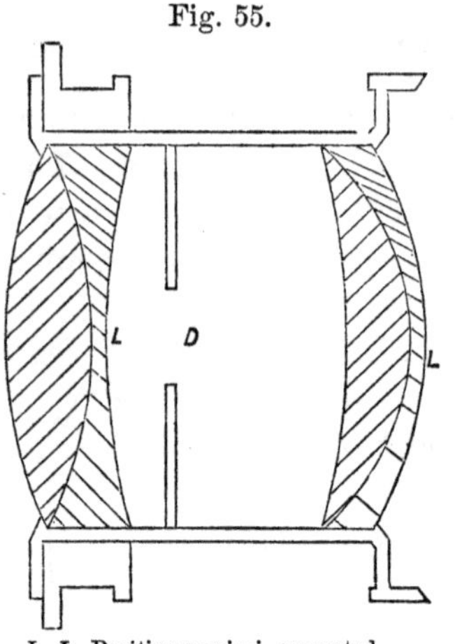

L, L. Positive menisci, corrected.
D. Diaphragm.
f, f. Flange.

covering the lens in the usual way with a cap. This feature has been also introduced into Zentmayer's lenses.

Ross's lenses may be separated, and each can be used as a single landscape lens.

§ 8.—Other Forms of Photographic Lenses.

Orthoscopic Lens.—This form which, like the portrait lens, we owe to Petzval, has been extensively used, especially in this country. Harrison manufactured many good objectives of this form; but on introducing the globe lens, he stopped making the orthoscopic, and this lens is now but little used here. In Germany it seems to have kept its place better.

The orthoscopic is a good copying lens, but slow, owing to its long focus, and the small stop generally used with it in copying. For taking views, a stop of considerable size may be employed; and, as it has a considerable depth of focus, it is by some much prized for landscape work; though this is rather in Germany than here. Small pictures of landscape scenery are well taken by the smaller orthoscopic lenses, because in them the focal length is not far from corresponding with that of the eye. But large pictures made with the orthoscopic require a lens of very long focus; and it results that planes of distance are not well rendered, the foregrounds become indistinct and inconspicuous, and distant objects look unnaturally near.

Busch's Pantascope consists of two corrected lenses with a central stop. It includes a very large angle of view, and has been highly spoken of. A very carefully constructed camera appears to be necessary for it.

Rectilinear, and Rapid Rectilinear.—Dallmeyer has lately introduced two new lenses under these two names, which, though similar enough to lead possibly to confusion, characterize very different lenses. The *Rectilinear* was introduced in 1867. A specimen examined by the writer was a good deal similar to the globe, but a better lens, including a wider angle, and apparently free from "ghost" or flare. The *Rapid Rectilinear* the writer has not seen. It is described as made of flint corrected by flint, in this resembling Steinheil's *aplanatic*, in which respect Dallmeyer claims precedence of Steinheil. It has just been introduced, and will probably prove a valuable instrument. The first includes an angle of 100°, the latter of about 60°, but is more rapid.

The Fitz Lens.—The late Mr. Fitz, of New York, just before his death, had completed a form of lens, which, however, does not seem to have been able to compete successfully with the other new lenses introduced about the same time.

The Ratio Lens was introduced a short time back by Mr. Harrison's successors. It consists of a pair of achromatized lenses of different sizes, and adapted so that the larger lens of one pair may become the smaller lens of a larger pair, in the same way as described in Zentmayer's.

Panoramic Cameras.—The theory of this very ingenious instrument, by which such beautiful results have been obtained, is as follows:—

Let J be the centre of emission of the cone of rays coming out from any objective, single, double, or triple, which finds its focus on the screen $S\ S'$.

Fig. 56.

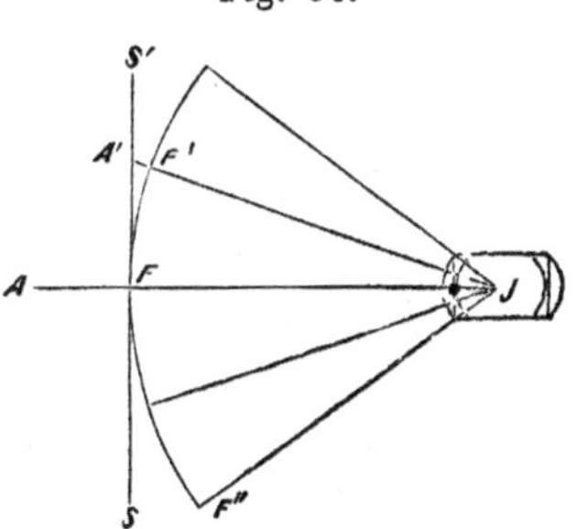

If now the lens be made to rotate horizontally, *on J as a centre*, the position of objects in the image formed on the focussing screen *will not change.* If the image of any exterior object, for example, falls at the centre F, the rotation of the lens will not cause the image of that body to move, but it will remain accurately at F until the lens rotates so much that it passes out of the field of view.

Now, to avail ourselves of this property, we must remember that when the lens is rotated so that its axis passes from the direction $J\ A$ to the direction $J\ A'$, its image is no longer in focus on the screen at A', but at the point F'; because the central ray is now in the direction $J\ A'$, and its focal length will be the same it originally was, viz., $J\ F$ or $J\ F'$.

The first idea for applying these principles would evidently be to use a sensitive plate of a cylindrical form, corresponding with the curve *F'' F F'*, and by means of a mask with a vertical slit, to conceal all the plate but a high narrow strip at the centre; then if the plate *F'' F F'* remained stationary, and the lens rotated carrying the mask with it, every part of the plate would be exposed successively.

But in the instrument now in use, this is otherwise managed. The sensitive plate occupies the position *S S'*, and is flat. It is masked, with a narrow opening at *F*, extending from top to bottom. As the lens rotates, the plate *S S'* is shifted sideways by a system of clockwork, which makes its movement exactly correspond with that of the lens, whether it be slow or fast, as the light may require.

As a curved plate, *F' F F''* would receive a perfect image from the rotating lens, masked as above explained, all that is necessary is, that the flat plate *S S'* should be shifted in such a way that when, for instance, the lens has moved so that its axis is in the direction *J F'*, then the plate shall have been brought up to *F'*, there to receive its image at its correct focus. And, evidently, if the plate be long enough, and the camera be rotated to a full circle, an entire panorama may be obtained.

This picture will be found to differ materially from one obtained in the ordinary camera. It will be in panoramic, instead of plane projection. The picture will not be an harmonious whole, which the eye sees whilst regarding its perspective centre, but as if the eye were directed always at the object opposite to it, in whatever direction it chanced to look, or, to speak more exactly, as if the eyes were directed in succession at all the vertical lines in the picture.

Another difference will be that from end to end (but not from top to bottom) the picture, no matter how large, will be in equally good focus. At the right and left extremities the picture will be as sharp as the middle. This is because the central part of the image only is used. Each part becomes successively the centre.

Again, the vertical slit at *F* may be made narrow at bottom and wide at top, so that the foreground will get a larger exposure than the sky; and this difference may be regulated at will, giving, if desired, to the sky an exposure of one-tenth or less than that which the foreground receives. It is this which has enabled

Braun to produce such wonderful cloud pictures in his Swiss scenery, and to get good definition of snow mountains against the sky and clouds.

The most successful application of this principle is at present Johnson's panoramic camera. It is patented, but the patent cannot cover the principle, which was understood many years before his application of it, and was applied to the construction of panoramic cameras.[1]

§ 9.—**General Remarks on Lenses.**

In the foregoing sections all the forms of lenses possessing any interest to the photographer have been described. It remains to say a few words on the use of them.

Portraiture.—The portrait lens is so far superior to all others for this purpose that none other is habitually used. When the light is strong, a tolerable portrait can be got with a triplet or Steinheil aplanatic or a globe; generally it is necessary to work out of doors to obtain a sufficient illumination, and avoid a very protracted exposure.

For card portraits the focal length needed for the lens will depend upon how much is to be included. For full lengths, very short focus lenses are commonly employed. For such as show part of the body, and even including the hands, lenses of six to eight inches focal length will be proper. For "cabinet size" lenses of eight to ten inches focal length will be needed. For $6\frac{1}{2} \times 8\frac{1}{2}$ plates and half length portraits, a ten inch focus lens will be suitable. For very short exposures, especially in taking children, "extra rapid" lenses are made, with very short focal lengths. Some makers make a difference in their lenses according as they are wanted for full lengths and for vignetted heads. In the latter case every effort is made for perfect definition at the centre; in the former a good definition all over the plate is aimed at.

Generally, the shorter the focal length, the less exposure will be needed; but the longer the focal length, the less exaggeration there will be in those parts that project, the hands especially.

Very ingenious arrangements have been adapted to the portrait

[1] See *Secretan, De la distance focale des Systèmes Optiques convergents.* Paris, 1855.

lens, with the object of changing the focus during exposure, in the effort to get a diffusion of focus, and, instead of having one part sharp to the exclusion of the rest, to maintain a certain average of sharpness over the whole. Even lenses have been made in which a certain amount of spherical aberration has been left uncorrected, in order to diffuse the sharpness. The late Mr. Clandet brought this whole subject prominently forward shortly before his death, and opinions are very much divided on the subject.

Flare or ghost in the camera is an image of the diaphragm. Let C be the centre of curvature of the second surface of the lens,

Fig. 57.

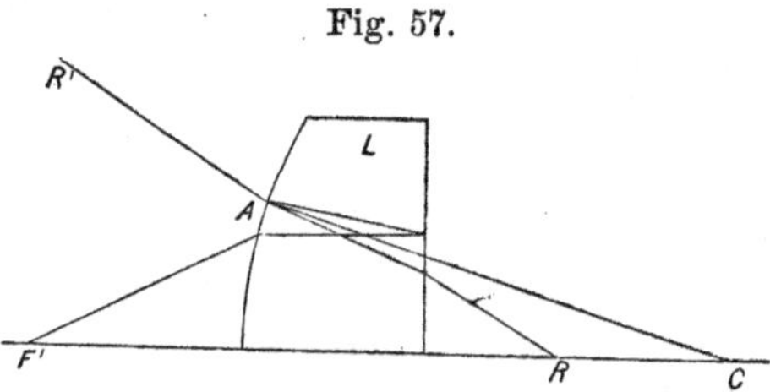

whose thickness is here intentionally exaggerated, in order to make the lines visibly distinct. A ray R, passing through the diaphragm, strikes the first surface, is refracted, and passes to the second. Here it is divided—most passing onwards in a direction R' to form the true image, but a part suffering reflection and returning to the first surface. Here most is transmitted, but a part is reflected again and returns to the second surface. The greater part is transmitted, and undergoing refraction is bent down to the axis at some point F', producing the flare.

Comparing Lenses.—A great deal of unintentional injustice is done by photographers in comparing lenses for want of taking the necessary precautions to make the test a just one.

It should invariably be borne in mind that the performance of a lens depends entirely upon its stopping down. Of two lenses compared, the inferior one may easily be made to seem the best, if it be used with a smaller stop, and no account be taken of the time of exposure.

It may be taken for granted that the sharpness, depth of focus, and size of good picture obtained will always increase as the size of the stop is diminished. This has led many landscapists to the use of extremely small stops habitually, esteeming it of little consequence to wait longer for the impression to be made. Several evils result therefrom.

1. It may be taken as an invariable rule that the larger the stop used, the more detail to the shadows will be obtained, always supposing that each trial has been made with a correctly timed exposure. Let us say that, with a half inch stop, fifteen seconds have been found exactly right. Now, using a quarter inch stop, we must, of course, expose for one minute.[1] The exposure will be correct; the picture will be the best obtainable with that size of stop, but the detail to the shadows will not be so good as in the former case.

2. It seems well established that a large stop always gives a bolder picture. A small stop, especially if less than one-thirtieth the focal length, leads to flatness.

3. A long exposure in the case of portraiture is a serious evil. Even with landscapes it is not unimportant, for, although the contrary has been affirmed, the difficulty of catching foliage still always increases with the length of the exposure.

But in comparing lenses of different focal lengths, the *absolute* size of the stop is not the criterion, but the *relative*.

For example, let it be required to compare the performance of a triplet of twelve inches focal length with a single view lens of six, the focal lengths being in both cases the absolute or equivalent, not the "back focus."

A proper average stop for a twelve-inch lens is half an inch; the stop is then one twenty-fourth the focal length, which may be conveniently expressed f24. The single lens, then, must also be tried with an f24 stop, in its case evidently one-quarter inch. Having taken with great care the best focus for each lens, let negatives be taken.

First, compare the definition at the centre. Some writers hold that the central definition of a good triplet exceeds that of the best single lenses. Others, equally reliable, maintain the opposite opinion.

Having settled that point for the particular case, pass from the centre towards the margin. What falling off the 6-inch lens shows at 2 inches from the centre, the 12-inch must not show

[1] The exposure must always be inversely proportioned to the *area* of the stop, and this area is proportional to the square of the diameter of the stop.

till 4. And to compare the marginal definition, the 12-inch lens must have its print cut 4 times as large. If it be tested on a 6½ × 8½ plate, the 6-inch lens must only be compared with a field of 3¼ × 4¼.

As for definition, so also for depth of focus. It must be examined under the same guarded conditions. To try two lenses together, with stops not corresponding to their focal lengths, is to obtain utterly unreliable results, and yet this is constantly done.

Take any common lens, cover its diaphragm with a piece of opaque yellow paper, and make a pinhole in it, not too small. There will at once be wonderful sharpness, and near and distant objects will be all in perfect focus at once. The principle of cutting off all the rays that do not meet the axis has been carried to great length, and the result is remarkable depth of focus and definition. But a negative so taken is worthless. The effect is flat, the exposure excessively prolonged, and contrasts too great.

To compare portrait lenses proceed as follows: Measure the focal length of the lens habitually used, and which is to be the standard of comparison, and that of the new one. As both are of the same construction, it will be sufficient to measure from the diaphragm to the ground glass. Measure with a pair of compasses the diaphragm you habitually use, and then set the new lens to the corresponding diaphragm in proportion to its focal length. If the one has, for example, a focal length ¼ longer than the other, let its diaphragm be ¼ more in diameter, and so on. Having repeated this, give the new lens the same exposure, with the same light, as the old, and a comparison of the results *under these conditions* will show which is the quicker, which gives the better definition, depth of focus, &c.

It is necessary, however, in all cases, to remember that even with proportionate diaphragms, lenses of different focal length cannot be accurately compared, as the proportion of performance always falls off as the focal length increases.

Selection of Lenses.—Much that has just been said in the comparison of lenses will necessarily control their selection; but some additional points need to be adverted to.

The *color* of a lens is always important. Place the lens on a perfectly white sheet of paper—any brownness of tint is a serious objection. In an old lens this may arise from the Canada balsam, with which the separate portions are cemented together, turning yellow. If this be thought to be the case, the lens should be taken to an optician to be separated, cleaned, and re-attached. The photographer is not advised to attempt this himself.

Bubbles in the glass are objectionable, because they tend to throw rays in abnormal directions, and to impair the brilliancy of the image. One or two small ones are not important, nor a sufficient cause for rejecting an otherwise satisfactory lens. But it indicates carelessness in the maker, as these bubbles are always visible in the disk from which the lens is made, and such disks should be rejected.

Striæ, hair-like or thready transparent lines, are very objectionable, and at once a sufficient cause for rejection.

Scratches.—Lenses will sometimes come from the maker with scratches, the result of careless handling of tools in setting, or of bad packing. Such of course are returned.

Centering.—To every lens there belongs an optical axis, a line perpendicular to the surface of the lens, and passing through its centre of curvature. Every achromatized lens consists of at least two portions, and it is necessary that these should be so arranged when attached together by the balsam used for that purpose, that the optical axis of each should exactly correspond. When two lenses or more are united to form an objective, not only must the parts of each be properly disposed, but the front lens must have its axis coincident with that of the back lens. This will depend upon correct mounting.

The usual way in which opticians test the correctness of the centering, is by making the tube containing the lenses revolve in an upright position, that is, with the lenses horizontal. If, now, a candle be placed at a little distance, and the eye be placed at a convenient position, the candle will be seen reflected from the surface as a bright point. Every surface of every piece of glass in the tube will send back a reflection. Next the tube is caused to rotate. Each lens that is correctly centered will continue to send its reflection back perfectly fixed and immovable; but any surface that is out of centre will cause its reflection to deviate more or less according to the amount of error. It is evidently not necessary that all the reflections should be seen at once, but they may be observed successively. This method of observing evidently renders it easy to fix which, if any, of the surfaces is erroneously placed, and in which direction is its error.

Another mode of observation is more convenient for the photographer, as not requiring the apparatus needed by the method just described.

The observer places himself in a dark room with a single candle. Standing five or six feet from it, he looks at it through the objective, inclining the latter a little until he sees a series of bright points, which are the images of the candle, produced by successive reflections from the different surfaces of the lens. When a lens has four pieces of glass in its construction, as in the case of the portrait, globe, orthoscopic, and some other lenses, the number of possible images is very considerable. These cannot generally be all found at once, but eight, ten, or more can be counted; a little practice, and altering the inclination of the lens materially aids in increasing the number.

If now the centering is perfect, it will be found that, by carefully adjusting the position of the lens, all of these reflections can be made to range themselves in a straight line. But if any one or more of the component parts is out of centre, this will be found impracticable. One or more of the bright points will remain obstinately out of line; and, when a little movement is made which brings them in, it will be found that some other image, previously in line, has slid out of it. When the observer, after very careful trial, finds that it is positively impossible to make all the images range, he will be justified in concluding that there is a fault in the centering.

Whilst this test is so easy that any intelligent observer can apply it at once, there is no doubt that it is a very severe one. A lens may perform quite fairly, and yet such an examination as this may reveal a defect. But there is no doubt that first-rate excellence is incompatible with such defectiveness.

It is also evident that the fewer the pieces of which a lens is composed, the less difficulty the optician will find in getting them all in correct line.

Quickness.—When lenses are tested with equal stops (in proportion to their focal length), their comparative quickness will depend upon the whiteness of the glass, the fewer number of surfaces that enter into their formation, and on the curves given by the optician: careful testing and this alone can settle the point.

Chemical Focus.—The correction for chromatic aberration is now greatly better made than formerly. To test whether a lens is properly corrected, select a newspaper printed with sharp-cut type, and paste a piece a foot or fifteen inches square upon a smooth piece of board. Set this up before the camera, with the columns vertical, but inclined in a slanting direction, so that one side, the right, for example, shall be a couple of inches nearer the camera than the left, keeping the board, however, exactly upright. Focus carefully along the central upright line, and copy it full size, or thereabouts.

Next examine the hair-strokes of the letters on the negative with a microscope. If the lens is properly corrected, the central line should be in the sharpest focus. If, however, it be found that a portion to the right or left of the central line is in better focus than the centre, then the correction has evidently been faulty. If the sharpest image is of a part *nearer* to the lens than the centre, the lens is *under-corrected;* if of a part further from the centre, the lens is *over-corrected.* In either case, it is said to have a "*chemical focus,*" that is, its chemical and visual focus does not correspond, a fault of the first magnitude, and sufficient cause for rejecting the lens entirely.

§ 10.—**Care of Lenses.**

A few words on the preservation and care of these beautiful products of science and art will not be inappropriate here.

When lenses have been out of use for some time, and have been carried to a distance, they should be carefully unscrewed and wiped out with a piece of soft clean chamois leather. The palm of an old white kid glove may be used, or a soft old linen handkerchief, but the leather is preferable. Nothing else should be used than the substances here named.

If the lenses have stood only for a short time, they may only require wiping on the exterior surfaces. They should first be examined, and if free from dust, it is better not to wipe them. Too much wiping is as bad as too little, and it may be set down as a general principle, that the less lenses are touched *with anything* the better; especially the fingers should never touch them.

With Dallmeyer's wide angle view lenses, convenient caps of morocco lined with velvet are furnished. This is an excellent arrangement, as dust is excluded, and the amount of wiping is diminished. These caps are also very convenient for covering and uncovering the lens. Such should be made and furnished with all photographic objectives. Something similar, or a light brass cap, to protect the back lens, would also be very useful with all lenses intended for field use.

It is a disadvantage to keep the lens in a cold place, and then, perhaps, suddenly remove it to a warm one. A dew may form on the lens while the image is being impressed, or before, and may escape observation.

Lenses should never be left lying where the sun, or even a bright light, can fall upon them, as strong light has a tendency to darken the color of the glass and increase the exposure necessary. For this reason, where stereoscopic lenses are occasionally used separately, this use should be divided between the two. If one of the pair is always used on such occasions, it will tend gradually to work more slowly than the other, so that the two can no longer be used advantageously together.

The care of the lens should also be extended to the brass mounting. If this is allowed to become dented, or is in any way roughly treated, there is danger that the centering may be interfered with, and the working of the objective thereby impaired. Second-hand objectives should always be severely tested before purchasing, and no one should be induced to acquire a lens in this way, unless he feels fully capable of judging the objective on its own merits by a careful trial.

CHAPTER VI.

PHOTOGRAPHIC PERSPECTIVE.

§ 1.—Nature of the Image formed by a Lens.

WITH the progress of photographic study there comes a general feeling amongst the more intelligent photographers that their art connects itself with Art especially so called, and that a knowledge of some of its fundamental principles should accompany the study of photography. Particularly, the photographer should have an elementary idea of Perspective. This must necessarily be gathered from appropriate manuals, for to explain it here, even in a very elementary fashion, would exceed the limits of this volume. The writer can only with appropriateness undertake to supply here what would be found wanting in any manual of perspective, viz., the application of the laws of perspective to the operations of photography.

Whenever a solid object is to be correctly represented upon a flat surface, it must either be laid out according to certain definite rules, as by the draughtsman, or the same thing must be accomplished mechanically, as done by the camera. In either case, the result is the same. The delineation of a solid body, or of a scene, or an edifice, as made by a draughtsman, is, in its essential features, precisely the same as that made by the lens; both, however, are subject to certain rules.

If we observe a building through a large pane of glass in a window, and if, our eye remaining stationary, we mark on the pane a series of dots, each exactly corresponding to some corner of the edifice, and then connect these dots, we may thus form a perfect outline of the building, every line of which will perfectly correspond to the same line in the building, covering it, as it were, as we look. This will be *one* perfect perspective drawing of the building.

If, now—still keeping our eye exactly opposite the centre of the pane—we draw back, so as to be farther from the window, the correspondence no longer exists, every line of the building has started *out*, beyond the corresponding line of the original drawing; and we obtain a *larger* picture than before.

By altering the position of the eye any number of different pictures will be obtained of the same scene, and these *correspond with the pictures obtained from lenses whose absolute focal lengths are equal to the distance of the eye from the pane of glass.*

If the arrow *A B*, fig 58, represent the edifice, *P′ P′* the pane

Fig. 58.

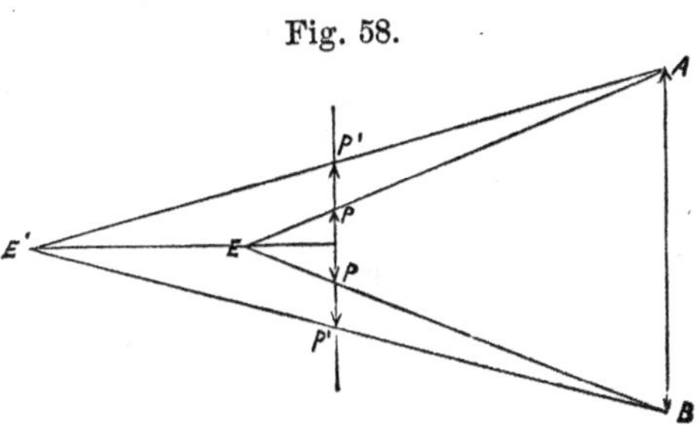

of glass, and E the eye, the edifice as represented on the pane will have the height $P\ P$. If the eye be withdrawn to E', the image will be enlarged to $P'\ P'$.

Now, if the eye be replaced by a lens whose focal length is the same as the distance of the eye from the pane, the image formed by that lens will be precisely the same as seen by the eye—reversed, of course.

The lens L forms on the screen an image I' (Fig. 59) of the arrow precisely as large as the image I seen by the eye when placed at L, upon the pane at I, the distance of the eye to the pane being the same as the focal length of the lens; that is, the distance from L to the centre of the arrow.

Fig. 59.

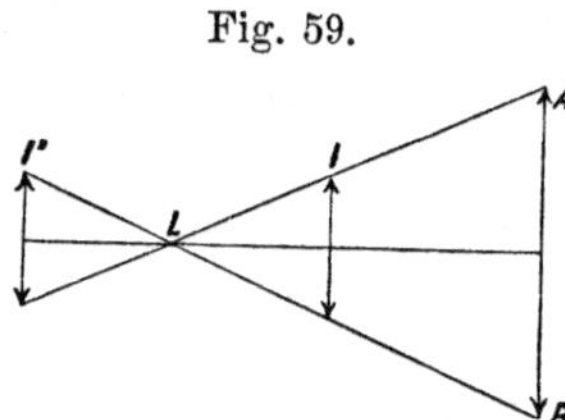

If now, keeping the eye at L, we move the pane I, backwards and forwards, we shall obtain any number of images of the object $A\ B$. By drawing lines from L to all parts of $A\ B$, it will be seen that the triangles are always similar; that is, any triangle $E\ A\ B$ (Fig. 58) will always be similar to the corresponding triangle $E\ P\ P$. All parts of the image $P\ P$ will therefore have the same proportion to the corresponding parts of the object $A\ B$. If any one dimension be altered, or if $P\ P$ be increased to $P'\ P'$ by drawing back the eye to E', all others will be proportionately changed. It follows, therefore (and this is very important), that all these images of the object will vary in size only; that is, they will be magnified or reduced images of each other; and as these images are identical with those formed by lenses placed at L (Fig. 59), having focal lengths respectively equal to any distance from the eye to the pane, we draw the conclusion that similar lenses of different focal lengths, placed at the same spot, give representations which differ from each other in size only. If the picture given by a small lens be magnified (for example, in a solar camera) to the size of the picture given by a large lens, the resulting picture will be identical with it, supposing the lenses to be perfect instruments. The perspective angles will be the same.

If $A\ B\ C\ D$ be the side of a house seen obliquely, the top and bottom lines, if continued, will meet at a vanishing point V, and the perspective angle *B V A* will be greater or smaller, according as we place ourselves nearer to, or farther from the building. The nearer we approach the nearer the point *V* comes in, and the more abruptly the apparent size diminishes from *A B* to *C D*. As any good photographic lens placed in the same position as the eye gives the same result, it follows that the nearer we go with our lens to the edifice, the sharper will be the perspective angle at *B*.

Fig. 60.

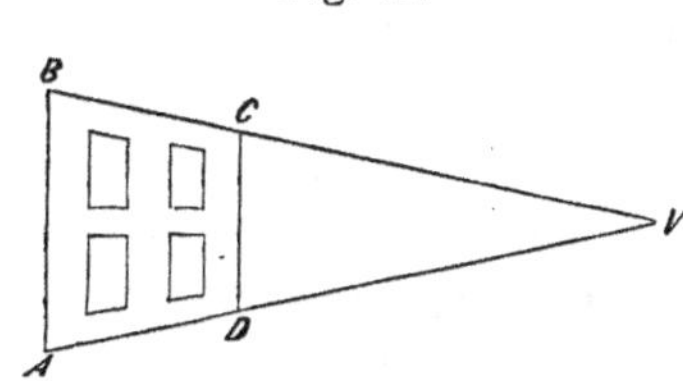

For example, the side of a house, which, when seen in perspective from a little distance, gives the effect *A B C D* (Fig. 61), changes as we approach, and assumes the appearance *A B c b*, with the much sharper angle at *B*.

So that the same lens which depicted this house from a distance

Fig. 61.

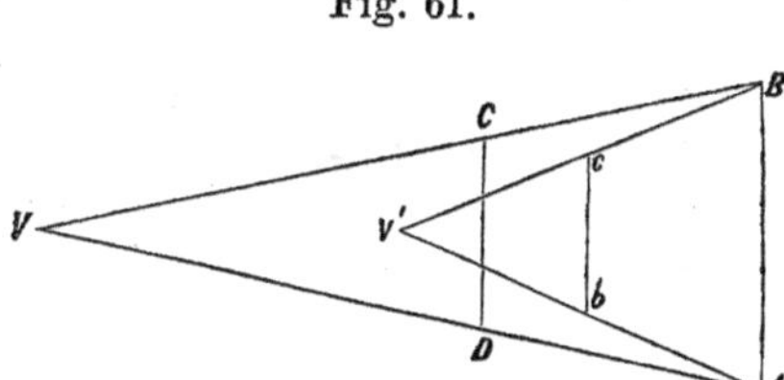

with the angles *A B C D*, will, when brought much nearer, give the effect *A B c b*.

This case is, therefore, to be very clearly distinguished from that which we before considered, and where the eye was simply brought nearer to or further from the plane on which the image was drawn. In the present case we suppose the plane itself to be removed from the building. In the first case the perspective angles did not change; in the second they do.

There is a certain subtlety in applying these principles to practice, which requires close attention. Although the character of the image as distinguished from its mere size, depends upon the distance to which we go from the object, and not upon the lens, yet, nevertheless, lenses of small focal lengths give almost always very incorrect pictures, because such lenses are brought too near to the objects, and the sharp perspective angle *c B A* results, which is always offensive, and may legitimately be termed incorrect, because it gives incorrect conceptions of the object delineated. A larger lens should be used, and taken to a greater distance. If, for example, it be required to photograph a large edifice, so that the image shall be only 3 inches high, and we take a 4-inch lens and go to such a distance as will secure the size required, we shall get a picture with the sharp angle *c B A;* but if we take a lens of 8 to 10 inches focus, and go to such a distance that the image is reduced to the same height, 3 inches, we shall get a natural angle *C B A*, the actual apparent height *A B* remaining the same in both cases.

The practical application of these rules is further somewhat complicated by the fact that it is necessary to take into consideration the actual size of the picture; for it is an unquestionable fact that the *eye will support perspective angles in a large picture, that it will not in a small one.*

If, for example, we take any small picture *c B A*, and magnify it considerably, we shall find that the perspective angles, before entirely too sharp, lose this effect, and seem natural. (The experiment is a surprising one, and must be tried to be appreciated.) This is one reason why the small photographs taken with very short focus lenses are so much improved by magnifying them. Their caricatured perspective, intolerable in such small pictures, becomes endurable in the large one. On the other hand, a large picture, in which the perspective is appropriate and suitable for its size, cannot be reduced without injury. Even if the reduction be absolutely perfect, as when executed by a copying camera, the character of the design is destroyed. Engravers know this, and know that a large architectural drawing cannot be reduced with advantage; and the same truth is recognized by all artists. Ruskin remarks that true perspective is infinite and unreducible in its nature. To every size of representation there is a certain size of perspective angle appropriate, or rather the appropriate size lies within certain limits, and these are only to be fixed by judgment and cultivated taste.

Farther, it is to be remarked, that as in every photographic image the focal length of the lens corresponds with the distance of the eye from the section on the window-pane before spoken of, it follows that every photographic picture, to give a correct impression, should be held from the eye at a distance equal to the focal length of the lens with which it was taken. It will be at once apparent that a view taken with a lens of 4 or 5 inches focus, cannot be held that near to the eye of a person with ordinary sight. It follows, therefore, that such lenses *never* can give truthful delineations of scenery. They may make pretty pictures, but these are wholly incorrect, as many must have noticed. A garden becomes a park. The farther part of a house is represented on so much smaller a scale than the nearer part, that the eye, accustomed to correct representations, is deceived, and imagines the farther part, by reason of its smallness, to be much farther away than it is. And thus the farther part being dragged away, the house appears to stretch much farther back than it does in reality, and consequently to be much larger. Distant objects are dwarfed down, mountains become hills, if they but stand clear of the foreground.

As we see objects best at about 10 or 12 inches from the eye, this would appear to be about the best focal length for a lens. Still, as the eye does not discriminate closely in these matters, and is very tolerant with limits, lenses of all focal lengths, from 7 to 15 or 16 inches, may be employed with advantage. Beyond this, the pictures become flat and tame, and the impression of solidity is insufficient. The round pillar looks like a flat pilaster.

In these cases the effect is, to some extent, corrected by removing the picture further from the eye. We can here alleviate the evil in a way that we could not with the short focus lens. Still, the effects are not good.

Perspective is not without its bearing upon portraiture. All portraits taken with short focus lenses are incorrect. The nose is represented upon too large a scale for the rest of the face, because it is nearer the lens. And it is still worse with the hands and feet, if visible. If two or more persons be included, their relative sizes are not properly preserved, unless they stand exactly in line side by side. This incorrectness becomes quite striking where one person stands behind the other, and a lens of 4 or 5 inch (absolute, not "back") focus is employed. The fault in all such cases depends upon the use of lenses of too short focal length, in order to work in a short gallery, and work very quickly.

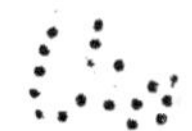

By using a lens of 7 or 8 inch focal length, and going sufficiently far from the sitter to get the reduction desired, all parts of the person will be harmoniously rendered, and the different persons composing a group will be represented in correct perspective proportion, whether near to, or at some distance from the foremost figure.

§ 2.—Plane Projection and Apparent Size.

Plane Projection.—In the foregoing we have always considered the perspective as referred to ordinary or plane projection, that is, the surface of the image is perpendicular to the line of vision. The eye looks in the direction $E\ C$ at the view $A\ C\ B$, which, as delineated, is supposed to be projected on the screen or paper $A'\ B'$, held perpendicularly to the line of sight E.

This enables us at once to fix the *apparent size* that any object will have in a plane projection, whether it be drawn or photographed. For suppose the paper to be held at one foot from the eye, that is, that $E\ C'$ is one foot. If the tree C is a hundred feet from the eye, that is, one hundred times $E\ C'$, which is now our scale, it will be diminished one hundred times. Therefore, if it is fifty feet high, it will be represented on $A'\ B'$ as half a foot. Precisely the same is true of a photographic representation. If the lens is at E, and has a focal length $E\ F$ of one foot, the tree fifty feet high and one hundred feet distant, will appear in the negative six inches in height.

Fig. 62.

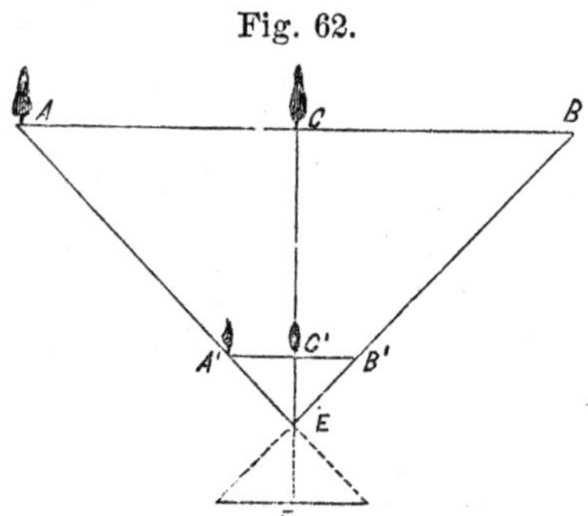

If another tree of exactly the same height be situated at A, then although that tree may be distant half as far again, it will be represented at A' of the same size as C'. It appears at first anomalous that two objects of the same size, at very different distances, should have an equal size in the image or picture; but this anomaly disappears by reflecting that, as the image is supposed to be held square before the eye, the image of the tree A at A' is *farther from the eye* than the image of the tree C at C', so that $E\ A'$ stands in the same relation to $E\ A$ as $E\ C'$ to $E\ C$, and therefore, if a sketch of a given size held at C' would exactly cover the real tree, then a sketch of the same size held at A' would exactly cover the real tree A.

It follows, therefore, *that all objects of an equal size upon a line* $A\ B$, *perpendicular to the line of sight* $E\ C$, *are represented of equal size in the plane projection* $A'\ B'$, *whatever be their distances from the eye.*

An instance of this occurs in all drawings of fronts of buildings or rows of houses, when the observer is supposed to stand exactly in front. In the picture the houses have the same actual height at the ends of the row, as in the middle, although they may be much more distant. So in the delineation of the front of the building, seen directly in front, the roof line is parallel to the base line, and shows no tendency to meet it. There are then no vanishing points, and we have *parallel perspective*, a form of representation always a favorite with the old masters.

§ 3.—Panoramic Projection.

This form of projection is never used in architectural delineations, and has only lately attracted attention in photography, from the introduction of the revolving camera.

In plane projection the image is projected upon a plane surface, as the name indicates; in the panoramic it is thrown upon one that is cylindrical.

The curved surface $A'\ C'\ B'$ receives the image, and as the point A' is no farther from the eye than C', it follows that of the two equal objects A and C A is represented smaller just in proportion to the actual distance, so that if $E\ A$ be half as long again as $E\ C$, the tree A will have only two-thirds the apparent height of the equal tree C.

Fig. 63.

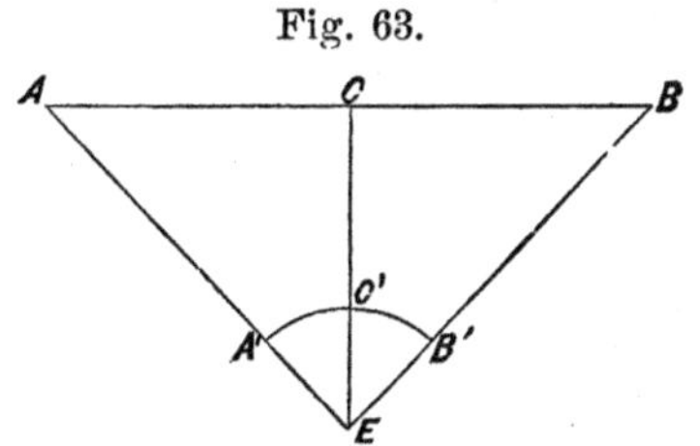

The representations afforded by panoramic perspective are correct only when they are received on a curved surface and so viewed. If printed on paper, the paper must be curved into the arc $A'\ C'\ B'$ of a circle, whose radius is the focal length of the lens with which they were taken. If such prints be laid flat (as they always are in practice), everything is distorted. With landscapes this may be tolerated, that is, the eye, if unfamiliar with the scene, may not detect the falsification, and the general effect may be pleasing. But as soon as this mode of representation is applied to architecture, its faults become strikingly apparent. If the front of a building be represented, the horizontal right line of the roof or cornice becomes a curve with the ends pointing downwards. The base line of the building becomes another curve, with the ends pointing upwards. All horizontal lines become curves, but vertical lines still remain straight, because the projection plane was curved only in a horizontal direction; it was cylindrical, and the vertical right lines in nature were all represented by vertical right lines on the cylindrical surface.

PART III.

PHOTOGRAPHIC MANIPULATIONS.

CHAPTER I.

THE DARK ROOM.

§ 1.—Regulation of Light.

THE dark room in which the operations of sensitizing and development are to be conducted, is most commonly made by partitioning off a portion of a larger room for this purpose. It consequently happens not unfrequently that this room is lighted only by an opening into the larger room, and has no window communicating with the exterior. This is a serious evil, and one to be avoided if possible. No sufficient ventilation can be obtained except from a window upon the street or yard, and for want of this, the operator's health is exposed to suffer severe injury.

The Window.—When access can be had to the open air, it is desirable that the window of the dark room shall not be so situated as to receive the direct rays of the sun. If this cannot be wholly avoided, it is better to have the sun fall obliquely, and later in the day, rather than perpendicularly, or in the morning; therefore a northwest exposure will be best, if it can be arranged.

It is much better to have a good light in the dark room than to work by a faint one, and this can always be accomplished by using proper precautions. The window need not be small, if it is properly protected.

There are two methods in common use: the use of yellow glass, and the coloring, or otherwise guarding of common glass.

The yellow glass sold in the shops, even when the darkest shades are used, is not in itself a sufficient protection. Even when direct sunlight does not fall upon the window, light enough will enter to impress a plate; this I can assert from experience. As an additional protection, a shade of brown holland is useful. In dark weather it can be rolled up, and a good light be obtained.

Pasting yellow paper, such as is made for common yellow envelopes, gives an excellent protection if the paper is stout, and if the sun does not fall directly on the window, this will, in many cases, be sufficient. The paper should be cut to the exact size of the panes, and attached by a border of paste. In this way the free open and shutting of the sash is not interfered with. The yellow glass is of course preferable.

By having not too small a window, the light, after being thoroughly divested of its actinic elements, will still be sufficiently abundant to render all operations easy. Ordinary print should be read with ease in the dark room, and this is not inconsistent with absolute immunity from fogging, if the precautions just mentioned have been suitably taken.

Fig. 64.

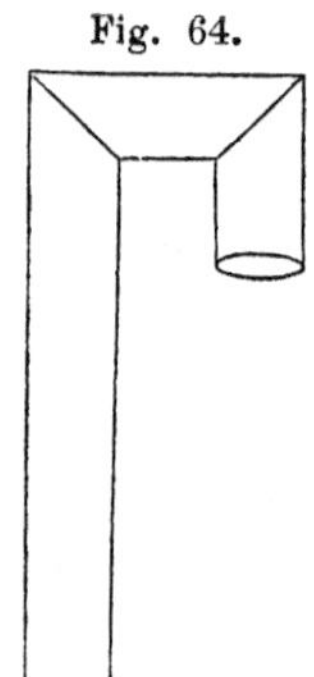

But a window for occasional opening, is not in itself, by any means, a sufficient mode of ventilation. In the roof of the room, a five or six-inch pipe should be set, the exterior part of which is bent twice at right angles, so as to point downwards; in this way neither light nor rain can enter. An opening communicating with the outer air, near the floor for the admission of air, is also very desirable. A slanting board is nailed against it, which freely lets pass the air, but excludes the light.

§ 2.—**Arrangement.**

The arrangement of the room will depend so much upon its size and shape, that it is difficult to give any general directions. But it may be said, that the place for developing should be in front of the window, and that near by it should be a sink with a tap for washing. The tap, in fact, should be so at hand that water can be made to flow over the negative at any instant to stop its development. This is very urgent, and any arrangement that does not accomplish this is exceedingly defective.

A good plan is to have a shelf eighteen inches wide round three sides of the room. The height of the shelf will depend upon whether the operator develops sitting or standing. If the former, the shelf should be just high enough to put the knees under, and no more. If standing, it should have a somewhat greater height.

If vertical baths are used for sensitizing, they should not stand on this shelf, but should be let into it, so that the top of the bath will be level with the shelf; at least this is advisable if it is intended to do this part of the work seated.

If the fixing is done in the dark room, the fixing bath and all utensils connected with this part of the work, should be as far as possible from the sensitizing baths, and the *utmost* care should be taken to avoid the introduction of the minutest portion of the hyposulphite into the silver bath, to which it would be fatal.

The figure below represents an arrangement adopted by the author, where it was a great object to save space. A wide shelf

Fig. 65.

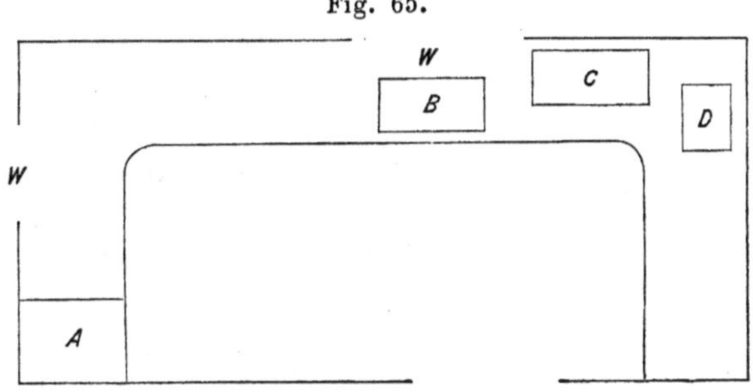

to be used as a table, runs round three sides. At *A* are the sensitizing baths, and near *A* is a small window of yellow glass, to coat the collodion and manage the sensitizing by. (This window is by no means essential.) Opposite to *B* is the principal window, looking north, and opening to the open air. In front of it at *B*, is the tray over which the developing is done. This window comes down so that the bottom of the lowest pane is level with the top of the table. A window with a high sill in a dark room is a great nuisance. At *C* is the sink with a tap of water over it. At *D* is the fixing bath of hyposulphite.

A double-kneed pipe is set into the roof, and air is introduced at the floor, as before described.

The dark room should be kept clean and free from dust. The chemicals that emit fumes should be kept elsewhere, and care be taken to avoid spilling hyposulphite solutions about. The temperature should not materially differ from that of the glass room. Ventilation should be maintained in it even when not in actual use.

For the sensitizing of positive paper any room properly darkened will answer.

CHAPTER II.

THE GLASS ROOM.

§ 1.—General Remarks.

No subject concerns the professional photographer more deeply than the glass room. Chemicals, lenses, and cameras he can always obtain of excellent quality from dealers of reputation, but in the construction of the glass room he must depend to a large extent upon himself, acting under such information and instruction as he can obtain. It is certain that a very clever operator will occasionally obtain good pictures in almost any glass room; this is not, however, what is wanted. The disposition of light should be such as to facilitate to the utmost the really difficult task of regular success.

If any intelligent observer will place himself in a room lighted from *several* different directions, and taking a looking-glass in his hand, will observe his own face, as he stands in very different parts of the room, with very different illuminations, he will see a wonderful change as regards feature, character, and expression. Now, the object of the glass room is to obtain from each face its best, and at the same time, also, its characteristic expression.

If the observer with his hand-glass carefully notices the effects of different lights upon his features, he will be especially struck with the three following facts:—

1. That a level light, coming directly in front, *flattens* all the features.

2. That a light directly from above produces an opposite effect, exaggerating the projection of the brows and nose, rendering the eyes cavernous, and drawing out the cheek bones.

3. That a level light from one side produces a most unpleasant effect, causing what is known as a "hatchet" expression of face.

Pursuing his trials further, he will find that the right light to use consists in a combination of the three into a *front-upper-side* light. To produce this light is the great object of the disposition of the glass room; bearing in mind that for different sitters, a variation of light must be at command, and that as the position, strength, and character of the light vary at different hours of the day, the means of compensating for, and correcting these changes, must be at hand.

§ 2.—**Ridge Roof Construction.**

By far the best light for the portraitist is the pure, soft, diffusive light that comes from a northern exposure. An abundant supply of this light is of the highest value. It is best, therefore, that the length of the glass room should be east or west, and that the north light should be received on one side. The best photographers all over the world are now pretty generally agreed in preferring what is known as the Ridge Roof System of Construction, a section of which in various forms is shown in the

Fig. 66. Fig. 67. Fig. 68.

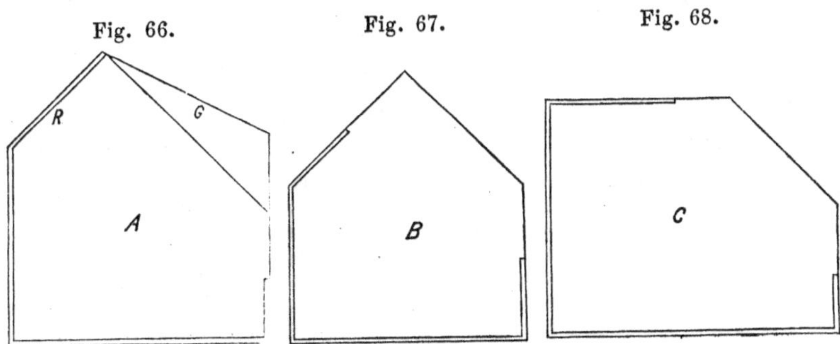

figures. The single line represents the glazed parts; the double line, ordinary walls, ceiling, &c.

A is the preferable form, *B* and *C* are much less to be recommended. In *A* the slanting roof may take the position of the line above *G*, or of that below it, or an intermediate one.

The form *A* may be still otherwise varied. Loescher and Petsch use a "lean-to" roof, that is, the glass *G* is continued all the way with the same pitch till it reaches the side wall, which is then much higher, and the roof *R* is thus superseded.

The dimensions adopted by these are[1]—

	FEET.
Length (east and west)	40
Breadth (north and south)	20
Height of south wall	16
" north "	11

The pitch of the roof is therefore 5 feet in 20. All the glass is provided with curtains which can be drawn. These photographers, in their construction, went upon the principle of admitting the chief light always in one direction, but having a complete and most extended choice as to that direction. Their general plan is to open each of the curtains on two-thirds of the north side a little, so as to throw the sitter in a half shade. Taken in this way, a very tame picture would be got. To give it character, a few feet of the top or side curtains are opened, and an upper light is let in, which at once gives relief and boldness to the face.

There can be no doubt that this is an excellent plan. Its idea is to place the sitter in a soft and harmonious, but insufficient light, and then by the introduction of a dominant light from a single definite direction, to produce as much shadow, previously deficient, as may serve to produce the desired relief. Work executed by these gentlemen strongly speaks for their system.

Mr. Henszey, of this city, has adopted a somewhat different system. The greater length of his room is north and south. Not that the design *A* is turned around, but simply *R* and *G* are made very wide, so that the sitter is placed against the south wall, and the camera at the north end. The difficulties that will at once suggest themselves in connection with this method of operating, are removed by having a large extent of glass completely controlled by curtains and pulleys.

Mr. Wenderoth's skylight is in form somewhat like that of Mr. Henszey, that is, it is figure *A* widened out. But the sitter has his back to the west wall, and the line from the camera to the sitter has the usual east and west direction. He has, in addition, arrangements for admitting light at the ends, and also a narrow line of opening just at the top of the south wall. This last, without the most careful management, must lead to cross lights, and is probably of no real use.

[1] See *Phila. Photog.*, III. 208, with illustrative figures.

The particulars of the construction of the glass room of a celebrated Parisian photographer, Reutlinger, have been given to the public. On the north side there is a perpendicular glazed portion, 22 feet long and 12 high. The glass roof has only 14 feet of width, protected by an awning controlled by pulleys inside, to cut off direct sunlight. The glass overhead is ground glass, and so are the sides as high as the eyes. The entire length of the room is about 44 feet.[1]

Any one of the forms of glass room which have been here particularly described, will, in good hands, give good work. The whole system used by Loescher and Petzch seems that most in accordance with sound principles, and without meaning in the least to detract from the excellence of the others, is that which is most strongly recommended here.

With respect to the glass employed, the general preference in this country is for using good window glass, and stippling it with blue inside. Abroad, ground glass is often used—here it is not liked. The use of blue glass is gaining in estimation in Germany.

§ 3.—Control of Sunlight.

An important consideration presents itself with respect to all the forms of roof and glazing just shown in section. Even if the roof looks directly to the north, it is impracticable to give it so high a pitch that the sun shall not shine over the ridge at midday, and it must also shine over the ends morning and evening, unless higher walls abut against them. Various efforts have been made by different photographers to obviate this difficulty. Some select a position where the walls of adjoining houses afford a screen, some run up board screens, others have used awnings moved by pulleys, most trust to excluding the sun by curtains and shades inside. These, indeed, are of course always necessary to regulate the amount and direction of light, independently of direct sunbeams.

Some, indeed, trust so entirely to inside shades to exclude the sun, as to prefer a southern exposure, softening the sunlight by shades, and getting it under management as best they may. The

[1] *Photographische Mittheilungen*, No. 41, p. 130.

solitary advantage that this system possesses is that in dull weather the southern light is stronger than the northern.

Some, in order to get every variety of light, use a ridge roof, with equal slopes north and south, both glazed, so that the principal light may be taken from either side, as may be found best suited to the weather and the sitter. But this has a most serious objection in the *intense heat* caused by it. The glass room becomes in hot weather a veritable hot-house. The sitters suffer—the chemicals do not work well.

To maintain a moderate temperature in the glass room is at best a difficult matter, even when not complicated by a southern exposure. A brick wall on the south side is a great protection, and there should be, if possible, a space between the southern slope of the ridge and the ceiling on that side. An excellent arrangement on all these grounds is represented in Fig. 69. At the upper angle of the ceiling *A*, a girder supports a wooden studding *B*. This allows an interspace *D* on the south pitch of

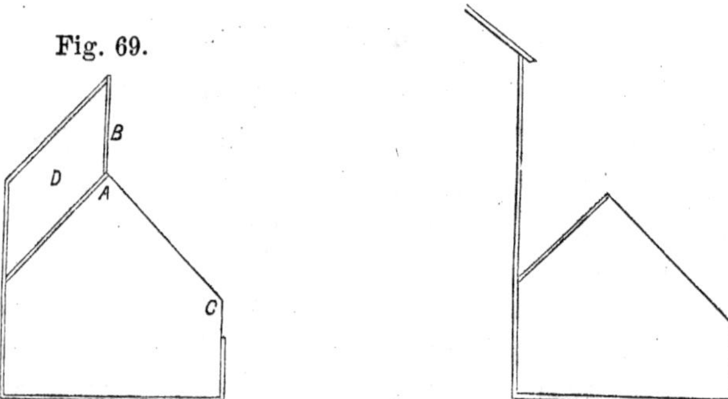

Fig. 69.

Fig. 70.

the roof—very effectual in diminishing the heat. The wall *B* tending to keep off the noon sun from the glazing *A C*.

It is evident that if the south wall supports a higher building adjoining, as shown in Fig. 70, somewhat the same result is attained. Such a form of construction requires especial care to render it water-tight at the junction of the roof and wall. The gutter in the angle must have a rapid pitch from back to front (which cannot be shown in the section), and must be thoroughly tinned by a good workman.

§ 4.—**Secondary Lights.**

In all these sections the sitter is supposed to be at the far end, and looking towards the spectator. He will thus receive on his left side a powerful light from the glass roof, whilst his right side will be comparatively dark.

Now, a difference in light on the two sides is desirable and even necessary, but this difference must not exceed a certain moderate measure. And the dark side of the face requires a *secondary light*, to give transparency to the shadows upon it. Three different methods are used for this end.

First, and most common, *reflectors* are used. Generally, a large screen covered with white paper, or white cloth, is placed on the side of the sitter, opposite the light. Some have used screens covered with silver paper; others, large mirrors.

Secondly, some have opened a window on the south side, and let in light directly on the dark side.

Thirdly, some object that these methods give false lights, especially affecting the expression of the eye, and, therefore, prefer to keep the south side of the room of a sufficiently light color to throw back a volume of soft white light, adequate to light up the shadows.

The brilliancy of the picture is always aided by excluding all extraneous light. The camera, therefore, should always be under an unglazed portion of the roof, and screens should be so arranged, that if the eye be placed where the lens is to be, it shall see no uncurtained glass. Too much glass is very objectionable, especially toward the direction of the camera. The air of a room always contains dust. The more strongly the dust between the sitter and the lens is illuminated, the more it will affect the picture, and always by taking from its brilliancy.

The *Tunnel System* is not to be recommended, though it is certain that good work has been done in this form of house, still the system is every way inferior to the ridge roof. In it, one end of the room, that in which the camera is placed, is lower than the other, and the vertical space between the two ceilings is glazed. Thus the strongest light is full in the sitter's eyes, at the same time that its quantity is almost always deficient, seriously incommoding the operator in dull weather, and producing effects inferior to the ridge roof, in good.

It has been said that few photographers succeed in their first attempts at building a glass house; that they require the experience of a first failure to attain subsequent success. Failures of this kind are expensive, and infinitely vexatious. They are best avoided by obtaining beforehand a clear conception of what are the conditions essential to success, and then carefully and thoughtfully applying them to the position which their glass room is to occupy. Sometimes splendid success comes by mere chance. Mr. Hughes gives an instance in which the portraits produced by a photographer in a country town in England were so excellent as to induce him to travel a long distance to see the maker. He proved to be a man of limited intelligence, who, however, had chanced to erect an excellent room, where an abundance of soft, pure light from the north was received to the exclusion of cross lights. The photographer knew that his work was excellent, and ascribed it all to his personal skill, neither understanding nor appreciating the merits of his room. Encouraged by success, he erected a new gallery in another town, intended to be far better than his old one, but was confounded to find that in it he could not make anything worth having.

One material difference that will be found between a well and ill-planned glass room is, that in the former work can be continued till a late hour in the afternoon, and even then, brilliant and well modelled portraits can be got. It is, therefore (and this cannot be too clearly understood), *no proof of a good construction that the operator can show a piece of first-rate work made in it.* A glass room can hardly be so badly planned but that in some sort of weather, and at some hour of the day, good work may be done in it. The well-planned room is one that is always in a condition to meet the operator's needs.

CHAPTER III.

PYROXYLINE AND COLLODION.

§ 1.—Pyroxyline.

THE manufacture of this substance has passed so much, in fact, so completely into the hands of those who make it their business, and who employ special methods, that it scarcely requires attention here, except in a brief way.

When any form of cellulose, such as cotton, paper, linen, &c., is exposed to the action of mixed nitric and sulphuric acid, a substitution takes place by which one or more molecules of NO_4, hyponitric acid, are taken up by the cellulose. Several different compounds are thus formed, and often simultaneously. When the acid mixture is too weak, the cellulose is dissolved with abundant disengagement of red fumes. When it is somewhat stronger, and used before the heat generated by the mixture of the acids escapes, pyroxylines suitable for photography are produced, thoroughly soluble in mixed alcohol and ether. With lower temperatures and stronger acids, the more explosive form of pyroxyline is produced, which does not dissolve well in the usual solvents.

As commercial nitric acid varies very much in strength, it is often found convenient to substitute nitrate of potash, and to increase the quantity of sulphuric acid, inasmuch as part goes to separate the nitric acid from the potash. It is also affirmed, that pyroxyline made with nitrate of potash, dissolves more easily, and gives a clearer solution, than that made with nitric acid.

The following is one of the most highly recommended formulæ for the production of photographic pyroxyline:—

Mix 200 parts of sulphuric acid of 1.84 (the full commercial strength) with 100 parts of dried and pulverized nitrate of potash, and keep them at a temperature of 147° to 150° F., which must be maintained during the operation. Stir with a glass rod till the lumps disappear. Then add 6 to 8 parts perfectly dry carded cotton. Agitate the mixture from time to time with a glass rod.

After the action has continued for from ten to forty-five minutes, empty suddenly into a large pan of water. Wash thoroughly and rapidly with plenty of water; finally with boiling distilled water.

During the whole operation the temperature must remain over 147° or the pyroxyline is of inferior quality, and if over 160° the cotton is partly dissolved, becomes shorter in fibre, and does not adhere so well to the glass.[1]

The use of ammonia in washing pyroxylines is rather dangerous, as the quality of the cotton is injured by it. Blondeau affirms that pyroxyline is a pentabasic acid and capable of combining with ammonia. Thorough washing with pure water is the most effectual treatment. Any acidity, either left in the cotton or acquired by it through subsequent spontaneous decomposition, tends to render the collodion very insensitive.

But, as already said, the manufacture of pyroxyline as a business is now so thoroughly understood, that it is no longer necessary for the photographer to prepare it for himself in order to have it good. On the contrary, it is probable that it would cost him much labor and some experience, to get it of as good quality as that which he can readily purchase.

The only facts of interest in relation to it that have been elicited of late years, are that the quality of the original cotton used has much to do with the resulting pyroxyline, and that in general the best cottons make the best pyroxyline—especially the American Sea-Island. Also, that different cottons require different treatment; the same mixtures of nitric and sulphuric acids, or of nitre and sulphuric acid, which give the best results with one description of cotton, will give inferior results, or perhaps fail, with another.

As to the keeping properties of pyroxyline, especially at temperatures above the common, there exists a great difference of opinion. It has been affirmed that pyroxyline exposed for several days to a temperature of 150° F. became uniformly decomposed, and that at the temperature of boiling water, some specimens explode. On the other hand, another experimenter declares, that pyroxyline was sealed up in a glass bottle and exposed in his garden for a year, the temperature of the inte-

[1] Belitzky, Br. J. XII., 4.

rior of the bottle having frequently exceeded 150° F., and was found at the expiration of that time to be unaltered.

That pyroxyline does easily decompose there can be no doubt. And, also, that that decomposition is greatly aided by light—even by diffuse light. I prepared at one time several different pyroxylines, which were placed in glass bottles and corked. One of these bottles was partly used just before leaving town for the summer, and was by oversight left on the table, where it remained for nearly three months. The room received a north light only, and no sunlight. At the expiration of the time just mentioned, the pyroxyline was converted into a moist, sticky, spongy substance, not one-fifth the bulk of the original cotton; the vial was filled with red vapors of hyponitric acid, and the cork much eaten away. Other bottles left in a closed closet had not suffered.

For this reason pyroxyline should always be kept in opaque cases.

M. Blondeau has published some new and interesting views on the subject of pyroxylines, which may be briefly expressed as follows:—

He considers pyroxyline to be a definite compound of *fulminose*, a substance isomeric with cellulose, and nitric acid. Of this fulminose little is stated except that it is decomposed at 140° F. into vapor of water and carbon. In the case of pyroxyline, the nitric acid which is in combination with the fulminose oxidizes the carbon to carbonic oxide, so that the products of explosion are carbonic oxide, nitrogen, and vapor of water.

Dr. Liesegang strongly recommends the substitution of *tissue paper* for cotton in preparing pyroxyline. The tissue paper is cut into strips and plunged into the acid mixture, which permeates it more rapidly and evenly. There is, therefore, less tendency to decomposition, and, it is affirmed, the product is more regular and uniform in its character. It is also claimed that it gives a remarkably smooth and uniform film when poured out upon the glass.

A variety of pyroxyline, called "alcoholic," has been introduced, but has been found of little use, even in our hottest summer weather, with the thermometer ranging from 90° to 100°. The ordinary pyroxylines, made up with perhaps a little more alcohol than in cooler weather, are preferred.

§ 2.—Collodion.

When pyroxyline is dissolved in acetic ether, it makes a perfect solution, but dries opaque. The solution of good negative cotton in a mixture of alcohol and ether has the inestimable quality of leaving behind it in drying an absolutely transparent film, not to be distinguished from the glass on which it lies.[1] It is, moreover, acted upon in some way by nitrate of silver, with the effect of adding greatly to the ordinary sensibility of iodide and bromide of silver, so that the "wet collodion process" is the most sensitive of known photographic methods, a fraction of a second being sufficient, under favorable circumstances, to impress a latent image, full of gradation and detail, in the camera.

The application of collodion for photographic uses has been claimed by Archer, Legray, and Bingham as their discovery; nor does it appear decidedly which is entitled to it.

The sensitizing or salting of collodion is effected by dissolving in it compounds of iodine and bromine, rarely chlorine, with bases. Fluorides, held now by Prat to be oxy-fluorides, to which considerable importance was at one time attached by the French photographers, have now gone quite out of use.

Formerly, the plain collodion was generally prepared separately, the salts were dissolved apart in a portion of the alcohol, and added subsequently. But as more care was taken in the manufacture of pure materials, and as the proper constitution of collodions came to be better understood, it became possible to prepare them so much more stable, that now it is more usual to prepare at once the collodion in the condition in which it is to be used. A good sound collodion, placed in a cool cellar, will keep two years, and is then by some preferred to fresh.

Also the use of excess of ether has been, to a large extent, done away with. Equal parts of alcohol and ether are now usually employed—an improvement originally advocated, I believe, by Mr. Sutton. The gain by this change is decided. More even coats are attained, because the collodion does not set so quickly, and casual draughts of air are less to be dreaded. The fumes are also less hurtful, and the cost is diminished.

[1] Some varieties leave a "dead" film, which is rendered transparent in the varnishing, and this is by some operators preferred. It is doubtful if such a film is as strong as a clear one.

The proportion of pyroxyline to that of solvent varies, according to the character of the pyroxyline itself, from 4 to 8 grains; 5 to 6 is the most usual with average pyroxylines. Some cottons, however, make a collodion so dense that the proportion must be lessened; others make it so thin that 6 grains are insufficient. Something will depend upon the character of the work to be done —for instance, negatives require a denser collodion than positives (ambrotypes).

§ 3.—Selection of Bases.

The selection of bases to which the iodine and bromine shall be united, is a matter of very great interest to the photographer. And this has been so well recognized that even exaggerated importance has been ascribed to it. The following will, it is believed, be found to be the sum of what is actually known on the subject.

It appears that the most permanent collodions are obtained when the iodine and bromine are combined with only a moderately powerful base. The alkalies tend to provoke decomposition, perhaps by attacking the hyponitric acid contained in the pyroxyline, whereby iodine is liberated, or at least enters into other forms of combination. Of the moderately strong bases, cadmium has been found to give such excellent results that it is very extensively used.

On the other hand, freshly-mixed collodion does not give as good results as that in which certain reactions, little understood as yet, have taken place between the constituents; and these reactions take place much more rapidly when an alkaline base is present. For this purpose *ammonia* is generally preferred. *Potassium* is very objectionable, because its bromide is very insoluble in the mixture of alcohol and ether used as a solvent. And even if the potassium appears in the form of iodide, yet as a bromide must be employed also, it follows, according to the well-known chemical law, that if the constituents present are capable of forming a combination insoluble in the solvent used, that combination will be formed. Therefore, if with bromide of cadmium we mix iodide of potassium in such proportion that if by the combination of all the potassium with its proportional amount of bromine, there will be more bromide than the liquid present can dissolve, then that excess will inevitably be formed and precipitated. *Sodium* forms a more soluble bromide than potassium, and the use of bromide of sodium, or of iodide of sodium, in the presence of bromide of cadmium, has been highly praised, but has never attained general acceptance.

Lithium forms a very soluble bromide, and its use in collodion has been very highly spoken of. Its higher price prevents its being more extensively used.

A curious difference exists between the actions of alkaline salts and of cadmium compounds in this: that the alkaline iodides and the bromides tend to render collodion thin and fluid, whilst the corresponding cadmium compounds render it thick and viscid.

For the various reasons here given, it is almost invariably customary to combine in collodion an alkaline and a metallic base. And it is exceptional to use any alkaline base except ammonia, any metallic base except cadmium.

Collodions made for sale must have good keeping properties, therefore in such the proportion of cadmium largely preponderates. Those mixed by photographers for their own immediate use, bear a larger proportion of ammonia, and this composition is generally preferred by portraitists.

Before touching upon the influence of iodine and bromine, which will form the subject of the next section, I must remark here that it is by no means indifferent in what form we add the respective substances to the collodion. It is a general law in chemistry, that when different salts are all completely dissolved in a solvent, the resulting combination will be independent of the form in which the substances were added. For example, if an equivalent of nitrate of potassium and one of chloride of sodium be dissolved in water, the result will be absolutely the same as if one equivalent of chloride of potassium and one of nitrate of sodium had been used. In each case the affinities are independent of the original form of the compounds.

It would be a great mistake to apply this principle to the preparation of collodion, as some might be disposed to do. The admixture of one equivalent of iodide of ammonium and one of bromide of cadmium would produce a quite different collodion from that afforded by the mixture of one equivalent of bromide of ammonium and one of iodide of cadmium. This is a point that cannot be too well understood.

The explanation is, that bromide of ammonium is a very stable salt, so likewise are bromide and iodide of cadmium; but iodide of ammonium is not. As received from the manufacturer it is apt to be yellowish, and to have a penetrating smell, apparently of iodine. It reacts quickly on the collodion and brings it soon to an orange shade, as is observable in collodions made with iodide of ammonium and iodide and bromide of cadmium. Whereas collodions made with bromide of ammonium and iodide of cadmium retain a pale straw-yellow color (if the pyroxyline has been quite neutral) easily for a year, and even more. What is curious is (at least so it has been in my experience), that those collodions in which the proportion of bromide of ammonium is large become darker than in those in which it is small.

Bromide of cadmium has a very remarkable tendency to thicken collodion, and sometimes even gelatinizes it so completely that the vessel may be inverted without spilling a drop. Therefore, when bromide of cadmium dissolved in alcohol is added to plain collodion, it should be in dilute solution, or, at least, not too strong. If a strong solution of bromide of cadmium be dropped into plain collodion, I have seen it cause threads and lumps in an otherwise sufficiently fluid collodion. These can be seen forming.

To resume, then. For all practical purposes, ammonium and cadmium are the great resources of photography as bases. Where the bromine is combined with the ammonium, and especially when the proportion of ammonium compound is not over the fourth part of that of the cadmium, a collodion is obtained which ripens within ten days or a fortnight, and then continues of excellent quality for many months, or, in a cool place, for years.

When the iodine is combined with the ammonia, and especially when this is used in larger proportions than above mentioned, collodions are obtained that ripen rapidly, and are fit for use in two or three days, or even in a few hours; but which become dark colored and insensitive, and give harsh pictures when kept. Whilst these are in their best condition, they are by some considered as giving the best possible results, and superior to those of the other class. It is only, however, when there is a regular and uniform consumption of collodion that this form can be employed without waste, or the risk of having a quantity of material on hand that has passed its best condition.[1]

§ 4.—Effects of Iodine and Bromine.

At first, iodides were used alone in connection with collodion. But as photographers were familiar with the influence of bromine, bromides were shortly after used with collodion. Experience led (by surprisingly slow degrees, however) to the recognition of the fact, that they were invaluable.

The manner in which bromides act is, however, still a point not thoroughly settled. It is a familiar fact that iodide of silver *solarizes* very easily, that is, the maximum effect of light is quickly reached, after which its action is reversed. So that with a certain degree of exposure, for example, the brightest lights may produce less impression, and come out in the development less strongly than others of inferior intensity. Bromide of silver has much less of this tendency, and a collodion containing bromide has much less tendency to solarize.

It has also been generally held, that the use of iodides was favorable to the effects of force and contrast, whilst bromide tended to softness and the correct rendering of half tone.

Some careful experiments made by the writer brought him to the conclusion that this view is by no means correct. That bromides tended fully as much, perhaps even more, to hardness and contrast than iodides; that softness of effect and the correct rendering of half tone depended upon the judicious combination of

[1] M. Regnauld has given the following summary of effects of different salting.

Iodide of Potassium renders collodion slow, but gives great density in the high lights. M. Regnauld recommends it for copying old engravings, and generally in subjects requiring marked contrasts.

Iodide of Cadmium.—Rapid, but tending to fog, unless a bromide is present, or the bath is quite acid. Chloride of zinc will also prevent the fogging.

Iodide of Ammonium.—M. Regnauld assigns to this iodide a tendency to give artistic perfection, but also a disposition to spottiness and inequality.

Such are some of the opinions that have been expressed on this subject, though others differ from them. The subject will be further referred to under the head of "Copying." Potassium has been excluded almost entirely (except for making ambrotypes) since so large a proportion of bromide has been introduced, because the bromide of potassium is very insoluble in the mixture of alcohol and ether used for making collodion. To keep it in solution, a watery alcohol must be employed, and this tends to give weak and rotten collodion films.

the two. For example, 2 grains of bromide and 4 of iodide gave a soft and well-modelled picture, whereas 2 of iodide and 4 of bromide gave a very harsh one.[1]

Another important function of bromide of silver is that of keeping the plate clean. It is certain that a bath which will no longer work with a pure iodide collodion, will give good pictures with one containing bromide. So with careless manipulation and impure chemicals, clean pictures may be got with a collodion containing bromide, when this would be impossible with a simple iodide collodion.

In the older formulæ employed for collodions, a great variety of substances were employed, and in some not only iodides and bromides, but also chlorides and fluorides. Then came a tendency to reject everything but iodides. Next this was modified by introducing bromides, and it is by no means impossible that we may yet find it advantageous to introduce a portion of chloride into our collodions.

The writer expresses this opinion, not with any positiveness, but as an idea which we may yet see realized. He has made many experiments on the development of positive prints on paper, and has been much struck with the superiority of chloride for this purpose. He believes that, at least when he first published this view, it was contrary to the prevailing opinions, according to which mixtures of iodides and bromides were preferred. But he found chloride of silver, though less sensitive and needing a rather longer exposure, to work far more evenly and regularly than the others, and he has little doubt that a grain, or perhaps half a grain to the ounce of chloride of zinc, would be found an improvement. A collodion containing three grains of chloride of zinc, ten of bromide of ammonium, and twenty-five of iodide of cadmium, to two and a half ounces each of alcohol and ether, and twenty-five grains of pyroxyline, would constitute a collodion which would probably be found to have superior qualities.

(Since the foregoing was written, the writer has shown that a perfectly invisible image upon chloride paper can be perfectly developed with as full detail as one upon bromo-iodized paper. This experiment has been repeated by others upon a collodion plate, and although the exposure required was longer, an excellent negative is stated to have been obtained. It was found necessary

[1] *Philadelphia Photographer*, III. 201.

to use a weaker fixing bath, as there was a greater tendency to dissolve than with the ordinary collodion film).

By some it has been argued, that the beneficial effects of the addition of bromide of silver are due to the fact that, as has been stated, bromide of silver is sensitive to less refrangible rays than iodide. That whilst iodide of silver was affected by only the violet and bluish-violet rays, the bromide was sensitive to the blue and even, to some extent, to the green.

Without discussing the question as to whether, under some circumstances, this sensitiveness may be exhibited, it results from Mr. L. M. Rutherfurd's experiments that, in the case of the collodion film, there was much uncertainty as to the extent to which the less refrangible rays affected the film; under some circumstances iodides gave a longer spectrum than bromides. But it was also rendered clear that the rays from which photographic effect was to be depended upon, the *working rays*, so to speak, for the photographer, were the *violet*. Where the violet distinctly passes into the blue, the effect on the collodion film was either nothing, or so small as to be not practically worth considering.

I pointed out, as far back as 1865, that the action of the green color of leaves upon the collodion film was very trifling and of little importance, and that leaves impressed themselves upon the film, not by the agency of their green, but of their white light.

In bodies generally we distinguish two sorts of light as emanating from them. One reflected from the surface, which is white, whatever be the color of the body, and the other emanating from the interior of the body, which is characterized by color. In some cases one of these may predominate almost to the exclusion of the other. Perfectly black objects send us only surface light, and in perfectly white objects the interior color is white as well as the surface color.

Now this surface light, which we scarcely take into account at all in our ordinary observation of bodies around it, so completely is it masked by the colored light, is, in fact, as I have elsewhere pointed out,[1] all that is really effective to the photographer, with the exception only of blue or violet-colored bodies. All bodies of blue-green, green, yellow, orange, and red colors impress themselves on the collodion film *solely* by virtue of the white surface

[1] *Philadelphia Photographer*, July, 1867.

light that accompanies, unperceived to us, the colored emanations which they give forth.

It follows from this that there is little use in endeavoring to find collodion that has a little greater range of impressibility. What we want is a film sensitive to the very faintest rays of white light, so that every faintest emanation of surface light shall act upon it by virtue of the violet rays which it includes.

Vogel has published some interesting experiments, from which he concludes that iodide of silver is more sensitive to strong lights, is more quickly impressed by them than bromide, but, on the other hand, that bromide is more sensitive to weak rays. Schrank has lately called this view in question, and gives as the result of special experiments made by him, that the beneficial influence of bromide depends upon its absence of tendency to solarization.

In view of this diversity of opinion, it is not surprising that the relative quantity of bromide to iodide, which gives the best result, is still unsettled. It has been positively ascertained that the bromide must not form less than 25 nor more than 50 per cent. of the whole salting. If 6 grains of salting to the ounce be used, the quantity of bromide must not be less than 1½ grain, nor more than 3. Most photographers approach the former rather than the latter limit. It may be said, however, that the proportion of bromide recommended has steadily increased for several years past, and with its increase has been a well-marked gain in the artistic effect of the photographs produced. The addition, moreover, of bromide has the effect of rendering the process far more certain. The bath will continue to work with a well-bromized collodion long after it has ceased to give any good result with a simply iodized collodion. The tendency to stains, fog, and other troubles in development is far less with a bromo-iodized collodion.

It now remains to give a few general directions as to the preparation and management of collodion, and then will follow some of the best formulæ in use.

To make the collodion, the cotton should first be weighed and placed in the bottle. Three-fourths of the alcohol are then to be added, and shaken up with the cotton. Next the ether is added, and the whole shaken till the cotton dissolves. If the cotton is exactly right, little or no visible residue will be left—a few filaments through the liquid, which, however, will not be clear.

This constitutes *plain collodion*, which may either be kept as such, or at once be sensitized. It is to be observed that plain collodion keeps *much better* than collodion sensitized with much ammonium salt, especially if iodide of ammonium of the yellow sort be used, but *not so well* as collodion sensitized with bromide of ammonium and iodide of cadmium. The operator will be guided by this in deciding in what form he will keep his collodion. As a general thing, the portraitist will make plain collodion and sensitize it as he wants it. The amateur will sensitize as soon as made, with bromide of ammonium and iodide of cadmium, with or without bromide of cadmium, or else use a good sort of commercial collodion.

Formula 1.

Alcohol and ether in equal quantities	1 ounce.
Bromide of ammonium	1 grain.
Bromide of cadmium	2 grains.
Iodide of cadmium	5 "
Pyroxyline	6 "

Formula 2.

Alcohol and ether in equal quantities	1 ounce.
Bromide of ammonium	2 grains.
Bromide of cadmium	1 grain.
Iodide of cadmium	5 grains.
Pyroxyline	6 "

These two are excellent formulæ. Collodion prepared with No. 1 will ripen in about two weeks and then keep for a year. No. 2 ripens more rapidly; of course, does not keep so well.

Prof. Rood's formula has been very largely used. It is:—

Alcohol and ether in equal quantities	1 ounce.
Bromide of ammonium	1 grain.
Iodide of cadmium	5 grains.
Pyroxyline, as required.	

It gives a good collodion of excellent keeping properties, but contains too little bromide.

Van Monckhoven's.

Ether	3 ounces.
Alcohol	4 "
Pyroxyline	50 grains.
Iodide of cadmium	25 "
Iodide of ammonium	25 "
Bromide of ammonium	12½ "

This also seems deficient in proportion of bromide.

The sensitizing is done by placing the weighed salts in a test-tube for small quantities, or a flask for larger, and pouring over them the remaining fourth of the alcohol, not at once, but in successive portions, allowing each to take up what it will before pouring it off. It is generally expedient to employ the heat of a Bunsen burner or spirit lamp to get the bromide into solution. It is not worth while to filter the solution—the simplest plan is to pour it into the plain collodion, shake well, and filter or decant afterwards.

Many operators regularly add a little solution of iodine to all their collodion, and there is no doubt that that system is the one that obviates the most completely all danger of fogging. Others prefer to depend upon the aging or ripening of the collodion.

Those who adopt the former plan of adding iodine to the collodion, should be extremely careful in acidifying the nitric bath. Perfectly neutral nitrate of silver should alone be employed, and before adding *any* acid to the bath, a plate should be tried with the collodion intended to be used, and if it works cleanly, then *no acid* must be introduced into the bath, or the sensitiveness of the film will be materially diminished. This point will also be adverted to in the remarks on fogging.

§ 5.—Clearing Collodion.

Two modes are adopted—decantation and filtration. The disadvantage of the former is that time is required for settling, and that there always remains a portion that cannot be got clear by decantation. Much trouble has been attached to filtering collodion that has no real, or at least no necessary existence.

Collodion filters are sold that do the work very well. The space in the throat, around the small tube, should be pretty tightly filled with clean sponge, not cotton, of which the filaments are just as bad a thing as possible to get into collodion. A piece of soft sponge should be left for two or three days in hydrochloric acid diluted with twice its bulk of water, until every trace of calcareous matter is got rid of. Then it should be left for hours in running water until every suspicion of acid is removed; then squeezed as dry as possible, and left in a place perfectly free from dust till dry; then put into a bottle and corked. A few ounces of sponge thus prepared will last for a very long time.

The whole art of filtering collodion is simply this: filter and leave the under or bottle part of the filter nearly full; then at any moment there is a stock of filtered collodion ready, with the great advantage that the air in the whole vessel being kept saturated with ether and alcohol vapor, the sponge does not dry up to a hard cake, but filters immediately when a fresh quantity is poured upon it, and continues to do so until finally choked up with sediment, when it requires to be replaced. Whenever the supply in the bottom part is removed, a fresh quantity is poured in at the top, and thus, even if the filtration goes on only by drops, it is of no consequence, the clear collodion is ready when wanted.

The small tube round which the sponge is pressed in must have the *small opening uppermost.* I prefer to bend it to an angle, which is easily done in any gas flame—the upper part thus turns to one side, and collodion poured into the top vessel, even carelessly, cannot get into the tube and run through without filtration.

CHAPTER IV.

THE NEGATIVE.

§ 1.—Selecting the Glass.

NONE but very careless operators will use a lot of glass indiscriminately. Every piece should be gone over and examined previous to cleaning it. The high price of plate glass in this country almost wholly excludes it from photographic use. If it could be obtained at the same cost as in England, France, or Germany, none other, or very little other, would be used. As it is, photographers for the most part content themselves with a quality of glass, usually of French manufacture, known as "photographic glass."

The best quality of the glass only should be purchased. It comes in boxes containing fifty square feet. Opening such a box, and sitting with his face to a well-lighted window, the operator examines every piece—

1. As to sufficient thickness. Thin plates break too easily in the printing process.

2. As to curvature, by running the eye along the edges: a slight curvature cannot always be avoided; but anything over a certain degree of bow is a sufficient cause for rejection. (See p. 23.)

3. As to blebs. Blebs are worse on the *outside* (the convex or bowed side) than on the hollow side, which is always that on which the collodion is poured. Any bleb on the outside is a sufficient cause for rejection, and many think that any bleb at all is sufficient to condemn the piece.

4. *As to scratches.* Some lots of glass by careless handling will be scratched. All pieces with scratches visible by transmitted or reflected light are to be rejected. And to avoid farther danger every piece after examination must have a sheet of paper laid between it and the adjoining piece. And this precaution must be kept up in every subsequent stage of the operations. Printed paper should never be employed for this purpose, but some common though clean sort. If glass is left for some time in contact with printed paper, a complete impression will be taken off upon it, and the difficulty of cleaning will be proportionately increased by the greasiness transmitted to the glass.

5. *As to surface.* Some pieces of glass must be rejected for roughness of the surface.

A close attention on the part of photographers to these points would have the effect of obliging those who manufacture photographic glass to work more carefully and deliver a better material.

§ 2.—**Making the Plate.**

The mode of pouring collodion upon the plate varies with different operators. Some pour upon the part of the plate nearest to the operator, and then pour off at the far right-hand corner.

Others reverse the matter, pour nearer to the far edge, and pour off at the near right-hand corner. The latter seems to be the best method, as the fatigue of holding the plate is rather less when so managed.

Let *A B C D* be the plate of the usual shape. Imagine a line drawn at *E F*, leaving the portion beyond it square. Now, evidently, the natural course (as directed in the Introduction) is to pour by beginning with the centre of this square. viz., *G*. The pool at first spreads equally and circularly. The operator by inclining the plate rapidly brings the pool down to *A*, then to *B*, then across to *C*, next to *D*, then (unless using a very thick collodion) sends a wave clear across the plate to *A*, which part having been the first covered, is the dryest and the thinnest. This sending back increases the thickness all over, but especially about *A*, and more nearly equalizes the whole plate. The moment the wave reaches *A*, it is sent back again to *D* and poured off.

Fig. 71.

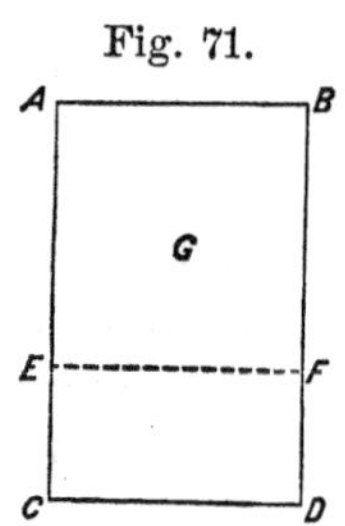

The whole of this operation, and especially the sending back, requires a light directly in front of the operator, and not too high. It is *essential* that the operator catch the reflection of the light on the film, by which he easily watches the wave go back, and stops the motion at the right moment.

Before pouring, the neck of the bottle must be carefully wiped free from dust, or a *collodion pourer* may be used, in which the top of the vial is covered with a cup of glass ground to fit it.

As now the film dries, the surface, which looked before perfectly smooth, will frequently show minute specks, which by capillary attraction cause the collodion to collect round them so that they form slightly raised spots. These are one of the great nuisances of photography, and one which no carefulness of manipulation will get rid of. The writer has even tried forcing collodion through thick filtering paper by the pressure of a considerable column, but the collodion so filtered produced them just as much as that filtered through sponge. These specks, so far as he can find, depend upon—

1. Minute filaments carried through the filter (if sponge) or coming from the filter itself (if paper or cotton-wool).
2. Dust on the plate before pouring.

3. Dust falling during the collodionizing.

Of course cause (1) is beyond helping, and is therefore the most serious of all. To obviate (2) brush the plate gently with a soft wide camel's hair brush, or rub gently and very moderately with chamois leather, just before collodionizing. Not using too much friction, or it will very easily become electrical and attract every mote in the atmosphere, and retain it obstinately.

Cause (3) is best obviated by having a special closet in the dark room for collodionizing. This is so desirable on hygienic grounds alone, that it should never be omitted.

Only experience can enable the photographer to decide as to whether a film showing some of these specks must be wiped off again. If intended for copying, it must, invariably, be rejected; and, generally, if for portraiture. In landscape work, one or two small specks are not likely to show in the negative.

This is on the supposition that the particles are filaments of wool, or cotton, or other inert substance. Sometimes there may be chemical dust, as of hyposulphite of sodium, in the atmosphere. In this case the speck, after sensitizing, will appear *darker than the rest* when viewed by transmitted light, and the plate is, of course, worthless.

Attention to the proper moment for dipping into the bath is necessary, because, if the plate be kept too long, it is insensitive, and tends to marbled stains; if plunged in too soon, it may split in the bath. But even if the film does not split, it may still not have been dry enough, and may exhibit an appearance which no one, without instruction, would ascribe to the right cause. Some portion of the film will assume a peculiar appearance, not easily described, but very observable. Perhaps a better idea can be given by saying that it has something the appearance of wax, the structure of a freshly-broken cake of camphor, or of fused nitrate of silver; neither exactly conveys the idea, but are perhaps as good comparisons as can be found. This appearance is rarely at, or carried to, the edges, which dry faster, but is generally to the interior of the plate, and mostly covers a few square inches of surface. It rather gives the idea of some decomposition to the collodion, than suggests its true origin.

§ 3.—Developers and Development.

The first agent used for developing was gallic acid. In time it was discovered that pyrogallic acid was in many respects preferable. Again, protosulphate of iron was recommended. This last had great difficulty in making its way, but has finally come into general use, as giving a softer picture, and answering with less exposure than pyrogallic acid.

When sulphate of iron is used for developing *instantaneous pictures*, no restraining acid is employed, but simply a very strong solution of the iron, 80 or 100 grains to the ounce. Such a developer cannot, of course, be kept on more than a very short time, and the image once forced out, recourse must be had to redevelopment, or to after intensification, to bring the image up to printing strength. Conversely, when a long exposure has been given, a good deal of restraining acid may with propriety be added.

Operators differ a good deal in their views as to the proper strength of the iron developer for ordinary exposures, using from ten grains of sulphate to the ounce up to forty or more. The following proportion will be found to give good results:—

Winter Developer.

Sulphate of iron	3 ounces.
Acetic acid	3 to 4 ounces fluid.
Water	40 ounces fluid.

Summer Developer.

Sulphate of iron	2 ounces.
Acetic acid	3 to 4 fluidounces.
Water	40 ounces fluid.

Adding four ounces of alcohol if the bath be an old one.

It has been proposed at various times to place a very great number of various organic substances in the developer. Experience has shown that almost any organic substance may take the place of acetic acid as a restraining agent, and sometimes with advantage; for some of these substances have a remarkable power of destroying the tendency to fog, so that the iron developer can be kept upon the plate like a pyrogallic developer. Thus redevelopment becomes wholly superseded, and the picture is always finished at a single operation. The substance that possesses this property in the largest degree is, as shown by the writer, *modified gelatine.* The writer published several formulæ for this purpose, and the subject attracted at one time very great attention. Many experimenters went to work at it, and published formulæ of their own. Since publishing some years ago the remarks on the subject that gave the initiative to all that has been written, the writer has remarked that the quantity of sulphuric acid necessary to modify the gelatine is absolutely so small in proportion that it exercises no hurtful agency upon the development, and *consequently it does not require to be removed by a subsequent neutralization.* This brings the preparation of the collo-developer to a singularly simple form, as follows: Take

Common glue	6 ounces.
Sulphuric acid	¾ fluidounce.
Water	9 fluidounces.

Boil these together for a couple of hours in a flask, replacing the water as it evaporates. Then throw in an ounce of granulated zinc, and boil for an hour and a half. Add water as it evaporates, and, when done, dilute to twelve ounces.

This syrupy liquid has the most extraordinary restraining power. A single drop is sufficient for three ounces of 30-grain iron solution; one ounce, therefore, of the above gelatine solution is sufficient for 1500 ounces of developer.

Two essential remarks remain to be made in reference to this process. It might be alleged that the restraining power is due to the sulphuric acid by reason of its powerfully acid nature; but the writer has, by careful experiment, demonstrated the fact that sulphuric acid does not tend to restrain development, but tends to fog. It is therefore clearly not the sulphuric acid that acts.

Again, it may be alleged that by the long boiling with zinc, the whole of the sulphuric acid must have been removed by the excess of zinc present. But the presence of the gelatine checks the action of the acid on the zinc so much that it was ascertained by careful experiment that when the operation is performed as above described, at the end of a boiling of an hour and a half, only *one-fourth* of the sulphuric acid was neutralized. This was ascertained by weighing the zinc before and after the operation, and determining the quantity of sulphuric acid corresponding to its loss of weight.

The action of the gelatine in this case in checking chemical action, presents a very striking analogy to its action in the development.

The collo-developer obtained by adding one drop of the gelatine solution, prepared as above, to three ounces of water and 90 grains of protosulphate of iron, develops rapidly and with less tendency to fog than the common iron developer. By somewhat increasing the quantity, the development goes on still more slowly, with still less tendency to fogging.

The Sugar Developer.—For the regular needs of the photographer no developer can be better than the sugar developer. The writer uses a formula of his own which he strongly recommends. It is as follows:—

In 32 ounces of hot water dissolve 10 ounces of protosulphate of iron. This is best done by letting a portion of the hot water stand over the crystals until it is pretty well saturated, pouring it off, and repeating it with a second and third portion. To this solution add 10 oúnces of white sugar and 3 ounces of acetic acid No. 8. This need not be filtered. It is the sugar developer in a concentrated form, and keeps indefinitely. To prepare for use take:—

Above solution	3 ounces.
Acetic acid No. 8	2 "
Water	10 "

Filter.

It is perhaps an improvement to add a little sulphate of copper. An ounce or two of it may be added to the 10 ounces of sulphate of iron. With it, or without it excellent results are got. The strength above given is suitable for winter, and may be diluted with from one-half to an equal quantity of water in summer.

§ 4. Local Redevelopment.

It will occasionally happen that after the deposit on a negative has reached a point such that whilst the denser parts have received all that they can bear consistently with giving full detail in the high lights in the print to be hereafter taken, the thinner portions, or some of them, might advantageously have more strength; that is, these thinner portions, though exhibiting fine details to the eye, may be thin to print properly. In order, therefore, to bring the negative into a condition to show the greatest possible transparency of shadow, that is, a clear rendering of details in the least illuminated portions, it may be very advantageous to resort to a *local redevelopment.*

This may be performed either before or after fixing. When done before fixing, there is more hope of adding to the details, when after, the operation can be performed more satisfactorily, because the operator sees far better what he is about. In the former case, although details not before visible may be rendered visible, yet it is doubtful if within the limits of this operation, detail so brought out, can be got up to printing strength. The proper hope of this operation seems therefore to be the bringing of visible details, too weak to print, up to printing strength, and this is better done upon the fixed and washed negative. I shall therefore so describe it. It will be understood, however, that if preferred, exactly the same operation may be performed upon the unfixed negative, remembering that the same precaution as to light must be then used as in the regular development, otherwise fogging will ensue.

If the negative has been allowed to dry, it will be advisable first to go round the edges with India rubber dissolved in benzole. The film must then be well wetted, is to be grasped by the left thumb and forefinger at one of its corners, and so held that those parts which are already fully dense shall be on the side of the plate farthest from the operator (in a landscape negative this will generally be the sky side); the plate is to be tilted a little, so that this far side will be a little the higher, and a solution of pyrogallic acid, silver, and citric acid, such as is usually employed for redeveloping, is to be dropped upon those parts where the additional deposit is needed. The plate being very wet, this dropping of solution will produce circles that slowly expand, and as they cease to expand wash down towards the edge near the operator, by reason of the tilting position given as above directed. As this takes place the operator holds the plate under the bath and washes off the solution. If the parts nearest to the operator will easily bear the additional deposit that they get as the solution passes over them, the operator proceeds more deliberately. If they are already pretty strong, he washes off almost as soon as the solution spreads to them. A few seconds suffice to wash away the solution, when the operator recommences, and this is done as often as necessary, even up to six or a dozen times.

By this mode of proceeding, spots and stains are avoided. If the solution were left to rest on any one part, a circular spot might result which would print lighter. But with a little care nothing of the sort need be dreaded, and the most satisfactory results can be obtained. The pyrogallic solution can be used pretty strong, but should be kept clear and colorless. The whole operation turns on not allowing the solution to be for a moment stationary anywhere, but washing it off as it ceases to spread, and recommencing. Of course, before washing, the greater part of the solution may be first drained off into the developing vessel.

§ 5.—After-Intensification.

The three stages by which the utmost possible density is acquired by a negative are—*development*, with iron, pyrogallic or gallic acid; *redevelopment*, by a second application of either of the foregoing reducing agents, not necessarily or even generally the same as at first employed, since iron is commonly followed by pyrogallic acid; and *after-intensification*, which last may be effected in a variety of different ways.

Redevelopment may be resorted to either before or after fixing, and in all cases is accompanied by an addition of silver solution. After-intensification is always applied *after* fixing, and silver is never used. The object of redevelopment is always to add more silver, without acting in any way upon the previous deposit. After-intensification adds no silver, but always acts chemically upon the original image, bringing it into a new combination more opaque to light.

Usually the second stage is omitted, the developed picture is intensified without redevelopment. It should be thoroughly understood by all students in photography that after-intensification is at best the remedy either of a mistake in the exposure, or else is rendered necessary either by a deficiency of illumination, or an exposure which for good reason has been greatly curtailed. Therefore, whilst a good knowledge of several modes of intensifying is necessary for the photographer, he should resort to them as little as possible. Where the exposure has proved much too short or too long, it is generally better, when practicable, to take another negative. It will cost but little, if any, more time; the experience of the first will enable the operator to time the second correctly, and the probabilities of a fine negative are decidedly greater.

Iodine.—When only a little additional strength is wanted, iodine may be employed. If a few drops of tincture of iodine be dropped into a quantity of water, the latter acquires a pale sherry wine color, and if poured over a negative gradually blackens it, or rather brings it to an exceedingly deep violet black. The application must be stopped at this point by washing off the solution as its continued action brings the plate to a light yellow color. The solution may either be flowed over the plate, replacing it with fresh as soon as it loses its color, or it may be applied as a bath.

Care must be taken that there are no undissolved particles of iodine present, as these may lodge on the film and produce yellow spots. For this reason many prefer to add a little iodide of potassium to the liquid, which enables it to keep more iodine in solution. This combination may be purchased at the druggists, under the name of "Lugol's solution," which may be diluted with twenty times its bulk of water and used.

Chlorine.—The blackening may be equally well effected by chlorine. Make a solution of bichromate of potash, 1 grain to the ounce, and add to each ounce 2 drops of hydrochloric acid. This solution is applied like the preceding.

Corrosive Sublimate.—If a saturated solution of this substance be diluted with ten times its bulk of water, it may be applied precisely like the preceding, and blackens the plate very effectually.

The foregoing applications all give a moderate degree of additional density to the image, though the latter acts more powerfully in this respect than the others. They also act alike in this, that if their influence be continued too long, the images, after having become black, become lighter again; in the first case pass to a yellow shade, in the two latter, to white. In this condition, the film is in all cases much *less* dense than at first. In this stage, however, they are fit for additional treatment, which may confer upon them a much greater density yet, as follows:—

Sulphide of potassium will not act much upon the silver film, but if by the continued action of either of the three first methods, the film has been brought to the yellow or white stage, and then a dilute solution of sulphide of potassium be poured over it, the image acquires an intense blackness, so intense, in fact, that all middle tints may be expected to disappear. Nevertheless, there do exist cases in which this treatment may be applied with very useful results. Negatives of line-engravings, especially such as are of the full size of the original, are often very successfully obtained by developing only till an ambrotype is got, and then, without any redevelopment, intensifying in this way. But it is to be said that, in skilful hands, equally good and quicker printing negatives of line engravings are got by the ordinary development and redevelopment, though they do not give prints which so easily tone to a perfect black as those yielded by the denser sort of negatives. Even, however, when these denser negatives are wanted, they may be still better obtained by the following:—

Cyanide of Potassium.—When a film has been treated with corrosive sublimate till the white stage is reached, there is often a little veiling produced, scarcely visible whilst the print has this light color, but visibly injurious after the blackening by sulphide has been effected. I have found it, therefore, useful to substitute *cyanide of potassium* for the alkaline sulphide. The cyanide solution must be very weak, one grain, or not exceeding two, to the ounce of water. It must be flowed over evenly, or applied as a bath, and must be washed off as soon as an even blackness is obtained. A continued action will cause the negative to whiten again.

This treatment gives great intensity, and, at the same time, keeps the transparent parts of the negative beautifully clear. For photographic operations in processes not intended to give half tones, it is exceedingly well suited, as well as for all cases where clean sharp contrast is a main object.

Schlippe's Salt—Scarlet Negatives.—This method of intensifying, which the writer introduced to photographic notice some years ago, has been largely used where great increase of intensity is needed, and with excellent results. The negative is first treated in either of the three first described methods: with iodine, chlorine, or corrosive sublimate, until the light stage is reached, and then, after washing, a dilute solution of Schlippe's salt (sulphantimonite of sodium) is poured over it. The negative instantly turns bright scarlet, presenting a remarkable and very beautiful appearance, and becoming very opaque to active rays.

The solution of Schlippe's salt should contain about ten grains to the ounce, and should be kept tightly corked. It, however, gradually deposits a precipitate, but if decanted from this it still acts well. The addition of a few drops of liquid ammonia prevents the precipitate and causes the solution to keep quite well. In this condition it does not give the bright-colored negatives before spoken of, but beautiful russet-brown ones, which are perhaps as non-actinic as those obtained without the ammonia. The color will also be found to vary a good deal with the extent to which the first application (of chlorine, iodine, or sublimate solution) has been allowed to act. The full scarlet color is got by allowing the first action to reach the full light stage, and applying the Schlippe's salt without ammonia.

Solution of Schlippe's salt is apt to stain the fingers red. A little weak solution of caustic potash or soda instantly removes this.

It should always be borne fully in mind that operations with either sulphide of potassium or Schlippe's salt should be carried on away from the dark room, as the sulphuretted hydrogen, of which a little is diffused in the atmosphere, may tend to cause fogging. It is also injurious to the health to breathe a sulphuretted atmosphere, therefore a thorough draft should be provided to carry off such vapors.

Permanganate of potassium has been highly recommended for after-intensifying by Mr. Wharton Simpson. A dilute solution is poured over the plate till the requisite intensity is obtained.

Uranium intensifying is now abandoned, because the negatives rapidly become denser in printing till worthless; after-intensification with sublimate is, to some extent, liable to a similar objection.

In such cases it has been recommended to expose them to a gentle heat for a length of time, which treatment is said to lower the intensity. In copies of engravings without half tint (line engravings and wood-cuts, but not mezzotints, lithographs, or photographs) this increase of strength is of little or no disadvantage; in such cases therefore the mercury may be used without hesitation.

These processes may be divided into three classes, according to the amount of effect that they produce. For a quite moderate increase of density chlorizing or iodizing may be used. For a rather greater, but still moderate result, sublimate solution is suitable. When a very decided increase is needed, chlorizing, iodizing, or mercurializing, in each case till the light color is reached may be resorted to, to be followed by Schlippe's salt or sulphide of potassium.

All the mercurial treatments weaken the film and render it liable to split in drying. If, therefore, a valuable negative is so treated, it is a prudent course to flood it with gum-water or solution of gelatine, the former about 30 to 35 grains to the ounce, the latter about 20 to 25. If intensifying is much practised it is well to have a solution of this sort on hand; it may be made to keep by adding either creasote or carbolic acid, one drop to every two ounces. The gum solution or gelatine is flowed over the plate for a half minute, worked in, and then poured off again, and the plate is reared up to dry. After thorough drying it is to be varnished. It has been affirmed that a plate so treated can be varnished cold without the varnish drying *dead.* On the whole, the gum-water answers better than the gelatine, and does not require to be warmed to liquefy it.

To Intensify Varnished Negatives.—The usual plan is to remove the varnish by soaking in alcohol or benzole, whichever has been used in the making of the varnish to be removed; then apply any of the intensifiers already described.

The complete removal of a lac-spirit varnish by alcohol is no easy thing, portions of gum remain behind and refuse to dissolve. Some, therefore, intensify without removing the varnish. Mr. Alfred Hughes' method is as follows: Dissolve iodine in spirit varnish, one grain to the ounce, and varnish the plate with this varnish, without removing the first coat. Drain it well off, dry, and expose to the light, when a considerable increase of intensity takes place.

When the operation has been performed by dissolving the varnish, the use of an alcoholic solution of iodine, two or three grains to the ounce, is to be recommended, and acts more uniformly than any aqueous solution would. Care should be taken not to leave it on too long, and it must be borne in mind that the alcoholic solution cannot be instantaneously removed, like an aqueous one, as it takes a few seconds for the water to moisten the plate evenly.

§ 6.—Negatives for Enlargement.

A negative intended to be enlarged from, should always be taken specially for that purpose. It is undoubtedly true that *some* negatives taken for ordinary printing are capable of being used for enlarging from; such are those that print easily in the shade. Usually, however, it is found better to take negatives expressly.

These must be thinner than usual, but it is not to be supposed that that thinness is to be secured by a brief exposure. On the contrary, *because* the development must be short, the exposure must be full, a little longer than usually given, so that the picture may flash up as soon as the developer is poured over it; and then, after a very few seconds, the plate is rapidly to be washed, lest the deposit should become too thick. Van Monckhoven, who is excellent authority on this subject, remarks that the details in the shadows should be scarcely visible, and the denser parts so thin that one can read through them, and see the smallest objects without difficulty. Also, that negatives which are too strong are best reduced by plunging them into a bath of one grain of perchloride of iron to each three ounces of water; then, after washing, apply cyanide, which will reduce the strength. The operation to be repeated if necessary.

The deepest shadows should be represented by perfectly clear glass. Veiling that would be unimportant in an ordinary negative, will unfit one for enlarging.

Varnish is objectionable for many reasons. The best results are got with negatives washed and dried without even a solution of gelatine or other preservative. Some, however, do not hesitate to apply protectives, but, if possible, they are to be avoided.

§ 7.—Retouching the Negative.

The remarkable effects which can be obtained by artistically retouching a negative have latterly attracted a great deal of attention to the subject; especially since portraits printed on paper have been received from Germany, in which the complexion exhibits all the beauty of a fine miniature. Inquiry has been made how such results have been obtained by Angerer, Grasshoff, Rabending, Milster, and others.

Retouching may be done on either the varnished side or the back of the negative. On the back it is useful when there are considerable masses of shadow, deficient in transparency. When there exists detail in the negative that cannot be printed, but comes out as black, or at least too dark to produce the desired effect, this may be obviated by the application of a smooth and uniform coat behind all such places, of some moderately non-active color. As, however, the marks of the brush must not show, and this is difficult to avoid, Dr. Vogel has recommended a simple and effectual plan of covering the whole of the back of the plate with a coat of varnish made by dissolving dragon's blood in alcohol. This varnish is then wiped away from all such portions as are sufficiently dense. It is quite obvious that even great faults in the way of excessive contrast in a negative may thus be somewhat ameliorated. It is scarcely necessary to say that negatives treated in this way must be printed in the shade, otherwise the edge of the varnish, unless exceedingly well applied, will be offensively distinguishable. More local retouching, however, is generally done upon the varnished side, and may be managed either with *Indian ink* or *black lead pencil.*

For stopping out small holes, Indian ink is generally used. A color which contrasts with the negative is always desirable, as it is easier to see what is done; therefore if a negative has been blackened by any after-intensification, it is more advisable to touch out holes with a red color. Vermilion is very effective, and seems to stand the sun pretty well. The indefinite permanence of Indian ink against all action of light is an argument in its favor that is not to be overlooked.

In skilful hands the black lead pencil gives very excellent results. A very soft pencil is to be taken, a Faber's B B, or B B B. The smoothness of black lead is much in its favor, and its facility for uniting strokes so as to give a uniform tint. On the other hand, care must be taken not to injure the negative, and the work must be managed with the utmost circumspection, for a stroke once made with the black lead cannot very easily be removed; whereas with the liquid color and camel's-hair pencil, the work may of course be washed out, and tried over and over till the operator is satisfied. If it is found that the varnished surface will not take the lead pencil, a coat of gum water must be applied.

A special arrangement is advisable when such retouching is to be done. A table is provided, with a slanting top, like a desk. An oblong piece is sawed out, and a plate of stout plate glass is set in permanently into the opening thus made. On this plate is rested the negative whilst undergoing retouching. As in this way the light is insufficient (a negative must always be retouched whilst looking *through* it, not *upon* it), it is necessary to make some arrangement to throw up light through the negative. For this purpose either a mirror or a sheet of clean white paper, stretched on a board, is placed beneath it; either that is used should incline towards the light.

Homersham, who has studied the art of retouching, especially on landscape negatives, recommends a different method of operating. He takes a badger's brush, cuts off the hairs at half their length, square, so as to have only the stump of a brush. Rubbing a transparent water color upon a saucer, and using as little water as possible, he takes up the thick color on the stump brush and dots it carefully and evenly on the back of the plate. Any strength of color may be got by successive applications, carefully waiting till the last is dry before applying a new one. This treatment he especially recommends for foregrounds of landscapes that are too transparent to print well, and become too black when the printing is continued long enough to get the best effects of the distance, as not uncommonly happens, owing to the better lighting of the distance. *Carmine lake* he especially recommends for this use. So, too, when negatives have been taken in cloudy, dark weather, they often have great softness, but exhibit insufficient contrast. In such cases a careful application of color to the negative will give density when required, and add to the force and character of the high lights.

The *pasting of paper* behind parts that are intended to be lighter is a well-known artifice; but it only answers well when the borders of the part to be influenced are pretty well defined. Some curious effects of light exhibited in this city have been so produced. A female face, for example, is raised upwards, and a beam of sunlight falls upon it from a window, lighting it up in a striking way. The beam and the effect upon the face are produced by pasting thin paper on the back of the negative, and printing in the shade. It is scarcely necessary to say that the paper must be selected with a very even grain and an absence of the lightish dots so commonly found in thin papers.

Architectural subjects lend themselves to artifices of this sort, because of the straight lines by which they are bounded; at the same time that in such there is less need of them, for the needful effects can always be got by proper management without these devices. The case is different in portraiture and landscapes. A complexion, such as is produced by retouching the negative, can rarely, if ever, be got by the regular processes of photography. The light and shade found in a landscape in nature is rarely the best possible—rarely such as an artist in painting the scene would take without alteration. In such cases the opening for skilful retouching is very evident.

§ 8.—**Other Artifices Connected with Negative.**

Other ingenious operations have been performed on negatives, either to remove objections or to produce particular effects. Thus Mr. Notman, of Montreal, has produced prints in which the effect of *falling snow* is very well represented. A white pigment is mixed up with water moderately thick, is put on a brush and flirted over the negative with a quick jerk. Snow-banks in these pictures were made in the studio of common table-salt, which also, when scattered over clothes and drapery, gives a very good imitation of the effects of snow caught in the folds. Clear ice was represented by plate glass resting on sheet zinc: figures in skating attitudes were posed on this. The positions of rapid skating motion were obtained by supporting the model in the desired position with Sarony's apparatus, the stem of which was concealed behind the leg of the skater which touched the ice.

One peculiarity of photography lies in the opening it affords for original devices of all sorts by the ingenious. This seems the proper place to mention a few of them.

Ghosts.—This name has been give to prints representing a shadowy figure through which all the objects behind it are distinctly seen. Such pictures are obtained by causing the model, after remaining standing or in a chair for a short time, to move suddenly away, whilst the exposure is completed without him. In such a case it is evident that the objects at first concealed by him will afterwards impress themselves on the film, and be visible through his figure.

Doubles.—A model may appear twice in the same print by having a couple of folding doors arranged inside the camera, a little in front of the film. One of these being closed, the sitter is taken on the other half. This then is shut, the other door opened (the lens being covered during the change), at the same time the sitter is transferred to the other side, and taken again in some different attitude, as, for instance, offering a glass of wine to his double across a small table. By accurate adjustment a man is made to shake hands with himself. The position of the doors causes them to be very much out of focus, so that they do not show in the image.

Moonlight Effects.—Although a negative of the moon itself can be easily obtained in the camera, the photographing of objects illuminated by moonlight is utterly impossible. Prints, however, from under-exposed and over-developed negatives often have a resemblance to moonlight views. For in effect if we observe a view by moonlight we shall notice that there is almost a complete absence of diffuse light. Objects in shadow are not lighted at all. A tree seen by moonlight exhibits a bright mass of light where the rays fall, with a moderate detail; in the shaded foliage there is absolutely no detail at all—it is a black mass. Now these effects are those that belong to badly-made negatives, with all their worst faults of exposure and development. But these same faults, when intentionally introduced and artistically managed, are capable of producing very pleasing effects. Ferrier, in Paris, has been particularly happy in some of these. The moon itself is produced by a piece of paper pasted on the negative.

Artificial Clouds.—In cases where the sky of a landscape has become much thinned by solarization, it may admit of painting-in clouds. This is done by the application of transparent water colors on the back, in imitation of natural clouds. No small skill with the brush is necessary to produce good effects. The description of clouds known to meteorologists as the *cumulus*, the *cumulo-stratus*, are those most successfully imitated. The photographer should bear in mind that the direction of light must correspond with that of the picture, and also that unless the sun is very low, heavy clouds are always darkest underneath.

§ 9.—Printing-in Skies.

To obtain clouds in this way the sky of the negative should be opaque, or very nearly so. A print is taken and the sky cut carefully out and rejected, following as nearly as possible, but in flowing lines, the outline of the landscape as projected against the sky. This is done immediately after the print is taken from the frame. Next, expose to light, when the whole becomes perfectly black, and fix without toning.

A good sky negative with suitable character of clouds and direction of light is taken, and the black mask above prepared is neatly attached to the back of the sky negative, *the white side next* the glass. The sky negative is now ready for use.

Prints for the landscape negative, when removed from the printing frame, are placed under the sky negative, and printed again. The black mask protects all but the sky, which receives the cloud image from the second negative.

Printing of this kind requires, of course, to be done in the shade, otherwise the line of the mask cannot be so well concealed. This object is best attained by having a border of sky in the mask—that is, not cutting too close to the landscape. With ingenuity and care beautiful results are got in this way, and effects can be obtained that, when exhibited, puzzle even the photographer who is not acquainted with the mode in which they are accomplished.

For example, if a dead tree, or a tree without foliage, as in winter, or with but small foliage, showing the sky through as in early spring, stand well out and detached from the sky, clouds may be printed in behind it, showing through the branches. This is done by cutting out all that part of the tree that is thus open, along with the sky, so that all such part of the tree is not masked. The clouds are then printed in, and as such a tree presents little or no aspect of light and shade in its slender branches standing against a bright sky, the second printing does not affect it otherwise than to make parts a little blacker, a result that is not injuriously noticeable in the finished print.

A splendid effect is produced by printing *reflected clouds in water*. It requires three printings. A scene is chosen with a wide expanse of water and sky. The sky and water are both masked; the sky first printed in, and then the cloud negative turned over so that what was before the top, becomes the bottom, and the film or varnished side is away from the paper. The reflection of the cloud on the water is thus obtained by printing *through the glass*, which gives it just the amount of indistinctness wanted, whilst every cloud and shade of cloud in the sky is faithfully rendered in the water. The deception is so complete that it is difficult to persuade one's self at first that the whole was not taken at once, and the reflected clouds obtained at the same time with the real ones.

The effects that may be obtained by these repeated printings in landscape photography are exceedingly beautiful. They have also been varied by being made the means of introducing figures into landscapes, as in Robinson's "Bringing Home the May," in which several pretty youthful figures of girls are introduced into the landscape. The difficulties, however, in such maskings are necessarily much greater than in simply printing-in a cloud picture.

The same general methods have been used for obtaining effects much more odd than pleasing—as, for example, a card portrait is printed of a man standing before his own tombstone, with his head severed from his body, and grasped by the hair with one of his hands. The trees and objects behind the portion where his head would properly be, are all perfectly well made out, so that the deception is complete. This is done by masking and repeated printing. There are several ways in which it may be thus managed, but the subject has not sufficient importance for the space the details would occupy.

§ 10.—**Negatives by Magnesium Light.**

Some successful applications have been made of the magnesium light to photography. Thin strands, coils, or wires of that metal, when set fire to, burn with a splendid blue light, very rich in actinic power; negatives may be very well taken by it. Interiors and parlor groups have been photographed at night by it, and pictures taken of caves, catacombs, and other places inaccessible to daylight.

The chief difficulty in obtaining good interiors results from the *directness* of the light. If one light be used, of course the shadows exhibit a total want of illumination. At least two are necessary, and this immediately introduces the danger of *double shadows*, an evil which is not known in the carefully adjusted light of the ordinary glass room. It has been tried to obviate this difficulty by burning one of the lights behind ground glass, but this has been found to diminish the illumination very materially. It appears that the background for magnesium photography should be much lighter than for daylight work, for reasons which I have pointed out fully elsewhere.[1]

Very ingenious lamps have been constructed for burning magnesium, especially one in which a draught of air, kept up by a chimney, is made to enter in front, and thus to keep the heavy white smoke of magnesia, which is generated by the combustion, from obscuring the light. It is affirmed by competent observers, that the effective light produced by a given quantity of magnesium is nearly doubled by this simple contrivance.

Mr. E. L. Wilson gives as the results of his experiments with magnesium, that one reflector should be placed about the height of the head of the sitter, at a distance of six or eight feet, and somewhat between him and the lens. The other should be rather farther off, lower down, and at the opposite side. The first of these should be supplied with from three to five tapers, the second with two to three. A half taper is burned quite near the sitter, whereby to focus. The exposure lasts as long as the tapers burn, viz., from seventeen to twenty-five seconds.

It seems probable that better effects would be got by raising the burning magnesium higher above the sitter, so as to correspond better with the effects of light ordinarily preferred.

A variation on this process has been introduced by Mr. Skaife, and consists in pointing, focussing, and leaving open the camera, by ordinary gaslight. Then a pyrotechnic mixture of magnesium, chlorate of potash, etc., is inflamed, and gives an intense light for a second. During this time, and whilst the sitter's face still retains its expression, an image is secured.

§ 11.—**Storing of Negatives.**

There are three ways of storing away negatives, that are in common use—plate boxes, shelves expressly made for plates, or

[1] *Philadelphia Photographer*, III. p. 53.

the plates are wrapped up in clean paper in bundles of ten or twelve each.

Plate boxes are made with either single or double grooves. In the latter, two plates are slid together into each groove, the film side out. Much trouble arises from the grooves in plate boxes not being made deep enough. The plates vary a good deal in size, although nominally intended to be equal, and the boxes sometimes shrink very much; so that in some, after having been made some time, the small plates will get loose instead of being confined, and, in other boxes, the plates a fraction over size will get fast. It has happened to the writer to be obliged to force out the side of a box to get out a negative. All these troubles should be avoided by making the grooves deeper. The edges of the groove should be rounded, not square.

Plate boxes should never be used for putting wet negatives into, both because the boxes should never be wetted, and because, if the washing has been imperfect, hyposulphite may be introduced. Nor should negatives just varnished be placed in them, as the edges of varnished negatives remain sticky after the face is dry. Nor should "dry" plates be dried in them; in a word, they are for storage only.

Shelves for negatives should be built very strong, and are better so placed that the window shall not be opposite to, but at one end of the room, on the side of which are the shelves, so that as they are drawn out they can be looked through to obtain the one sought.

Negatives wrapped up in paper have been found to keep better than in any other way. Cases are described in which some of a lot of negatives have been stored in boxes, some wrapped in paper and laid flat, where those in boxes have cracked, and those in paper have stood perfectly. The reason appears to be, that plates sliding separately into grooves are exposed to changes in the atmosphere to a much greater extent than those securely wrapped up and pressed closely upon each other.

It is evident that considerable care should be exercised in the selection of paper to be interposed. Printed or soiled paper should be rigorously excluded. Blotting paper is too porous and hygroscopic. An ordinary quality sized paper, not too hard and stiff, is the most suitable.

The outside paper should be good, strong wrapping paper.

Paper saturated with India-rubber varnish would doubtless be better than any other. For amateurs who have but small numbers comparatively of negatives, the plate box is so much the more convenient form that it will probably be always that used.

CHAPTER V.

AMBROTYPES AND FERROTYPES.

ALTHOUGH ambrotypes almost belong to the past, a few brief remarks will be made on the subject here for the benefit of those who may desire to make them. A really fine ambrotype is a very beautiful thing, but for the most part, they want contrast and breadth of effect.

An ambrotype is nothing but a thin negative. When a negative is held up to the light, those portions on which the light has acted in the camera are more or less opaque, and the lights and shades in the original are reversed in the negatives.

But the negative is formed of grayish-white silver powder, so that if it be viewed by reflected light, and held against a black background, those parts which looked dark by transmitted light, appear light by reflected, and the transparent parts, which permitted the light to pass through when viewed by transmitted light, look dark in the ambrotype, because their transparency permits the black background to be seen through.

Formerly, a different bath was thought necessary in the two sorts of work. Now the same is generally used, although many perfer to acidulate it with one or two drops more of nitric acid.

A formula for collodion (if a special collodion be desired, which is not absolutely necessary) will be found in the Introduction, p. 40.

The developer is the same as for negatives, a little more acidified. Or, when *brilliant whites* are wanted, take—

Sulphate of iron	250 grains.
Acetic acid, No. 8	half an ounce.
Best granulated nitre	30 grains.
Water	20 ounces.

As the bath becomes older, add a little alcohol to cause the developer to run smoothly. If there is any disposition to fog, increase the dose of acetic acid. Stop the development as soon as the image comes out enough to be seen in light reflected from the surface of the plate.

Where dead whites are wanted omit the nitre.

Melainotypes and ferrotypes are ambrotypes taken on plates of thin varnished iron instead of glass. The operation is in all respects similar. They may be said to constitute the most ordinary and least artistic of photographic products.

Opinions vary very much as to the best means of getting good results. The points are these, that a very clear, clean picture must be got. This of course is most easily effected by the aid of acid. The acid may be applied in various ways. For example, the bath may be made more acid than usual with nitric or acetic acid, and used with the ordinary collodion and development. Or an ordinary bath may be used with a very ripe collodion, or one to which tincture of iodine has been added; or a very acid development may be resorted to. It naturally follows that whilst very clear pictures are got in this way, there is an absence of detail often observable. The right plan is just to carry the acidification far enough to get clean glass in the darkest shadows and no farther. Of course the slightest veiling is fatal to the ambrotype.

Collodion made with alkaline iodides and bromides ripens quickly; some therefore omit entirely the cadmium salts from collodion intended for ambrotypes. Others employ cadmium and ammonium and add iodine, and others, as mentioned in the Introduction, consider potassium essential.

Alabastrine Positives.—The body of both the negative and ambrotype is composed of nearly pure silver, which has a grayish tint, and is deficient in brilliancy. This defect injures the light and shade of the picture, and recourse is sometimes had to mercury in the form of corrosive sublimate to whiten them.

The following formula may be used:—

Corrosive sublimate	40 grains.
Protosulphate of iron	20 grains.
Common salt	15 grains.
Water	2 ounces.

The first effect is to make the picture grayer, but the whitening soon sets in.

CHAPTER VI.

PORTRAITURE.

§ 1.—The Portrait Camera.

THERE is no doubt that portraits can be successfully taken with the simplest possible camera, but there are cases which make it desirable that certain adjuncts of construction should be present. These which every operator who desires to produce first-rate work should have all the *sliding front* and the *swing-back.*

The object of the swing-back is this. If lines that are perpendicular in nature are to retain their perpendicularity in the picture, the plate on which they are received must also be perpendicular. It is, however, *not* essential that the cross section of the lens should also be perpendicular, but it may be inclined if the sensitive plate is maintained in its proper position. A swing-back renders this possible. A few bellows-folds intervene between the focussing slide and the body of the camera, and permit the former to revolve a short distance on a horizontal axis. Thus the camera may be tilted, and nevertheless the focussing screen (and sensitive plate) may retain the necessary vertical position. As in portraiture the camera will be often tilted, this will keep the vertical lines, as of columns, &c., straight.

In another form of swing-back the axis is vertical, permitting of a sidewise movement, which is valuable in taking groups where one end of the group is nearer to the camera than the other. The nearer part of the group has, of course, a longer focus than the farther, and the sidewise movement permits this to be accommodated in the position for the plate.

The front which carries the objective should slide in a pair of vertical grooves. This permits to raise or depress the objective, whereby the centre of the picture may be thrown above or below the centre of the plate. This is the *sliding front.*

The object of these arrangements is as follows: If we wish to take a standing figure, we wish to give the effect of the figure as seen by a person also standing. Now if we lower our camera stand so as to bring the lens half way between the head and feet, we get the whole figure, it is true, upon the plate, but we get the effect of the figure as seen by an eye placed no higher than the camera. The shape of the nose is thus altered, and the whole symmetry of the face spoiled; the neck is shortened, and the effect otherwise more or less injured.

Therefore we must raise the camera at least as high as the shoulders. The first effect of this is to throw the head nearly into the centre of the plate and to cut off the feet. This may be remedied—

1st. By inclining the camera downwards. This tends to distort the vertical lines, and here the swing-back comes into play and straightens them, or,

2d. By lowering the sliding front. As the front is lowered, the image moves down the plate, and takes its proper position.

This last arrangement has this notable advantage over the first that the best definition which in the portrait lens correctly focussed is that of the central pencils, is got for the head, precisely as if the bust only were taken. In the first arrangement the middle of the body is formed by the central pencils and receives the best definition. On the other hand, the lowering of the sliding front has this disadvantage, that the feet and lower part of the picture are then formed by pencils more excentric than enter into any part of the picture in the other case. Each method has its advantages and its evils, and in some cases the one, in some the other, will be proper.

A *repeating back* enables the operator to make the image of a lens fall in succession on different parts of the sensitive film, thus with two lenses and a repeating back, four or more card portraits are taken on one plate.

§ 2.—Management of Light.[1]

The play of light upon the sitter must be regulated partly upon certain general principles of illumination, and partly according to the needs of the particular case.

The general principles are—

[1] See also chapter on the "Glass Room," and that on "Light and Shadow."

That there shall be no *cross light;* never shadows visibly cast in more than one direction.

That the light on the side away from the glazing shall be maintained as subsidiary.

That there shall be no false light, especially no false reflection from the eyes.

That there shall be no excess of illumination in some one or more parts of the picture, otherwise the eye will be *led away* from the face, instead of *led to it,* as takes place in a judicious distribution of light and shade.

That the shadows, wherever they may be, shall invariably receive a sufficient illumination that their details may impress themselves with strength enough to show agreeably in the print. There must be no dark patches destitute of detail.

That the highest lights shall not be so illuminated but what they shall be full of detail. A bald head, for example, must not run into a light background, as is occasionally seen. White hair must preserve all its details. The play of light and shade over white garments must be thoroughly well preserved, and all white patchiness rigorously excluded.

Conjointly with the above, two different systems of illumination may be used. There is that almost universally adopted, in which the effect of the picture is made as nearly as possible to imitate what we commonly see around us. The part of the room, for example, in which the model sits, is made, in its play of light and shade, to resemble ordinary rooms.

There is another and very effective system occasionally used in which some of the effects generally produced by distinguished portrait painters in their work, are imitated. The object of this system is to allow no light, except that which stands in some definite relation to the face. It was the dictum of a celebrated painter that a portrait ought to be two-thirds dark.

To obtain this effect in photographic portraits, a dark background and dark hangings are used. Dark clothing is worn, especially dark velvets, whose play of light is always exceedingly effective to photography. Whatever of light is permitted in the clothing must "lead up to the face," that is, so far as it is permitted to catch the eye, the eye must pass directly from it to the face. All this, of course, is more easily effected in women's vestments than men's; still the application is not confined to the former. The borders of the picture are all kept dark, and, in fact, the shadows are accumulated in order that the light may tell as effectively as possible. When well managed, this method produces very striking and beautiful results, but it requires considerable artistic knowledge and feeling on the part of the photographer.

§ 3.—**Exposure.**

A correct knowledge of the time of pose comes only with long practice and through many failures. Not only does the light of the glass room vary continually in strength, but different complexions and different clothing will alter the needful time. Moreover, the photographer's task may be greatly increased in difficulty if a style of clothing, unsuited to the character of the sitter, chance to be worn by him or her. It would, in fact, be very advantageous if the photographer could always direct in advance, after personal observation, what description of clothes should be worn during the pose, for it by no means follows that clothes most becoming to the wearer under ordinary circumstances will be most appropriate before the lens. The element of *color*, which enters so largely into consideration, as to suitableness and effect, here disappears, and the only question is as to the rendition of light and shade on the film. A photographically suitable clothing is, therefore, not at all one in which the colors harmonize with the character of the wearer, but one in which the photographic effect of the color harmonizes with the photographic character of the face and hair. To get a clear insight into this matter it will be necessary to begin by considering the relation between the skin, eyes, and hair.

A clear white skin will, of course, impress its image rapidly on the film. If the hair be fair, all will go on well and harmoniously. But if a white skin be combined with dark hair, the exposure will have to be more accurately timed, it must be continued until the details of the hair are fully out, and yet must be stopped before the face is overdone. Conversely, where light or white hair accompanies a red or dark complexion there is danger of the hair being overdone and the details lost in it before the face is duly taken. These are faults that are constantly seen in card portraits, and constitute difficulties to be understood and conquered.

Dress.—The clothes worn may evidently add a further complication to such of these difficulties as exist, or may produce them where they did not. Let us suppose that a lady with dark hair and complexion presents herself to be photographed, attired in white, or light blue or purple. It will follow that by the time that justice has been done to the face, the fine gradations of shade in the dress may be lost, or if preserved, it can only be by great skill and some good fortune on the part of the photographer.

The difficulties occasioned by contrast are, however, now less unmanageable than they formerly were when iodide of silver alone was used, and we see less tendency than formerly to black spaces destitute of detail, and white ones prefectly flat: these blemishes are now comparatively exceptional, and such work is always destroyed by the intelligent photographer who prizes his reputation.

Some photographers keep two kinds of collodion on hand. One sort for regular use, the other containing more bromide, to be employed where too much contrast is apprehended, especially where masses of white drapery are to be taken, in which case the proportion of bromide may rise to one-half. For regular use such collodions are liable to the objection that they yield thinner pictures and require more redevelopment.

§ 4.—Development in its Relation to Portraiture.

Some assistance can always be had in difficult cases by regulating the development. The writer has attempted, in papers written upon the subject of negative development, to demonstrate the true character and the rules by which it is governed, and as a correct understanding of this is of much importance to the portraitist, a few words may advantageously be said on the matter here.

The stronger the developer, that is, the more sulphate of iron it contains, and the less restraining acid, gelatine or sugar, the more rapid will be the precipitation of the metallic silver that forms the picture. *Just in proportion as the silver falls more slowly it is more subject to the attraction of the most strongly impressed parts of the silver.* In a slow precipitation the most strongly impressed parts of the film will get a larger proportion of the deposit than in a rapid precipitation. This fact which has been thoroughly established both by theory and practice, is of the highest importance, and is the key to all the peculiarities of iron development in the wet way.

If, then, danger of a flat picture is feared, either by reason of—

1. An absence of contrast in the subject;
2. Too uniform an illumination;
3. Too long an exposure;

We should apply a weak developer, in order to increase the contrast.

On the other hand, if we have reason to dread a harsh picture from—

1. Excess of contrast in the subject itself;
2. Insufficient light;
3. Light badly controlled, so that it is excessive in places and insufficient in others;
4. Too short an exposure;

We should apply a strong developer to diminish the contrast by favoring a more equal deposit of silver.

The application of these principles to special cases is sufficiently obvious. If it is evident that the main difficulty of the work to be done will lie, for example, in getting relief and form into a quantity of white drapery, we shall need a slow development, in order that the faint shadows which are to give life and form to the white mass, shall not be overwhelmed by a rapid deposit of silver.

But if, on the contrary, it is specially desired to obtain detail in deep shadows, a strong developer will force the depositing silver to find all the faint impressions in these shadows and bring them out on the sensitive film.

A comparison of this section and the former will lead directly to the sufficiently obvious conclusion that exposure and development stand to each other in opposite relations. A highly illuminated object will demand a short exposure and a long development with a weak developer; a badly illuminated object will do best with a long exposure and quick development with an energetic developer.

Where both these conditions are present in one subject; where part of the subject points to a short, and part to a long exposure, we encounter what is in fact the central difficulty in photography, to wit, the obtaining of delicate detail in high light and dark shadows at once. In accomplishing this we see amongst photographers every grade of success and of failure. Whilst much must necessarily be left to the talent and ingenuity of the operator, a few very useful remarks can be given—especially this: that *too short an exposure is always fatal.* It is irremediable; if the impression is not sufficiently made on the plate, of course it cannot be brought out. The photographer will therefore invariably expose till he gets his detail in the shadow, at least sufficiently, and then will exert all his efforts to save the detail in the high types by a slow and careful development. In all such cases, if redevelopment be necessary, silver must be added *with the utmost caution.* The very useful property of bromide of silver of resisting solarization, of allowing the impression received in the high lights to remain stationary until the darker portions can sufficiently impress themselves, furnishes the best means of meeting such difficulties as those here in question.

It is not sufficient, however, to endeavor to overcome these difficulties, the difficulties themselves must to some extent be removed. Light must be so controlled that the illumination on the actinic surfaces must be restrained, and that on the shadows and non-actinic portion must be increased until the two can sufficiently be combined in one development.

§ 5. **Causes of Unsatisfactory Results in Portraiture.**

1. *Too much Front Light.*

Excess of front light produces *flatness.* Light is too equally distributed over the projections and depressions of the face, so that these lose their character, and the face assumes an unmeaning expression, sometimes even a stupid or silly one. Such a light also throws, as Schrank has well remarked, too much illumination on the centre of the forehead, the ridge of the nose, the chin, and the cheek bones. What is worse still, it produces a bright reflection in the centre of the eye, precisely where the dark pupil properly appears, thus reversing the natural aspect, and at times giving almost the effect of blindness. Of all defects of lighting, excess of front light produces the most inartistic effects, and the most thoroughly displeasing pictures.

2. *Too much Side Light.*

Excess of side light produces a too unequal illumination of the two sides of the face, gives an excessive projection to the nose, and a hatchet shape to the face. The effect upon the eyes is sometimes very curious, causing them to look utterly unlike each other in consequence of the difference in the amount of light that they receive. Still the effects of an excess of such light are not so bad as those of excess of top or of front light. The best effects require a difference of illumination on the two sides, which may in skilful hands be carried to a very considerable extent. Nevertheless it is easily overdone, and such attempts demand good management.

3. *Excess of Top Light.*

This error produces effects precisely the reverse of those of excess of front light; all the features become hard and projecting; a heavy frown settles on the brow; the eyes appear deep set and cavernous; the nose is enlarged, and any hollows about the mouth are greatly and unnaturally increased. A black shadow is produced directly under the chin, sometimes almost producing the effect of a beard.

4. *Too even Illumination.*

It is easy to fall into an error the reverse of all the foregoing by diffusing the illumination too generally. This is most apt to occur in operating under a flat, low glass roof, where the light comes in around the sitter from a variety of angles and directions. The result is a soft, characterless picture, which finds little favor, and deservedly so, whilst at the same time those unacquainted with the subject cannot tell why the picture is so unpleasing, for it is undoubtedly like the original, and there is no prominent objection to seize upon. At the same time there is the greatest of all objections, viz., that the portrait is totally devoid of merit, and gives the face with its least interesting and acceptable expression. The fault here spoken of is one that has received too little attention, some photographers refusing even to recognize it, and thinking, when they produce these pictures, that they are doing creditable work; they do not, however, find the sitter or the sitter's friends to agree very cordially with them.

5. *Insufficient Illumination below.*

When the illumination is at the same time chiefly horizontal, and yet is not carried low enough on the side, it may result that whilst the upper part of a sitter is well illuminated, the lower part is not. There results from this a want of detail in the shadows of all the lower part of the figure, a defect which can only be remedied by an alteration in the system of lighting.

6. *Insufficient Light.*

As it must always be the object of the operator to work well with a short exposure, a deficiency of light is one of the most serious evils to which he can be exposed. I may, for example, cite the case of a photographer in this city, who, after putting up a complete gallery, found his light so deficient that he was led to adopt the after intensification of his negative with mercury as a regular system—a bad and dangerous one every way, worse by far than even an expensive alteration in his defective glass room. His case was by no means a solitary one. It is far better, in constructing a glass room, to err by having too much light, the excess of which is so easily shut out, than to make the opposite mistake. When the mistake has been made, it is better for the professional photographer to recognize it at once, and remedy it radically by introducing more glass at any cost. In doing so, however, he should work neither at random nor in a hurry. He should first carefully ascertain by study in which description of light his glass house is most wanting, and proceed with a view to remedying that deficiency in the introduction of the additional glass. If his glass room has abundant top light, it would be folly for him to introduce his additional glass on the roof, and so on. The explanations already given will enable him to detect in what direction his glass room tends to err, and in arranging to admit more light he will be in a position to get exactly the kind of light which he most wants. Thus, in remedying a fault, he may, if he takes care and study, succeed in making his room better than if that fault had not been committed, for he may succeed in distributing his light more scientifically than if he had at first arranged to admit enough. It is in this, as in so many other cases in photography, the man who thinks carefully first over what he wants, and chooses, after reflection, that which is best fitted to afford the desired result, will always in the end succeed. One who can only learn through continual failures, will be weary before he can reach success. Every failure met with should be required to yield its fruit in the way of useful experience; and this should be made a fixed rule by every photographer.

§ 6.—Backgrounds.

The subject of backgrounds is one of no small importance to the portraitist, and one often of no small difficulty. Without care, tact, and ingenuity, his productions are apt to be exposed to the imputation of sameness. Every one has become thoroughly tired of the column and the balustrade, which might as well now be banished once for all. The heavy curtain has also been a good deal employed, but it is too useful to be definitely dispensed with.

The end of the gallery should be colored of a soft bluish-gray, and will form a useful background for taking groups of several persons. Special backgrounds usually consist, when plain, of colored cloth sold by the dealers, and which is usually stretched on a large frame furnished with feet, rolling on castors. These are of various shades, according to the effect desired. The photographer will need at least three—dark, light, and medium. Views are sometimes sketched on canvas stretched on similar frames. Considerable tact and skill are necessary for the production of really good pictorial backgrounds.

Sometimes a very beautiful effect is produced by having the upper part of the plain background lighter than the lower. This is especially useful in the case of three-quarter figures, or those which include from the head to the knees; the light part is made to correspond with the head, gradually softened opposite the shoulders into the dark shade of the rest. This calls attention to the head and throws it out, with an effect which, when well managed, is excellent.

Another useful effect which has attracted considerable attention of late years is that of inclining the background so that either side, right or left, shall be nearer than the other, taking care that the screen is turned towards the light, not against it.

It is common in photography to act on the principle that with a plain and indefinite background no furniture shall be introduced, and that, on the other hand, if any furniture be visible, the background shall correspond and complete the room. This is, however, not so absolutely necessary as some suppose. For example, if a three-quarter figure be represented, standing at the side of a small table and occupied in any way, as with papers, letters, flowers, work, &c., the picture may be finished with a plain, or better, a simple shaded background, such as just described, and thus the photographer is relieved from the incessant use of a limited stock of combinations.

It is a most serious mistake to crowd quantities of objects, such as vases, urns, bouquets, etc., into the picture. This only results in distracting and confusing the attention. Certain points, where lines of direction reach the floor or a table or other object, often need imperatively to be supported by some object; this part of the subject will be treated of more particularly hereafter. A foreground is often relieved by characteristic objects, grouped, not scattered. But then they require to be handled with taste and according to rule, and must never be strewn about or huddled together promiscuously.

When a whole sitting figure is represented in profile, the point at which the back legs of the chair reach the ground will invariably and absolutely need to be supported. No rule is so commonly violated as this, and none with worse results, for the figure will always appear to be slipping out of the chair, because its lines want their due support. This it will not be always easy to give; the position is, therefore, especially for a male figure, an objectionable one. If for any reason it is especially desired, the photographer must introduce some object, such as a stool, best with drapery, or characteristic objects over or on it. With the female figure the difficulty is less, for its own drapery may be so disposed as to give the support required.

A vignetted bust undoubtedly possesses advantages over any other description of photographic portraiture: it is that form in which the shortcomings of our methods are best overcome. It may therefore be doubted whether, in the introdution of the cabinet size, it has been wise to endeavor to exclude the vignette. The whole plate vignette heads which were formerly made, and are now so rarely seen, were far more effective than the little card heads that have taken their place.

When pictorial backgrounds are employed, it is necessary that the lens should be directed at the point of sight, that is, at the point to which, in the drawing of the background, the spectator's eye was supposed to be directed, namely, the point at which the line of vision cuts the horizon. If, as may happen, this point is not very easily distinguishable, the lens should at least be directed at the horizon line of the picture.

It is affirmed that Salomon, whose pictures have been so generally admired, uses a plain buff background producing the shading entirely by regulating the light. Others obtain good effects by using a background of brown paper, shading it off with white crayon in a light and sketchy way.

If it be desired that the print shall show parallel strokes of shading over the shoulders and round the head in imitation of crayon drawing, it is evident that this result can be attained by marking on the background a central spot for the head and sketching large, coarse shading around it. In this case black crayon or charcoal should be used on a light buff ground. Such backgrounds will need to be in sliding frames, balanced with weights that they may be raised or lowered to bring the centre into exact correspondence with head.

The appearance of the grain of drawing paper is sometimes given to the finished and mounted photograph by passing it, before quite dry, through a press, together with a piece of coarsely grained paper laid on the surface of the print.

CHAPTER VII.

LANDSCAPE AND ARCHITECTURAL PHOTOGRAPHY.

§ 1.—**Selection of Lenses.**

In the taking of views, the collodion and bath used, and the general manipulations will be the same as in portraiture. The same lenses, however, are not appropriate, although a portrait combination will produce a view, sometimes even quite successfully. Nevertheless, it is never worth while to waste time and patience with an inappropriate lens, unless under very exceptional circumstances.

Of late years, opinions have been very much divided with respect to the comparative merit of different combinations. The single view lens at first used almost exclusively for the work, included so narrow an angle that instead of views, "bits" only were obtained. When, therefore, the Globe lens was first introduced with its wide angle of view, it was hailed with a sort of enthusiasm.

The Triplet shares with the globe its correct rendering of perpendicular lines, but not its width of included angle, and it has the further objection that, having a third lens, there is the greater thickness of glass to pass through, and three additional surfaces for reflecting light. Notwithstanding these drawbacks, the lens is a very useful one. It works with a large stop, always a great point, and the equalization of illumination over the field is good. The best triplets made are probably those of Dallmeyer.

The same maker has modified the ordinary view-lens by achromatizing it with three thicknesses of glass instead of with two, as hitherto. In this way the image continues clear and sharp to a greater distance from the centre, and a very useful lens is obtained, known as the wide angle view-lens. The angle which it includes is less than that of the globe, but sufficient. The $8\frac{1}{2}$ inch focus lens of this sort is a most excellent instrument, and covers a $6\frac{1}{2} \times 8\frac{1}{2}$ inch plate exceedingly well with a stop of $\frac{1}{25}$th focal length, or about $\frac{1}{3}$ of an inch diameter. It may even be worked with the next larger stop, or by using the next smaller, can be used with an 8×10, though, of course, not quite so satisfactorily. Like the ordinary view-lens, of which it is a modification, it can only be used for views that do not include any architectural subjects, unless, indeed, they are small in size and subordinate in character.

For architectural subjects the triplet gives excellent results, though the operator must be able to recede to a sufficient distance. This difficulty is largely obviated in Zentmayer's lens, which includes a large angle with excellent definition and perfectly straight lines. The same may be said of Dallmeyer's "Rectilinear" lens. Both of these are very valuable, especially for views taken in cities, where it is mostly impossible to find a point for the camera sufficiently removed from the buildings to be taken to make the use of the triplet possible. Both are better than the globe lens in almost every respect. For further information on the subject of selection of lenses the reader is referred to the special descriptions of the respective forms.

There is one point connected with the use of lenses for architectural subjects which is not generally as fully understood as it might be. Many views of buildings exhibit a peculiar tilted appearance, as if they would fall forward, and this is always accompanied by a sharpness of the angle of the roof. A corresponding sharpness is visible at all the corners. A right-angled corner is so represented as to give the appearance of an acute angle.

This defect is always ascribable to the use of a lens of too short focal length. To give a thoroughly correct view, with true perspective effect, the focal length of the lens should be about the same as the distance from the eye at which the print will be held in viewing it. As this distance will generally be not less than 8 or 10 inches, nor more than 16 or 18, true representations will only be got by using lenses with focal lengths between these limits. The explanation of this will be sufficiently evident by considering what was said on the nature of perspective delineation in the chapter on that subject. It was there shown that any perspective delineation represented a section of the cone of rays coming from the object to the eye, and that the image formed by any lens corresponded with the section taken at a distance from the eye equal to the focal length of the lens.

The image or picture, therefore, formed by any lens, is only correct when held from the eye at a distance equal to the focal length of the lens, and even the most distorted-looking pictures taken with a short focus lens become perfectly correct when placed close enough to the eye.

Therefore the photographer, in taking an architectural view, will always use a lens of 10, 12, or 15 inches focus, unless insurmountable difficulties compel him to do otherwise.

In taking architectural subjects (but not landscapes) the camera must *invariably* be levelled with care. A detached level may be used, but a universal level countersunk into the camera is better.

§ 2.—Choice of Conditions.

As landscapes are always seen with disadvantage under a noonday sun, so photographs taken under similar circumstances are mostly unpleasing; and as photography tends to exaggerated contrasts of light and shade, the result is all the worse. Many experienced landscape photographers therefore avoid bright days, and like best of all those times when the sky is covered with white clouds through which the sun occasionally breaks. If a glimpse of sun can be secured at the end of an exposure, the best of all effects is got, and this may be compared to the effect in nature of the softened sun late in the afternoon, and we all know the magical influence of such light even upon the tamest of scenery. It is therefore a good plan, if there is hope of a burst of sun, to cover the lens a little before the proper exposure has been given, and then, when the sun comes, to expose for a moment, and so light up the picture without getting harsh contrasts. These last may in extremely bright weather give an effect of snowiness in the high lights, which is in the highest degree displeasing.

The time during which the lens may be covered to wait for this sun will depend upon the weather. In moist or cool weather, much more time may be prudently allowed than in hot or dry. Great care should be taken not to disturb the camera in opening and closing. For this, the morocco lined with velvet caps, furnished with the best English lenses,are very recommendable, and work better than the common brass caps.

As the sky is apt to be over-exposed, it may often be advantageously shaded during part of the exposure. This may be done by holding the hand or other object in front of the upper part of the lens, and near to it, moving it continually. To accomplish the same object, sky shutters are often made to the lens or to the camera, but it is difficult to use these without disturbing the camera. In landscape taking, the photographer will avoid the use of the smallest stop. The object of the stop should be clearly understood. In the case of the view lens, it is to obtain depth of focus, to have the distant and the moderately near objects simultaneously in focus. With both the triplet and the view lens, diminishing the size of the stop improves the definition and crispness at the margin. When these objects have been sufficiently secured, no further diminution of the stop is advisable, as the image loses in character and boldness, in addition to which the time of exposure is of course increased.

All the most experienced photographers are agreed, that a

view should invariably be taken with the largest stop that the conditions of the case will permit. As soon as a satisfactory definition is obtained, farther reduction of the stop should be avoided with the utmost care. A small stop produces a flat picture without gradation of distance or atmosphere. A large one gives a bold clear view, with the objects in the respective planes of distance well made out. Objects that with a small stop seem pressed together, with a large one stand well out and show what they are. The photographer cannot be too strongly enjoined not, in order to obtain a microscopic sharpness, to sacrifice the general character and expression of his view. Of course, good definition cannot be dispensed with. But when the operator finds that he cannot get this without a very small stop in using any of the ordinary forms of lenses, he may be sure that he is straining the lens, making it do work for which it is unsuited, and therefore that he cannot expect the best results.

A photographer may visit scenes of great natural beauty, and may be deeply impressed by them. He may labor very hard to reproduce them in his negatives, and yet, after much effort, he may obtain but unsatisfactory results. Some will, under these circumstances, lay the blame on photography, and affirm that the indifferent results spring from the incapacity of the method to yield what is wanted. Others will not perceive the deficiencies of their own pictures, and think they have all that can be expected; whilst others, again, with a truer sense of the beautiful, will be disheartened by the difference between what they have seen in nature, and what they have been able to carry away.

In a landscape, the best effects are to be secured by *contrast.* In photography, as we have no effects of color, our contrasts are limited to those of *line* and those of *light.*

Contrasts of line or form are always relished by the eye. The effect of the mountain is enhanced by the levelness of the plain at its base. A picture that should represent a plain with no elevation, or simply an elevation with no plain to contrast with it, will always be deficient. Other, and beautiful contrasts of line, are often seen in a rolling country, even where there is no plain and no great elevation.

Contrasts of light and shade, technically called chiaroscuro, are the life of all pictorial representations. They give us, in a great measure, our ideas of the form and relative position of bodies.

Negatives taken in dull weather are necessarily deficient in this quality, whilst those taken in clear sunshine often present contrasts too harsh. A weak sun often gives beautiful effects, and as the sun is less powerful when low, this, as well as many other advantages, is obtained by working at such times.

Whilst contrast is all important in photography, it is to be carefully remembered that too much of it is even worse than too little.

If a negative be taken with insufficient exposure, and then this be attempted to be made up in the development, it will most frequently happen that the silver instead of being deposited so as to keep up the regular graduation of tone, falls too much upon the lights. Thus the picture becomes *hard*, and if the fault has been great, it becomes snowy.

In some classes of subjects, snowiness is not easily avoided. If a landscape be in parts very brightly, and in others very badly, lighted, the photographer finds himself in the dilemma that either he exposes and develops too long for the one part or too briefly for the other. In printing his negative he may find an absence of detail, accordingly, either in the lights or shadows. This difficulty is inherent to the nature of the subject, and may be too great to be overcome. The best advice that can be given is to expose for the worst lighted part and use a rather weak developer, and develop very cautiously. If redevelopment be found necessary, study the character of the image so far obtained. If it still shows great contrast, use pyrogallic acid liberally, adding silver very cautiously and slowly. If the long exposure given has controlled the contrasts so much that a flat picture is feared, reverse this, and be liberal with the silver and sparing with the pyro.

Cast Shadows are such as retain more or less of the form of the object that casts them, as distinguished from the more indefinite shadow that comes from some less distinct source. Such shadows are often the source of exquisite beauty in landscapes. A level foreground of grass is apt to be flat and unmeaning—the shadow of a tree cast across it gives it at once life, character, relief. The landscapist cannot pay too much attention to such effects of foreground.

Generally, the more that shadow is *diversified* the finer its effect. A large dark shadow of a tree is far less beautiful than one in which the sun penetrates the leaves and falls in irregular broken forms upon the ground.

When it is required that a house shall appear in the foreground, a diversified shadow upon its walls has an extremely good effect. In neither case, however, must the lights and shadows be too much broken or the effect will lack breadth. Parallel patches of light and shadow are especially ugly.

The tree, the great beauty of the landscape, offers peculiar difficulties in photography, owing to the non-actinic color of its leaves. For this reason it has been thought advisable to use much bromide in collodion intended for landscape photography; the true explanation of its utility has been already given. Smooth and highly polished foliage, ivy especially, is far more beautifully represented in the photograph than rough or dull, because of the greater quantity of which light reflects from is surface. Prof. Towler has well remarked upon the advantage of photographing foliage immediately after a rain, and whilst the leaves are still glistening with moisture.

It is generally advised in photography to have the sun well behind the camera. This, however, is a rule of very doubtful validity. When the sun shines full upon a group of trees in the middle distance, or even in almost any part of the picture, the forms of the individual trees are never well made out, and the result is apt to be a mere mass of brilliantly lighted foliage. Often the separate twigs and boughs may stand out in consequence of dark shadows falling between the leaves, but the beautiful rounded effect of each particular tree is only well thrown out by a good side light. The inferiority of effect produced by having the sun directly or nearly behind the camera, is in this respect most striking, and the landscapist should resort to this mode of light only in exceptional cases. The exquisite beauty of the rounded forms of individual trees is too precious to be sacrificed short of paramount necessity.

One reason why this light from behind has been extensively used is that it is the least exposed to *blurring*. Whenever dark masses stand out against a bright sky, the light has a tendency to get round and intrude upon the shadow; an effect that arises from reflection from the back surface of the glass. The writer has shown elsewhere that the partial opacity of the film scatters the light that passes through it, in every direction, so that portions reach the back at very oblique angles and may return to the face at considerable distances from where they entered. To a large extent this may be avoided by wet red blotting-paper or the backs of wet plates and glycerine plates (a precaution which should *never* be neglected), and by painting the backs of dry plates. Still better with certain sorts of dry plates, as the writer has pointed out, by impregnating the sensitive film with red litmus, details of which system will be found under its appropriate head. With a side light, and still more with a front light, there is far more danger of this trouble than with a light from behind. That, however, is a reason for applying the preservative and not for adopting what is apt to be a disadvantageous system of lighting. Atmospheric effects of haze are best got by a side front light. Vogel has executed some beautiful pictures in which rays of light are seen upon a faint mist, the rays being broken by the branches of trees.

The disadvantage of the entire absence of sun is often successfully conquered by artistic workers, such as Bedford, Wilson, and others in England, and by some of our good landscapists in this country. In the shade, however, nature is always tamer than when lighted by the sunshine.

An agreeable diversification of the foreground is a capital point in a landscape. It has been already remarked how much this is aided by shadows. Almost any characteristic and prominent objects will have a good effect; logs, stones, and, still more, rocks, bushes—anything that breaks the level, and changes the lines, also attracts and pleases the eye—not in itself, but in the general character that it imparts. It may generally be affirmed, that scarcely anything can so much detract from the effect of a landscape as unbroken foreground, level in form, and uniform in light. Such a foreground will mar, if not destroy the effect of the finest objects. The artistic photographer will always change his position to avoid such a foreground; or, if he is tied down to a particular spot from some imperative cause, he will, if possible, have some object, such as a log, a large stone, or a trunk of a tree, thrown where it will relieve his lines, as explained more fully beyond.

The same objects will appear so differently in different lights, that the pains-taking photographer will not hesitate to wait or to return when he finds the illumination to be unsuitable for his purposes. There is a story told of a distinguished landscapist that he once waited three weeks to get good weather and a particular effect of light upon a scene that he had come to photograph. There is some contrast between this and the rapid worker who points his camera at everything that catches his eye, and exposes his dozen of dry plates in an hour or two. It should be laid down as an axiom by every worker, that a *good* negative is *very* valuable, a tolerable negative worth absolutely nothing. It is at least as troublesome to print a tolerable negative as a good one, and the prints from the tolerable one are not worth the pains they have cost in printing. Twenty copies from a good negative are valuable for exchanging against prints from good negatives belonging to others; but twenty prints, each from a tolerable and different negative, are nearly worthless. No multiplication of indifferent results will give good ones, and the experimenter will derive more satisfaction from a single thoroughly good negative than from a score or a hundred of indifferent or tolerable ones. Good results will come only with care, thought, close observation, and a resolution to have things right at any cost of time and trouble. Care taking soon becomes a matter of course, and the habit once acquired, is invaluable.

§ 3.—Focussing.

In landscape photography as a general rule the focus must be taken on the objects in the foreground. Want of sharpness in these is a fatal fault. This much admitted, the question arises, how is the rest of the landscape to be treated?

Some persons are as anxious for sharpness in the distance as in the foreground, and will exhibit a print with the boast that the extreme distance will bear a microscope. As the eye cannot see natural objects in this fashion, it can scarcely be right to depict them so. And when we examine the works of the great masters of landscape painting, we find that, with the power to draw their distances precisely as they pleased, they did not think right to make them sharply cut.

We find that, as distance softens down outlines to the eye, so when outlines are softened down, the eye infers distance.

Not that this principle is to be carried to excess, and made an excuse for blundering work. It is only that the same sharpness is not to be exacted in the distance as in the foreground; especially as this can only be attained by the use of a very small stop, which greatly mars the boldness and life of the image.

As a general rule, the photographer will focus on the foreground at a point half way between the middle and the corner, but will rack in the back just as far as he can whilst keeping this portion perfectly sharp. And then will use a stop just so small, and no smaller, as will enable him to get a good effect in the rest of the picture.

§ 4.—**The Wind.**

One of the most serious difficulties that the landscape photographer has to contend with lies in the wind. A very large part of the beauty of most landscapes depends on the foliage, and it is necessary that this should remain quite still in order to be satisfactorily depicted.

The difficulty that arises from this source is greatly enhanced by its uncertainty. We may set out in perfectly still weather, and reach our place of destination in a gale, or reluctantly give up the expedition by reason of the wind, and see it, when too late, entirely subside. This is annoying enough to those who have their full time at their disposure:—doubly so to those who are restricted to occasional opportunities.

It follows that the photographer, even while avoiding windy days for work, which he is strongly recommended to do, will occasionally find himself exposed to its effects. It is best then to attempt only such landscapes as have no foliage in the foreground. This part of the picture should consist of immovable objects only—rocks, logs, dead trees which have lost their smaller branches. Even water is far less objectionable than foliage. In weather in which wind is dreaded, the photographer will chiefly need his longer focus lenses, 10, 12, or 15 inches, as with such the foreground of the image can be made of objects at a greater distance from the camera.

It will also occasionally happen that hollows and ravines can be found protected by precipitous banks crossing the direction of the wind, in which perfect stillness exists, whilst the wind is blowing hard elsewhere. It is within the recollection of the writer that he once ascended a hill to take a distant view, and found the wind blowing such a gale that there was no hope of steadying the camera. Shortly after he found a ravine in which a wall of rock lying at right angles to the direction of the wind afforded a complete protection, and the foliage was so completely steady as to afford a good picture.

For the most part, however, it is a waste of time to attempt to photograph landscapes in windy weather. The evil effects of very slight winds may be materially diminished by observing one or two precautions.

When light branches are projected against a bright sky or clouds, the least motion of the leaves allows the bright light of the sky to pass in behind them. The result is that the leaves appear shrunk away and blurred,[1] an effect very often seen and most displeasing. If the sky is very dense, and prints perfectly white, such branches should always be painted out. A similar result follows when branches are projected against the reflection of the sky or water, or against any bright object.

Again, where boughs with glossy foliage well illuminated stand out against deep shadow, and are moved by wind, they carry their bright reflection with them, and their image is extended, in place of being shrunk away as in the previous case. Each leaf, in place of being small and sharp cut, as we would wish to have it, is large, blurred, and undefined.

Therefore, if the air be somewhat in motion, the landscapist will do well to avoid foliage in either of these two positions, which are those that produce the worst effects. For when foliage standing before other foliage, and nearly equally illuminated, is moved, the result, though anything but pleasing, is not so very injurious as in the other cases.

On those priceless days when the light is neither too strong nor too weak, and the foliage perfectly still, the photographer will do well to turn his attention especially to those landscapes in which the chief beauty lies in the foreground. Foliage should be intro-

[1] When no paper is placed behind the plate (or color in the film or on the back of dry plates) the same result may be expected by reflection from the back of the plate, quite independently of any movement of the leaves.

duced quite near to the camera, the nearer the better, provided it can be kept in good focus together with more distant objects. Projecting boughs seen against the reflection of sky in water, so objectionable in the former case, may now be made to produce the most charming results, especially when accompanied by their reflected images.

When it is intended to photograph immovable objects in a heavy gale, it is very desirable to find, if possible, some suitable support, such as a wall, a rock, or the stump of a tree, on which to place the camera, which is then steadied by placing on it a heavy stone. Perfect steadiness may in this way be obtained. In the absence of these resources, a cord may be fastened to the screw under the table of the tripod, and a heavy stone be tied to the other end, and let to hang down. Or it has been proposed to tie a loop in the cord, reaching just short of the ground, and to put the foot into the loop, and thus hold steady the camera.

It remains to say a word respecting the wind, in its relation to long and short exposures.

It has been said that the wind does not act more injuriously upon a long exposure than upon a short one, the effect having the same average in each case, in proportion to the exposure. This view is, I am persuaded, erroneous. The wind rarely blows steadily (such weather is to be particularly avoided), but generally in puffs. And these puffs are apt to come at intervals, such that, by watching, a short exposure can be caught between them, when a long one cannot possibly.

It is an excellent plan in such weather, both for long and short exposures, to throw the cloth over the camera in such a way that it rests just on one side of the tube. In case of a puff of wind, it can be dextrously brought over the lens without shaking the camera, and the exposure can be suspended till the foliage is again quiet. The same can be done with a well-adjusted shutter, or even with a cap; but in these cases more dexterity is required to avoid deranging the apparatus, as will be readily found by a comparative trial.

§ 5.—Toning of Landscape Prints.

Although remarks on this point belong technically rather to the head of printing, yet they are so closely connected with the general subject of Landscape Photography, that I have preferred to give them a place here.

A landscape print is subject to none of the conventional rules of color that hold to a large extent with portraits, and even to some extent with architectural views. Every pleasing tone is appropriate—light brown, deep brown, warm brown, dark purple, purple black, steel gray, and pure black. All of these do well. Blue black is unpleasing, and is presumably never got intentionally, but results from accidental over-toning.

All the warm shades up to black do well, as has just been said, and a wide range of them gives a most agreeable diversification to a collection of views. It will be found, however, that *every negative has some particular tone that gives its best effects.* This is a fact that every photographer of refined artistic taste will perceive and feel: it becomes, therefore, in the highest degree desirable to be able to say approximately of any negative in advance, or on seeing the first proof taken, what toning will best suit it. The following remarks may afford some clue to this knowledge.

Some negatives that have been taken with a highly favorable illumination, and have been developed exactly right, will exhibit so exquisite a combination of contrast and harmony of light and shade, that they will look well with any toning. They have no defects to soften, and can hardly be spoiled in the printing. For this higher class of negatives, a rich warm purple black, best obtained by the acetate of soda or by the benzoate toning bath, will be the most suitable.

Starting from a supposed perfect negative, we gradually pass down to less excellent effects. In all, we shall suppose that both the denser and thinner parts are full of detail (for if either lacks it the negative will not be worth printing), but that these parts, though each full of detail, do not work well together. If the printing be stopped when the thinner parts are right, the denser have not produced their best effects; if it be carried on until the latter are right, the former are too heavy and dark.

Now, this is a fault which may exist in every variety of degree. If it exists to a large degree, the negative is worthless; if only to a slight one, the intention here is to point out what course of action will render such a fault the least conspicuous.

The lighter and the warmer the color, the less this bad effect will be noticeable, a fact, I believe, which has never been pointed out before, though possibly some may have acted on it. A print *must* be exposed until the detail is out in the high lights, otherwise it is a complete failure. The effect therefore of the discordance here spoken of, is always to produce heavy black shadows, without detail, and the lighter and warmer the toning, the less offensive will be these dark masses, and the more of detail will be left in them. An observation of this rule will go far towards getting a fair print from a *somewhat* faulty negative. But it must be understood in the clearest way, that beyond a certain point the want of harmony is an irretrievable one.

Conversely it is evident that if a negative lack contrast, either from the subject having been too monotonously lighted, or from an over-exposure, a pure black toning, without too much over-printing, will do what can be done towards affording a good result.

If these precautions be neglected, and if, for instance, a negative in which the contrast is already too great, be toned up to full black, the result will be that its faults, instead of being softened will be aggravated. And if the photographer is unaware of, or does not appreciate, the principle here laid down, he may never obtain more than a passable result from a negative which, properly handled, might give a really good, though not a first-rate, print.

CHAPTER VIII.

COMPOSITION.

§1.—Landscapes.

A SUBJECT like this, to which the attention of photographers is more and more drawn, cannot be passed over in this manual; but the limits to which it is necessarily restricted will permit of a brief discussion only, of a few important points.

Cultivated taste has learned that the representation of a landscape gives a completely satisfying effect to the mind most easily by complying with certain general conditions which have been reduced to fixed rules. Too slavish a compliance with these leads directly to mannerism and sameness, but some acquaintance with them cannot but be of the highest use to every intelligent photographer.

Lines of Direction—Balance.—In examining any picture we may discern certain lines of direction. These lines may be of one prominent object, or may depend upon the directions of the principal portions of a succession of objects.

It is a rule that these lines of direction should *support each other*, as in Fig. 72, where the longer line is supported by the shorter. The longer line may, for example, be that of a distant range of mountains, and the shorter that of a tree in the foreground; or both lines may depend partly upon distant and partly upon near objects—it is immaterial. The essential point is only that the characteristic lines of the picture shall balance each other. But

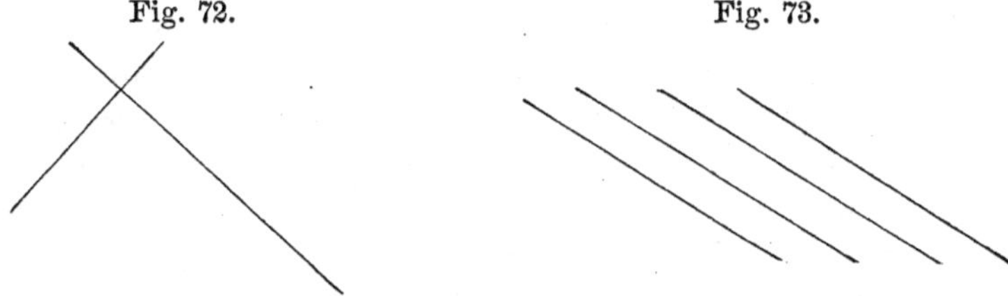

Fig. 72. Fig. 73.

if the lines be all in one direction, as in Fig. 73, or even if not quite parallel, there is a want of balance, and the idea of weakness and of falling is given. Moreover, the effect of the repetition of direction is generally unpleasing, though it is occasionally used to convey the idea of receding distance. In any case, however, it is necessary that these lines should be balanced.

A succession of perpendicular (see Fig. 74) or of horizontal (Fig. 75) lines is, for the most part, unpleasing. As an example

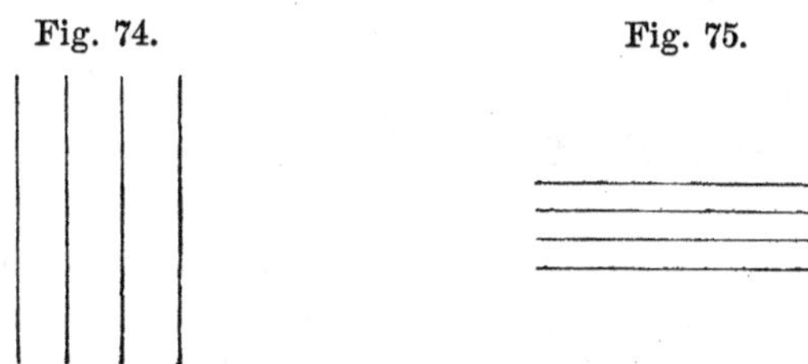

Fig. 74. Fig. 75.

of the former, we may take a row of straight-stemmed trees, the effect of which is infinitely less pleasing than if their directions are diversified. Parallel horizontal lines are rarely allowable;

sometimes, however, they are employed by artists in "parallel perspective"—that is, where buildings are represented in full front view.

The Diagonal Line.—According to the direction into which the principal lines of the picture fall, the composition is distinguished into angular and circular. The diagonal line, the simplest form of angular composition, is exceedingly well adapted for representation of perspective, especially when, to get a better range of effect, the distance is placed at one side of the picture.

Fig. 76.

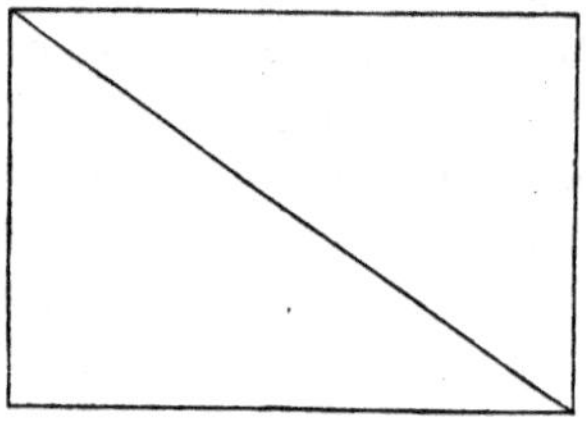

It is by no means necessary that the principal line of direction should proceed directly from one angle to the other. This angular line of direction should always be *supported*—that is, the eye carried along it should not be dropped vaguely, but fall upon some object, which, though it must be distinct, need not be large. This object is termed the "*ruling point.*" An inspection of landscapes and groups executed by artists will show how far ingenuity has often been taxed to hit upon some object of this sort in which to terminate a line of principal direction. In one of Leslie's paintings, one figure is made to rest a hand (rather awkwardly) upon a table, in order that the hand may furnish such a termination. In country scenes, a dog, or a fowl, or any other small object in keeping with the general subject will be introduced into the foreground. A little examination will show that its exact position has been determined by a line of principal direction, and that the object has been placed at its exact intersection with the ground. The universality of this practice seems to indicate that it is correct; the principle is evidently that, after the eye has been carried from one to another of the striking features of a picture, it should not finally fall blankly upon nothing, but that there must be some sufficient object upon which to rest. In most cases the resting point or ruling point is made dark on a lighter ground, though in some cases a lighter object than those that surround it is used.

A beautiful and familiar instance of the balance of opposing lines of direction is seen in mountains, the opposite sides of which rest on each other like an inverted Λ. So a gap between two mountains gives lines that balance each other in the form V.

Circular Composition.—Curved lines of direction are often introduced with very fine effect. Views of lakes, or of curved reaches of rivers, will be apt to fall into this form, and it is also seen in many compositions of rural scenery.

The Foreground.

The foreground is the portion generally most under the photographer's control, and those who desire to obtain the greatest success will spare no pains in the selection of this part of their picture.

The foreground should be diversified. A level unbroken foreground of grass or meadow cannot be expected to give a good effect. It weakens the effect of the distance, and deprives the picture of much of the character that it ought to possess.

A portion of the foreground should be occupied by some dark object, whose effect will be materially enhanced if brought into immediate contrast with some of the highest lights of the picture. The best effect is for the most part attained by placing the dark object in the foreground under the farthest distance. This gives great tenderness and softness to the distance, causes it to recede from the foreground, and at the same time supports it by lending firmness and foundation to it. Too much attention to this point cannot be given by the landscapist, who will, however, often have his patience and ingenuity taxed to the uttermost to find anything like a satisfactory foreground to his pictures.

The Distance.

The distance should never find its place exactly in the middle of the picture, which by such a disposition becomes divided, as it were, into two equal halves.

A peculiar pleasure is given when the eye is conducted from the foreground to the distance by lines of direction. These lines may be one or both banks of a river or stream, a picturesque road, or other object. The leading should be rather by broken and diversified lines than by straight ones.

A certain pleasure is communicated when objects in the middle distance are repeated in the farther distance. Such a repetition is not to be by the same object, but rather by some other object in strict keeping. This rule is closely allied to one in painting. It is laid down in painting that if a particular color be introduced in one place only, it has the effect of a spot or blot; the color must be carried through the picture, or at least part of it, by recurring here and there. As in colors, so in objects. If trees are seen in the foreground or middle distance, the eye is gratified by seeing them reappear in the distance. If a cottage or other building be a conspicuous object in the foreground, the eye likes to see something similar in the distance.

The effect of a high light in the extreme distance is greatly enhanced by placing a dark object in the foreground directly under it. This acts partly by throwing the distance farther back, and partly because the light becomes lighter and the darkness darker through contrast.

Contrast.

Some of the highest pleasures which the eye is capable of enjoying depend upon contrast. Contrast is of various kinds. Of *light*, where the artist throws his deepest darkness against his highest light, thus strengthening both. Of *size*, where the greatness of the majestic oak is made more apparent by the shrubs or bushes at its base. Of *form*, where the grand elevation of the mountain is further ennobled by the level lake or plain at its foot. Of *character*, as when the graceful lines of pine-trees are contrasted with rugged roughness, as in Alpine hills. Of *season*, as when winter snows look down from the mountain upon summer verdure in the valleys beneath. Of *mass*, as when light clouds, the lightest of all visible objects, rest upon mountains, which, of all natural objects, give the most striking effect of weight. In a word, the beauty of contrast is that which most completely pervades all nature. All our ideas are formed by comparison, and contrast is comparison in its most vigorous form.

Repetition.

The repetition of lines of direction, as has been already said, is for the most part unpleasing. Introduced into a group, it gives the effect of a range of figures on a frieze, or the composition of a pre-Raphaelite painting. In landscapes it is equally objectionable.

But the repetition of objects themselves is often very pleasing. The echoing of a near object by a distant one has been already spoken of, but perhaps the greatest beauty of repetition is where we see objects mirrored in calm water. Few persons are so utterly destitute of the sense of the beautiful as not to appreciate, however imperfectly, the charm of this exquisite reflection. The commonest object may in this way be rendered beautiful and attractive. A log, a branch, a boat, insignificant in themselves, immediately acquire a charm by being repeated in the water. Often the inversion that accompanies reflection materially adds to the charm by the variety which it affords, or by forming, as a reflection often does when looked on in connection with the object itself, a charming symmetrical figure.

Atmospheric Effect.

When a scene in nature, embracing objects at various distances from the spectator is depicted upon a flat surface, we are enabled to distinguish between objects near and distant, in two different ways.

One of these is *Linear Perspective*, treated of elsewhere. By virtue of it, distant objects are diminished in size and brought closer together, thus giving to the eye the information that they are proportionately remote.

But the effect of linear perspective is greatly enhanced by another agency, to which the name of aerial perspective, or, better, atmospheric effect, has been given.

The atmosphere in its usual conditions is not wholly transparent, but interposes an exceedingly delicate veil, imperceptible indeed as respects neighboring objects, but becoming more evidently distinguishable as the distance increases. The eye is thus greatly aided in judging distances, which it unconsciously computes by the extent to which the softening effect of the atmosphere reaches.

If this softening effect of the atmosphere be studied, it will be found to act as follows:—

1. *It diminishes contrasts.*—Dark shadows lose something of their darkness, high lights of their brightness. This opposite effect of the atmosphere on light and on shade needs some explanation. Lights lose part of their brightness by reason of the slight opacity of the atmosphere through which they pass. But the darkness of the shadows is partly lighted by the light which

falls, not on them, but *on the atmosphere through which they are viewed.* We have a familiar example of this in the sky itself, which is only the deep shadow of the outer darkness of space viewed through a not perfectly transparent medium, which medium is itself lighted up by the sun. In clear weather, the sky is deepest in color, because there is less opacity in the atmosphere to receive and reflect the sun's light. On a high mountain the sky is darker still, and at very great elevations appears almost black.

2. *It obliterates details.*—Smaller objects and parts of objects easily distinguishable when near by, cease to be so in proportion to the distance to which the object is removed, and of this the eye takes due note and recognizes the cause.

3. *It softens outlines.*—The dead limb of a tree near by, for example, cuts boldly and sharply on the sky, but the outline of a trunk upon a hill in the middle distance is already somewhat softened, and the outlines of distant mountains are still more so.

Consequently atmospheric effect tends to give soft grays and middle tints to distant objects and to efface all sharp contrasts of light and darkness. Lines also cut each other less sharply. In nature we find a very wide range of variety as to this influence. When the air is very free from moisture, as on some of the arid plains at the base of the Rocky Mountains, atmospheric effect almost disappears, and distant objects appear unnaturally and deceptively near. It is not too much to say that the capacity of the eye for judging correctly of distances is actually destroyed. From this extreme we may pass through every degree to the other, when the air is so laden with mist that near objects seem farther and distant objects disappear altogether.

It is a curious fact, and one of the highest importance for the photographer to understand, that both the process which he uses and his lenses themselves, may have a great influence on the amount of atmospheric influence which will appear in his pictures.

There are certain photographic processes by which the distance is rendered with more sharpness than others. In the common wet process, for example, the tendency is to slightly increase the actual atmospheric effect in the scene photographed. In the glycerine and honey process the atmospheric effect is always increased to a greater extent than by the wet process. With the dry processes the distance is more apt to be sharp cut, and clear.

The lens has likewise something to do with this rendering, though its action has been by some writers a good deal exaggerated; it is the size of the diaphragm used that has more to do with the atmospheric effect than the lens itself.

A large diaphragm will always tend to *increase*, a small one to *diminish* aerial perspective. This is caused in two distinct ways co-operating to the same result. For a small diaphragm will always greatly increase the depth of focus, so that when the focus has been taken, as it always must be, on near objects, a small diaphragm will cause the distance to be in sharp focus also. This will increase the detail of the distance, and as it has been already shown that one way in which atmospheric effect shows itself is in tending to obliterate detail, the greater depth of focus necessarily tends to counteract the effect of the atmosphere. Again, a small diaphragm always tends to harshness of contrast, and it has been also shown that aerial perspective especially shows itself by diminishing contrast. Clearly, therefore, aerial perspective will be produced in direct proportion to the size of the diaphragm. This explanation tends to throw additional light upon the fact stated in a previous chapter, that a large stop materially aids the effect of distance by placing objects in their proper planes of distance from the eye.

It is, however, sufficiently apparent, from what has been previously said, that lenses will differ somewhat amongst themselves, independently of the diaphragm, as to the rendering of atmospheric effect, inasmuch as some have greater depth of focus than others.

Those photographers who are accustomed to plant their cameras in front of any conspicuous object, satisfied if it covers enough of their plate, and if they can get a clean negative of it, will naturally, in the same spirit, endeavor to get the same sharpness in the distance (so far as practicable) as in the foreground. Such will be found working with small diaphragms, and acid baths, and getting technically perfect negatives, which will yield prints that no one cares to look at a second time, prints which are a reproach to photography.

It must at the same time be very clearly understood that the writer is as far as possible from wishing to say that a photographic landscape should show a clean cut foreground, and a hazy, woolly-looking distance. No rules must be carried to excess, or the truth and beauty that result from them are destroyed by exaggeration. That objects several miles away should be as distinct and sharply cut as those near at hand, is unnatural, or at least occurs in certain regions and in peculiar states of the atmosphere only, with which we have not here to do. It cannot be right, therefore, and it certainly is not pleasing to an educated eye, that they should be so represented in a photograph or in any other form of delineation. As already said, the landscape painter, with this matter under his absolute control, always softens the distance.

§ 2.—Portraiture.

What has been said in the foregoing section finds its natural application also to portraiture. Lines must be balanced and supported; light must be brought out by opposing it to shade, in portraiture as in landscape work.

To give an agreeable and graceful effect to a single standing male figure, has always been a difficulty which has taxed the genius of artists to evade. When a man clothed in our modern habiliments stands erect, the lines of his arms and legs fall into parallelism with his body, and the objectionable effect of parallel perpendicular lines has been already pointed out (Fig. 74). There is perhaps no effectual way by which, in our ordinary portrait, this difficulty can be disposed of, unless some characteristic occupation or position can be adopted. A soldier, for example, may rest upon his musket, a fisherman may have his rod so disposed as to afford a supporting line, and so on, but as the great mass of those who present themselves to be represented by the camera, do not care to figure in connection with any particular vocation, it follows that for the most part the best that can be done is to adopt a sitting posture, not in profile unless the back legs of the chair can be supported, and try to relieve this by surrounding objects. Good effects are often obtained by representing the sitter as either engaged in some occupation, reading, playing on some instrument, examining some object, or often better, as having just turned from having so done.

When several male figures are introduced together, their lines may be made to support each other, but here, again, a photographic difficulty is introduced—the necessity of keeping the heads to a certain extent in the same plane of distance.

The ingenuity of the photographer will often be here taxed to a severe extent. He may be aided by the following observations:—

Where two or three heads are present, they should rarely be placed, as so very often seen, on the same level, but should form a pyramidal arrangement, or else fall into the diagonal line. Or the middle head may be the lowest. If a fourth head be introduced, it may either fall into one of the lines of the above forms, or the lozenge-shaped composition may be adopted. If more than these are present, they may either have a place in the principal arrangement, or a secondary group may be formed.

A group of three persons will generally be the most manageable. Somewhat less so with two or four. When the number increases, difficulties are multiplied, when it diminishes to one, the difficulties of getting a satisfactory attitude are, as already said, most serious. A standing portrait of a man gives almost invariably the effect of a person placed for the express purpose of having his picture taken, and this is apt to be made worse by the conscious look generally assumed by the person.

The same remarks apply, though to a somewhat less extent, to female portraits. The form of the dress considerably relieves the difficulty, as it represents two opposing inclined lines which tend to support each other. Nevertheless, single portraits of standing female figures are apt to bear a stiff appearance, unless in the hands of very artistic photographers. When sitting, however, this is wholly changed. The drapery can be very much varied, and a great support can be got by regulating the folds of the dress so that these shall run in directions which shall relieve and support the other lines of the picture, that is, that some of the lines of drapery shall oppose and support the lines produced by the direction of the body, the position of the arms, &c. The position of the arms can often be regulated in sitting figures, both of men and women, to greatly aid in balancing the lines of the body; and here a thousand expedients come in to give occupation to the arms and explain their position.

In groups of female figures, or of men and women together, the same remarks as those made respecting the positions of the heads, for men, of course apply.

Two useful observations remain to be made before we close this very brief section on an important subject.

The lines which connect the heads of a group, form always the principal lines of the picture. Such lines should never be permitted to simply run out and end in nothing, but when carried by the eye to the bottom of the picture, should fall on some object, precisely as already explained in landscape composition. Thus, if a line of direction, when extended by the eye, reaches a table, for example, at the point of intersection there should be placed some small but very distinct object, dark on a light ground, or light on a dark ground. A book, an open letter, or, still better, some object characteristic of the taste or occupations of one or more of the sitters, will be suitable. If a line of direction reach the floor or a wall, the same principle of course holds good.

Again, a line in some parts of the picture, whose direction crosses that of the main line of the picture, will give an excellent effect by supporting it. This line may be anything, a cane or staff, any object whatever, even the line of an arm. *It* need not cross the line of direction, only so that its direction does so.

Thus, let *A B C* be the heads in any group. *A B* will be the most important line, opposed and balanced by *A C*. But, also,

Fig. 77.

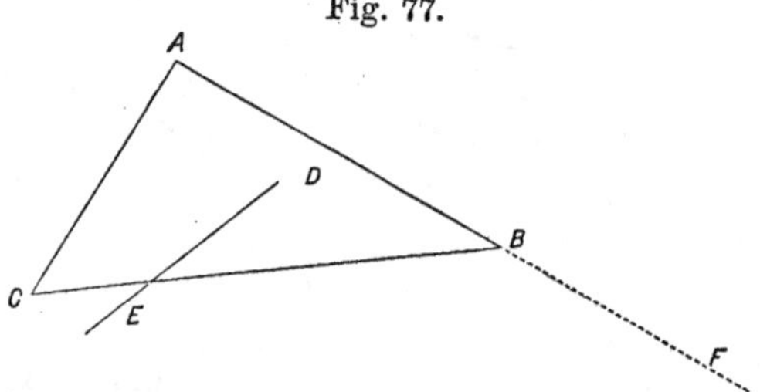

some other line, *D E*, if introduced, will greatly support the line *A B* and balance the picture. And where the line *A B* if continued would terminate at *F*, on the ground or elsewhere, there should be some object for it to rest upon, as explained above.

§ 3.—**Management of Light.**[1]

Our perception of the inequalities of surface, of relative distance, and in fact of the shape and position of bodies generally, depends almost wholly upon light and shadow.

[1] See also *ante*, Remarks on causes of unsatisfactory results in portraiture.

Take, for example, an outline drawing of a building. The eye, chiefly by habit and education, understands that a solid body, and not a flat surface, is intended to be depicted. I say, the eye *understands*, for it seems more like a deduction than a perception.

If now the artist washes in even only a single shade of neutral gray behind each projection, how these projections suddenly start out and strike the eye! As if by magic the whole building has assumed a visible solidity, and if the work has been correctly performed and the shades duly graduated, the eye instantly recognizes the length, breadth, and depth of the edifice, and is able to derive whatever pleasure its justness of form is fitted to afford.

Any photographer who frequently passes a public building with many projections, such as are especially to be found in gothic architecture, and who will stop and carefully study the effects of different lights upon it, will be amply repaid, and will learn more by a few minutes given twenty or thirty times, or still oftener, than by a year's random photographing.

At times the light is so exceedingly uniform and so broken by clouds, that every portion of a building will be almost equally lighted. So far from this being an advantage, the structure will be found on critical examination to look extremely flat and tame, and if photographed in such a light, its photograph will also be deficient in relief. This great uniformity of light may occur with various amounts of illumination, and though more common in dark weather, will sometimes be seen when the light is tolerably good.

When the clouds are thinner, a considerable quantity of direct light (without notable sunshine) may pass through them. In this case projections cast faint shadows, and the relief is greatly improved.

With still thinner clouds, *faint sunshine* passes through. The inestimable value of a very faint sunshine every experienced photographer will fully recognize. Photographs of natural scenery, taken in the absence of sunlight, are apt to be tame and monotonous. A faint sunlight gives an exquisite relief and life to the whole, with beautifully illuminated shadows.

When the sun is fully out, and especially towards the middle of the day, the contrasts become excessive, and before the details in the shadows impress themselves, the high lights suffer.

The case of a building has been chosen as an example, but precisely the same holds good with portraiture. The shape of features, the character and expression of the face, all these depend upon light and shade and their due management.

In examining the work of professed portraitists, we constantly observe the faults here pointed out as being so easily seen and judged in a building, which last, from its invariable position and (so to speak) expression, enables us to compare the effects of different lights so very advantageously. These faults lie, on the one side, in too uniform a lighting, by which the features are rendered flat and the expression stupid, or at least less intelligent than the original; and, on the other, in too great contrast of lighting, whereby the character of the features is exaggerated, and the expression rendered stern and hard.

These two generic faults represent the Scylla and Charybdis of the portraitist, and, with the varying lights of the day, will require his most intelligent efforts to avoid.

CHAPTER IX.

ON COPYING.

COPYING by photography falls into three classes:—

1. Copying oil paintings and drawings in color.
2. Copying mezzotints and lithographs, and drawings in Indian ink and sepia, &c.
3. Copying line engravings, woodcuts, pen and ink drawings, and pencil drawings.

These three classes will require different treatment, but all the varieties in one and the same class will require the same, or nearly the same, management.

Old oil paintings, in which the backgrounds have become very dark and the colors have lost their brilliancy, are especially difficult to copy, in fact, in many cases, it will be impossible to obtain really satisfactory results. It is possible that, in some cases, Dr. Vogel's plan of applying a yellow varnish against the thinnest parts of the negative obtained, so as to diminish contrast, might be advantageously employed with the result of getting increased detail.

The best instructions that can be given, are to use a pretty wide stop, give a long exposure, and use a collodion containing equal parts of bromides and iodides. As many collodions will not bear the very long exposure required, it is probable that the glycerine process might be usefully applied, though, of course, with still farther prolongation of exposure. But a glycerine plate does not deteriorate by exposure, whereas many collodions will not bear more than ten or fifteen minutes; often, not so much. (See also Chapter XV., Remarks on keeping plates.)

In the second class above enumerated, we included subjects which, though in monochrome, present *gradation of tint.* These will require to be treated through all the stages, very much as views, and with the same care to avoid harshness and excess of contrast.

On the contrary, the third class will require a widely different treatment. With these the object will be to get, not to avoid, strong contrast. The originals are composed of only white and black, the half tints depending upon the presence of more or less of each of these constituents. A white and black negative will therefore be wanted.

But it is an entire mistake to suppose, as was for a long time believed, that this was best accomplished by the use of a collodion containing little or no bromide. The author of this book long since pointed out that copying was best done with ordinary landscape collodion. Iodide of silver is more sensitive to a strong light, bromide to a weak light. Now, as line engravings require to be copied with a very small stop, the light is always weak, consequently bromide is needed; and this view is fully supported, both by direct experiment and by common experience.

To obtain a fine copy of a line engraving, in which the hair lines are to be faithfully and sharply reproduced, requires a good lens, well managed. The stop must be very small, not exceeding *f* 60, or one-sixtieth in focal length. The lens should be a large one.

Copying is the most delicate and difficult branch of photography. The faint light admitted by the small stop cannot form a brilliant image; the attraction to the developer is therefore weaker, and the tendency to the production of stains is greater, whilst no department of photography requires so absolute an absence of stains as this. Consequently, photographers generally confine themselves to the central parts of the plate, or at least leave a border of an inch or more around the image, as it is the borders that are most exposed to these troubles.

The bath must necessarily be in good order, giving clean blooming negatives. The developer must have a full, though not excessive, dose of acetic acid. The development must not be prolonged, but be rather a brief one, and if a very strong negative be wanted, recourse must be had to after-intensification.

The best means of effecting this is to place the plate in a solution of corrosive sublimate until it becomes entirely white, and then to flow it with cyanide of potassium. The cyanide instantly blackens the negative, whilst at the same time it clears away all tendency to veiling, if any existed.

Another excellent method is to chlorize the plate and then to apply Schlippe's salt. (See article on After-intensification.)

But for the most part, an ordinary development followed if necessary by a re-development, after fixing, will be sufficient, remembering, however, that neither development nor re-development should be pushed. The re-developing liquid should be used no longer than it is quite colorless, instead of serving, as in other work, as long as it is clear. Heavy deposits of silver, if allowed, will evidently clog up the finer lines.

The lens to be used should be one free from distortion. The Zentmayer and the globe form are perhaps the best, though the distortion of the triplet is so very slight, that except for work requiring absolute exactness, as for example engineering and other topographic work, it may properly be employed. The Dallmeyer Rectilinear lenses, and Ross' Doublet are also suitable. The orthoscopic copies excellently. It must never be forgotten that to get the hair lines clean and sharp a very small stop is essential.

Mechanical Appliances.—When an old picture is to be copied, it will be well cleaned and then be hung up in the sunshine. Fix the camera so that each corner of the picture shall be equally distant from the centre of the front lens, and take care that all parts of the picture shall be equally illuminated, also that the direction of the sunlight shall be such that no reflections shall reach the lens.

The copying of engravings and smaller pictures may be done in the same way. But it is more convenient to make a special arrangement as follows:—

A long board, about the width of the camera, is provided, with a raised edge on each side. Upon these, there slides a block which carries a large board which it maintains always in an exact vertical position and exactly at right angles to the length of the board, being controlled by guides underneath. At one end a raised box carries the camera at such a height that the centre of the lens is opposite to the centre of the board, which centre is permanently marked by the intersection of two diagonals from opposite corners, drawn in strong black lines upon the board. If then a drawing be fastened so that its centre corresponds with the centre of the board, we know at once that it is in the right place. The board is shifted backwards and forwards according to the size of the reproduction wanted. If, as advised by some, the board is stationary, and the box which carries the camera moves, then there is a disadvantage, that when it is pushed in far, the focussing becomes troublesome from the necessity of bending so far over the board. A still better plan is to have both the board and the box fitted with guides.

If the board has lines parallel to the sides, as well as diagonals, drawn, the placing of objects to be copied is facilitated.

The drawing, print, etc., can then be placed at once in the exact centre of the board, and is at once ready for focussing.

Plans may be well copied by simply laying them on sensitized paper and exposing. This gives a paper negative, which is to be laid on other sensitized paper and exposed—if the resulting positive is not strong enough, it is brought up by development. Plans of several feet square, made for the Treasury Department at Washington, are thus beautifully multiplied by Mr. Walker, the photographer of the department.

CHAPTER X.

THE STEREOSCOPE.

THIS ingenious invention of Prof. Wheatstone depends upon the fact that the two eyes see the same objects differently in consequence of their difference of position. If we view a collection of objects, as, for instance, trees in a grove, and then moving our position by a few yards, we view them again, their relative positions will seem changed. A smaller change produces this in a lesser degree, and even the space between the eyes corresponds to a change of aspect, which, small as it is, aids greatly in fixing relative positions. This will be better exemplified as follows:—

Let the polygonal figure (Fig. 78) be viewed by the eyes *E* and *E′*. Its distance from them and its size may easily be imagined such that the eye *E* will see the five sides, 1, 2, 3, 4, 5; whilst *E′* will see the five sides, 2, 3, 4, 5, 6. The eye has, by long experience, unconsciously learned to combine these two portions of the polygon, and to understand thereby that it is a solid body, and not a mere projection on a flat plane.

Fig. 78.

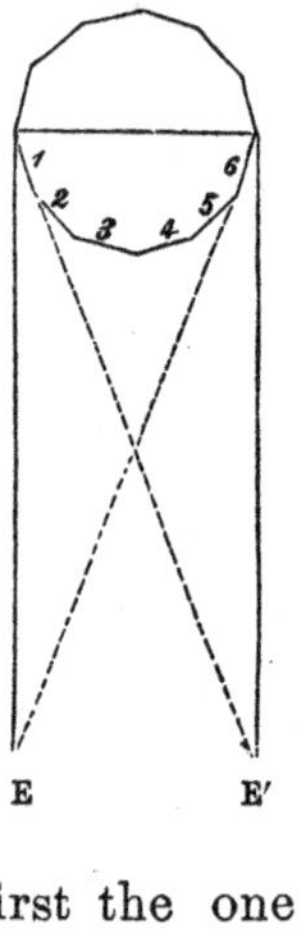

If we suppose, instead of the polygon at Fig. 78, that we look at a pillar, of a portion of which that polygon is a section, the mind realizes that it is a solid body by its consciousness that the one eye sees partly round it on the one side, and the other upon the other side.

If then, whilst viewing any scene, we close first the one eye and then the other, it is evident that we shall see slightly different scenes with the respective eyes, the combination of which two scenes gives us a distincter sense of distances and positions, than what would result from observation by either eye separately.

Now, if we place two lenses in positions of distance corresponding with that of the two eyes, each will be capable of producing an image corresponding with those seen by the separate eyes. And if these pictures be placed side by side before the eyes, and each be looked at by one eye separately, these two images may be combined by the brain precisely as the two views seen by the eyes in observing a landscape. Such pictures are made in the *stereoscopic camera*, in which, however, the lenses are placed somewhat farther apart than the distance which separates the human eyes, it having been found by experiment that the effect so obtained is more striking than if the actual distance between the eyes were maintained with the lenses, which also it would not be easy to carry out in practice.

All the operations with the stereoscopic camera are precisely the same as with the ordinary, except the mounting of the prints when finished. These should be cut with care to a convenient size, keeping the centres of the cut prints to correspond as nearly as possible with the point directly opposite the centre of the lens.

In pasting, they must be reversed, that is, the print which is on the right hand side as printed, must be mounted left. It has, however, been shown that this may be avoided by cutting the sensitized paper to twice the length of the negative, and folding its ends till they meet at the centre.

The figure represents the paper loosely folded. *B* and *C* are pressed down till the edges *E E′* meet. The sensitive side of the paper is outermost. Apply the side *B C* to the negative; a print is taken. The sheet is then turned round and the other side printed. Cuttting through at *A*, and opening out, *B* and the piece behind it give one print, and *C* and that behind it, another, each with the sides correctly placed for mounting, and not needing to be reversed.

Fig. 79.

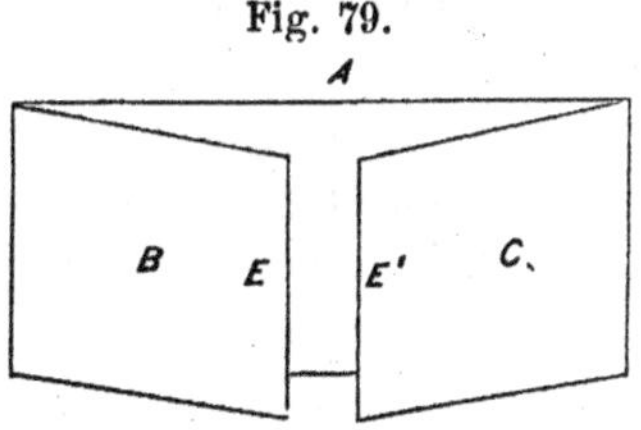

The stereoscope, which for some time enjoyed an almost unbounded popularity, has latterly been much less prized. Larger views from half size to 10×12 are capable of so much more artistic effect, that they are taking the place, and deservedly, of the stereoscopic slides, and will, no doubt, increasingly in future.

CHAPTER XI.

MICROPHOTOGRAPHY AND MICROSCOPIC PHOTOGRAPHY.

THE first of these processes has for its object the production of extremely small images of objects intended to be viewed by the microscope. The second is the impression upon a collodion film of the image seen in the microscope.

§ 1.—Microphotography.

If a negative be placed in a suitable apparatus and its image extremely reduced in size, be thrown by a very short focus lens upon a sensitized albumen plate, that image may readily be developed by appropriate means, and a sharp fine positive image be got, which when viewed by a sufficient magnifying power may exhibit satisfactory detail if all the manipulations have been well performed. The process evidently involves no real difficulty, except that the image is so exceedingly small that its development requires to be followed by the microscope.

The form in which this description of work first attracted public attention was in the reproduction of objects which by magnifying were made to exhibit striking details, lettering, for example. A monumental tablet, for instance, reduced until much smaller than a pin's head, when placed under the compound microscope, showed many lines of lettering, all perfectly distinct.

Subsequently, however, M. Dagron gave a new impetus to the matter by substituting for the microscope a modified Stanhope lens, having one end a plane surface, to which the microscopic print was attached permanently by Canada balsam. These lenses were manufactured out of glass rods at an infinitesimal price, and enormous quantities have been sold in Paris. In this country they have never become popular, and space can be spared here for a brief description only.[1]

[1] The writer is informed that this work is carried on commercially by Mr. Morrow, of New York.

A long box, open at both ends, is provided. At the far end is a slide to receive the negative with a plate of ground glass to diffuse the light beyond it. At the near end there is placed a plate of glass ruled with fine lines, whose position corresponds with that which the sensitive film is to occupy. Just in front of this is fixed the very short focus lens, movable by a rack and pinion. This is brought to focus with the magnifier and with the aid of the ruled lines. The sensitive plate is then substituted. In good weather the exposure is about two or three seconds.

The dark slide is movable, so that after each exposure it is advanced a step, and another image is taken. With Dagron's instrument, eight can be taken in succession on one plate, but with a different multiplying apparatus contrived by Dubosq, ninety can be taken on one plate.

A lens is used to watch the development. After all the operations are finished, the images are carefully examined with a compound microscope, and all that are any way imperfect are rejected. The good ones are warmed, touched with Canada balsam, and pressed firmly on the Stanhope lens, through which they are intended to be viewed.

§ 2.—**Microscopic Photography.**

In microscopic photography the images are enlarged greatly above the natural size. The operation differs from ordinary enlarging, both in its object and method.

In ordinary enlarging, the object is usually to reproduce from a small negative, a large paper picture, though we also may obtain enlarged negatives on glass. But in microscopic photography, the object is to get negatives, large or small, of microscopic objects, often enormously enlarged.

Dr. Woodward, of the U. S. Army, has so far exceeded all other experimenters in this direction, whose results have come under the writer's notice, that his method of operating will be given in preference to any other.

Outside of a southern window is placed a Silberman's heliostat, which reflects a beam of light upon the mirror of a microscope. This mirror is outside of the shutter, and throws the light through a tube set in the shutter, into the microscope, which last is just inside in a horizontal position. At the outer extremity of this tube is placed a plate glass cell, filled with a solution of ammonio-sulphate of copper, the object of which is to let only the violet rays pass, at the same time that it reduces the light so much that the eye can bear the full light of the sun in focussing. Two steel rods, passing through the shutter, are attached to the mirror, and enable it to be regulated in position from the inside.

A black velvet hood arranged round the stage of the microscope prevents the escape of any rays of light into the room.

With high powers, an ordinary achromatic condenser is found advantageous; it is placed between the inner extremity of the tube and the object glass. Objectives properly corrected for use with violet light were manufactured expressly by Mr. W. Wales, of Fort Lee, New Jersey, and were found perfectly satisfactory. The plate-holder, properly centred, slides on a horizontal walnut frame by which it is held perpendicular to the axis of the microscope and can be clamped at any distance, not exceeding nine feet from the stage. A round rod reaches from the microscope to the plate; at the end nearest to the microscope this has a grooved wheel. By turning the rod, the operator regulates the focus whilst standing by the plate-holder.

Standing by the microscope, the operator puts in an eye-piece and focusses in the usual way, adjusting the light by moving the mirror outside by the aid of the steel rods. Next the eye-piece is removed, and, going to the plate-holder, the final adjustment is made by turning the round rod, and viewing the image with a focussing glass directed upon a plate of glass placed in the plate-holder.

All being now ready, the sensitive plate is placed in the holder and exposed for a time, which may vary with the illumination and the amount of enlargement, from less than a second up to twenty minutes.

The objective alone is sufficient for low powers, but for higher ones an achromatic concave is introduced into the upper part of the body of the microscope, and enlarges the image six or seven times linear. This concave has a regular aperture of 28°, and is one inch diameter.

In some cases a ground-glass must be interposed in the solar pencil to prevent the production of interference bands.

"By these contrivances," says Dr. Woodward, "we have been enabled to produce pictures of the utmost sharpness, and perfectly satisfactory in every other respect, with powers up to two thousand and five hundred diameters and these pictures bear a further enlargement of from six to eight diameters in a copying camera. We have thus obtained excellent pictures up to ten thousand diameters."

Ordinary collodions were found to work very well. For great enlargements, where the light was weak, a collodion containing two grains of bromide of magnesium and five of iodide of magnesium was found useful, the deliquescent action of the nitrate of magnesium formed preventing the drying of the film.

In operations of this kind, it may be remarked that the precautions elsewhere recommended for keeping the plate in good order for a length of time, would be doubtless useful. These are, to use from two to two and a half grains of bromide, agitate the plate continuously in the nitrate bath, and remove it the moment the oily streaks disappear. In this way undecomposed bromide remains in the film, and permits of prolonging the interval between sensitizing and developing. In this course of proceeding, sulphate of copper must invariably be excluded from the developer, or brown fogging will result.

An ordinary nitrate bath with a collo-developer was used by Dr. Woodward, and after-intensification with mercury, or with Schlippe's salt.

With the very highest powers, such as Powell & Lealand's one-fiftieth objective, the correction of the objective to suit the violet light was found to be so small as to be practically unimportant. But with one-eighth, for example, it was found to be essential. As a general thing, images taken with the one-eighth and enlarged, gave results as good as those obtained directly with the one-fiftieth.

Drs. Woodward and Curtis have obtained many beautiful microscropic photographs by this process, which is exceedingly well adapted to increase our knowledge of the structures of animal and vegetable tissues. One of their most successful amplifications has been that of the Pleurosigma angulatum, of which they have obtained good photographic prints on paper, magnified up to nineteen thousand diameters. A curious result seems worth mentioning. It is well known that in the case of some pitted tissues, observers have differed; some describing these pits as seen when immensely magnified, as round; when others have seen the same as hexagonal. Now these prints, when viewed closely, appear to have the openings circular, but when held at a distance, the effect is hexagonal.

CHAPTER XII.

DEVELOPMENT ON PAPER.

§ 1.—Positive Development on Chloride of Silver.

DEVELOPMENT on paper requires to be differently managed according as we wish to obtain positives or negatives. These operations will be considered under different heads, commencing with positives.

Positives may be developed on paper with the aid of either iodide, bromide, or chloride of silver, or with a mixture of these substances. From his own trials, the writer long since decided on chloride as being the best, and the process published by him several years ago has been largely adopted with or without considerable variations.

If paper be impregnated with chloride, bromide, or iodide of silver, be exposed for a short time under a negative, and then be thrown into a saturated solution of gallic acid, a picture will soon be developed, which will go on increasing in strength, and, when satisfactory, may be taken out, washed, and fixed. Such was the original idea of development, which we owe to the Rev. J. B. Reade, though it was shortly after taken up and perfected by Mr. Fox Talbot, to whom, by many, it has been ascribed. Both these experimenters operated with iodide of silver, and turned their attention rather to negative development than positive. Some years later, Blanquart Evrard took the process up, used a mixture of bromide and iodide of silver, fumed with hydrochloric acid, and toned his pictures with hyposulphite and gold. His results were magnificent, and for a while it was asserted that none of his pictures had ever been known to fade. With increasing lapse of time, however, this has ceased to be true, and his pictures have in some cases faded.

The process which the writer brought forward was based upon

the use of lead in connection with gallic acid. It had been known before that the addition of acetate of lead to gallic acid greatly increased its powers of action, but as a precipitate was formed rendering the liquid muddy, this objection interfered with the use of the lead salt, and the fact remained without application.

Having ascertained that gallate of lead, the precipitate formed when acetate of lead was added to gallic acid, was soluble in acetic acid, the writer applied this observation to development both positive and negative, and with excellent results, especially in the former case. The economy of gallic acid was enormous, the rapidity of development was heightened, and what was of far more consequence, the clearness of the development was greatly enhanced, so that of all kinds of development, this was the safest and least liable to accident. The course was so regular and uniform that many prints could be developed at once, and the bath kept in working order for a longer time and with a greater number of prints. This was probably because the large quantity of acetic acid used restrained the precipitation of the silver, whilst the action of the lead expedited the development.

The following are the details of this process.

For a twenty-four ounce developing bath, dissolve four grains of gallic acid in a few ounces of water, and add about half an ounce of a solution of acetate of lead, thirty grains to the ounce, of which a stock may be conveniently kept on hand. A thick white precipitate falls. Next add acetic acid till this precipitate redissolves—a little excess of acetic acid does no harm, but is rather beneficial. Filter this and dilute to twenty ounces. To four ounces of water add a few drops of solution of nitrate of silver from the positive printing bath, and mix with the rest.

These various operations should be performed a short time only before the bath is wanted, as naturally it will not keep.

The development may be effected either on plain or on albumenized paper. It is commonly believed, universally it might be said, that development on albumenized paper is impossible, but this is a mistake. The treatment of the paper must be different, but either sort will develop in the foregoing bath.

To develop on plain paper, float it for one minute upon a five grain solution of sal-ammoniac. Sensitize on a nitrate bath acidulated with tartaric acid. A weak bath will be sufficient—say twenty grains of nitrate of silver to the ounce. Good results can be obtained with half this strength, but for general use it is not advisable to economize the silver so much. It is almost superfluous to say that this sensitizing, and the placing in and taking out of frames will be performed in a room by yellow light, and not as in the preparation of ordinary positive paper. The same care in excluding white light as in the wet collodion process, must be exercised.

The paper, when dry, is placed under a negative and exposed to light, direct sunlight is best, for from fifteen to sixty seconds, according to the light, the season, and the negative. The writer advises to continue the exposure until the image reaches a pale chocolate color. Some stop at the pale violet, good results are got either way, but the former seems preferable. Of course the frame must not be opened for examination.

It is a mistake to assert, as some have done, that no details are got in the development that were not visible faintly in the print when taken from the frame. On the contrary, much that is not any way visible, comes out distinctly in the development.

In fact I have proved this capacity of chloride to yield details in development, which were originally invisible in rather a striking manner. Taking a piece of paper sensitized with a chloride only, I placed it behind a negative, and burned a single magnesium spiral at a little distance. On removing the paper nothing was visible, but the careful application of a developer brought out the image with all the details in a surprising manner. The details were as full as if iodide of silver had been used.

When, then, the print is judged to have been sufficiently exposed, it is removed from the printing frame, and plunged evenly and quickly into the developing bath. With the bath above described, the development requires about five minutes to complete it. The prints should generally be a little stronger than they are intended to be when finished, for they lose a little in the fixing.

As soon as the print is judged to be sufficiently developed, it is thrown into water to stop the action, and is then toned with gold precisely in the same way as with any other positive on paper.

It will be seen that the above bath, though containing only one-sixth of a grain of gallic acid to the ounce, acts much like an ordinary developing bath, made twenty times stronger. This shows how remarkable is the agency of lead in increasing the activity of gallic development.

For albumenized paper a much larger dose of tartaric acid is here advisable. Take—

Nitrate of silver	1 ounce.
Tartaric acid	50 grains.
Water	12 ounces.

Float on this ordinary albumenized paper for two to three minutes, and then proceed otherwise as before.

Paper prepared in this way, although albumenized, bears development very well, and gives good results. Not so good, however, either on albumenized or plain, as with sun-printing, though sometimes not far behind. Still, it must be said that when the sun's light is left to do its perfect work, that work is better and more completely done than when we break it off just commenced, and force our solutions to complete it. It would seem that it could not be otherwise. And, although the development can be effected on albumenized paper, it is more difficult and much less certain than on plain.

This last described paper has good keeping properties. If placed in a tight tin case, thoroughly protected from light, it shows but little tendency to spontaneous decomposition, and I have succeeded in developing a perfectly clean picture, after an interval of at least ten days after sensitizing.

Modifications have been proposed of my process, but the alterations have scarcely the importance to deserve specific notice. I shall refer to them, however, so that any who please to experiment with them, may do so.

Libois directs to dissolve 1 drachm gallic acid in 4 drachms of alcohol, and 1 drachm acetate of lead in 12½ ounces water. Take

Rain water	50 ounces.
Solution gallic acid	½ drachm.
" acetate of lead	6¼ drachms.

After mixing, add a little glacial acetic acid to redissolve the gallate of lead which falls.

Salt with chloride of ammonium, adding a little citrate of sodium thereto, to assist in keeping the whites clear.

This last recommendation is evidently erroneously conceived.

To keep the whites clear, a moderate addition of tartaric acid (3 or 4 grains to ounce) added to the sensitizing solution, is useful (tartaric is better than citric). But the addition of a neutral salt, such as citrate of sodium, to the salting bath, cannot help the clearness of the development.

Dr. Kemp's modification consisted in using *basic* instead of ordinary acetate of lead. As basic acetate of lead is prepared by adding oxide of lead to common acetate, so that the base is in larger proportion, and as, immediately after the gallic acid is added, acetic acid in excess must be added, it is difficult to see but what the same effect must be produced as when we start with the neutral acetate.

§ 2.—Negative Development on Paper.[1]

Calotype Process.—Float paper on a 20 grain plain solution of nitrate of silver, and then, after drying, upon a 25 grain solution of iodide of potassium; on the first solution for one minute, on the second, ten minutes. Dip in water to wash off the excess of iodide and dry. In this condition the paper keeps well, if protected from light.

Make now 6 ounces of cold saturated solution of gallic acid, dissolve 300 grains nitrate of silver in 6 ounces of water, mix the two and add an ounce of strong acetic acid. No more of this sensitizer should be made than is needed, as it will not keep more than a few hours. Therefore in sensitizing a few sheets it is better to make much less and brush over the paper instead of floating. Whether dipped or floated the solution is left on but a minute; the sheet is dipped into water, the excess of moisture blotted off with bibulous paper, and the sheet is ready for use. A very brief exposure is sufficient to form an image which will go on strengthening in the dark, or may be hastened by washing over with the sensitizing mixture, just above described, and holding to the fire.

This process gave excellent results, and was long a great favorite, until the collodion process superseded it. The negatives so obtained may be paraffined as follows.

[1] An interesting negative process on paper, by Mr. H. J. Newton, will be found in the *Philadelphia Photographer*, vol. iv. page 187. The writer regrets that space will not allow him to extract it in full.

Paraffining.—Take a fine translucent paraffine candle—not the paraffine that resembles spermaceti, but the very translucent sort—and scrape it down to shreds with a knife or piece of broken glass. Strew some of these on a piece of filtering paper, lay the negative upon them, put more shreds on the negative, then another piece of filtering paper, and iron with a right warm, but not hot, flat iron. If on looking at the negative it is not found to be moist all over, put more shreds on the dry part, and repeat.

Wax Paper Process.—Legray showed that paper might be first waxed, and that even after this, it would take up sufficient iodide of potassium if immersed in the solution, to admit of sensitizing on solution of nitrate of silver and exposing in the camera. Serum of milk, or whey was found useful in this process, and the writer has used it with good effect in developing positives. After waxing good photographic paper with fine bleached wax, soak it for an hour in—

Serum of milk	25 ounces.
Milk sugar	½ ounce.
Bromide of potassium	48 grains.
Iodide of "	180 "

To obtain whey, heat the milk to boiling, add a very few drops of acetic acid till it turns, then the white of an egg to clear, and filter through paper. Milk sugar can be had of the druggist. Dry and put away between folds of paper. Sensitize, when wanted, on a 35 grain solution of nitrate of silver to which glacial acetic acid has been added in the proportion of one ounce of acid to 14 of bath. Immerse in two waters successively, dry between folds of blotting paper. Expose either between two pieces of plate glass, or else paste the edges of the paper over the edges of a piece of glass. Develop with a saturated solution of gallic acid, to which nitrate of silver has been added in the proportion of one grain to two ounces of gallic acid solution and a little acetic acid. Probably the lead developer, already described, would be every way better. (See Section 1 of this chapter.)

§ 3.—Paper Enlargements.

Life sized portraits may evidently be obtained in the same way as ordinary portraits, provided we proportionately increase the size of the lens. But unfortunately the defects of lenses increase with their size, and this is especially true with respect to depth of focus. The larger the lens, therefore, the more difficult it will be to get different parts of the subject simultaneously in focus, and consequently, while it is by no means impossible to take life-sized portraits direct, it is much more common to effect this object by enlarging with the aid of a solar camera from a small negative, generally made expressly for this purpose (see p. 139).

Enlargements, printed by the solar camera, may be finished in the camera, that is, the whole work may be done by sun-printing, precisely like printing in a frame. But the method of development is also practicable, and this may be done in the manner already described, by chloride development, or at the option of the operator, the negative process on bromo-iodized paper may be used, of course without taking means to render the paper transparent. But as the negative process is specially intended for those cases where the illumination is very weak, as in the camera obscura, and as the light of the solar camera is always abundant for chloride development, that process will give the most satisfaction, provided, as before said that the operator desires to develop, and not to finish in the usual way. Also when the picture has been supposed to be finished and has been found to be too weak, development may be resorted to, to bring it up.

§ 4.—**The Solar Camera.**

The apparatus for enlarging from a small negative may be arranged in several different methods; these instruments are known as solar cameras.

Woodward's Camera.—In this instrument the solar rays are received upon a mirror of silvered (not quicksilvered) glass, whose office it is to reflect them horizontally. They then pass through a plain convex *flint* glass condenser of 8 inches in diameter.

Fig. 80.

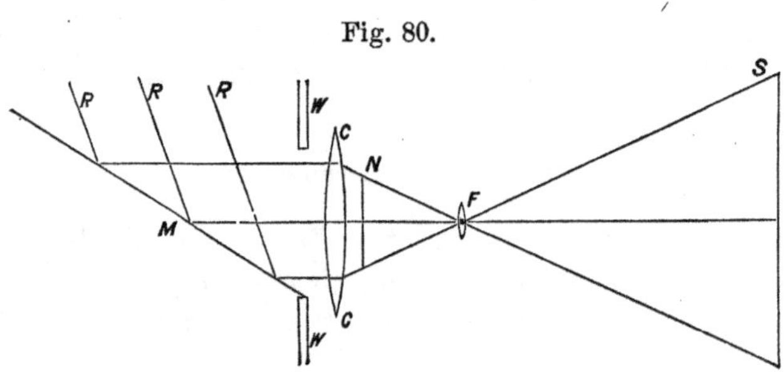

R R R, parallel rays from the sun falling upon the mirror *M*, which reflects them horizontally through the opening in the wall *W W* of an apartment. Inside is the condenser *C C*, which converges them to a focus *F*, where a photographic objective is placed. A negative *N* being interposed between the condenser and the objective, its magnified image is formed on the screen. In Woodward's apparatus the lens at *F* is an ordinary portrait objective.

The mirror *M* is mounted with racks and pinions, and requires to be moved every few seconds to keep the rays horizontal.

Van Monckhoven's Camera.—The objection made to Woodward's apparatus has been that the condenser was not large (8 inches diameter), and consequently the working was slow. The size could not be increased without introducing much spherical aberration and injuring the sharpness of the image.

To avoid this evil, Van Monckhoven introduced a negative lens behind the condenser, a thin meniscus, and also replaced the objective by one of a construction devised by himself.

Light is thrown upon the apparatus in the same way as with Woodward's. Or a *heliostat* may be very advantageously applied to any solar camera. In this instrument the mirror is regulated by clock-work, so that it moves with the sun and takes always such an angle that the rays reflected by it fall horizontally upon the condenser.

Very good work has been executed with Van Monckhoven's camera.

Other Solar Cameras.—The same optical principle which was adopted by Woodward, has been made the basis of a number of different arrangements, by Shive, Roettger, Fontayne, Gales, Carbutt, and others. In Shive's, Roettger's, Fontayne's, and Carbutt's the direct rays of the sun are used without a reflector. The difference in these instruments depends upon the mechanical contrivances applied to carry out the optical arrangement. In all a plano-convex lens is placed with its convex side to the light. Between its posterior surface and its focal point the negative is introduced. At its focal point the photographic objective is placed and the image is thrown upon a screen in the back of the camera. Roettger claims for his, to which he gives the name of "parallactic," a greater facility for following the sun's path. The most recent modification is Carbutt's, which is itself a modification of Stuart's; in it the whole tripod moves. The base of the tripod is a triangle, moving upon a hinge at one corner. The corner falls directly under the condensing lens; this gives a facility for making a great angular movement in a very little space. The apparatus is mounted permanently in a room at the top of the house. A section is removed from the south end of the roof to admit the direct sunshine.

It will be seen that the only modification of the optical principles of Woodward's camera which has been made is that of V. Monckhoven, who introduced the negative meniscus into it, to correct the spherical aberration, and thereby enable him to use a larger condenser. The size of the condenser is of material importance, for on it depends the intensity of the image. Woodward's condenser was eight inches in diameter, while V. Monckhoven was enabled to raise his to twenty. The time required for printing an enlargement of a given size with the two would be approximately inversely as the squares of the diameters, namely, as 400 to 64, or as 6 to 1, or thereabouts.

§ 5.—**Printing by the Solar Camera.**

Little special need be said on this head. Albumenized paper is attached to the screen, and the image gradually appears, requiring a time which may extend from half an hour to many hours to reach full strength.

This slow printing, requiring, as it does, incessant attention to keep the apparatus duly placed as respects the sun, unless the operator possesses a heliostat, is very objectionable and annoying, and therefore leads to the extensive use of development in order to shorten the time. This part of the subject has been already explained.

Efforts have been made to shorten the time required for sun-printing. That of M. Van Monckhoven founded upon the use of *nitroglucose* has been well spoken of, but does not seem to have passed into general use. The nitroglucose process may be used either for direct printing or for enlargement.

Nitroglucose is prepared by adding one part of pulverized sugar to one of sulphuric acid previously mixed with one of monohydrated nitric acid. After an action of about five minutes the mass is to be removed from the acid and washed with cold water. This crude nitroglucose is purified by dissolving in alcohol and precipitating by adding water, in which it is insoluble.

This nitroglucose, according to Dr. V. Monckhoven, does not precipitate nitrate of silver, but acquires that property if its alcoholic solution is kept for eight or ten days at a temperature of 110° F. Its application is as follows: the paper is passed through an alcoholic solution ten grains to the ounce, is hung up to dry, and is then immersed for two hours in an ordinary salting solution. Next, sensitized on a twenty-five grain plain solution of nitrate of silver and hung up to dry. So prepared it keeps for many months.

In use, the paper is exposed in the solar camera for about a minute, and is then developed with gallic acid 5 grains, water 10 ounces, glacial acetic acid 50 minims. The author of the process claims for it, that a gallic development causes *albumenized* prints to turn yellow in the whites, whereas with the nitroglucose process the whites remain perfect. Now when the development on albumenized paper is carefully conducted on the principles laid down in this manual, the whites do not turn yellow. Moreover V. Monckhoven observes that the operation for making nitroglucose is so delicate that the method would be useless were it not for a modification discovered by him and as yet unpublished.

The writer has himself prepared nitroglucose and found no difficulty whatever in it. He has found it advantageous to substitute one-half of *fuming* sulphuric acid for the ordinary acid. The mixed acids must be allowed to cool thoroughly in a covered vessel after mixing, powdered sugar is then stirred in, enough to make a thin paste. Soon a kind of grayish dough makes its appearance, which is at once removed with a spatula and thrown into water. This is continued till the dough ceases to form, when a little more sugar may be added, though its yield will be much less in proportion than that of the first.

The nitroglucose must at once be kneaded up with water to get out the excess of acid with which it is saturated, and which by remaining in it might cause its decomposition. For completer purification the nitroglucose is dissolved in alcohol and precipitated by water. The alcoholic solution should be poured into water (not the reverse) with constant stirring. The nitroglucose separates a thin dough, which is to be washed by agitating with several waters, and then should be kept under water.

CHAPTER XIII.

SILVER PRINTING.

Elementary directions will be found in the First Part. Here will be given some special remarks on the various branches into which the subject divides itself.

§ 1.—Selection of Paper.

The paper preferred in this country almost universally is the Saxe paper, of which the genuine is manufactured by Steinbach, and of which there are many imitations. Some of Marion's paper is also sold here, often as "Saxe paper," even as the writer has seen done, with Marion's name water-marked on the edge. "Rive" paper is little known here, nor Canson. Whatman's paper, much liked in England especially for negative work, scarcely finds its way to this country.

The qualities required in paper are—to be made of good stock—that is, fine clean rags; to have had the chlorine used for bleaching thoroughly removed, as also the antichlor (generally hyposulphite of sodium). Chlorine left in the paper tends to injure the fibre, but is otherwise of little importance, but even the slightest traces of hyposulphite make ineffaceable stains and discolorations. A print thrown by mistake into hyposulphite washings, turns black all over, the hyposulphite being decomposed and sulphide of silver formed; of course a similar reaction takes place when hyposulphite is left in the paper—faint traces make brownish spots, visible in the sensitized paper before printing.

Again, the paper must be free from all kinds of metallic grains, which, without care, are liable to drop into the pulp. Metallic dust, abraded from the machinery, forms imperceptible specks, which, however, reduce the silver from the nitrate bath, and make spots in the print.

In this country, prints are almost universally made upon white paper. In Germany, paper tinted faintly with rose color is also used. A warm effect is thus given, which tends to relieve the cold white and to form an agreeable variety. Such paper might be advantageously introduced here.

§ 2.—**Albumenizing Paper.**

Few operators take the trouble to albumenize their own paper. But as original experimenters require to understand every portion of the processes of photography, and as it may happen that photographers may desire to print where albumenized paper cannot be got, the writer gives the formula which he has used with good results.

Take the whites of perfectly fresh eggs and add thereto, liquid ammonia in the proportion of five drops for each egg. Measure the quantity, and take six grains of sal ammoniac for each ounce of albumen. This may be dissolved in an ounce of water for each five eggs, or if very high albumenizing is desired, it may be dissolved in the smallest possible quantity of water.

Add the sal ammoniac solution, and let the whole be beaten up to a froth, so that no liquid portion be left. Set away for twelve hours or more (a cool damp place is best), and pour off the liquid portions which have settled out of the froth. These are perfectly clear and free from foreign matter.

The albumen thus prepared is placed in a flat pan and the papers rested on it for three or four minutes, and then lifted off and hung up to dry. The faster the drying the higher the gloss, and, therefore, these papers when prepared commercially are often dried in rooms kept at a suffocating heat.

In small experiments the albumen may with a little dexterity be applied with a broad (two inch or more) camel's-hair brush. With care, streaks may be avoided.

Some have recommended the use of glacial acetic acid (three drops to each egg) instead of the ammonia. Lyte remarks that this tends to yellowness in the whites of the prints, and my experience has been the same.

In place of beating up, some filter through three or four folds of damp muslin. It has also been recommended to iron the paper after drying, to coagulate the albumen: at one time, this was considered essential. But dry albumen does not coagulate by heat, and, moreover, with a nitrate bath in good order, the albumen is always thoroughly coagulated. If ironing is done, the sheet must be placed between folds of paper.

In the salting considerable latitude is allowable. Formerly, strong salting was more customary than now, and twelve grains of sal-ammoniac to the ounce was usual. More lately the quantity has been diminished. An absurd secrecy is practised by many makers of albumenized paper as to their salting, and this introduces some uncertainty as to the proper treatment: strong salting requires a stronger bath, and with paper of which the salting is not known, some trials may be requisite to determine the appropriate bath.

The weaker salting now used is much less exhaustive upon the positive printing bath, but it is not quite sure that the pictures so produced are quite as permanent.

In the preservation of albumenized paper, two things are to be borne carefully in mind. First, that if the paper be kept in a moist atmosphere, it will not give brilliant prints. This is because the salt used becomes to some extent dissolved in the hygroscopic moisture absorbed by the paper, and is drawn by capillary attraction into the body of the paper; thus the silvered surface is less perfect. This is more the case with common salt, chloride of sodium, and less with chloride of barium, than with chloride of ammonium. Common salt is the most deliquescent, chloride of barium the least soluble of the three.

On the other hand, excessive dryness is to be avoided, the coat of albumen becomes too horny and not sufficiently permeable.

Generally speaking, the fresher the paper the better, and the less chance of defects.

Decomposed albumen is always hurtful. If it be kept so long before applying to the paper as to acquire a bad smell, it must be rejected. And if the paper be kept in a very moist place, the albumen may putrefy on the surface of the paper.

§ 3.—Salting Plain Paper.

In salting ordinary paper, the most various proportions of salt have been recommended. Two, three, or four grains to the ounce are about a recommendable proportion, and give good results. A little gelatine may be advantageously introduced; the latter should not exceed two grains to the ounce, and may be less.

The following may be taken:—

Chloride of ammonium	30 grains.
Gelatine	16 "
Water	10 ounces.

By some, chloride of barium is preferred. The greater equivalent weight of this substance requires that it should be used in larger quantity. As follows:—

Chloride of barium	200 grains.
Gelatine	45 "
Water	30 ounces.

A difference of opinion exists as to the proper mode of preparation. High authorities recommend that the paper be drawn through the solution. But as it is the invariable object to keep the materials on the surface, it is perhaps better to float the paper for a few moments in the bath. In any case, it is desirable that it should be rapidly dried, before the solution soaks too much in.

§ 4.—**Sensitizing.**

Good silver prints may be obtained by several different modes of sensitizing, and the practice varies very much in different countries. Both albumenized and plain paper may be sensitized on either plain nitrate of silver or ammonio-nitrate baths, and the paper so prepared may be used with or without fuming. First-rate results may be obtained in either way. The use of ammonia, whether in the bath, or subsequently, or both, is to save a portion of the nitrate of silver by working with weaker solutions.

In Part I. of this manual, the English process was given, as being the simplest of all. The same is largely used in Germany; in neither of which countries does the same belief in the economical effects of ammonia exist as here. In America, the use of ammonia is very general, therefore some of the best formulæ will be given here:—

Dissolve an ounce of nitrate of silver in twelve ounces of water, add liquid of ammonia until the whole of the precipitate at first formed is redissolved. Divide this liquid into two portions, add to the one-half pure nitric acid, until it turns blue litmus paper red; mix and filter.

This formula, published by a skilful professional operator, Mr. Fennemore, in the *Philadelphia Photographer*, may be taken as representing the weakest bath with which really good results can be got, and most printers would find it necessary to give such paper ten minutes fuming.

From this point we may advance to 50, 60, 70, or 80 grains of silver, treating it in the same way.

The treatment may also be varied; nitric acid may be added in larger quantity, as if two-thirds, or three-fourths of the ammoniacal solution be acidified, instead of one-half. On this bath, however made, the paper will be floated for one minute in warm weather, and two or three in very cold. Too long floating is as bad as too short, the object is always to keep the silver upon the surface; that which soaks into the body of the paper is little better than wasted.

After the sheet has floated for a proper time, it is to be pinned or otherwise fastened up to dry. Buff shades to the room, if wide enough to cover the window jambs, will be a sufficient protection; if too much white light be admitted, the high lights of the prints cannot be expected to be satisfactory.

Where a weak bath (30 to 40 grains) is employed, it has been found an advantage to dissolve about an equal quantity of pure nitrate of sodium in it. *Sugar* in the printing bath has been found to impart keeping qualities, at least in winter, to the paper.

The following formula of Mr. Bovey includes both these additions:—

Water	80 ounces
Nitrate of silver	6 "
" soda, pure	3 "
White loaf sugar	¼ ounce.

Management of Bath.—The positive bath by use soon turns yellow and loses strength. The first trouble is to be remedied by shaking up with half an ounce to an ounce of kaolin, according to the size of the bath. The strength must be kept steadily up to the mark originally fixed, and this is either done by watching carefully the character of the prints, and adding silver liberally as soon as they show any signs of deterioration, or by means of the *argentometer*, a sort of hydrometer expressly made for the photographer, and which, by sinking more and more deeply into the bath, indicates the exhaustion of the nitrate of silver. With the age of the bath, however, its indications become less reliable in consequence of the accumulation of other nitrates in the bath. It must, therefore, be calculated that an old bath will require *more* strengthening than indicated by the argentometer.

§ 5.—Fuming.

A convenient and close-fitting wooden or tin box is provided with a door, and either pieces of cork are attached to the sides near the top inside, or else cords are stretched across. To these the dry sensitized paper is attached for fuming. This operation lasts for ten minutes, and is best performed only a few minutes before printing.

In a saucer at the bottom of the box is poured some strong liquid ammonia. The quantity is not very important; for a small box and a dozen or twenty quarter sheets of paper, an ounce and a half to two ounces will be sufficient. For a large box and twenty or thirty whole sheets, two dishes with two or three ounces in each will be sufficient, if the ammonia be good. (The liquid ammonia of commerce is very variable in strength.) Carbonate of ammonium has been recommended by Dr. Liesegang as an advantageous substitute for the liquid; the mode of operating is precisely the same, except that a larger quantity is employed, and may be used many times.

It is best that the fumed paper should be exposed to the air for ten or fifteen minutes, to allow the adhering ammoniacal fumes to pass off, before laying it upon the negative.

§ 6.—Printing.

Before placing the paper in the frame, it is necessary to be certain that it is perfectly dry, otherwise the negative may be injured. The paper, especially if albumenized paper be in use, must be set in the frame neither roughly nor carelessly. For it is to be always borne in mind that a negative is a delicate thing. Even the best lac varnish is no protection against rough handling, and a slight scratch may easily occur in some place where touching out may be either impossible or nearly so. The paper should never be drawn over the plate, especially when pressed close to it. It must be laid flat down in its proper position, and the pads laid easily and squarely down upon it and secured by the back.

Printing may be done either in the direct rays of the sun or in diffuse light; the choice between the two will depend upon the nature of the negative, and the preparation of the paper must be regulated accordingly.

The characteristic of printing in the sun is softness, of printing in the shade, strength and contrast. Nevertheless, prints made in sunshine are mostly the stronger, simply because strong, hard negatives require sun-printing. And so, soft prints will often be found to have been executed in the shade, because taken from very thin negatives which could not be made to yield a good print in any other way. For want of understanding this, very contradictory and erroneous statements have often been published on the subject of sun and shade-printing.

A photographer will, for example, start out with the intention of printing in the shade, and will make all his negatives very thin with that intention. If these negatives were printed in the sun, the prints would be utterly worthless. By the time that the shadows were deep enough to stand toning and fixing, the lights would be discolored and the prints spoiled. To examine his prints and observe his mode of printing might lead to the conclusion that shade-printing gave soft prints, whereas the fact would be that the thin negative gave soft prints in spite of the mode of printing.

Another will prefer bold vigorous negatives, and will develop and redevelop till he gets them. These, if printed in the shade, until details were got in the high light, would lose all transparency of shadow, which would be converted into black patches. The exposures would be tedious and the prints bad. But exposed to a bright sun, the intense rays pierce through the dense parts of the negative and give us the details to the lights before the shadows are overdone.

Farther, it is to be remarked that both the salting and the nitrate bath must be regulated so as to act as a counterpoise to the printing. With a thin negative the bath must be a rich one, or the picture will tend to flatness. A bold negative will print well upon a less highly sensitized paper. In this lies the explanation of the much discussion over strong and weak printing baths, some succeeding with what fails with others, all depending upon the nature of the negative. Again, when, by accident, a very hard negative is taken which gives a harsh black and white picture, its prints may be improved by using an extremely weak sensitizing bath (prolonging the floating of the sheet upon it proportionately). It has even been said that extremely hard negatives, so hard as to be unserviceable in any other way, have been made to yield good prints by washing the paper after sensitizing it, so as to remove all free nitrate, then drying and exposing.

The proper degree of salting will always depend upon the strength of the sensitizing bath and correspond with it. A rich nitrate bath should follow high salting, and the reverse. Where it is wanted to get a soft print from a very hard negative the salting may be reduced to one or two grains per ounce of water, to be followed by a weak printing bath of 20 to 30 grains nitrate of silver.

Another remark of importance is this, that the image produced by a strong light stands the subsequent operations better than that produced by weaker light. A print made in direct sunshine is less reduced in toning and fixing than one made in the shade. Consequently, a shade-print requires more over-printing in the frame than a sun-print. The sun-print is undoubtedly the stronger picture of the two, and I think that, other things being equal, its chance of permanence is greater than that of the shade-print.

§ 7.—The Pressure Frame.

The construction of the frame is of too great an importance not to receive a word of comment here. Two very serious troubles arise from bad pressure frames, breakage of negatives and blurred prints. Pressure frames generally distribute the pressure very badly.

Take an ordinary piece of glass, the size of the frame, lay it in, put in the pads you commonly employ; take hold of the frame in both hands, the fingers on the back, the two thumbs resting on the glass near the centre. Press forcibly with the thumbs, until the glass moves back a little, and observe the amount of resistance. Next bring the thumbs up to one end, and press there; you will probably be surprised to find how much less the resistance is there, and consequently, how unequal the pressure.

This inequality is a principal cause of the breakage of negatives in the frames, and is also a disadvantage to the print, for wherever the contact is not good the sharpness of the print will be impaired, and this more so with shade printing than printing in direct sunlight. After trying carefully and comparatively many sorts of frames, the writer has come to have a very decided preference for the old form of bar-frame. The frame has two bars at back, hung to one side. When they are pressed down the two ends of a spring underneath the bar are forced down upon the back. This gives a more equal pressure than any other form of printing frame tried. Large frames require three bars; two are sufficient up to ten by twelve size. Many of the frames that are manufactured and sold largely are quite worthless. The form just described is recommended exclusively.

Many operators are extremely careless as to what padding they use between the back of the frame and the print, considering that anything is good enough, mill-boards, old newspapers, &c. This is quite wrong; such inelastic substances cannot give good contact, and always endanger the negatives. Moreover, as the material for this purpose lasts indefinitely, it is worth while to provide it right, once for all.

The one thing that is better than anything else is piano-cloth. This is a soft, thick, green felt-cloth; when really good it is about a quarter of an inch thick. It is expensive, costing about seven dollars a yard, but as that quantity will make pads for twenty whole plate frames, the cost is not worthy of consideration when the safety given to the negatives is considered. A single thickness is sufficient, and a fine, elastic, equable pressure is obtained which is invaluable. If by long use the felt has become flattened down, all that is necessary is to slightly wet it and let it dry.

The next best substance to this is probably a good thick flannel—woollen or cotton; the former is the more elastic. Whatever substance is used should of course be of some non-actinic color.

The *time* required for printing will of course vary extremely; in extreme cases, from a minute or two to many hours. The prints are to be examined by carrying the frame to a dark corner, loosening one end of the back, opening it and observing the condition of the print. Particular care is necessary to avoid injuring the negative with the nail in lifting back the print. The usual test of sufficient printing is when the shadows begin to bronze. At this time the highest lights should be either still quite clear or only just commencing to darken, so little that it will be removed in the subsequent operations and the white left pure. If in sun-printing the whites begin to darken before the shadows are sufficiently printed, it is a sign that the negative is thin and will require shade-printing. If in shade printing the shadows are fully printed before the details in the high lights are got, it is an indication that sun-printing is needed, and if this defect appears in sun-printing, it is a hint that the negative in use will require paper less highly silvered.

§ 8.—Vignetting.

When the print softens into a white border it is called a vignette, and this mode of printing offers a beautiful variety. The negative is usually taken in precisely the same way as for ordinary printing and the difference is made in the printing, though the effect can be very well produced once for all in the negative if desired, as will be presently explained.

Vignetting with a Frame.—This is the most usual way. The negative is placed in a frame on the face of which are springs which confine blocks of wood; in these blocks oval holes are cut, widening on the under side which is next the negative. On the upper side, farthest from the negative, tissue paper is pasted to soften the light.

Vignetting frames are also made expressly. These commonly have pieces of tin set in front, provided with wire rings, over which the tissue paper is to be pasted. For large negatives a convenient vignetting frame may be made by tacking a piece of stiff pasteboard upon the front of the frame. In this a hole is cut of the size desired, and this hole is covered with tissue paper.

Vignetting glasses are sold in which a deep orange enamel is applied to the border, leaving an oval space in the middle, of clear glass; of course the color is shaded off at the edges of the oval. This glass is to be placed in the frame between the negative and the light.

Any one accustomed to photographic manipulation may prepare such glasses for himself, by photography. Cut a small piece of oval hard wood, smaller than the part of the negative that is to be printed. Prepare a collodio-chloride, or albumen plate for positive printing, lay the little block on it, and expose to diffuse light, turning the plate now and then. It is evident that the part of the plate that is covered by the block will be completely protected, and the portions round it will be shaded off. Or, by reversing the operation, and using a hole in a shield instead of a block, a reverse vignetting plate may be got, that is, a shaded centre in a transparent border. This may be used as a negative from which any number of vignetting plates may be prepared, either by contact printing or by development. The writer cannot recommend this as being a very easy method, but it is perfectly practicable, as he knows from having devised it and used it several years since. More lately, it has been proposed and advocated by others in print.

Vignetting with Cotton.—A piece of stiff mill-board is tacked to the front of the frame, in which an opening is cut considerably larger than the size of the portion of the negative which it is intended to print. White cotton wool is pressed under the mill-board and allowed to project beyond it, until only that part of the negative is exposed which it is intended to print.

Vignetting with Paper.—In this case and in that immediately foregoing, the part of the negative that is to be printed is exposed uncovered. A piece of thin tissue paper is cut with an opening the size of the part of the negative that is to be fully printed; then another piece with the opening a little larger, and so on for a considerable number. These are pasted together and form a graduated shield, acting somewhat like the vignetting glass already described. By fastening this paper shield on the glass side of the negative and printing in the shade, the lines of the successive layers of paper can be concealed.

Vignetting with a Lens.—This ingenious method is practised by some professional photographers to the exclusion of all others, and has the advantage of great rapidity. A burning glass of some size (four to six inches in diameter) is set in a wide frame, or a piece of thin board. The negative is placed with silvered paper behind it in an ordinary frame, and the concentrated sunlight through the lens is allowed to fall upon the face. The lens is kept moving with a little circular motion, confining the light to the parts intended to be printed. In from ten seconds to half a minute the printing is finished. As the heat, as well as the light is concentrated by the lens, it is necessary to have a thin piece of plate glass in the frame between the negative and sunlight, to prevent injury to the negative.

All these methods give excellent results. The last is evidently only applicable to small heads, but the writer has seen beautiful vignetted cards made by it.

We next come to *vignetting on the negative.*

Vignetting by Development.—When the dark slide comes from the camera, the back is opened and an opaque shaded object of the shape and size of the vignette desired, is laid on the back of the plate, which then, and without removing from the slide, is exposed for a few seconds to weak diffuse light. When the image is developed, of course all parts of the plate not protected by the opaque screen just described are developed black in consequence of the second exposure. As the image is invisible at the time the opaque screen is applied, this last must of course have been arranged in such a way by the image, as seen in the camera, as to make sure of the screen being correctly applied.

Vignetting by a Screen.—Another method has been proposed. A large white screen is to be prepared with an oval opening. This screen is to be placed between the camera and the sitter, who is thus seen through the oval opening. The screen being white, reproduces itself by opacity on the negative, and being so much nearer to the lens than the sitter as to be completely out of focus, it of course has an indistinct shaded border. There seems an objection to this plan, that it tends to throw so much white light into the lens. It has also been proposed, instead of a large standing screen, as just explained, to have a small one, only a few inches from the lens, and attached to the camera itself, capable also of being regulated in distance and position.

These last methods are rather exceptional; the use of the tissue paper fastened over openings in wooden blocks or on metal rings as above described is almost universal.

§ 9.—**Toning.**

After the prints are removed from the frame, they may either be thrown directly into water or may first be trimmed; the latter method is found preferable by those who operate on a large scale.

The prints are washed by placing them one by one in a pan

of water where they all lie for a short time. This water is to be repeatedly changed, and of course is to be saved, at least the two or three first washings. It is rich in silver, which is to be thrown down as chloride by common salt. A neglect to wash the prints sufficiently is liable to produce two evils, a yellowing of the whites in the toning bath and a difficulty in toning; these troubles may come separately or together. This is the case especially with the toning baths now commonly in use. Those toning baths into the composition of which sulphocyanide of ammonium or hyposulphite of sodium enters, do not present this difficulty, and although it is best to wash the prints before toning in them, it is not absolutely necessary, nor need it be so carefully done.

The principle of toning is the substitution of gold for silver in the print. If a washed print be simply thrown into a dilute solution of chloride of gold, it will tone, but the acidity of the solution will lead to a great reduction in the strength of the picture. It is, therefore, needful in some way to neutralize the acidity, which may be done with carbonate of sodium, carbonate of calcium, or certain salts that have an alkaline reaction, such as phosphate of sodium, acetate of sodium, or borate of sodium, each of which substances forms the foundation of various toning formulæ. The explanation of their action is this: the soda or other alkali present becomes converted into chloride, which enters into combination with the chloride of gold, forming, for example, in the case of soda, chloraurate of sodium. The acid previously in combination with the soda is set free, but being in all the above cases a weak acid (carbonic, phosphoric, acetic, boracic), is without injurious influence on the bath. In fact other combinations of alkali with weak acids may be substituted. The writer has obtained excellent results with *benzoate of potassium* which he some time since proposed for making the toning bath with, and which has been very favorably reported on by others. *Tungstate of sodium* has also been used with good effect. Certain acids have a reducing effect upon salts of gold; oxalates and formiates cannot be used for this reason. Citrate of sodium has been used and was highly recommended some years back, but is now little employed.

VARIOUS TONING FORMULÆ.[1]

Alkaline Carbonate Toning Bath.—To make this very popular bath the gold solution is simply rendered alkaline with bicarbonate of sodium; the following proportions may be used:—

Water	32 ounces.
Chloride of gold	1 to 3 grains.
Bicarbonate of sodium	5 grains.

Mix twenty-four hours before using.

The gold gradually tends to precipitate from this bath, whereby it becomes inactive. Some operators, after using, add just enough hydrochloric acid to make it turn litmus paper red, and then, before using again, add enough bicarbonate of sodium to cause it to turn red litmus paper blue. In this way it keeps indefinitely.

Calcio-chloride Toning Bath.—A solution of chloride of gold is made, one grain to each ounce of water, and a couple of grains of precipitated chalk to each ounce are added and shaken; next day it is ready for use, diluting each ounce with ten to twenty of water.

This bath tones much like the preceding; gives brown, purple-black, or black tones, and by overtoning, blue. Succeeds best with paper sensitized on neutral baths.

Acetate of Sodium Toning Baths.

Chloride of gold	10 grains.
Water	80 ounces.
Acetate of sodium	1 ounce.

This bath differs considerably from the foregoing. It will not give black tones, no matter how prolonged its action, but gives splendid warm purple shades that cannot be excelled and cannot be equalled by the common carbonate of sodium bath. It must be placed in a warm spot for some hours before using.

Benzoate Toning Bath.

Bicarbonate of sodium	5 grains.
Benzoic acid	10 "
Chloride of gold	1 grain.
Water	10 ounces.

Give warm tones similar to the preceding. This bath, originally proposed by myself, works satisfactorily and keeps very well.

[1] *It should be clearly understood* that in winter the baths must be made stronger, and must be gently warmed. This applies to all.

It acts, perhaps, a little more uniformly than the preceding. Instead of the benzoic acid and bicarb. sodium, an alkaline benzoate may be employed.

Although any of these, or of the following, can be used for almost any purpose, yet certain baths will always have uses for which they are specially adapted. Landscapes should be toned only with the acetate or the benzoate bath. Small heads, as, for example, card portraits, are best toned with the carbonate bath. Reproductions of engravings, needing a pure black, may be toned with the carbonate, but still better with the chloride of lime bath, to be presently described.

The following special formulæ have been adopted and published by experienced and successful photographers :—

Notman's Formula.

Water	210 ounces.
Acetate of sodium	1 ounce.
Bicarbonate of sodium	¾ "
Nitrate of uranium	16 grains.
Chloride of gold	12 "

Keep twenty-four hours before using. When about to use, add eight grains more gold, and continue to add according to the quantity of prints toned.[1]

Shepard's Formula.

Chloride of gold	4 grains.
Water	1 ounce.
Neutralize with powdered chalk.	
Chloride of lime	4 grains.

Let stand a few hours; pour the whole, including sediment, into twenty ounces water; shake well; let stand over night, and pour off the clear part.

After use, return to bottle, shake up, add gold in proportion to prints toned, and a grain of chloride of lime for every grain of chloride of gold, or thereabouts, keeping the bath smelling faintly but distinctly of chlorine.[2]

This bath gives a variety of good shades up to full black. In fact, a pure black seems to be obtained more easily with a chloride of lime bath like this, than with the other formulæ. The bath keeps in order for many months, always ready for use.

[1] Philada. Phot., III. 252. [2] Ibid., II. 109.

§ 10.—Toning and Fixing Baths.

It remains to speak of certain baths which effect at once the toning and fixing. These are made either with hyposulphite of sodium or sulphocyanide of ammonium.

Hyposulphite Fixing and Toning Bath.—If two ounces of hyposulphite of sodium be dissolved in eight ounces of hot water, a grain of chloride of gold previously neutralized with carbonate of sodium (ammonia or phosphate of sodium will not answer) be added *after the hyposulphite has dissolved and been stirred up*, we obtain a mixture which, after half an hour's standing, fixes the print, at the same time toning it to a rich purple black.

Great fault has been found with this mode of toning, and it is certainly less safe than the foregoing. If used a few hours after mixing, and if a very moderate number of prints be fixed in it, they are as permanent as those treated separately. But, after standing, or if more than a very moderate number of prints be fixed in it, these are sulphur-toned and speedily fade and turn yellow.

Good tones are more easily got by separate toning than by this bath, which often gives coppery tones when it is difficult to find a reason why.

Sulphocyanide Toning and Fixing Bath.—The writer believes that he was the first to show that a toning and fixing bath could be made with a sulphocyanide and chloride of gold. His experiments were made in 1865, and are referred to the British Journal for 1866, p. 460 and p. 508. A solution of sulphocyanide of ammonium mixed with chloride of gold is quite free from the objection of fading. But the prints must be left some time in a second and fresh bath of sulphocyanide, otherwise a silver compound remains in the paper, and eventually darkens.

To prepare this bath, I precipitate chloride of gold with a very few drops of ammonia, and redissolve with sulphocyanide of ammonium. This rose-colored solution, if used fresh, stains the lights rose-color. But if kept twenty-four hours, it becomes colorless, and then no longer stains the lights. Dr. Liesegang finds the addition of a little sal ammoniac very advantageous.

When toning baths lose their toning properties, there frequently remains gold in them which has passed to an inactive state.

This can be thrown down by making the bath acid with a little hydrochloric acid, and then adding a few drops of solution of sulphate of iron. The gold falls immediately as a brown powder, which may be collected and preserved.

§ 11.—Fixing the Prints.

After the toning is finished the print is passed through clean (but not necessarily distilled) water, and is thrown into the fixing bath.

Until lately, the substance exclusively used for fixing positives on paper has been hyposulphite of sodium. Within a year or two the sulphocyanide of ammonium has been proposed as a substitute on the ground that the prints were thereby secured from the injurious action of partly used hyposulphite, which causes fading.

When either chloride or nitrate of silver is added to a solution of hyposulphite of sodium, decomposition takes place with formation of tetrathionate of sodium,[1] an unstable substance which readily undergoes farther decompositions. Tetrathionate of sodium will itself tone a print very beautifully, entirely without the aid of gold; its toning action seems to depend upon the formation of sulphide of silver, an intensely black substance, so that this process may be likened to some extent to the blackening of a collodion picture with alkaline sulphide, with this difference, that the action of alkaline sulphide is far more powerful and extends to chloride and iodide of silver, which it blackens readily and intensely. Tetrathionate of sodium, or rather the hyposulphite bath containing this substance, will not do this, nor will it attack the albuminate of silver which remains to some extent all through the substance of the picture. The toning bath spares, therefore, the whites of the albumen print, which a solution of alkaline sulphide would turn brown.

The tendency to fade seems to be distinct from this production of sulphide, although it mostly accompanies it. The mere production of sulphide of silver could not cause fading, for sulphide of silver is a very permanent substance. This we see abundantly

[1] Tetrathionic acid S_4O_5 differs from hyposulphurous acid S_2O_2 in having one-fifth less oxygen.

proved in the case of negatives which have been treated first with solution of iodine and then with a bath of sulphide of potassium, and which have no disposition to fade, even by long keeping. The addition of three or four grains of bicarbonate of sodium to the ounce of fixing bath, is useful as checking somewhat the tendency to fade.

Sulphocyanide of ammonium was brought forward as replacing hyposulphite with great advantage, and as yielding very permanent prints.

Hyposulphite is generally used for fixing positives by dissolving it in four times its weight of water. When perfectly fresh, such a solution will fix a print, kept moving in it, perfectly in five minutes. It is observed, however, that as a general thing it would be quite unsafe to trust to such rapid action. Ten, twelve, or fifteen minutes is a good time; it may be extended to the latter amount in the case of deeply-printed positives, or the shorter time may suffice for lightly-printed ones, which might be too much weakened by a longer action of the fixer. Generally speaking, the print tends to gain in permanence by a prolongation of the action; some which the writer left for over an hour in a joint toning and fixing bath exhibited remarkable resistance to the destructive agencies of various tests which he applied to them.

No more important advice can be given to the photographer than *Do not spare the hyposulphite.* Even a fresh bath should not be used for too many prints, and a bath which has stood over night after using, should be *unhesitatingly* rejected, because the decomposition goes steadily on, and such a bath is in much worse condition the next day than it was at the end of the day of use.

It is always difficult to induce photographers to act upon correct principle as respects the toning bath, not merely on account of the expense of the gold solution (it requires a better toned print to withstand the action of the fixing bath when the latter is fresh and in right condition for the permanency of the print), but because it is easier to work with a decomposed fixing bath; so much so that ten years ago it was even recommended to start decomposition in the bath by substances purposely added. But the photographer who really desires to do justice to his work will not allow himself to be swayed by such considerations, and may be assured that with a little care he will obtain admirable tones that will resist the fresh hyposulphite and give prints that will not disgrace him by turning yellow and fading out.

§ 12.—Washing.

The subject of washing is one that demands the greatest care on the part of the photographer, and there is an almost positive certainty that unless it be done systematically and thoroughly, the prints, however carefully managed in other respects, will rapidly fade. To work thoroughly, the water must be used abundantly, and must be continually changed.

If prints be thrown into a tank and a stream of running water be made to flow into it for several hours, a few prints may be satisfactorily washed. But if the number be large, they will interfere with each other, and the washing will be more or less imperfect.

The simplest contrivance for obviating this difficulty is to have a plug in the bottom of the tank which can be removed from time to time and the tank emptied. Both the time of washing and the quantity of water necessary are in this way very much diminished, but care is necessary that the prints be not drawn into the orifice.

To obviate the necessity of attending to the washing and removing and replacing the plug, a siphon may be adapted to the tank, which will come into operation as soon as the water reaches a given height. Considerable care must be taken in the arrangement of the siphon to make it do its work regularly. To empty the tank the water must of course run out faster than it is supplied; the diameter of the siphon must therefore be larger than that of the supply pipe, especially as the water comes from the street mains under a stronger pressure than it runs off, and therefore it is supplied faster than the mere proportion between the pipes. This larger size of the siphon introduces this difficulty, that the water tends simply to drain off through it, instead of starting the action of the siphon and so emptying the tank.

The stream of water should, in all cases, be thrown against the side of the tank; this gives a rotary motion to the whole body of water and keeps the prints constantly moving, a most important consideration, and which should never be neglected. The flow of water through the siphon will be regulated as to rapidity by the difference between the length of its legs. The greater length given to the long leg, the more rapid the flow of the water, and the less danger of draining off without starting the siphon.

Other and more complicated plans for supplying the water have been proposed, such as carrying a pipe round the inside top edge, and piercing it with holes, so as to sprinkle the surface of the water with small jets. But unless these are so contrived as to send slanting streams and so keep up a rotary motion, this great advantage is lost.

An ingenious arrangement consists in dividing the tank into two parts by a compartment, underneath which and under the bottom of the box is placed a fulcrum on which the tank balances backward and forward with a see-saw motion. The compartment that is uppermost receives the stream of water till it reaches a certain height; it then rocks over, and the other side receives the water. Meantime the first side is emptying out, and when empty, rises again and again fills. In a narrow compartment or drawer under the tank and attached to it a quantity of bullets are placed loose. These roll from end to end, and by their weight prevent the end that is lowest from rising too soon.

In whatever way the photographer elects to wash his prints, he must satisfy himself that the work is done effectually. The mortification which must be experienced by those who have distributed handsome looking prints at finding them turn yellow and fade, cannot be otherwise than very great, and nothing has acted upon photography so unfavorably as the universally recognized uncertainty as to the durability of the most attractive productions.

There are several ways of testing whether hyposulphite is completely washed out. Two simple but not very accurate methods are the following:—

1. Touch the white of the print with a little weak solution of nitrate of silver. If a brownish mark is made, it is certain that the print is very imperfectly washed.

2. Touch the white of the print with a little *very* dilute solution of iodine in alcohol. A blue mark indicates that the print is pretty nearly free from hyposulphite. Before using this test it should be ascertained that the particular paper used is sized with starch. To fix this point, touch a piece of the paper before sen-

sitizing with a little very weak solution of iodine in alcohol, on the back. If no blue stain is produced, there is no starch in the sizing and this test cannot be used.

3. By far the best test is the following: Take a clean beaker, or even a two ounce vial, provide a small piece of white blotting paper, on which make some irregular marks with a glass rod dipped in weak solution of acetate of lead.

Fill the beaker or vial nearly full of water, add a few drops of sulphuric acid, and mix. Then put in a part of the print to be tested, several square inches at least, and drop in ten or twenty grains of granulated zinc and immediately cover the mouth with the blotting paper marked with acetate of lead, which must be still moist. Leave the whole for ten or twenty minutes. If the markings turn brown, it is a proof of insufficient washing. Prints that will stand this test may be considered as thoroughly washed, which cannot be said of (1) and (2), which are less exact.

It is necessary to be sure of the purity of the sulphuric acid and zinc employed, and the best way to accomplish this is to try the experiment *à blanc*, that is, go through it *without* the print to be tested. If then the markings become brown, it is a proof that the materials are impure. This preliminary trial entails very little trouble, as one may immediately proceed to test the print, adding it to the other materials, and, if necessary, a few drops more acid to keep up a very gentle escape of gas.

Where sulphocyanide of ammonium is used as a fixing agent, it is probable that a materially less amount of washing is sufficient. But care must be taken that the fixing has been effectual. This may be ascertained by covering one half of a print and exposing the other half to a bright sunlight for three or four hours, or better, a day. If any differences in the purity of the whites is perceptible in the two halves, the fixing has been insufficient.

§ 13.—**Finishing the Print.**

The fixed and washed print will next require to be trimmed and mounted.

When very large quantities of prints are trimmed, machines are made that cut them out of the required shape at a single blow. This method is peculiarly suited to portraits, especially card portraits. Landscape prints require more attention, and the trimming can often be so regulated as to improve the general effect.

An extremely convenient arrangement is to procure a thick plate of glass with its sides exactly at right angles to each other, and to rule on it with a diamond a number of lines parallel to the sides. Then resting the plate on the print, some one of these lines is kept parallel with a vertical or horizontal line of a building, the horizontal line of water, or in the absence of any of these, with the line of the horizon itself. Then a sharp blade is run round the edges.

Fig. 81.

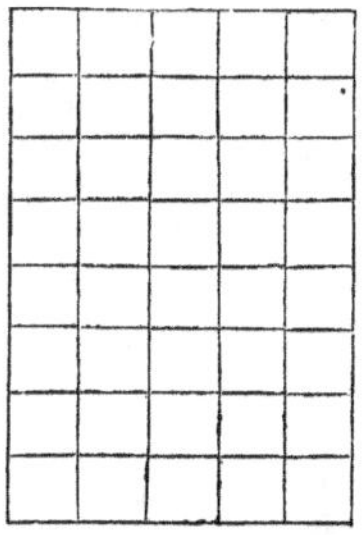

It is convenient to have one end of the plate dome-shaped. The edges should bevel a little, receding as they rise ftom the print; the ruling should be on the *under* side.[1]

Some operators use brass frames. These are very objectionable, as fine fragments are chopped off and ground into the paper, eventually making stains. Steel edges to glass plates are excellent, but brass edges to glass plates are bad.

The trimmed print is next to be attached to the mount with some adhesive substance. Glue is undoubtedly the best, but not the least troublesome, and is therefore less used than paste and gum.

Whatever is used should be applied freely, and a few minutes given to swell, otherwise the print cannot be applied smoothly and evenly to the mount.

Too little attention is paid to the quality of the pasteboard used for mounting. If this contain hyposulphite of sodium, used as "antichlor" by many papermakers, the eventual destruction of the print is almost certain, as in damp weather enough moisture penetrates to transfer the hyposulphite to the print. It has been affirmed that three-fourths of all the mounts in the market give indications of hyposulphite when tested carefully.

It is therefore no small protection to the print, to have a

[1] These plates are made and for sale in London, but, I believe, not here. Mr. B. Shoemaker, of this city, has made me one of 8×10, a larger size than is kept in London. I presume that when they are better known here, they will be kept by dealers.

lithographic "tint" printed on the board for mounting, and extending a short distance beyond the print all round. In this way the transfer of soluble ingredients from the mount to the print is rendered well-nigh impossible. As various adhesive preparations adhere much less well to thick "photographic tints" than to ordinary paper, it is generally necessary to use good glue, otherwise the prints readily peel off.

In damp weather, the drying of the adhesive application between the two hard surfaces proceeds slowly, and care must be taken not to pile up the prints too soon, or the evaporation may be checked, and the paste or other material may mould, and immediately stain the prints.

Rolling.—Prints after mounting are always rolled, usually in powerful presses between steel surfaces. This forces together the fibres of the paper, gives a hard fine surface, darkens the print a little, and improves its appearance materially. It is best done just before the print is dry after mounting.

Encaustic paste is prepared by dissolving white wax in essential oil of lavender, or any other volatile solvent, to a pasty consistency. This mixture well rubbed into a print with a tuft of flannel, adds considerably to the transparency of the shadows, and, in many cases, decidedly improves the picture. It has also a favorable influence upon the durability of the print. Salomon, whose prints are remarkably fine, gives the following formula:—

Pure virgin wax	5 ounces.
Gum elemi	44 grains.
Benzole	2 ounces.
Essence of lavender	3 "
Oil of spike	66 drops.

CHAPTER XIV.

FAILURES IN PHOTOGRAPHIC OPERATIONS.

THE beginner in photography will be very apt to find that, after proceeding reasonably well for a time, his success suddenly terminates for some reason quite undiscoverable to him. He appears to be proceeding exactly as before, yet he cannot get the same results. A very simple and useful course will be to change each of his materials in succession, collodion, bath, and developer, and so endeavor to detect the proximate source of the trouble. This plan does not always, however, succeed, for the new material substituted may have precisely the same fault as the old; it may not be in any respect bad or impure, but may be simply unsuitable to the other materials with which it is employed.

Not only the beginner, but even the experienced photographer will occasionally find that things go wrong; no one can claim entire immunity from photographic troubles. For these reasons the writer has endeavored to make this chapter a very complete one, believing that it will be very frequently referred to, and with advantage. He has collected the information here given partly from personal experience, but also very largely from other sources in various languages. For convenience of reference, it has been carefully classified under different heads:—

A. DEVELOPMENT.

I. *Failures Common to Negatives, Ambrotypes, and Ferrotypes*—

Sec. 1. Fogging.
" 2. Thinness of Film.
" 3. Irregularity of Film.
" 4. Transparent Mottling at Corners.
" 5. Defects in the Image.
" 6. Splitting of the Film.
" 7. Want of Sharpness.
" 8. Streaks.
" 9. Transparent Spots and Pin-holes.
" 10. Opaque Spots, Comets, &c.
" 11. Lines.
" 12. Stains.
" 13. Miscellaneous.

II. *Failures belonging especially to Negatives.*
III. *Failures belonging especially to Ambrotypes.*
IV. *Failures belonging especially to Paper Development.*

B. FIXING.

I. *Failures from Imperfect Fixing.*

C. SILVER PRINTING.

I. *Failures Common to Glass and Paper Work.*
II. *Failures Peculiar to Silver Printing on Paper.*
III. *Failures Peculiar to Collodio-Chloride Printing.*

A. DEVELOPMENT.

I. *Failures Common to Negatives, Ambrotypes, and Ferrotypes.*

§ 1.—Fogging.

Fogging is a trouble that affects different operators very variously: some are very frequently, others almost never affected by it. The learner may expect to be frequently troubled; the experienced operator will have learned how to avoid it, except, perhaps, when he works under unusual conditions, or with chemicals different from those which he habitually employs.

Before proceeding to the particular sources of fogging, some observations of a general nature may advantageously be made.

General Remarks.—When a case of fogging presents itself, a careful study of the appearance of the plate will often afford a clue to the source of the trouble.

A fogged plate may present a uniform sheet of blank fog all over, without a trace of a picture. Or an image may come out with more or less strength, but, after showing itself, may presently become covered with a dense deposit of silver. Or, finally, the fogging may be very slight, leaving all details of the image perfectly visible, but ruining it by veiling the deep shadows sufficiently to prevent them printing to a full rich black.

The above various cases are alike in this, that the action of the fogging is *uniform* all over the plate. We, therefore, presume that the trouble lies either in the chemicals, the light, or the atmosphere of the dark room, and, if we cannot get rid of the evil by the addition of a little iodine to the collodion, we must commence a series of systematic trials (see beyond), to detect the source of the trouble. We do not, however, in the above case, suspect the camera. For, if the camera leaks light, the effect of that light is invariably partial and irregular. The unequal contraction and expansion of the wood round the flange, into which the lenses are screwed, will often produce a crack; this will give a mass of fog somewhat denser in the middle, and shading off towards the ends of the plate. A hole in the bellows body will produce an irregular mass of fog on some part of the plate on which the light falls. If the dark slide does not fit tight, the fogging will mostly be at one end of the plate. A crack in the shutter will produce a bar of fog, lengthwise of the plate, and shading off on both its sides. Cracks in the woodwork will send in fan-like masses of light, and so on. These appearances will aid at once in the detection of the cause of the troubles (see also, beyond, "White Light").

Another very valuable distinction is drawn as follows:—

A *superficial fogging*, one that rests *on* the film and not *in* it, and can be rubbed off with the finger, is always attributable to the chemicals, never to exposure to white light, which last always produces an action in the interior of the film.

Therefore, if the fogging be internal and not superficial, it is most probably owing to intrusion of light; this cannot be affirmed with entire positiveness, but is the most likely cause, for faults in the bath, collodion, &c., most generally give rise to superficial fogging. That is, fog from chemicals is *generally* superficial; superficial fog is *always* from chemicals.

1. *Chemicals in Fault.*—Generally speaking, when fog shows itself, and when the presence of white light is not suspected, the first thing done is to treat the bath.

But, in all such cases, the first step should be invariably to try another collodion, or to add a little tincture of iodine to that in use. Iodine tends to make the bath slightly acid. Therefore, the addition of acid to the bath, or iodine to the collodion, is, in each case, a step in a somewhat similar direction. And it would at first seem more correct to add the acid to the bath, as that brings the bath at once to the requisite point of acidity, and stops there, whereas, by adding iodine to the collodion, every plate tends to render the bath more acid.

But, in practice, it is found that the results of the two treatments are very different. Sometimes a very little iodine will effect a cure when acid seems to have no effect. For example, the writer has seen a bath made of fused nitrate of silver absolutely refuse to give a clean picture, even when acidified beyond what is proper, and yet work excellently by adding a very little iodine to the collodion—a collodion which was not new, but had worked perfectly a month before, in cooler weather with a nearly neutral bath.

When a neutral nitrate has been used, acidulation should not be carried beyond one drop of nitric acid or twenty-five drops of No. 8 acetic acid to every fifteen ounces of bath, and this much is only allowable when the nitrate of silver was free from acid. When the acidifying has reached this point, if the picture is not clean, the remedy is most certainly needed in the collodion. And it must never be forgotten that these treatments with acid or with iodine are but necessary evils, and that the more nearly neutral the bath and collodion, the more rapid will be the work.

The bath, however, may have been alkaline, and may therefore need neutralizing and acidifying. This will be ascertained by introducing a piece of red litmus paper. Alkalinity may arise from having introduced an alkali intentionally, especially if ammonia have been added, previous to sunning. Bicarbonate of sodium renders a bath rather neutral than alkaline, and is the only substance that should ever be employed for removing an excess of acidity. Or alkali may have been carelessly introduced, when glasses cleaned with caustic soda or other alkali have been insufficiently washed before collodionizing.

The use of fused nitrate of silver, that has been kept too long in a state of fusion, or heated to too high a temperature, may tend to produce fog. Remedy: add very dilute nitric acid very cautiously, or try an older collodion.

An old bath, highly charged with impurities, may lead to fogging. As a palliative, add bicarbonate of sodium till a permanent precipitate falls, and then expose for several days to the sun. Filter, and acidify if necessary.

Sometimes an old bath will lead to fogging, not by reason of impurities, but simply by having become too weak by mere exhaustion of the silver. This will be more apt to happen with baths whose evaporation is checked by being kept covered. Remedy: add crystals or fused nitrate of silver.

Or the *collodion* may be in fault. A very new collodion, especially one containing little or no alkaline salt, particularly if used with a nearly neutral bath, will sometimes refuse to give clean, bright pictures.

In this case, especially if the collodion be very pale, it is well to add to it a little tincture of iodine, and so apply the remedy to it rather than to the bath. Or the admixture of a little old (but not too old) and more highly colored collodion will be found useful.

The *developer* may be in fault. If, when thrown upon the plate, it becomes almost immediately muddy, more acetic acid is wanted. Or, a developer that has hitherto worked well, may cease to do so in consequence of a change of weather and temperature.

It has been affirmed that *excess of acetic acid* may produce fogging.

If copper be used in the developer (sulphate of copper, blue vitriol), and the plate have been left in the bath for a time insufficient to convert all the soluble iodides into iodide of silver, *brown fog* may be produced by the formation of iodide of copper in the film.

Old specimens of pyrogallic acid used in developing or redeveloping, have been known to produce *blue fogging.*

2. *White light* will, of course, cause fogging. As already said, a careful examination of the appearance of the plate will generally indicate whether light has been admitted into the dark room, or has made its way into the camera, because, in the first case, its action extends uniformly over the whole plate, in the other it does not, but mostly appears in bars, fans, brushes, or long slanting rays, the positions of which will always aid in tracing out the cause, remembering that the more indistinct the boundary of the fog, the farther is probably the opening or leak from the plate.

A few systematic trials will always force out the source of the fault.

Develop a plate without exposure and without removing it from the dark room. If no tendency to fog appears, the fault was clearly in the camera or dark slide. Then sensitize a plate and carry it into the glass room in its dark slide. Leave it a minute, and develop it again without having exposed it or withdrawn the shutter. If it then fogs, the leak is in the dark slide; if not, then it must be in the camera.

Let us, on the other hand, suppose that the plate fogged, when developed, without having been removed at all from the dark-room. Then the fault is, either that white light gets into the dark-room, or the chemicals are in fault.

A simple way of deciding this, is to try a plate at night. Use only a candle or lamp, well protected with yellow glass. Sensitize a plate, lay it on a dark object, put a worthless negative over it, and carry it into another room, in which is a gaslight, turned on. Hold the plate a foot from the burner for fifteen seconds, taking care that the back is perfectly protected. Then carry and develop, by the light of a lamp or candle, behind yellow glass. If a clean picture comes out, it is a proof that white light gets into the dark-room in daytime. If it fogs still, when tried thus, the chemicals are wrong, and must be changed, one after another, until the wrong one is detected.

This simple but systematic and exhaustive search will invariably lead the operator straight to the source of his trouble.

If the foregoing examination shows the fault to be with the camera, it must be carefully overhauled. Carelessly made cameras are quite worthless, and a great many such are exposed for sale. The writer dislikes walnut, although this wood is so great a favorite, because it cracks so much, and prefers mahogany, and next to it, cherry. Look, therefore, carefully for cracks. Examine if the shutter works close in the dark-slide. Notice if a hole has been worn into the bellows body. But the commonest place to crack is the camera front, which often splits at the screws that fasten the flange in. When a crack once appears, do not trust to filling it up, but get a new front. A crack slowly widens, and so leaves a space between the edges and the filling. A crack may, however, be neatly mended by a good workman. The front is cut half way through at the crack, for half an inch each side, and a piece set in. Then if the crack widens it can do no harm. and another crack is not likely ever to form, as the tension that caused it has been relieved.

When a camera is used in the open air, it must invariably be covered with a thick cloth. Strong light, especially direct sunlight, will make its way through almost any camera, unless so protected.

Insufficient blackening of the interior of the camera may also lead to fogging.

3. *Sunlight falling directly upon the lens* may cause fogging, though this result does not necessarily follow.

4. *Atmospheric Causes.*—The sources of fogging may depend upon impurities in the air. These may be of several sorts.

A. *Chemical.*—Fumes of various sorts may cause fogging. Ammonia is especially to be avoided. See that the ammonia bottle has a well-fitting glass stopper—not a cork. Sulphuretted hydrogen, arising from exposure of solutions of sulphide of potassium, is even worse.

B. *Certain organic substances* have a tendency to cause fogging. The vapor of turpentine and of fresh paint. The smell of kerosene lamps in the dark-room does not seem to be hurtful, as might be supposed.

C. *Foulness in the air* is liable to cause fogging. Emanations from drains, cesspools, and the like, or any putrefying or decaying organic matter. Emanations from stables are always ammoniacal, and tend to fogging. It should be borne in mind, that immunity from these sources, at one time, is no proof that they may not be acting at another. *Dampness* acts very remarkably as a vehicle for odors, and emanations may rise in wet weather so as to cause fogging, when they would not at other times. Independently of this, the *state of the barometer* controls currents and movements of air remarkably. When the barometer is rising, a room will be supplied with air from channels quite different from those that act when the barometer is falling. Drafts of chimneys are always worse with a rising barometer. Whether *carbonic oxide*, the gas which flues are intended to carry away from fires, will cause fogging, the writer cannot state, but no one is justified in permitting this most dangerous gas to escape into apartments by defective flues. Its danger is not greatest when it asphyxiates, for then the evil is noticed in time, and remedies are applied. But if inhaled continually in small quantities, it causes diseases of the brain and spine. Leakage of illuminating gas may cause fogging.

5. *The Water.*—It is affirmed that the use of calcareous or ferruginous water may cause fogging.

6. *Errors of Manipulation.*—Under this head the following are to be classed:—

a. *Plate left too long in the bath.* This, especially in warm weather, is a fruitful cause of bad plates. When the plate is perfectly free from oiliness it is ready for removal.

b. *Too long a development*, rendered necessary by too short an exposure.

c. *Insufficient washing* off of the developer, so that enough remains to act.

d. *Considerable over-exposure with a large stop* will produce fogging, or rather an appearance closely resembling the effect of fog.

In the case of glass positives, fogging, when superficial, may be wiped off carefully with soft cotton-wool.

7. Finally, it may be remarked, that *excessive temperature* of the weather may so precipitate the action of the chemicals as to lead to fog. Therefore in very hot weather less iron and more acetic acid must be used, than for ordinary summer weather, or the collo-developer may be substituted.

§ 2.—Thinness of the Film.

A thin gray film—so appearing when removed from the sensitizing bath, may be caused by too strong a bath, which at first acts rapidly upon the film, but gradually diminishes its density. This is the case with *ordinary collodion.* With a collodion containing bromide only, intended for the dry process, thinness of the film results from *too weak* a bath.

A thin bluish film, with wet plates, indicates insufficient salting of the collodion, or insufficient time in the bath. With collodio-bromide plates, it indicates that the collodion has not stood long enough after sensitizing.

§ 3.—Irregularity of the Film.

Crapy Lines.—1. Too watery alcohol or ether.

It has been lately stated that when there is too much water in collodion, it may be removed by putting some pieces of gelatine into the collodion. This abstracts water, and swells up. There is no danger of any dissolving.

2. Neglect to rock the plate from side to side, after collodionizing. This fault is most apt to occur with a thick collodion. If this is the case, thin with equal parts alcohol and ether. Before deciding, however, that the collodion requires thinning, the operator, if not experienced, should endeavor to satisfy himself that the fault is not in his manipulation, for a good thick film is always desirable, and thinning should not be unnecessarily resorted to.

The larger the plate the thinner must be the collodion. A small plate can be managed with a collodion which will inevitably give crapy lines when used for a large one.

Structural Markings.—I do not know any better name to apply to what the French photographers call a *moutonné* film, from its resemblance to the sky when filled with litttle broken clouds, dotted over the sky like flocks of sheep (*ciel moutonné*). This appearance is generally local, not extending over the whole plate, and arises from immersing the plate too soon after the collodion is poured on—not waiting till it sets. Those parts of the plate that had not set properly will have this appearance, whilst the rest is all right. Such films must, of course, be wiped off.

Ridges.—1. Too much pyroxyline in collodion. 2. Too much alcohol and too little ether. (Both these defects are cured by adding a little ether.) 3. Excess of ether may, however, produce a similar effect. 4. Bad cotton, tending to gelatinize; or the collodion may have become too thick by the agency of bromide of cadmium. The action of this substance upon collodion is very remarkable, and varies extremely at different times.

Collodion that has thickened through the agency of bromide of cadmium, may be made to work by mixing with very fluid collodion. Much circumspection is, however, needed. The mixture should stand for several days, with occasional shaking, and then be carefully filtered.

Want of homogeneity in the collodion must result in the irregularity of density and streakiness. If different collodions be mixed without sufficient shaking; collodion that drains off from the plate is always denser, and sinks to the bottom if drained off into other collodion. By standing a long time, the mixed collodion may become homogeneous by diffusion, but it is unsafe to trust to this.

Again, suppose the drainings from the plates have been received, as they always should be, into a separate bottle, and that a quantity of such be filtered in a collodion filter, of which the bottom part is already partly filled with collodion, each drop will sink to the bottom, and the two collodions will remain quite separate. If poured out, and handled carelessly, there will be formed an irregular mixture which cannot diffuse itself with perfect regularity over glass plates.

Therefore, collodions either should be kept thoroughly separate, or, if mixed, should be mixed thoroughly by shaking, and then be either filtered in separate lots, or allowed to settle separately. Those curious to observe the action of collodions in mixing, can tinge one portion with a little rosaniline, by which means it can be distinguished in its movements.

§ 4.—Transparent Mottling at one Corner of the Plate.

This is owing to the heat of the fingers. It will be found that these marks always come at the corner by which the plate was held whilst being collodionized. Often if the plate be held up to the light before putting into the dark slide, these irregularities will be perfectly visible.

What is remarkable, is that, in the great majority of instances, the plate can be held without this result following. It appears to come only with certain temperatures and conditions of the atmosphere, and principally in cool weather. The remedy is to fold up a piece of paper, and keep it between the finger-ends and the bottom of the plate. In fact, this sort of marking is so great an annoyance where it comes, and so irregular in its coming, that it is a good plan always to use the paper: it is little trouble, and the cure is perfect.

In making dry plates this precaution should never be neglected.

§ 5.—Defects in the Image.

Image strong but coarse. Too much pyroxyline.

Image fine but weak. Too little pyroxyline.

Too Much Contrast.—1. Under exposure followed by over-development. 2. Too little pyroxyline in the collodion. 3. Too much iodide. 4. Too much bromide (over one-half) produces the same fault, and not, as has been hitherto erroneously maintained, too little contrast. 5. Acidity of collodion. 6. Use of old, red collodion. 7. It has been said that alkalinity of collodion may also produce the result.

Too Little Contrast.—Over-exposure.

Too Much Vigor.—Powerful, slow printing negatives, requiring sunshine and long exposure to print, come with a thick, highly salted collodion, and rich nitrate bath. Such will need to print with a weak positive bath and sunlight.

Too Little Vigor.—Good negatives, except that they are thin yet very delicate and full of detail, are got with fluid collodion, lightly salted and sensitized in weak baths. Such will need a rich positive bath and printing in the shade.

This fault may arise from under or over-exposure, the effects of which are, however, different. In the under-exposed image, the least defective parts will be the high lights of the object, which will in general be good, and the worse lighted parts will be defective. Where the picture is over-exposed, the reverse will be the case. Generally speaking, in an under-exposed picture, especially after redevelopment, the contrasts will be too great. An over-exposed picture will be gray and feeble, and deficient in contrast.

Weakness may also arise from exhaustion of the bath, in which case it must receive more nitrate of silver.

A very common course of weak images is the using of too much developer, and the flowing of it over the far edge of the plate. The operator should always bear in mind that the image is to be formed by the silver in the bath solution with which the collodion film is soaked. If he applies his developer so as to greatly dilute the bath solution, especially if he washes it off, the picture will necessarily be weak, and more silver must be supplied in the shape of redevelopment.

It should, therefore, be the study of the operator to use no more developer than is really necessary to cover the plate quickly and evenly with, and to let no more than he can help flow off the lower edge.

§ 6.—Splitting of the Film.

1. *Splitting in Sensitizing Bath.*—1. Immersing too soon in the bath, before the film is properly set. 2. Ill-cleaned, greasy, or damp glass. 3. Omitting to roughen the edges. 4. Too much alcohol in the collodion. 5. Too much salting. 6. Alcohol too watery. 7. Immersing the plate too roughly.

2. *Splitting in Washing.*—Bad quality of pyroxyline; also, the faults above enumerated may exert their influence in the washing as well as in the sensitizing.

3. *Splitting in Drying.*—This may also be the fault of the pyroxyline, but it is apt to result from the treatment which the

film has received. Much redevelopment with pyrogallic acid and silver is very apt to cause the film to split. Treatment with mercury for forcing (which see) also makes the film very tender. Remedy: coat the rest of the plates (when warned by one splitting) that are in danger, with a solution of gum in water, about thirty grains to the ounce, or with one of gelatine, about half as strong. This will not take the place of varnishing, which must be done as usual, unless but few copies are wanted and little value is attached to the plate.

Splitting in drying may also arise from an insufficient quantity of pyroxyline in the collodion, or from too large a proportion of ether. Too alkaline a collodion gives a weak film.

§ 7.—Want of Sharpness.

1. The necessity for having the sensitive film occupy the precise position of the ground glass, has been before dwelt on. Without the nicest attention to the perfect adjustment of the camera in this respect, perfect sharpness is impossible. Careless focussing may also have been done. And some lenses have no focus at all, but may be racked in and out for half an inch, without great variation, being really sharp nowhere. Such are, of course, worthless, and with a bad lens *nothing* can be accomplished.

2. *Camera Moving During the Exposure.*—This may arise from carelessness, or from the wind. A simple mode of avoiding the latter, consists in fastening a string to the under part of the tripod head which hangs down and ends with a loop reaching nearly to the ground. The foot placed in this loop and pressed forcibly down, holds the camera securely in its position, supposing always that the legs rest on a hard surface. On a yielding surface, the legs might sink during the exposure, enough at least to destroy the sharpness.

3. Want of coincidence between the chemical and visual foci.

4. *Blurring.*—The bright lights of a picture sometimes encroach on the neighboring shadows, in consequence of being reflected back from the inner surface of the glass. This can be avoided by painting the back with tincture of annatto, or any non-actinic color, or, more simply, by applying a piece of wet red paper to the back.

In preparing certain sorts of dry plates, the writer has shown the very great advantage that may be obtained by adding tincture of litmus, reddened by acetic acid to the preservative bath. The film is thus colored red, and needs no other protection against blurring.

§ 8.—**Streaks.**

There are two causes that are especially fruitful in streaks which may utterly ruin the negative.

1. *Removing too soon from the Negative Bath.*—When this has been done, oily looking branching lines may be seen at once, if the reflection of a light be caught on the surface (for this reason the light ought to be arranged with special reference to observing the surface of the plate as it is removed from the bath). These streaks will appear in the development.

2. *Repellent Action of the Film on the Developer.*—The developer for an old bath must always contain a certain amount of alcohol to keep up its relation with the bath solution. When the negative bath is charged with alcohol and ether, the developer may cease to mix quickly and evenly with the bath solution on the plate, and may collect on it in ridges; under these ridges the plate develops faster, and consequently they are represented by dark streaks in the image. One point is especially worthy of attention. Often the developer on the film is in a condition that it just barely holds together in an even film so long as the plate is level, ready to break into ridges the moment the plate is tilted up to look through, for the purpose of judging whether it is sufficiently developed. The moment this breaking up takes place, the development becomes unequal, and streaks are formed. Numbers of otherwise successful plates are spoiled in the development in this way, and the danger must constantly be borne in mind. Generally it may be said that (unless the operator is quite sure that his materials have no tendency to this defect) it is a safer way to let the iron development go as far as is judged safe, then *first* wash it off, and then hold up to the light and examine. Unless the picture flashes up very suddenly and quickly, it is safe to let the iron development do all it can, before washing. Then wash off; if the negative is found, on looking through it, to be of the right density, all is right. If not, redevelop

with pyrogallic acid, citric acid, and nitrate of silver, taking care not to pour on the solution till every atom of the pyrogallic acid is dissolved, or to keep the pyrogallic acid in solution.

When, in examining a negative, it is found that along the edge which was farthest from the operator during development there are streaks, especially branching streaks, the operator may be pretty sure that the fault arises from the cause here described. And, if he doubts it, let him watch the plate from the first application of the developer to its *complete* washing off, making sure that the film was unbroken and even for every second of time. On that negative the streaks will be absent, always supposing it was not removed too soon from the negative bath. (See 1.)

Where a great tendency exists in the negative bath to form these streaks, it is well to agitate the plate during immersion, from side to side, as well as up and down. In fact, this last is a very good practice for habitual adoption. A repellent action in the film may arise from the use of too strong alcohol and ether in the collodion. Such films dry rapidly, do not take the nitrate bath well, and repel the developer.

Blanchard has remarked that the keeping qualities of plates may be greatly increased by using a good proportion of bromide, two to two and a half grains to the ounce, and removing from the bath as soon as the oily lines disappear—further, hastening that time by keeping the plate constantly in motion from its first entrance into the bath. In this way some of the bromide may remain undecomposed by the silver bath, and, decomposition continuing after the removal from the bath, the concentration of the nitrate of silver and its consequent evils are prevented. He affirms that in this way he has been able to keep a plate for three hours. Such plates must be developed without sulphate of copper in the developer, or brown fogging will result.

3. *If the table* is allowed to be sloppy, it will follow that the bottoms of the developing vessels will become wet. When they are turned over in throwing the developer on the plate, there will be a tendency in any liquid adhering to the bottom, to run along the side and mix with the liquid poured out from the vessel upon the plate. Such a result can hardly fail to produce ugly stains.

4. *Inequalities of Temperature.*—It has been affirmed that when a material difference in the temperature of the bath and developer exists, this may be the cause of streaks.

5. *Streaks Descending more or less Perpendicularly from the Upper Part of the Plate.*—During exposure the bath solution drains down to the edge of the plate, and tends to flow thence upon the edge of the dark frame. When collected there in a drop, it easily rises again by capillary attraction as the film becomes drier by standing and mounts up the film again, so giving rise to a streak. Remedies: 1. Wipe out the dark slide. 2. Attach a piece of blotting board to the edge of the plate. 3. Drain better after removing from the bath and before placing in the dark slide.

Another source is changing the position of the plate after it has drained after removal from the sensitive bath. If the plate after draining be turned so that what was the bottom becomes a side, the change in the direction of the currents will produce streaks that infallibly ruin the negative.

Neglect to keep the dark slide always in one position till the plate is out of it will evidently produce the same result.

In a word, the plate after it has *once begun to drain*, must remain with the *same side down* till, by the completion of the development, danger is ended.

7. *Streaks along the Border, or working in from the Borders.*—1. If the film becomes loose at any part of the edge, hyposulphite may remain under it and escape complete removal by a short washing. If then the plate be reinforced with pyro and silver, brown streaks may result. 2. Redeveloper getting under the film.

§ 9.—Transparent Spots.

Pinholes.—Even to experienced photographers pinholes are a source of no small trouble. They consist of small transparent dots in the negative, and are occasioned by the presence of opaque matter adhering to the plate and interposing between the light and the plate. During the subsequent operations, these are removed, and the portion of iodide beneath having been sheltered from the light, dissolves out in the hyposulphite. These pinholes have been traced to the following sources :—

1. Dust in the bath—remedy, filtration.
2. Crystals of iodo-nitrate of silver floating in the bath.

Iodide of silver is capable of dissolving in nitrate of silver, and certain conditions of the bath appear greatly to favor this solution. A new bath may be pretty thoroughly saturated with iodide of silver and yet give no pinholes, whereas an old bath can at times scarcely be kept free from them, and, even if removed by appropriate treatment, they quickly return. The treatment is as follows:—

a. Add a few drops of solution of sal ammoniac and filter. This is a palliative; the pinholes mostly soon return.

b. Take *one-half* the bath, and pour *it* slowly *into* a quantity of water about its own bulk (do not reverse this), that is, if you have a thirty ounce bath, pour fifteen ounces of it into fifteen ounces of water and filter. Add the rest of the bath, without filtration, and then add, in summer thirty, in winter forty grains of nitrate of silver for each ounce of water added, unless the bath was at the time impoverished, in which case, of course, the addition must be larger. Sun it, and filter.

In some states of the bath this treatment will give effectual relief for a considerable time. But an old bath seems to acquire an increasing tendency to dissolve out the iodide of silver from the plate and precipitate it in these irritating crystals. When it is found that this tendency to recur is obstinate, it is better to

c. Evaporate the bath to dryness in a porcelain basin, and fuse it. The fused nitrate may be used as new (remembering that it contains alkaline nitrates), and if the fusing is perfectly done, the bath is as good as if made with new nitrate. Often it will *not* require acidulating, and acid should not be added till it is found that a trial plate is fogged without. Or, the bath may be placed amongst the silver residues, for reducing.

3. Another source has lately been brought forward as causing pinholes, viz: the presence of sulphuric acid, or sulphates, in the water. Trouble from this source is rare: no satisfactory mode has been brought forward for remedying it. *Fusing* is in this case ineffectual. The bath should be placed amongst the residues.

Large Clear or Hazy Spots.—1. When the developer is not swept along the upper edge as here recommended, but poured over the plate in the same manner as the collodion (as is practised by some operators), a transparent spot, half an inch or more in diameter, is very apt to be formed unless the operator rapidly moves the hand which pours on the developer. This spot is caused by the washing away of the bath solution, so that when development sets in, that part of the film is deficient in free nitrate of silver, and is proportionally weaker in effect. 2. Collodion poured too suddenly back into the vial, making an irregular film. 3. Bad cotton, which does not thoroughly dissolve in the fluid, and which has not been properly filtered. 4. Bad collodion, too thick, or with alcohol and ether badly proportioned (*i. e.*, alcohol should be ⅓ to ½, ether ½ to ⅔). 5. A new bath, not saturated with iodide of silver will corrode the first plates. 6. An over-strong bath may produce the like effect. 7. Keeping too long before developing may produce roundish hazy spots, especially when the bath is acidulated with nitric acid. Apparently this happens most easily in hot weather when the evaporation is most rapid. The *glycerine preservative* is advantageously kept on hand to meet such cases, as it keeps good for years, is always ready, and is simply applied to the ordinary sensitized plate.

As mentioned elsewhere, small transparent spots in a negative should always be touched out with opaque color. This causes them to print *white* spots in the print, which are easily retouched and brought up to the surrounding shade. But a transparent spot prints dead black, and this is much more difficult to manage and the blemish is never so well concealed.

Rings.—If the collodion bottle be *held too high above the plate* in collodionizing, rings may appear in the development.

§ 10.—**Comets and other Opaque Spots.**

The name *comet* very aptly designates those larger or smaller spots with tails, opaque in the negative and showing more or less white if printed, so that unless but a few prints are wanted, and the photographer is willing to touch out the comet's mark, the negative may generally be considered as worthless.

The heads of these comets mostly are towards the direction from which the developer came, and the tails pointing to the side on which it ran off. They may be caused by anything that forms reduction at some chance point. A fragment of undissolved pyrogallic acid, unfiltered solutions of sulphate of iron, organic dust on the plate, or in the sensitizing bath, or floating on its surface, any of these causes may produce comets. Their appearance may be taken as a plain indication that one or more of the solutions worked with wants filtering.

Or, suppose that hyposulphite is spilt about the room. The

grating of the feet on the floor or carpet grinds off dust, which is charged with hyposulphite. If the glass be rubbed immediately before using it becomes electrical, and every floating mote near it is drawn to it. These are imbedded in the collodion, and on plunging the plate in the bath they become centres of reduction. Sometimes these are even observable as dark spots on removing the plate from the bath. But if the proportion of hyposulphite is infinitesimal, they may escape attention on withdrawing the plate, and cause comets.

If this dust is about the room, it can scarcely but get into the dark slide, and then in moving, especially if roughly moved, it may be transferred to the plate and lead to comets.

Metallic hinges to the dark slide will sometimes grind off particles of metal which may be transferred to the plate. Each becomes a centre of reduction, and must lead to the formation of a spot of some sort, probably a comet.

Imperfectly filtered collodion may give rise to opaque spots. Also, neglect to wipe thoroughly the lip of the vessel from which the collodion is poured.

Where any cause of comets is present, a strong developer tends naturally to aggravate the evil. A rather acid developer is the easiest worked with, but does not give as fine results, viz: as much transparency of shadow. At the same time it diminishes the tendency somewhat to stains, and helps detail in high lights, such as white dresses in portraiture, or a strongly illuminated distance in landscapes; also fine lines in copying *line* engravings (not mezzotints, photographs, lithographs, or India ink drawings), for all of which a well balanced, *i. e.*, moderately acidified, developer is needed. Finally, the developer, if not kept in continual motion over the plate, may allow particles of metallic silver to fall, which presently become nuclei of development.

§ 11.—Lines.

1. *A pause*, however momentary, in the immersion of the plate produces a line, generally as thin as a hair, at the place where the pause took place. With a vertical bath, such a line is necessarily a straight one. With a horizontal bath the most curious curves and sinuous lines are seen. If the horizontal bath has

not been deep enough to cover the plate with a single wave, but pauses for a fraction of a second, the mark of that pause will inevitably appear in the development, and the negative is of course ruined. Remedy: with a vertical bath immerse the plate with perfect regularity. With a horizontal bath, have plenty of solution, raise the bath at one end, place the plate in at that end, raised so high that the solution leaves it, and then, at the same time, lower that end and let the other end of the plate fall gently in.

2. *Wavy Lines at Edges.*—Developer too small in quantity, or too slowly applied, especially where the plate has been kept some time after leaving the bath.

3. *Fine Parallel Vertical Lines in Direction of Dip.*—I have seen this result from sulphate of iron in the silver bath, thousands of such lines being thus produced.

4. *Two Images at once.*—Badly cleaned glass, on which there remains enough of a former image to come up under the developer.

5. *Crystallization through the Film of the Fixed Negative.*—Insufficient removal of hyposulphite by washing.

§ 12.—**Stains.**

Marbled Stains.—"Oyster-shell" stains of reduced silver, with a gray metallic surface and in curious curved and arabesque patterns occasionally make their appearance. They are exceedingly peculiar and unlike any other stains, and have occasioned much speculation and discussion. The best information that can be given respecting them is that they come from too long an interval between collodionizing and plunging into nitrate bath, too strong a developer, or too long a development, especially with sulphate of iron. But they may also arise from scum on the surface of the bath which is taken up by the plate and is subsequently developed by the action of the developer. According to some reliable photographers, iodide of ammonium in the collodion tends strongly to the formation of this species of stains. They usually, however, indicate too long an interval between collodionizing and development, most commonly between collodionizing and sensitizing. Remedy: Let the operations follow each other more rapidly. If this cannot be, use more bromide, agitate the plate the whole time that it is in the bath, and remove it from the bath the moment the oily lines disappear.

In very hot weather these stains will show themselves upon plates otherwise every way perfect, even with a bath quite sufficiently acidulated, and with a collodion containing iodine. The longer the interval between the operations, the larger and more numerous they are. They appear to depend upon the drying of the collodion film on the surface.

It is therefore advisable when such a tendency appears: 1. To carefully wipe out the dark slide with a wet cloth, in order superficially to wet the surface. 2. To place a piece of very thick moist blotting paper behind the plate. 3. To diminish the intervals before the development as much as possible. 4. If necessary, to roll the dark slide in a damp cloth.

Stains of this sort are very superficial, and, by dexterous manipulation, may often be entirely removed. The surface of the collodion is to be thoroughly wetted, best with alcohol, and a piece of *very* soft paper is well moistened, and a point of it carefully and repeatedly drawn over the stain. Unless the pressure is exceedingly gentle, the film gives way, but when care is taken, the stains disappear wonderfully. The writer has seen a third of the surface of a negative covered with these stains, and yet has succeeded in getting rid of them with care and patience. A kind of very thin brown paper, made of jute, is that which has been found to answer best. It becomes exceedingly tender when wet. The operation is best performed *after* fixing.

Brown Stains.—If it is desired to reinforce *after* fixing with hyposulphite, careful washing is necessary before the pyro and silver are applied; if traces of hypo remain in, or under the film, a brown stain of sulphide of silver makes its appearance the instant that the redeveloping solution is put on the plate.

These stains are also said to arise from using pyrogallic acid with too little acetic acid, when the water is hard (limestone water) and sometimes from white light admitted to the dark room. Redeveloper getting under the film will stain brown.

Irregular Markings are said, in some cases, to arise from the use of too strong alcohol and ether in the collodion. Mr. Terry mentions a case as occurring in a gallery in which not a perfect negative had been made in a week, and where the trouble was at once removed by adding a few drops of water to the collodion.

It had been made by the photographer himself; absolute alcohol was used instead of 95 per cent.[1]

§ 13.—Miscellaneous.

No Image at all.—In copying by a bad light, if too small a diaphragm be used, and a much too short exposure be given, with insensitive chemicals, the developer may fail to bring anything out. A very exceptional case.

Insensitiveness arises either from too acid a condition of the negative bath or from the use of too old acid, or dark collodion. If from the latter cause, it will be at once removed by substituting a collodion in good condition. And if the old collodion be not too defective, it may be used up by mixing with some that has been very newly prepared of thoroughly neutral materials, preferably with cadmium salts only, and which by the admixture of an older collodion will at once pass into good condition.

It is usually collodions made with alkalies that become insensitive. Cadmium collodions will keep in cool places for several years.

As to the proportions in which to mix new and old collodions, one part of old may be added to three, four, or five of new, according to circumstances. If the old collodion be quite dark, it will hardly be safe to add in larger proportion than five. Over-acidity of the bath is generally the result of tampering with it—as a general rule, after your bath is once rightly made, ascribe all troubles to anything else, and apply no remedies to it, until you are certain that it is in fault. If you have by mistake added too much acid in making it, you may add bicarbonate of soda very cautiously until a precipitate falls, filter and acidulate again.

3. *The Film after Cyanide Fixing Solution, shows a Bluish Color.*—Insufficient washing after development so that iron remains on the plate.

II. *Failures belonging especially to Negatives.*

1. *Too Little Density.*—1. Too weak a bath. 2. Too strong a bath. 3. Over-exposure. 4. Too short a development. A be-

[1] Really absolute alcohol is rarely to be met with in commerce. The difference between 95 per cent. alcohol and absolute, is over 25 drops of water to the fluid ounce, rather more than 5 drops to each hundred. It will thus appear how important it is to understand the exact strength of the materials used.

ginner is often so afraid of fogging that he cuts short the development when the negative has only reached the ambrotype stage. 5. Insufficient illumination.

2. *Excessive Density.*—1. Over-development, especially with under-exposure. 2. Too much salting.

3. *Solarization*, results from over-exposure. For a film exposed to light for a gradually increasing time gains in strength up to a maximum point, then remains stationary for an exceedingly short time (in case of iodide of silver), and then loses again in the over-exposed parts, showing little tendency to take a deposit under the developer. A great disposition to solarization in a collodion indicates an insufficiency of bromides; the tendency of bromides is greatly to prolong the stationary point just spoken of.

III. *Failures belonging especially to Ambrotypes.*

A. Want of detail in the lights. Over-exposure.

B. Want of detail in the shadows. Under-exposure.

C. Grayness of lights may arise from the use of hyposulphite, which gives a less brilliant picture than cyanide. Or the development may have been pushed too far.

D. Want of depth in the shadows. Insufficiency of acetic acid in developer.

E. Want of contrast may arise from over-exposure or too neutral a bath. Highly bromized collodions are less suitable than those made chiefly with iodides (see formula, article *Ambrotype.*)

IV. *Failures in Paper Development.*

Much that has been already said applies itself necessarily to working with paper, especially the remarks on *fogging*, and effects of *under* and *over-exposure.*

Harshness.—Too much iodide.

Stains are often ascribable to handling with not perfectly clean fingers. Indeed, so absorbent is paper, that almost any touch will become visible to the developed print, even with very clean fingers. The addition of bromide has a great tendency to check the staining; and in the case of positive printing by development, where extreme brevity of exposure is not important, it will be found best to develop on chloride of silver.

The use of very weak gallic acid in connection with a lead salt and acetic acid, as proposed by the writer, and explained elsewhere, exposes less to danger of stains than other modes of development.

Sunk-in Appearance.—All development tends to this effect; developed pictures are always less brilliant than sun-prints—the picture does not so much lie upon the surface. Nor is it easy to state the causes upon which a more or less sunk-in effect depends, though the quality of the paper appears to have very much to do with it. It is far more difficult to find a good paper for developing upon, than for ordinary silver printing. When the photographer finds paper that will yield a bright print by development, such paper should be carefully placed aside for this use, and an exact note should be made of the details of the method which was found to give good results with it.

B. FIXING.

Feathery Markings over the Plate.—Yellowish feathery markings are owing to insufficient fixing. These may appear at any part of the plate, most frequently, however, at the corner at which the collodion was poured off. At times a yellow shade is left over the whole plate; this indicates a still more imperfect fixing.

When this fault is not noticed until the plate has been washed and dried, particular care is necessary; for plates thrown into hyposulphite a second time are almost certain to become loose, or to split in some part of the operation, either in the fixing, or washing, or the drying; therefore, the best precaution is to take a six or eight grain solution of India-rubber in benzole, to pour out an ounce or two of it into a pan, and tilt the pan upward at one side, so that the solution may lie in the angle opposite. We thus have a pool the length of the pan, and about one-fourth of an inch deep in the middle. The four edges of the plate are to be plunged in this successively, giving each a full minute to allow the varnish to soak in, and also to allow the previous side to drain and dry before it becomes the top. The plate thus cemented fast at the edges, will stand the necessary treatment without difficulty. After re-fixing and washing, coat with gum-water or dilute albumen, dry and varnish.

C. SILVER PRINTING.

I. *Failures common to Glass and Paper.*

1. *Weak Gray Prints.*—Use of negatives destitute of light and shade, generally from over-exposure or bad manipulation. Also may arise from bad paper.

2. *Harsh Black and White, or Snowy Prints.*—Over-developed negatives. Strong negatives, which would give good prints with sunlight, may produce this fault in printing by diffuse light, especially if the light is weak, or the nitrate bath very rich.

3. *Whites turn yellow.*—Throwing the prints into the toning bath without thoroughly removing the nitrate of silver by washing, tends to yellowness of the whites. Also exposure of the sensitive surface to light. Old hyposulphite causes the same fault. Paper kept too long after sensitizing. Remedy: sugar in the nitrate bath, where it is intended to keep the paper more than a few hours.

4. *Prints weakening in the Toning Bath.*—Use of bath too soon after making. Insufficient printing.

5. *Prints refuse to tone.*—Toning bath badly made (see article on *Toning Baths*). Too acid or too weak a printing bath. Adulterated chloride of gold, or exhausted bath. Insufficient washing before immersion in the toning bath; the other extreme, excessive washing before toning, is said often to produce the same effect. Too cold a temperature; the bath generally works better at blood-heat.

6. *Prints lose too much intensity in fixing.*—Insufficient printing, but oftener too thin a negative; or may arise from too weak a positive bath.

7. *Toned and fixed print too red.*—Insufficient toning. Continue the toning till the redness is gone, when the print is held up to the light, and looked through, but avoid over toning.

8. *Fixed and toned print too blue.*—Over-toning.

9. *White Spots.*—Air-bubbles.

II. *Failures Peculiar to Silver Printing on Paper.*

Stains in the Print as it comes from the Frame.—1. Soiled fingers handling the paper. Too much care can never be taken in handling photographic paper. The sources of stains by soiled or moist fingers undoubtedly often *precede* the purchase; in this the professional photographer has a great advantage over the amateur, that his paper is purchased in quantities, and so undergoes far less fingering. Two corners of the sheet, whether whole or cut up, should at once be folded down at the commencement of operations, and no other part of the paper be touched from first to last.

2. A very common source of stains is the presence of very fine metallic particles in the paper, produced by the grating of the mill-machinery. These particles, however infinitesimal, become causes of reduction, and inevitably make stains.

3. Imperfect removal of hyposulphite used in bleaching.

4. Foreign substances of almost any sort, constituting invisible imperfections in the paper. These may act in several ways. They may diminish the penetrability of the paper locally. Such portions will take up less silver and print lighter than the rest. Often these foreign matters can be detected by holding the paper up to the light and observing its regularity.

5. Irregular distribution of resin or other sizing material through the paper. Resin easily combines with silver, making a sensitive compound. If the resin is not equally distributed, the quantity of silver compound will vary accordingly.

6. Reflected light from bright objects near the printing frame.

7. Printing by sunlight through a window frame, with irregularities in the glass.

8. Paper not well floated on the bath, or left on it an insufficient time for the equal absorption of nitrate, causing irregular marbled stains.

9. Impurities floating on the surface of the printing bath, taken up by the paper.

Spots appearing in the Toning.—Neglect to keep the prints moving. Where one print rests upon another, the action of the toning bath is slower, and a spot results. This is a very common source of trouble unless the necessity of care is borne steadily in view.

Spots in the Fixing. Adhesion of prints to each other in the bath, by neglect to continually move them.

It seems almost needless to say that any acid introduced into the fixing bath, either by accident or intentionally, leads to fading.

Prints have a sunk-in or mealy appearance.—Insufficient albumenizing. Bad paper. Old and foul printing bath. Too much salting. Old albumenized paper that has not been kept thoroughly dry, especially if chloride of sodium has been used for salting. Dampness causes the chloride, which should be wholly in the layer of albumen, to penetrate into the body of the paper.

Black Dot with a White Tail.—If the pin to which the sheet hung to dry, was put through a wet place, a local reduction follows with this result. Pins left for some hours in an old cyanide fixing bath become silvered, and are exempt from this trouble; silver may be dissolved in cyanide for the purpose.

Failures appearing only in the Toned and Fixed Print.—Troubled appearances in the substance of the paper. 1. If the chloride of silver has not been thoroughly, or rather has been very imperfectly removed, the print has a mottled look on holding up to the light, and as this remaining chloride of course darkens by continued exposure to light, the mottled appearance becomes with time more perceptible. This imperfect removal may arise from not leaving long enough in the hyposulphite bath, or from the exhaustion of the bath, or, possibly, by exposure to light before fixing. The first are the most probable causes. Remedy: use hyposulphite of sodium liberally; one pound to twelve or fifteen sheets is none too much. Make no more than you want, and begin each day afresh, under no circumstances using a bath a second day, even if but a single print was fixed in it the previous day.

2. Cases have been observed in which the prints were in perfect order when toned and fixed, and yet exhibited stains after the final washing. This has been found to arise from the use of *zinc* vessels, or a zinc bottom to the washing trough. The more thoroughly the vessel is cleaned, the worse the spots. Remedy: varnish thoroughly the whole surface of the zinc.

Over-contrast.—If necessary to print from a negative too harsh, the excess of contrast can be reduced by exposing the paper to light for a few seconds, or a minute, before placing it in the printing-frame.

Blurred Spots.—A bad frame may not have brought the paper home to the glass everywhere. Many printing frames are very defective in this, that they throw all the strain into the middle of the plate, thereby endangering the safety of the negative, and getting bad definition at the edges, which is apt to be attributed to a falling off in the power of the lens. Try your frames always with a piece of plain glass, fastening down the springs and pressing up the glass with the thumbs on various parts in succession, to find how the pressure produced by the springs is distributed. The old pattern, with bars at the back, is the best by far.

Blistering of the Albumen—1. Peculiarity of the albumen film which will not bear the sudden change from the fixing bath to pure water without endosmose. Remedy: let the prints lie for a short time in a weak intermediate bath of hyposulphite, between the regular fixing bath and the washing. 2. Acid washing after toning in an alkaline gold bath containing alkaline carbonates.

Fading of the Prints.—Insufficient washing. Old hyposulphite fixing baths. A solution of hyposulphite of sodium in water keeps perfectly. But if used, it should be rejected, and not employed on any subsequent day to that on which it just had prints thrown into it.

Black specks showing first after Mounting.—Appearances of this sort may almost invariably be traced to the agency of fine metallic particles. These, by the aid of atmospheric moisture, gradually act upon the print and produce the specks. They come—

1. By trimming the print upon a brass plate. The point of the knife detaches fine particles of metal, these are by the pressure forced into the print and soon make stains upon it. Glass or hard wood should be used to cut on.

2. By using a brass form to trim by. Particles are abraded and enter the print in the same way as before. Steel or glass forms should be used exclusively.

3. By using Bristol board for mounting on which borders or designs have been printed in gold or bronze. The designs are printed in varnish and the metallic powders are rubbed on; grains adhere elsewhere than on the design, and are not entirely removed in the subsequent brushing, but eventually destroy the print.

III. *Collodio-Chloride.*

Fading is said to be owing to the use of albumen as an understratum.

Bad Tones.—Citric acid in collodion. Substitute tartaric.

Sunk-in Prints.—The opal glass may not be suitable.

Splitting of Film.—Use of ground opal glass.

CHAPTER XV.

OUT-DOOR PHOTOGRAPHY WITH WET AND PRESERVED PLATES.

§ 1.—Wet Plates.

WHEN negatives are to be taken at a distance from the dark-room, we are obliged either to work with a tent, to use "preserved plates," or to resort to "dry plates," which last method will be considered in subsequent chapters.

Sometimes, indeed, we may prepare a plate by the wet method and carry it rapidly to some distance, expose, hasten back, and develop. If this can be done within twenty minutes, it will generally succeed. If thirty are required, success will sometimes be attained; if an hour, rarely. The following are the troubles which will be apt to show themselves:—

1. Fog.
2. Marbled stains.
3. Transparent or hazy spots of various sizes up to one-quarter of an inch diameter, generally nearly round.

Fogging is not a very common trouble, and seems to depend on newness of collodion, for which a riper must be substituted.

Marbled stains are very apt to come, especially in hot weather. After a careful study of this source of trouble the writer advises as follows: (see also remarks of Blanchard, *ante*, 242.)

1. Use a rather ripe collodion and immerse the plate into the sensitizing bath as soon after coating as possible. In hot weather just as soon as the drops cease to fall. If the film is slightly loosened by the bath at the corner from which the collodion was poured off, it will not be important.

2. Withdraw the plate as soon as the oily marks are gone.

3. Use a watery collodion. A collodion *too* watery will show crapy lines in the finished negative. Short of this the more water the better.

4. Apply thick wet blotting paper on the back. This must not be *too* wet, or it will make stains by running down the back of

the plate and getting round the bottom and irregularly diluting the liquid on the film.

The *hazy spots* are very annoying and troublesome when the exposure is very long; difficult by their size to touch out and ruining the picture if left in. They appear to arise from a concentration of the bath solution reacting upon the iodide of silver in the film. The presence of acid, especially of *nitric acid*, has seemed to the writer to increase this tendency. For plates that are to be kept, acetic acid is far better than nitric. The addition of a few grains of acetate of potash or soda with a little acetic acid, will change a bath from a nitric to an acetic bath. The proportion is roughly about a grain to five or six ounces of bath. Dissolve in half an ounce of water and pour slowly into the bath, stirring. The cloud of acetate of silver at first formed will speedily disappear.

This is the best information that can be given for the preservation of plates in their natural condition. It is greatly to be regretted that some method cannot be found for keeping them for ten or twelve hours with the full sensitiveness of the wet process. All preservative processes that are really practicable and that succeed easily, tend to diminish sensitiveness of the plate, and this is unquestionably a serious evil in every way. Whoever will discover a method by which plates can simply be held over without injury to them for half a day, will confer a great benefit upon photographers.

Tents and Boxes.—When the distance of the object makes it clearly impossible to carry a wet plate, we must either use a dry one, or else take the means with us for preparing wet plates on the spot.

In using a *tent* the operator works inside. With a *developing box* he passes his arms through sleeves provided with India-rubber rings, and watches his operations through yellow glass let into the front of the box. Of the two methods the former is the more satisfactory. With the box there is more danger of spilling hyposulphite and so exposing the delicate operations of photography to the effects of hyposulphite dust.

Of tents, probably Carbutt's is as convenient as any. A still more convenient mode of operating is with a *van*, either altered or built for the purpose. An exceedingly convenient arrangement has been made by altering an old barouche, the front part being arranged with an operating table and racks for bottles, the photographer sitting on the back seat to sensitize and develop.

The tripod itself may be made the support of a tent by simply stretching an ample black cloth over it, and kneeling or sitting on a block, stone, or stool. A piece of yellow muslin set in, lets in light to work by, and water is introduced from a vessel outside by a flexible tube.

§ 2.—Instantaneous Photography.

When objects in motion are to be photographed it becomes necessary that the exposure should be so reduced that the movement shall be inappreciable. To these exposures the name of "instantaneous" has been applied, although they are in many cases reduced to a small fraction of a second. Various contrivances have been devised for effecting them. The most usual and one of the best is to have a slide attached to the camera front, capable of moving up and down in a groove. In its centre is a circular opening of an inch or two in diameter. When the slide is up or down it covers the lens, but in descending it uncovers it for the space of time that the circular opening takes to pass the front of the lens.

The following are the conditions under which it is possible to take instantaneous views:

1. *The Chemicals.*—The bath should be thirty grains, new or nearly new, and nearly neutral. The collodion should be just old enough to work. The developer must contain no restraining acid and be simply an eighty grain solution of sulphate of iron. The development must be very brief, or such a developer will produce fog.

2. *The lens* must produce a strong bright image. The portrait lens may be used, à triplet, a Dallmeyer "rapid rectilinear," and instantaneous views have even been got with view lenses. The stop must be the largest that can be made to give an image of satisfactory character. As the images of short focus lenses are the brightest, it will be much easier to take instantaneous views with such.

3. *The subject* must not present difficulties too great. The illumination must be good everywhere, and there must be no strong contrasts. Objects in motion will be much more easily taken

when their line of movement is somewhat inclined. An object passing rapidly, directly in front of the camera, will be exceedingly difficult to catch successfully, it is, however, accomplished.

Mr. Chapman recommends after the iron development has done all that it can, to wash it off and to apply an alkaline development with pyrogallic acid (see Chap. XVI.); when this ceases to act, to finish with acid pyro and silver in the ordinary way.

§ 3.—Preserved Plates—The Glycerine Process.

The preserved plate stands intermediate between the wet and the dry. Of various preservative processes the glycerine and honey, first brought prominently forward by Mr. W. H. Harrison, is the best. A plate coated and sensitized as usual is plunged without previous washing into a bath prepared as follows:—

Price's glycerine	2 ounces.
Pure honey	2 "
Ordinary bath solution	2 "
Water	2 "
Glacial acetic acid	8 drops.

These are well shaken up and set in the sun for a few hours, or still better, a day, then half an ounce of kaolin is added, well shaken up, and the whole, after standing for a day, is filtered into a bottle. A large funnel with a filter in it is left permanently in the neck of the bottle. When wanted for use a sufficient quantity is to be poured into a pan. After using it, it is poured back into the funnel; it is a saving of trouble to have the funnel large enough to carry the whole at once; the mixture is then always through and ready for next day. The glycerine keeps the filter moist and ready to filter well and rapidly.

The sensitive bath is a common acetic bath, a bath acidulated with nitric acid does not work well. The usual formula for the glycerine preservative does not include the acetic acid as above, but the writer has found a marked advantage from adding it.

As above directed, the preservative bath contains about eight grains of nitrate of silver to the ounce. By use it becomes continually richer in silver, and thereby deteriorated—from eight to ten grains is its proper dose. Therefore we must add glycerine and honey, and if necessary a little water from time to time to maintain a correct proportion. After such addition it must invariably be sunned and shaken up with kaolin again.

The *development* of these plates takes place in the ordinary way with an iron developer, or with a pyrogallic one. In the former case, an exposure about three times as long as for wet collodion is proper. With a pyrogallic development a longer exposure is needed; this mode is preferred by Mr. Harrison, as allowing of more latitude in exposure. The writer's trials have worked best with iron development; for this purpose he does not like the plain iron developer so much as the sugar developer. (See p. 132.) The development is generally best done in a pan. The edges sometimes become a little dry, especially if the plate has been kept six to twelve hours; and then these do not take the developer evenly, and the edges may be defective even when all the rest of the plate is good, unless developed in a pan. A red transparent sky indicates over-exposure.

The deposit in the glycerine film is very fine; it seems to lose more in fixing than common wet plates; on the other hand, the deposit is rather less actinic and more opaque to light. The negatives print well. There is no disposition ever seen to detaching of the film, and no under-stratum is required.

The principal difficulty with this process lies in a tendency to harshness; not that this invariably is present—on the contrary, harmonious and soft negatives are often obtained. But shaded foliage presents great difficulties; often the details cannot be forced out, and black masses appear in the positive print; also bright distances are apt to be not well rendered, but become too opaque. Well-lighted views, presenting no excessive contrasts, are very well rendered by this process; it may be said that for such it is equal to the wet. Filtration before each using is necessary.

CHAPTER XVI.

DRY PLATE PHOTOGRAPHY—MANIPULATIONS COMMON TO ALL PROCESSES.

§ 1.—General Remarks.

THE prejudice which for a long time has existed against dry plates is steadily diminishing. It affirmed these objections, that dry plates were uncertain; that they yielded results inferior to the wet process; that they were very troublesome to prepare.

The sources of uncertainty in dry plate work have, to a large extent, gradually yielded to patient study. The results, in the hands of intelligent and careful photographers, have proved very satisfactory. With respect to trouble of preparation, the writer has devoted many months of continued study to the perfection of one of the processes—the collodio-bromide, and has succeeded in putting it into a shape which costs actually no more trouble to prepare than wet plates. It is certain that we have now a variety of dry processes, all capable of yielding excellent results. Before proceeding to the consideration of the separate methods it will be convenient to describe certain details of a general nature, namely, the Preparation of the glass, Drying the plates, Care of them when dry, Alkaline and acid development.

§ 2.—Preparation of the Glass.

In the selection of glass the photographer is advised to use new glass only, unless he means to coat the entire surface with a substratum; and this for two reasons, first, because the marring of a plate that has been carried many miles by a stain resulting from imperfect cleaning is so serious an annoyance; second, because the more continued development necessary for a dry plate has more tendency to evoke latent stains than in wet process. For the same reason, glass with stained surfaces, such as is sometimes found in the market, should be carefully rejected. Glass which has been packed in hay or straw should also be avoided, or the photographer may find the marks of the straw stains develop in his skies. The dry plates (and this is one of their advantages) do not, generally, give opaque skies; however, any imperfection in the work is most apt to show itself in the flat tint of the sky. Photographic glass, as delivered by the dealer, should always be packed with nothing between the plates, and nothing should ever be placed between plates of cleaned glass but pure white blotting-paper.

We next come to the preparation of the plates for receiving collodion. The tendency of drying and wetting collodion films is to detach them from the glass, and the extent of this tendency varies in different processes very much. In the *Coffee Dry Process*, for example, of Col. Baratti, there is very little tendency of the film to slip; in some others very much more. But, as even in the coffee process the films will occasionally get loose, it is better *always* to apply the protection. It is not much trouble—in fact so little, that supposing that without it one plate in ten only would be lost, the trouble of applying it to the other nine would be fully compensated by the saving of the tenth. And in most dry processes it is indispensable. The two best protectors are *albumen* and *India-rubber dissolved in benzene;* either is all that could be desired. There are two ways of applying—*edging*, and *covering the whole plate.* In the writer's opinion, where the whole plate is to be covered, albumen is the better—India-rubber for edging. These modes will be so described, but the reader will bear in mind that there is no objection to reversing the system if preferred.

Edging with India-rubber.—To prepare the solution, take the freshest, cleanest, pure India-rubber (not the vulcanized, but the pure gum). It is best to get a solid piece rather than the sheet, and the softer the better. Cut it into thin slices, and cut these up into shreds. Place an ounce of this in twenty-four ounces of good benzene. As very much depends upon the benzene, it is best to get it of the manufacturers of aniline colors.[1] The smell of really good benzene is much less offensive than that of the

[1] Kurlbaum, or Poizat & Co., of this city, are recommended. True benzene, that made from coal tar, is necessary; that made from petroleum does not answer; this, and the use of impure gum, explains the difficulty often encountered in making this most useful preparation.

impurer sorts; but its quality is still more important in connection with its solvent powers. If the benzene be of good quality, in twenty-four hours the gum will have swelled up enormously; shaking will then disaggregate it a good deal; after which, if the bottle be stood in warm water, or placed near a hot-air flue for half an hour, solution will be complete. If the operator finds any serious difficulty, he had better pour off the benzene, and moisten the gum with half an ounce of chloroform; let this act for a day or two, and then add the benzene. (The writer has not found this needful.) For use this solution may be diluted with four times its bulk of benzene.

If this solution is to be used for edging only, it need not be filtered, but simply left for two or three days to settle, and be then decanted; but if the whole plate is to be covered, it is necessary to filter it through paper, which is troublesome—for which reason the writer advises albumen when the whole plate is to be covered.

Edging is, however, in all cases an ample, in fact, an invaluable protection. It is rapidly and easily done in the following way: Take a stout glass rod, ten inches long, and a medium sized camel's hair pencil (the hair part should be not over half an inch long, and one-eighth thick), and tie it with cord to the piece of glass, so that it will lie flat against the glass, with its point half an inch from one end. Put enough of the India-rubber solution into a wide-mouthed bottle to rise to and moisten the brush. Run the pencil round the glass plate, keeping the side of the rod against the edge of the plate; and the brush will give, without trouble, a neat and regular edging from one-eighth to three-sixteenths of an inch wide, according to the pressure applied. The width of the edging should be regulated a little according to the size of the plate, three-sixteenths for a four-fourth plate. The brush must be re-dipped in the solution for each side, if the plate be larger than four-fourth, otherwise the film of rubber left will be too thin. In three or four minutes the edging will be sufficiently dry to proceed to collodionize; if this small interval be not allowed, the coating cannot be so well done.

Plates may be edged *after* they are sensitized and dried, or immediately before developing; but it is exactly as much trouble to adopt these latter plans, and the protection is *far* inferior; the adhesion of the film is much better when the India-rubber is applied directly to the glass.

There is another method of applying the edging, which is ingenious. Tilt up one side of a porcelain pan about an inch, and pour into it enough rubber solution to lie in the lower corner about three-sixteenths of an inch deep. Rest the edges of the plate, one after another, in this, which produces a band such as desired.

Having used these methods, the writer finds the first the least trouble, as the bottle is always ready for use at the instant. In one case, however, the latter method is decidedly better. If the photographer has prepared his dry plates without any protection, and, after beginning his development, finds his films slip, he will wish to save those that have not yet been moistened. In this case the immersion of the edge seems to protect the plate better than the application of the brush, because of the abundant quantity of liquid afforded for soaking through the film, and attaching it to the glass.

Covering with Albumen.—After this manipulation has been acquired, it may be done with surprising ease and rapidity; but a little practice is required to do it right. First remove any bubbles from the surface of the albumen (repeat this between every plate) with a pointed piece of blotting-paper. Brush off the surface of the glass with a wide soft brush. Pour on the glass a sufficient quantity, avoiding to attempt it with too little; hold down the lip of the vessel as close as possible to the glass to avoid making bubbles. When a sufficient pool has been made, take a thick clean glass rod, four or five inches longer than the width of the plate. Resting this flat on the surface of the pool, carry the liquid up to the far edge and corners; next bring it down to the near edge. Send the bulk of the liquid back to the far edge; rest the rod on the plate up by the far edge, and then bring it down with one clean, slow, steady sweep to the near edge, carrying the bulk of the liquid with it. Drain off at the near right hand corner, precisely as in varnishing.

Other modes may be used for covering the plate; the above is that which the writer employs; it is easy when once mastered, and gives a particularly good, smooth surface, free from those annoying lines that form in drying when the plate is not evenly covered. After draining into a separate vessel, the plate is reared up to dry in a place thoroughly free from dust; and the pourings off are, at the end of the work, to be filtered back into the bottle. This precaution is, however, scarcely necessary when the albumen is used as here proposed, merely as a substratum, though very necessary for albumen which is itself to carry the sensitive preparation. The albumen is prepared by beating it up to a snow, and after allowing it to subside for some hours, diluting the liquid which collects with five times its bulk of water. The edging with the rubber solution is the least trouble, and the writer has never seen a single case in which its protection failed.

§ 3.—Drying the Plates.

The plates, when coated and sensitized by any of the processes subsequently to be described, will require to be thoroughly dried, which is accomplished in either of three ways—by the Drying-Box, by Heat, or by Spontaneous Drying.

In *drying in a box* there is the great advantage of perfect freedom from dust and other accident. But as in a close box the desiccation would be extremely slow if not artificially aided, it becomes necessary to put into the box some substance capable of absorbing moisture, which shall keep the air perfectly dry, and thus dry the plates quickly and perfectly. This has generally been effected by the aid of chloride of calcium, which is placed in lumps in a dish at the bottom. But the writer has introduced, and himself invariably uses, the far preferable plan of *drying by sulphuric acid.* A pan, capable of holding from one-half to three-fourths of a pound of acid, is introduced into the bottom of the box, and keeps the air thoroughly dry until it is so weakened as to lose its effect. It will work well until it has absorbed about twice its own bulk of water; and in view of this expansion, the vessel should be selected capable of containing three times and more the bulk of the acid placed in it, otherwise the acid must necessarily in time overflow.

The advantage of this system of the writer lies in that the chloride of calcium when liquefied by the moisture absorbed, must be dried, first over the stove, and then be melted in a crucible or pot. This troublesome operation has greatly restricted the use of the drying-box, and has sent operators to the other methods. But this difficulty is completely removed by the use of sulphuric acid, which is so extremely cheap that, even if thrown away, the cost would be insignificant. No waste is, however, encountered; for the dilute acid, as it comes from the box, is in excellent condition for mixing with a saturated solution of bichromate of potash for cleaning plates. The advantages are sufficiently evident.

As any acid fumes are destructive to dry plates, it may be asked how this powerful acid can be employed with impunity. The explanation lies in its entire absence of disposition to rise in fumes. The writer carefully tested the effect of this method upon the sensitiveness of dry plates by preparing two exactly alike (by the coffee dry process), and drying one in the box, the other in a dark closet, with the aid of hot water. With equal exposure and identical development the advantage was on the side of the plate dried over sulphuric acid. The drying is more perfect, and the slightest trace of dampness takes from the sensibility of a dry plate.

As respects the arrangement of any drying-box, there is a certain amount of difficulty. The writer always uses a form the idea of which he partly took from M. Davanne. The box has two glass tubes which run from end to end parallel, about three inches apart, and about six inches from bottom. About four inches from the top twelve similar tubes, parallel, and about two inches apart, run crosswise to the first; like the first their position is horizontal, but they run from side to side, instead of from end to end. If, now, a plate of glass be let down so that one of its corners passes between and rests on the two lower tubes, its back can rest on one of the upper tubes. Of course, as many can be put in at once as the number of the upper tubes—in this case, twelve. It is easy to regulate the whole so that it will answer for several sizes; the writer's accommodates half size, whole size, and 8 by 10. The advantage of this plan lies in its perfect cleanness; the plates never touch any absorbent substance with wood or paper, which can give to one plate what it absorbs from another. They touch nothing whatever but the glass rods, which can at intervals be wiped clean with a wet cloth.

At the bottom of the box is a long, narrow door for sliding in the pan of sulphuric acid; a cup will not do. There must be a considerable surface of acid exposed—at least so it is more effective. A piece of black muslin is tacked upon this door so as to hang in front of it when shut. The cover of the box must not be hinged, but simply slide over the top, thus excluding light effectively. The whole inside must be blackened; this is easily done by mixing up fine lampblack with about half its bulk of powdered gum-arabic, into a thick paste with water, and rubbing on with a piece of flannel. A good proportion of gum prevents the lampblack from detaching itself as dust, to the detriment of the plates.

Tubes are used simply because they are stronger than rods, and lighter; can be used about five-eighths to three-fourths of an inch diameter. After they are all in place, a strip of wood is nailed permanently over the ends of the holes, through which the tubes are inserted, to keep the light out. A well-constructed box of this kind can be left in a light room without the plates suffering, though, as a precaution, I always throw a cloth over it.

A simpler but less compact mode of making a drying box is simply to take an empty box, set a pan of acid in the bottom and a range of empty tumblers round the sides. In each tumbler set the lower corner of a plate, and let the upper rest against the side of the box. Cover up securely from light and from change of atmosphere.

Drying spontaneously is effected in a dark cupboard, or even on shelves in a dark room. Drain the plates for a minute or two, not more, on blotting paper, and then set them in the cupboard, each with the lower end resting in an empty tumbler, its upper corner against the wall. Some allow the plates to dry on blotting paper; this has the disadvantage of keeping the lower end very long in drying, and so risking unequal action in development.

Drying by Heat may be effected either by filling a very large bottle with hot water and rearing up the plates against it, or by filling a wedge-shaped tin vessel with hot water and laying a plate against each side. Such a vessel is easily made by any tinman; it should have an orifice at one end of the top which may either be closed by a brass screw lid or by a common cork. The edges on the bottom should turn up a little. Another method is to have a piece of tin bent across the middle and its edges turned up. A leg is made at each corner, or the whole supported in any convenient way. A Bunsen's burner, lamp, or candle is set underneath, at a considerable distance below the tent-shaped piece, which is thus kept warm by it. The writer cannot speak of this method from personal experience, having always used the others, and preferably the dark box. It has, however, been well spoken of.

Whatever method be used, *the drying must be thorough and perfectly regular.* If it be stopped, and the plates be examined, a line may be expected in the developed negative at the place to which the drying had advanced at the time of the disturbance. For this reason the mode of drying must never be changed whilst it is in progress. A plate that has begun to dry spontaneously must never be hurried by applying heat, nor must one that has been heated be removed from its place till dry. *Regularity of drying* is a need so absolute that any carelessness may be expected to ruin the plate. In this respect drying in a box, after the exact manner here recommended, is extremely satisfactory, and drying lines on the plates are things unknown.

§ 4.—Care of Plates when Dry.

A great barrier in the way of dry plate work has been its reputed uncertainty. As knowledge has advanced the sources of this uncertainty have become much better understood.

A dry plate, as taken ready for use from the drying box, is essentially and necessarily a very delicate thing. Well prepared and well preserved, the time for which it will retain its condition of sensitiveness is very remarkable. Coffee dry plates have been preserved, according to Col. Baratti whose process is now much used, for periods of from one to two years, and although requiring of course a longer exposure, were in excellent condition. Collodio-bromide plates have crossed the Atlantic uninjured; some of the Liverpool Dry Plate Company's sent me by Mr. Mawdsley were found in good order months after their preparation and after their voyage. These came packed in light boxes grooved like ordinary boxes for storing negatives, which boxes were fastened up in India-rubber paper. Collodio-bromide plate prepared by the writer with the aid of a lead bath, as hereafter to be described, had lost nothing of their sensitiveness or clearness of development when tried at the end of five months.

The causes of injury to dry plates are—1st. Insufficient protection from light. 2d. Exposure to damp air. 3d. Exposure to injurious fumes.

Exposure to light must of course be carefully guarded against, remembering that extremely faint light may after a long period produce a deterioration which would not happen in a few hours —so that boxes, slides and cases for keeping plates for days or weeks must be far more carefully protected than where the plates are to be used in a few hours.

Exposure to dampness seems to be specially injurious. M. de Constant, of Lausanne, in a written communication to the author, observes that after various disappointments, for which he blamed the supposed uncertainty of the process, he discovered that the true cause was the formation of slight dews on the plates by damp air.

It is a law that when a colder body is brought into a warmer atmosphere, saturated or nearly so with moisture (not necessarily misty however) that a condensation takes place on the surface. If plates be taken from a cold cupboard into a warm room, a dew will very easily form on them. Or suppose that whilst a room is cool, warm damp air be let in, and that it penetrates into the closets or cases in which plates are kept, the dew will form not uniformly, but in myriads of little beads, and the plates are lost. The drying box is peculiarly safe in this respect, as the air that penetrates is dried as fast as it comes in—perhaps for the reason that because this method of drying the writer has personally had no unpleasant experience of his own in this direction.

Noxious Fumes.—Any reducing vapor or gas must destroy plates. Sulphuretted hydrogen, or any foul emanation from drains or water-closets, chemical vapors of many sorts, probably also carbonic oxide, the so called "gas" that comes from badly drawing stoves. Sulphurous acid would also destroy plates. Resinous wood used for drying boxes or for plate boxes, or freshly-varnished wood surfaces would be very suspicious.

It will be observed that all of these sources of trouble point amongst other things to the necessity of the complete exclusion of external influences. And this can, perhaps, in no way be better effected when plates are to be carried to any distance, and preserved for any time, than by enclosing the cases in thick brown or dark green or red paper, saturated with India rubber varnish. Where this cannot be procured commercially it might easily be made by the photographer himself. The joints of the paper must of course be pasted down with the varnish also.

§ 5.—**Ordinary, or Acid Development of Dry Plates.**

The common development of a dry plate is made with pyrogallic and acetic or citric acid, and closely resembles the development of a wet plate with the same materials.

There is one distinction, however, which it is very important to have well understood. Dry plate work tends to harshness, therefore the development must be so conducted as to favor softness and the bringing out of detail. This is best done by applying plain pyrogallic acid first dissolved in water, about one grain (some prefer two or three) to the ounce. Then a solution of nitrate of silver ten grains, citric acid fifteen grains, water one ounce, is added with extreme caution, a drop or two at a time.

The slower the development, the more cautiously the silver is added, the softer and better will be the negative. Only when a flat effect is feared, should the silver be added rapidly.

§ 6.—**Alkaline Development.**

Perhaps in the whole range of photography there is nothing so remarkable as the alkaline development. That the action of an alkali, unaided by silver, should be able to force out an image, and that, too, with even more power than the strongest silver developer, is one of those wonderful results which has been reached by patient investigation and intelligent experiment.

Mr. Henry T. Anthony, of New York, and Mr. Borda, of Philadelphia, deserve the largest share of the honor of this discovery, and Major Russell, of England, it is who has done most in utilizing it, in fixing its conditions, and putting it into its present most valuable shape. The late Mr. Glover and Mr. Leahy are also entitled to their share of credit for independent work in this direction, though in a less degree than the gentlemen previously named.

Mr. Anthony was the first to observe the extraordinary accelerating influence of ammonia both on plates dried without preservatives and on tannin plates. He communicated his results to Mr. Borda, who carried on Mr. Anthony's investigation, and ascertained that ammonia applied after exposure would *develop the image.* The result, however, was accompanied with some uncertainty. Mr. Glover traced out this uncertainty as depending on the more or less dryness of the plate, and remedied it by bringing the plate to a proper condition of dampness to be acted upon by the ammonia fumes. Mr. Leahy simplified the matter by substituting solution of ammonia for the fuming. Major Russell worked out the details with great accuracy, showed that alkaline solutions could be used advantageously with pyrogallic acid, and made the useful discovery that the action of the new developer could be controlled by the addition of solution of an alkaline bromide precisely in the same way that developments with silver were controlled by acid. He pointed out that just as the ammonia seemed to replace the silver (when both were used with pyrogallic acid) so the bromide of potassium might replace the acetic or citric acid. This property of bromide he did not find by blind trial, but sagaciously deduced it from his experiments, on the action of negative baths on bromide plates, in which he found that fogging was caused by immersion so long that all the soluble bromides in the film were decomposed. Clean plates, where bromides only were used in the collodion, could only be got by stopping the action of the bath *before* all the soluble bromides were decomposed. Reasoning back to the alkaline development he was led to add to it an alkaline bromide, and found its action precisely that which he had attributed to it in connection with the negative bath. This observation perfected the alkaline development, a mode of operation of infinite value to photography; perhaps in its present complete form it is entitled to a place alongside of the introduction of collodion.

Such, it is believed, is a perfectly just statement of a subject on which there has been much controversy, except on the part of Mr. Anthony and Mr. Borda, who seem to have never made any vindication of their claims. Whatever merit be ascribed to the other gentlemen, to them is undoubtedly due the discovery of the alkaline development. But by the labors of the other gentlemen that discovery was greatly increased in value.

The alkaline development consists essentially in evoking the latent image by an alkali; either carbonate of ammonium, or bicarbonate of sodium, or liquid ammonia may be employed.

The first is generally preferred, and will be that recommended here. The development is held in check by bromide of potassium.

The following formula is that which the writer employs, and has the advantage that equal quantities of each of the solutions are employed, whereby the trouble and the chances of mistake are diminished:—

Sol. 1.—Dissolve one-quarter of a pound of carbonate of ammonium in twenty ounces of tepid water.

Sol. 2.—In five ounces of alcohol dissolve three hundred grains of pyrogallic acid.

Sol. 3.—In twenty ounces of water, dissolve one ounce of bromide of potassium.

All these will need to be filtered. They keep well. As carbonate of ammonium is decomposed by hot water, tepid water will be best to use. Put the lumps of carbonate in a deep vessel, and barely cover with water. After standing some hours, with occasional shaking till saturated, pour off into the filter, and add more water. In this way the whole will be got into solution in the above quantity of water.

The developing mixture is obtained by adding half a drachm of each of the above solutions to six ounces of water. The plate must first be thoroughly wetted, and then the liquid is applied. Some pour it backwards and forwards on the plate, but the writer strongly recommends always to develop dry plates in pans, and to give much more time than can be allowed where the plates are developed in the hands. Levelling stands are far less convenient than pans.

In this mixture the plate is left till the detail is fully out. Half an hour is often needed, but if the light has been strong, much less time may be sufficient. If the plate has been underexposed, more may be required. When the detail is fully out, add twice as much carbonate of ammonium as at first used—that is, to six ounces of water let the second dose be one drachm. Intensity will soon come; if it does not, add half a drachm of the solution of pyrogallic acid, and give whatever time is necessary.

In this way the development is completely made with alkali; but it may be stopped when the detail is fully out, and be finished with solution of nitrate of silver, pyrogallic acid, and acetic or citric acid. This part of the process exactly resembles the ordinary redevelopment of a wet plate, except that, after washing off the alkaline developer, and before applying the redeveloping solution, the plate should be rinsed off with weak acetic acid, to ensure the perfect removal of the alkali; otherwise fogging may be expected. And if the alkaline developer be not washed off before the acetic acid is applied, bubbles of carbonic acid will form under the film, and detach it from the glass.

The advantage of the use of the alkaline development in either of the above forms lies in the greatly diminished exposure necessary.

The photographer, in undertaking a dry process, will do well to remember that although some may be worked with ordinary collodion, yet generally an old, ripe, red collodion should be used. The cotton should be of the intense powdery sort.

It was necessary, before passing to the description of individual processes, to state that which applied equally to all. Having done so, we shall now consider the special processes for producing dry plates.

It will be impossible, within the limits of this manual, to describe all the dry processes that have been proposed, or even successfully employed; the best that can be done is to give those that are the most general favorites.

Dry plates may be divided into two classes, viz., those in which the plate is collodionized in the ordinary manner, and then sensitized in a negative bath, and those in which the nitrate of silver is added to the collodion.

CHAPTER XVII.

DRY PROCESSES REQUIRING THE NEGATIVE BATH.[1]

§ 1.—The ordinary Tannin Process.

THIS process is here placed first, not by any means as being the best, but as being the first dry process that obtained any satisfactory measure of success.

The collodion for the tannin process should be made of intense cotton, not ordinary negative cotton; should be salted with a liberal supply of bromide (Formula 2, p. 124), and is best when a little reddened by age.

After sensitizing in an ordinary nitrate bath, it is well washed off with water, and then plunged into the following preservation bath:—

Tannin	150 grains.
Water	10 ounces.

Many prefer to add honey (in the proportion of about a quarter of an ounce) to the above solution.

After the application of the tannin solution, the plates are dried in any of the methods already described. Some operators wash the plates after tanninizing, and consider that their sensitiveness is thereby increased. Exposure eight times that of the wet.

Develop with plain pyrogallic acid, adding solution of nitrate of silver very cautiously, or the alkaline development may be applied to diminish the exposure.

A very pure and colorless solution of tannin is said to be obtained by dissolving six parts of tannin in twelve of hot distilled water, and, after cooling, one part of ether is to be added; after standing for a few hours, the solution is to be filtered, and is then ready for use.

Quassia has been lately recommended as a substitute for

[1] The photographer who is unfamiliar with dry plate work, is recommended to read the preceding chapter carefully before attempting any of these methods.

tannin: two hundred grains of quassia chips are to be extracted with a pint of boiling water; add half an ounce of honey and substitute for the tannin solution.

§ 2.—Russell's Tannin Process with Bromised Collodion.

This is the most rapid dry process that has yet been invented, and that by which the instantaneous pictures on dry plates can best be obtained. Its peculiarity lies in this, that the collodion contains bromide only and no iodide, and that the nitrate bath is made extremely strong.

Collodion:—

Ether	5 ounces, fluid.
Alcohol	5 " "
Bromide of cadmium	80 grains.
Negative cotton	45 "

It has been commonly said that almost any cotton will answer, but there is no doubt that an intense specimen is preferable. The collodion cannot be used till at least a fortnight after mixing, and improves for a month or two.

The bath should be of sixty-five to seventy or seventy-five grains of nitrate of silver to the ounce, with a drop of nitric acid to every three ounces of bath.

The essence of success with this process, as Major Russell determined after very many trials, lies in this, that a trace of bromide of cadmium must remain at the back of the film unconverted into bromide of silver. Therefore, collodionize a plate to begin with, and leave it in the bath until a clouding begins to show itself at the back of the film.

Note the exact time required for this, which will probably be somewhere between five and fifteen minutes; *reject the plate*, and leave in the rest one or two minutes *less* than the time at the expiration of which the cloudiness appeared on the first. The object is to leave the plate in nearly, but not quite, long enough for the appearance of that indication that the silver bath has acted clear through to the glass.

These plates are now to be thoroughly washed under a tap, or by placing them successively in four or five pans of water, and agitating well in each.

To eight ounces of albumen, add one ounce of water and

twenty-four drops of glacial acetic acid. Strain, and, after half an hour, add half a drachm of strongest liquid ammonia. Next, dissolve one hundred and fifty grains bromide of potassium in eighty ounces of water, and add six drachms of albumen, prepared as above. In this mixture leave the plates five minutes, moving from time to time.

Wash again in several pans, to the third of which add a little acetic acid in the proportion of one drop to each ounce of water. Give another wash in common, and then one in distilled, water.

Drain the plates, and then tanninize them in a solution of fine pure tannin, fifteen grains to the ounce, with one ounce in twenty of alcohol, well filtered. Use the tannin bath for one set of plates only.

The above is the form of this process as described by Mr. George Griffiths, a very successful worker with it. He saves some trouble in washing by having a sort of grooved plate box without a bottom, or sufficient merely to keep the plates from sliding through. In this half a dozen are placed at once, and are carried together through the successive washings by plunging the whole rack into the vessels containing the washing water, or solutions, respectively.

It will be seen that this is a laborious and complicated process. The plates must be left for a long time to sensitize, and yet care must be taken to time that sensitizing exactly according to conditions which must be ascertained afresh for each batch of plates. The treatments after sensitizing are numerous; the washings troublesome. The inducement is, of course, to obtain plates of extra sensibility, for instantaneous or rapid exposures. Either alkaline or acid development may be used. In the latter case, apply plain pyrogallic first, adding nitrate of silver and citric or acetic acid, both very cautiously, to avoid harshness.

§ 3.—**The Coffee Dry Process.**

This process is due to Col. Baratti, of Florence. It is one of the most regularly and easily successful of all the dry processes. The writer works it as follows: the proportions are Baratti's.

Infuse an ounce of coffee in ten of boiling water with half an ounce of white sugar. This keeps eight or nine days, and is employed by simply pouring over a plate excited in the ordinary way and washed. De Constant has kept these plates two years in good order. Or the preservative may be conveniently applied as a bath. It must, of course, in either case be filtered.

Any collodion giving a good thick film may be used. Edge with benzene rubber varnish (see Chap. XVI. § 2), at first, if the plates are whole size or over.

The exposure is five times that of wet collodion. An iron development answers, but scarcely as well as a pyrogallic. The plate is moistened, and then treated with weak plain pyro, the details come out, whereupon a drop or two of silver and acetic acid solution are added. Finally push with pyro, citric acid, and silver.

Care must be taken not to push the development too much, or the plates become hard and dull. Alkaline development may be employed to diminish the exposure, very advantageously.

§ 4.—**Hot Water (Collodio-Albumen) Process.**

This branch of dry plate work has always been highly esteemed for the durability of the sensitive plates, the softness of the image, and the great safety from sliding and slipping of the film. A favorite form of the collodio-albumen is known as the *hot-water process*, from the fact that the albumen is coagulated by hot water, as first proposed by Dr. Ryley. W. Fairweather describes it as practised by himself in the following manner:—

Acidulate the bath with acetic acid, using from three to four fluidrachms to twenty-five ounces of bath. As the images are apt to be too strong and dense, he dilutes his collodion with an equal bulk of mixed alcohol and ether by which it was everyway improved, especially as, by standing or filtering, impurities were separated which otherwise would have remained; the main object, however, was to avoid excessive density in the high lights, an exceedingly common fault in all dry plates except the collodio-bromide (Chap. XVIII.).

The plate, after being sensitized, was put into a bath of distilled water for a couple of minutes, and thence into a second. This was repeated with each plate until the whole number were thus treated.

Five ounces of water and twelve drops liquid ammonia were added to each white of egg, well shaken up, left to stand over night, and then filtered through two thicknesses of a silk handkerchief. Holding the washed plate carefully at one edge, pour over it the prepared albumen, working it well in, and carrying it always up to the very edges. Then pour off.

Meantime the operator has a small kettle of boiling water over a gas flame, and pours into a pan enough boiling water to cover a plate, then slides a washed sensitized plate into it, takes it out, rinses with cold water, and sets it in the rack to dry.

Develop with an eight grain solution of plain pyro till an image appears, then add a little solution of nitrate of silver ten grains, citric acid ten grains to ounce. Over-development to be most carefully avoided.

These plates keep for months, and a considerable time may be allowed to elapse between exposure and development, always a more dangerous interval than that between sensitizing and exposure. Exposure long, double that of the last.

§ 5.—Malt-Albumen Process.

The collodio-albumen and malt processes are sometimes combined, and the result has been highly praised. The following are Mr. Nicol's directions in substance:—

Remove the plate from the nitrate bath, and set it to drip into a tumbler. Transfer to a porcelain pan, and cover with water; rock till greasiness disappears. This is done three times, and the plate set to drain on blotting paper.

Take ten ounces good strong ale; add the white of one egg, and beat up well; filter through paper, and pour over the plate when brought to the condition just mentioned. If many are to be made, it may be applied as a bath. Dry spontaneously or artificially.

The exposure is shorter than for tannin; about three or four times as long as for wet plates.

Develop by first moistening the plate, and then pouring on a two or three-grain solution of plain pyro. In three to four minutes the detail will be visible by reflected light. Pour back, and add a few drops of solution of nitrate of silver, twenty grains, citric acid twenty grains to one ounce of water, which will bring up the intensity to printing strength. Care must be taken not to over-develop, as the color is very non-actinic.

In case the plain pyro does not bring out the image, pour it off, and add a few drops of weak ammonia, or of a twenty-grain solution of bicarbonate of sodium, or ordinary carbonate of ammonium. This will at once bring it out, after which the plate should be well washed at once, and re-developed in the usual way with acid, pyro, and silver.

The preservative keeps for a week in hot weather, and a fortnight in cold.

§ 6.—The Gum Process.

In this process a solution of gum-arabic is used, twenty grains to the ounce, as a preservative. The plates are collodionized and sensitized exactly in the same way as for the tannin or coffee process, are then washed off under a tap, and plunged into the gum solution; or this is poured over and worked in.

This process is more rapid than any other with a negative bath, except the tannin with bromized plates. It gives soft pictures with good detail—not, perhaps, as vigorous as the coffee plates, but more soft. As the gum renders the film very transparent, it is much exposed to blurring; therefore it will be necessary to paint the backs carefully with annatto, or lampblack, or Spanish brown mixed up with gum-water; or probably the writer's method of using red litmus in the preservative bath might be very useful with these plates.

Develop with plain pyrogallic acid, adding acetic acid and a little silver as the details come out, and keep up the action of the developer until the required strength is obtained; or apply alkaline development. Beautiful negatives are obtained by this process. Mr. Gordon uses the iron collo-developer.

§ 7.—Morphia Process.

This method, introduced by Bartholomew, gives sensitive plates; but whilst some have succeeded with it, others have failed, and the plates are not certain to keep more than four or five days—in some hands still less, in others, much more.

The plate is sensitized as usual (a ripe collodion, with tolerably intense cotton, is in *all* dry processes to be recommended), and, after washing, is left for a few minutes in a solution of acetate of morphia, one grain to the ounce. It is then taken out, drained, and dried.

The writer has found a decided advantage, in this process, in adding a few drops of acetic acid to the morphia solution. A drop of glacial acid to each ounce of solution is amply sufficient.

Develop either with plain pyro, precisely as with the last, or an iron developer may be employed. The writer has never found iron answer as well for dried plates as pyrogallic acid, and most operators prefer the latter mode. Mr. Newton has substituted the tincture of opium (ordinary laudanum) for morphia solution, diluting largely with water.

CHAPTER XVIII.

DRY PROCESSES WITHOUT A NITRATE BATH—COLLODIO-BROMIDE PROCESSES.

THE first idea of sensitizing collodion by the addition of nitrate of silver is due to M. M. A. Gaudin. The negative work with a sensitized collodion was further improved by Dr. Liesegang, in Germany, and by Messrs. Sayce and Bolton, in England. Dry plates are extensively and very successfully manufactured commercially by Mr. Mawdsley, either by Sayce and Bolton's process or by some modification of it. The writer believes that he has materially improved this method of operating by introducing into it the use of a lead salt, and by otherwise simplifying the method. This process of Sayce and Bolton will be first given, then that proposed by the writer.

§ 1.—**Sayce and Bolton's Process.**

In all the forms of the collodio-bromide process the collodion is made to contain bromide of silver in suspension. For it is a peculiarity of this substance that when it is formed in the presence of collodion in place of immediately sinking to the bottom it is capable of remaining for a considerable time in suspension, and while in that condition the mixture can be extended on glass, and affords a sensitive film fully as perfect and as regular as can be obtained in any other method without exception.

A collodion is prepared containing bromides only. Sufficient attention has never been called in any publication on the subject of the collodio-bromide process to the great importance of having proper cotton; hence, many have complained of thinness of the image and difficulty of intensifying. With the commercial plates this is never the case. Examined, they give evidence of having been made with intense cotton and with collodions that have been kept till fully ripe.

Supposing then that the operator has procured a short powdery cotton made with weak acids at high temperatures and a little yellowish in color (the Helion No. 1 manufactured commercially is suitable), he proceeds to make his collodion as follows:—

Alcohol	10 fluidounces.
Ether	10 "
Bromide of cadmium	60 grains.
Bromide of ammonium	20 "
Pyroxyline	140 "

Place this collodion aside for a month to ripen.

When wanted, add to each ounce eleven grains of nitrate of silver, rubbed to very fine powder. Shake well at intervals of an hour or two, set aside for six to twelve hours to settle, decant carefully the clear part, and use it for coating precisely like any other collodion, taking great care to avoid crapy lines.

When the film has set, wash it under a tap and sensitize in a fifteen grain solution of tannin. Drain it off and dry.

Develop either with acid, pyrogallic acid and silver, or with alkaline development. Mr. Sayce at one time recommended an iron development, but the other methods have generally been preferred. The back of the plate to be covered with annatto.

§ 2.—**Lea's Collodio-bromide Process.**

As the result of a very long and careful series of experiments the writer found that the collodio-bromide process might be both simplified and improved by using a preservative bath that would *dispense with all washing*. He thus not only avoided much trouble, but got a more sensitive plate.

A very powdery, short, intense cotton should be selected, "Helion No. 1" answers well, and made into collodion as follows:—

Collodion.

Alcohol	15 ounces.
Ether	15 "
Bromide cadmium (12½ to ounce)	375 grains.
Bromide ammonium (2 grains to ounce) . . .	60 "
Pyroxyline as above (7 grains to ounce) . . .	210 "

This collodion should stand two weeks at least, or, better, still longer.

When wanted for use this collodion is to be sensitized twelve hours beforehand with 21½ grains of finely-pulverized[1] nitrate of silver to the ounce, is shaken several times at intervals of half an hour or an hour, and is either decanted after resting for six hours or more, or else filtered.

At this point it is proper to call very special attention to a difficulty that has beset every one in commencing with any collodio-bromide process, otherwise so easy. The plates are found to be very insensitive, giving a pale image difficult to intensify.

Sensitized bromide collodion when first made gives thinnish blue films. By degrees a peculiar reaction takes place between the ingredients, and a film so opaque is obtained that the window bars of the dark room cannot be distinguished through it when held up. *In this stage only* is it fit for use.

Now when a wholly fresh lot of bromised collodion is first sensitized it may require a day or several days to reach this stage. But afterwards there is no trouble. The operator makes it a rule to sensitize at least twice as much collodion as he expects to want. To his residue he adds a measured quantity of the plain collodion, sufficient to replace what he used, and shakes up. In this stage the mixture will keep for weeks, probably for months, because the bromide is now in excess. The amount of plain collodion added is always noted on the bottle, which should have yellow paper pasted round it and be *always* kept in the dark room. Then when wanted to use again the operator adds *as much nitrate of silver as corresponds to* that quantity added.

[1] The pulverizing must be continued till the powder is as fine as flour, and has lost every trace of grittiness.

In this way the operator goes on indefinitely without loss or waste. The portion left over from the previous use is not only saved, but it so acts upon the fresh that in twelve hours after sensitizing the whole mixture is fit for use. It has acquired the property of giving opaque, highly sensitive films.

If, therefore, the operator wishes to coat his plates in the morning, he sensitizes the night before, shakes up several times thoroughly and at intervals, and next morning his collodion is in good condition. Or if he intends to coat at night, he sensitizes early in the morning of the same day, always remembering that when he begins *at first*, or at any subsequent time *without a residue over* from a previous operation, he must allow more time. For a first beginning, the writer recommends to proceed as follows:—

Take, say eight ounces of the collodion and sensitize it. It will require $8 \times 21\frac{1}{2}$ or 172 grains of nitrate. Shake at intervals for twelve hours. Then add four ounces of plain collodion. Shake at intervals for several days. Lastly, twelve hours before you wish to coat the plates, add the nitrate corresponding to the four ounces ($4 \times 21\frac{1}{2} = 86$ grains), and shake well at intervals of several hours. The object of this proceeding is to get the collodion into the *opaque condition*, afterwards it will simply be necessary after each use to supply as much plain collodion as will make up for what has been used, and, twelve hours before the next use, to sensitize with the corresponding quantity of nitrate of silver.

To get the collodion clear, it may either stand and be decanted or be filtered. The writer has sometimes used the one, sometimes the other, preferring on the whole to filter. The filtering is done precisely in the usual way, through sponge in a collodion filter. If decanted, it should rest for six hours previously.

To *coat the plate*, pour on exactly like other collodion. After covering the plate and before pouring off, *send back a wave to the far corner*. This is a good plan with all coating, but with collodio-bromides it is *essential;* if not done, a curved line of cloudiness will be visible on the upper end of the plate, and this will print lighter than the rest. In pouring off raise the plate but *very little and very slowly;* rock it carefully.

Previous to coating the plates should be edged with India-rubber dissolved in benzene; they should stand five minutes or more afterwards before coating. The brushing off with a soft wide brush to get rid of dust, should be done *immediately before coating*, and not before edging.

The plate, as soon as set, should be dipped into the preservative bath (*without washing*).

Preservative Bath.

Water	6 ounces.
Lead solution (¼ ounce acetate of lead dissolved in 2 pounds of acetic acid, No. 8) . . .	1 ounce.
Gallic acid (1 ounce gallic acid dissolved in 4½ of alcohol)	¼ "

This will be suitable for 4×4 size plates, 8×10 will require nearly double.

The plates after remaining in this solution till all oiliness disappears, are taken out and dried. Raising one end rather suddenly so as to send a wave over the plate, tends to wash off bubbles and motes. The solutions need to be filtered when first made, but I have not found it necessary to filter the bath itself.

The directions here given apply to all collodio-bromide processes. The foregoing, however, is much the least troublesome, and the writer's preservative bath *dispenses with a previous washing.* These directions are minutely given, and seem for that reason much more troublesome than they really are. The reader may be assured that there is no process by which plates are so rapidly prepared as by this. The *washing* of a plate is more troublesome than the applying of a preservative bath; in this process there is no washing; all other processes ever proposed, without exception, need at least one washing, many several. There is less manipulation in this than in any other process, and when the comparison is made with the collodio-albumen processes the contrast is very great indeed.

Character of the Negatives.—A great advantage in this process lies in the absence of disposition to choke up the high lights, so common with dry plates.

Keeping Qualities.—The keeping qualities leave nothing to be desired. The writer prepared some plates in April, and put them into slides for use. He was prevented from using them, and they lay in the slides over the intensely hot summer of 1868 till the middle of September, when they were found to be in perfect order and seemed not to have lost anything of their sensitiveness.

Development.—Use either the alkaline or the acid development (see Chap. XVI.). The writer prefers the alkaline. Exposure about three to four times that for wet. There is no danger of over-exposure, the longer the exposure the quicker and more satisfactory the development.

It should be remarked that these plates begin their development slowly, but gain steadily and regularly, and with no disposition to fog or stain, though they often look very dark.

Use of Litmus.—As the best, most effectual, and simplest mode of preventing *blurring*, that is, light reflected from the back surface of the glass and interfering with the purity of the image, the writer colors the film with a water color, and selects litmus. A strong solution of litmus is made by covering the cakes with hot water, covering the vessel and letting it stand, best in a warm place, for twenty-four hours. The soft mass is thrown on a filter and washed with hot water till, with one-quarter pound of good litmus, about sixteen ounces of very intense solution is got. To this add one-fourth alcohol to make it keep.

This litmus solution when added to the above described bath, in the proportion of about 3 drachms to 6 ounces of bath, colors it deep blood-red, by reason of the acid contained in the bath. The plates come out light rose color, and this coloration, so effective against allowing light to pass, is applied without the least inconvenience. So far from detracting from the sensitiveness of the plate, it adds to it; it requires no special means of removal, but disappears spontaneously in the development and washing, and no trace remains in the fixed negative. Nor does it interfere with the keeping. The plates kept from spring till autumn as abovementioned, had been thus treated.

The writer has published several other forms of the collodio-bromide processes, but believing this to be the most useful he has selected it for description here, and excludes the rest for want of space, except to say that by at least one of them, results almost if not quite equal to those of the above are obtained. Alcoholic solution of aloes is made by boiling good aloes with four times its bulk of alcohol. Fifteen drops of this is introduced into the sensitized collodio-bromide, and well agitated. After coating plates with this mixture, they need nothing but washing and drying, and give excellent pictures. De Constant modifies this process of the writer by substituting balsam of Tolu for the aloes. In his hands both the Aloes and Tolu gave results as rapid as the wet process.

CHAPTER XIX.

PHOTOGRAPHIC VARNISHES.

THE extreme importance to the photographer of having a first rate varnish is sufficiently evident. Often, however, the fault of bad storage is laid to the charge of the varnish. If negatives are so left that they are exposed to damp air and to continual changes of temperature, hardly any varnish will stand well; at least it will be safest not to trust to its doing so.

Spirit varnishes have alcohol for their solvent; others are made with *benzene*. Even the same gum-resins leave a different coat when they have been applied with a different solvent. Benzene varnishes may be applied with less heat than spirit varnishes, but they render the negative more transparent than the former. Spirit varnishes should always contain some essential oil; oil of lavender is the most suitable, there should be of this not less than five nor more than ten per cent. of the spirit.

Lac is the best of the resins employed, it is hard and tough. Fine shellac makes excellent varnish, except that it is too highly colored. Bleached lac is, therefore, better.

Sandarac is largely used in many commercial varnishes. It gives a very pale varnish, but it is a more brittle resin than lac.

Jalap resin dissolved in twenty-four times its weight of alcohol has been highly extolled as a photographic varnish; its high price, however, stands in the way of its use.

These are the principal resins employed. *Dammar* and *Mastic* are sometimes used. *Copal* gives an excellent varnish. It is high colored, however, and very difficult to dissolve. *Canada Balsam* is often taken to mix in with other resins; the writer has however satisfied himself that, when fairly dried into a resin, it is much more brittle than bleached lac, and darker colored by a good deal.

The principal objection to bleached lac is that it is not altogether soluble in alcohol, whereby a portion, about twenty per cent., is lost. This, however, is a small consideration in comparison to obtaining a first-rate varnish for valuable negatives. Even this objection, it has been affirmed, may be avoided by using shellac, and decolorizing it by shaking it up with, or filtering through, animal charcoal.

The toughness of a varnish appears to be increased by the addition of essential oil to the solvent. Essential oil of lavender is generally employed, and gives also a pleasant aromatic odor to the mixture, though this, of course, is of little importance in comparison. Sandarac varnish seems to need the essential oil much more than lac varnish: an instance has been mentioned in the journals in which a professional photographer lost thousands of negatives by the use of a sandarac varnish made without lavender.

Sandarac dissolves rapidly in alcohol, bleached lac requires to be left for two or three days in contact; best in a warm place. The lumps of the lac should be broken down pretty well, but powdering is quite superfluous. At the end of some hours or days, according to the specimen of lac, and the temperature of the room, the lumps will have disappeared and the undissolved part will have a yellowish muddy appearance. At intervals it should be well shaken up.

The filtering of a lac varnish is a troublesome matter. If time can be spared, it is very much better to let the mixture stand for a week or two and decant the clear part. The residue must be filtered through paper, which is a slow and tedious operation, during which the filtering funnel should be covered with a glass plate to check the evaporation of the alcohol.

The following formula is the one employed by the writer:—

Alcohol	24 fluidounces.
Essential oil of lavender	1½ "
Bleached lac	3 ounces.
Sandarac	1 ounce.

This will make the varnish thicker than necessary. It will be therefore a good plan to proceed as follows: Put the lac only in the alcohol, and after shaking at intervals and letting stand, decant. To the residue add about one-fifth the original quantity of alcohol, and shake up and again decant. If this last be allowed to stand some time and be carefully decanted, the residue will scarcely be worth filtration. The two portions of liquid can then be mixed, the sandarac and lavender added, and the whole filtered through paper, which is then extremely easy, as the only difficulty is where the pores of the paper are stopped by the fine particles of undissolved lac.

Those who prefer to use Canada balsam in connection with lac and sandarac can employ the following formula:—

Bleached lac	8 ounces.
Sandarac (picked)	4 "
Canada balsam	1 ounce.
Alcohol	3 quarts.

A little more alcohol may be used to wash the residue.

Some photographers prefer a varnish composed entirely of sandarac as a basis; I therefore give a formula, but with a negative recommendation, not believing that this resin has the necessary qualities.

Sandarac	4 ounces.
Chloroform	5 drachms.
Essential oil of lavender	3 ounces.
Alcohol	25 "

The chloroform is not of very certain utility, but the lavender must on no account be omitted or diminished. The second quality of essence of lavender answers perfectly well.

The following formula has been highly recommended, and was patented in Germany:—

Alcohol	20 ounces.
Bleached lac	2 "
Venice turpentine	200 grains.
Sandarac	100 "
Mastic	50 "

A varnish will sometimes dissolve away the film. This may arise from either of two causes, too great strength in the alcohol or a slight acidity. The first can be remedied by the addition of water in the proportion of from three to ten drops per ounce or even, if necessary, more. The latter by addition of very little liquid ammonia.

As to applying the varnish to negatives or positives, see p. 37.

CHAPTER XX.

TREATMENT OF RESIDUES.

EVERY photographer should endeavor to avoid wasting the valuable metals that he employs, but the extent to which this care should be carried will depend largely upon the scale on which he carries his operations. It would be, for example, a waste of time for the amateur to attempt to extract the silver from his hyposulphite solutions, but the professional photographer should never reject them without first removing the silver, unless indeed he operates upon a very small scale. But the amateur will always wish to recover the silver from baths, positive and negative, that have become useless.

Residues may be worked in two ways, either the dry or the wet. Both are chemical manipulations of the very simplest order, can be explained in a few paragraphs, and can be readily mastered by any man of ordinary intelligence. The writer would recommend the professional photographer to use the dry way, and the amateur, the wet.

§ I.—The Dry Way.

Old Baths.—These will be thrown down with common salt. Take good coarse but clean salt, make a strong solution of it in any convenient vessel of glass or wood. Pour in the baths with constant stirring. Make sure that the salt has been added in excess, or large quantities of silver may be wasted unknowingly. To assure yourself of this, first give the whole a most thorough agitation, then let stand some hours to settle, take off some of the supernatant liquid, and add to it a little clear solution of salt. If no precipitate falls and no cloudiness is produced, the operator may feel assured that all the silver is thrown down as white chloride of silver, changing to violet whenever exposed to the air.

This chloride must next be washed. The liquid over it is carefully and completely drained off, clean water added in abundance, the whole thoroughly well stirred up and allowed to settle, then poured off, and this is repeated several times; the oftener the better. The vessel should be capacious, so that the chloride of silver, after settling for some hours, should not form a layer extending one-tenth the height of the water in the vessel.

The chloride of silver after being washed and dried, is put into a crucible, after being mixed thoroughly with half its weight of dry carbonate of soda and one-quarter its weight of clean sand. The crucible should not be plunged suddenly into a hot fire, or it will almost surely crack. But a few live coals should be put into the furnace, then a thin layer of fresh coal, then the crucible on that, and more fresh coal heaped round it. Bring the fire gradually up to a bright red heat, and when the silver is melted, stir it up with an iron rod.

Cuttings and Spoiled Prints.—These should be carefully burned in any convenient vessel, the ashes gathered up, and these may be added to the foregoing. Some have advised to heat the ashes with nitric acid, but this does not exhaust all the silver, and the nitrate of silver obtained is too impure for use without reducing it.

Hyposulphite Baths.—The silver is best extracted from the old fixing baths, positive and negative, by precipitation with liver of sulphur (sulphide of potassium). The silver is thus thrown down as sulphide of silver. This sulphide of silver is a heavy black powder, from which the sulphur is recovered by melting with an equal weight of saltpetre. But in doing this, two precautions must never be omitted.

First, the sulphide must be heated red hot *by itself* (that is, before the admixture of the saltpetre) in an iron pot. The object of this is to burn off the sulphur powder thrown down along with the sulphide of silver, and which, if it remained with the sulphide of silver when melted with the saltpetre, might cause dangerous explosions.

And secondly, it is necessary to be certain that the whole of the sulphide of silver is decomposed. This may be materially aided by stirring the mixture after it has been some time fused, with an iron rod, and continuing this for some time.

The writer, believing that all photographic operations should be carried on with nitrate of silver of the best quality, not only advises not to mix the silver got from the sulphide with that reduced from the chloride, but either to dispose of it to a refiner for further purification, or else to purify it by dissolving it in nitric acid, and adding this solution to the spent baths, to be with them precipitated as chloride. Many will doubtless hold this to be excess of caution, but a bath, and especially all negative baths, ought to be beyond suspicion.

Gold-Residues.—The least troublesome way of managing them is undoubtedly that recommended by Davanne, to acidulate the spent toning baths; add thereto solution of precipitate of iron, and to add the precipitate obtained by the addition of the iron solution to the chloride of silver, and place them in the crucible together. Then the lump of silver contains the gold alloyed with it, and when the silver is dissolved in nitric acid, the gold remains behind.

The residue containing the gold, after nitric acid has dissolved all that it can dissolve, may be treated with hot nitro-hydrochloric acid (nitric acid one part, hydrochloric acid two parts), in which it easily dissolves.

§ 2.—**The Wet Way.**

This method is here recommended chiefly for amateurs who wish to work over their positive and negative baths. A gallon precipitating jar is to be about one-third filled with a solution of clean salt, and the baths are turned into it and thoroughly stirred up. After the chloride has settled, and leaves the liquid clear, a portion of it is placed in a clean glass, and tested with more solution of salt, to make sure that the precipitation is complete. After being well washed by repeatedly stirring up with water, and pouring off again, the water is finally poured off closely, a little sulphuric acid is added, and then a lump of good zinc. For each pound of silver an ounce of sulphuric acid and a half-pound of zinc will be ample. The chloride rapidly shows signs of blackening, and this slowly proceeds until the whole of the metallic silver is revived in the form of a grayish black powder.

At the end of about two days, during which the contents of the vessel should be occasionally shaken, the operation will be complete. The lump of zinc is removed, a little more sulphuric acid is added, stirred up, and the whole left for some hours. The revived silver is then washed precisely in the same way as the chloride, with eight or ten waters (first breaking it well up with the fingers), and is then ready to dissolve in nitric acid. To effect this solution, place a quantity of nitric acid of good quality in a vessel which it does not fill over one-fifth or one-sixth. Throw in the silver powder, waiting between each addition till the effervescence subsides, and avoiding *most carefully* to inhale any of the red fumes evolved; to which end the operation should be performed under a well-drawing chimney. When all the silver is dissolved, the solution, which is always very acid, is to be filtered, evaporated down, and either crystallized or fused; the writer decidedly prefers the latter.

In fusing nitrate of silver care must be taken to use a sufficiently large porcelain basin; for if, when the solution is very much concentrated, it reach nearly to the edge of the basin, it is liable to perform what is known to chemists as "travelling"—that is, it will creep over the sides, and a crust once established, more and more will get over by capillary attraction, make a crust on the outside, and run down, half crystallizing and half fused upon the table. The writer once left a capsule with nitrate preparing for fusion, for a short time, and on returning found over half a pound outside. Capsules of Berlin or Meissen porcelain only can be trusted for fusing nitrate of silver.

This method of operating gives satisfactory results if carefully carried out. The zinc used should be pure. The Bethlehem zinc, sold in the Atlantic cities of America, is excellent for this purpose. Granulated zinc is not near so good for use as zinc in lumps, for, though it may work a little faster, there is always danger of small portions being overlooked and remaining in the silver, failing to be dissolved by the acid. The Bethlehem zinc comes in ten-pound ingots. Instead of granulating it, set it on a good fire till it is nearly ready to melt at the corners; remove it, and it will be found that when thus hot it will break up under a hammer with the utmost facility.

With many photographers it will be an object to have as little to do with chemical manipulations as possible. Such cannot do better than to sell their residues to some fair-dealing reducer. The residues should be kept in fair condition, and the three sorts kept separate, viz., chloride, from throwing down old baths with salt; sulphide obtained from fixing baths by precipitating with liver of sulphur; and lastly, ashes from clippings, failures, etc.

CHAPTER XXI.

VARIOUS PHOTOGRAPHIC PROCESSES.

§ 1.—Glass Transparencies by Development.

THESE may be made with wet collodion in the camera, or dry plates made in various ways may be exposed under negatives and have positives developed on them.

Where it is intended to print in the camera, by far the best method is to have a camera expressly constructed for this purpose, with two bellowses and two racks and pinions. Suppose the bottom of an ordinary camera to be extended in front, another camera to be attached, and beyond, a frame to receive the negative. In this way a *total exclusion* of diffuse light is effected; no ray can reach the lens except through the negative. The frame containing the negative at the front can be racked in and out, as also can the dark slide and focussing screen at the back; the lens occupies a stationary position between the two.

It is scarcely necessary to say that the negative for this purpose must have precisely the same properties as those intended for enlargement (see p. 139). It must not be dense; print must be easily legible through the densest parts. The deep shadows must be represented by clear glass, free from all trace of veiling. The negative is to be adjusted against a white cloud, and the plate prepared and developed in the usual way. Once adjusted, any number of copies may be made in succession.

Transparencies may also be obtained by the wet process without the use of the camera. A wet plate is prepared in the ordinary way, and after *thorough* draining, strips of thin letter paper are laid on its face near the edges where it is not important to get the image, and the negative is laid face down on these, which preserve it from actual contact. It is then held for half a minute or thereabouts, according to the density of the negative, under an argand burner, and development is effected in the usual way. A dense negative will not answer.

The treatment of the positive after development will depend

upon the object in view. If the object be to produce a picture to be viewed in the stereoscope or hung against a window, the plate after fixing will be blackened with corrosive sublimate, or better will be treated with iodine and then with sulphide of potassium. (See p. 135.)

If the intention is to produce an enamel by Grüne's process (which see), the plates will be toned with bichloride of platinum.

The same results as the above are got by using a dry plate, exposing under the negative in a frame for a few seconds to diffuse daylight, or for about a minute under an argand gas burner, or to magnesium light; the latter being the most certain, as when the quantity of magnesium required for one operation has been once determined, it is easy to repeat without danger of error.

The Albumen Process.—The albumen process, which was used for making negatives before the discovery of the collodion method, and which was superseded by it, gives finer transparencies on glass than any other method in use. A good deal, however, depends upon the personal skill of the operator. It was, for example, long believed that Ferrier's magnificent specimens were produced by some secret process of his own, but eventually it appeared that he used the regular method, as follows:—

The whites of twenty fresh eggs are taken, clear of yelk. Iodide of potassium one hundred grains, and five grains of iodine, are dissolved in a little water and added to the albumen, and the whole is beaten up in the usual manner. As in this process it is of the greatest importance that no dust shall settle on the plates, it is necessary that the operating room should be cleaned the day before by wiping off the floor, walls, and woodwork, with a wet cloth. Shortly before commencing, the floor is to be sprinkled with water.

A stout iron plate is fixed in a horizontal position over a gas burner, or any other efficient lamp. The albumen having been poured off perfectly clear, is then extended over the plate (absolutely clean), an operation which is aided by first breathing gently on it so as to let the moisture condense. Four silk cords have each a little hook at the end, the other ends are tied together and held in the hand; the hooks are slipped under the plate, which is then supported by the cords. In this way it is suspended over the hot plate and a rotating motion is given to the threads, which keeps the albumen distributed over the plate; presently it is dry.

These plates are stored away, and when wanted for use are sensitized in an acid silver bath prepared as follows:—

Nitrate of silver	1 ounce.
Acetic acid (glacial)	2 ounces.
Iodide of potassium	2 grains.
Distilled water	14 ounces.

From a quarter of a minute to a minute is needed for sensitizing, after which the plate is rinsed under a tap, and laid in fresh water; then dried in any way suitable for dry plates.

The exposure is made in a suitable frame for a few seconds. The development is made by plunging into a bath of gallic acid, one grain to the ounce. Silver is gradually added until the plate acquires the desired density. Ferrier is said to have toned his transparencies by first plunging them in a weak sublimate solution, and then, after washing, into a one-grain solution of chloride of gold.

Transparencies may also be made by sun-printing, as in the following sections, substituting ordinary for opal glass.

Transparencies for the Lantern should not be dense, but have the same characteristics as negatives for enlargement (p. 139).

§ 2.—Albumen Positives on Opal Glass.

These beautiful pictures may be obtained in several ways; but the wet and dry collodion processes do not give pleasing results, and are quite inferior to the albumen process, and the collodio-chloride process. The latter will be presently described. The particulars of the former have been just given when used in connection with a development; but, for opal glass, it is preferable to make a sun-print directly upon chloride of silver.

Clear albumen by heating it to a froth, adding first to twelve ounces of albumen a quarter of an ounce of clean, pure sal-ammoniac dissolved in an ounce and a half of water. Coat the plates, dry, and sensitize.

The silver bath is made by dissolving two ounces of nitrate of silver in sixteen of water, acidulating with acetic acid.

When albumen positives on opal glass are thoroughly well made, they exhibit greater force and more transparency of shadow than collodio-chloride work. They are, however, extremely slow in printing, and the success of different operators has been very various.

Positives on glass appear to require longer and more thorough washing than negative glass work, to preserve them from fading.

§ 3.—Collodio-Chloride Process.

When chloride of silver is precipitated in the presence of collodion, provided the precipitation is gradual, the chloride does not fall to the bottom, but remains suspended in the liquid. In this condition it may be poured over glass or paper. After drying, the plate may be printed, toned, and fixed without difficulty.

In this city, the collodio-chloride process on opal glass was suspected of giving pictures very liable to fade, and some of our best operators abandoned it in consequence. Latterly it has been affirmed that this fading depended upon the use of a substratum of albumen, and that when the collodion was poured directly upon the glass, the permanence was satisfactory. Without undertaking to pronounce a positive opinion on this question, I shall give the details of the process.

Mr. Simpson, who first published the process, directs as follows: To each ounce of collodion add—

Nitrate of silver	7½ grains.
Chloride of strontium	2 "
Citric acid	1 grain.

The object of the citric acid is to give vigor to the print. Ordinary collodion with equal parts alcohol and ether is advised; the pyroxyline about six grains to the ounce.

To keep the film on the glass, an edging of albumen is useful, or of India rubber dissolved in benzene (see p. 262), but it should not be extended beyond the edges. Print till the shadows are bronzed, which requires a little less time than for paper prints. Over-printing is less objectionable than under-printing, because under-printed proofs are worthless, whilst over-printed ones make good transparencies, or may be reduced with a weak solution of cyanide of potassium. Tone with alkaline chloride, very weak.

To fix, leave for five minutes in hyposulphite, one ounce; water, ten ounces; a brief washing is sufficient.

More recently the *Photographisches Archiv* gives the following details as yielding excellent results:—

In one drachm of hot water dissolve one hundred and twenty grains of nitrate of silver, and pour it into a bottle containing six and a quarter ounces of absolute alcohol, which in cold weather should be first made warm by standing in warm water.

Add next one hundred and sixty grains of good pyroxyline, shake, and pour in seven and three-quarter ounces of ether, and agitate the mixture, which, if the alcohol and ether have been full strength, will not be clear, but have a grayish-white look. Add further, Canada balsam, twelve drops.

Dissolve in another bottle—

Chloride of lithium	15 grains.
Tartaric acid	15 "
Alcohol	1½ ounce.

Let this fall into the collodion drop by drop. If this part of the operation be hurried, instead of the fine milky chloride that remains suspended in the collodion, a clotted precipitate will be obtained that will go to the bottom. Shake well after each addition.

The collodion is now ready for use. It must of course be made and preserved with perfect protection from light. Tartaric acid is found to give a better tone than citric, or any other acid that has been tried. The amount of lithium used is so small that its higher cost is unimportant. It is used because most chlorides are extremely insoluble in collodion. Wothly has lately affirmed that *hydrochloric acid* may be substituted for chlorides.

After a moderate over-printing, the film is to be first moistened with water and then toned with alkaline chloride of gold, using a grain of chloride of gold to each five ounces of water, or an old acetic or phosphate (or, doubtless, benzoate) bath may be used. The print must in all cases be varnished. Solution of copal in benzene is recommended as excluding dampness better than spirit varnishes.

Collodio-chloride paper printing gives finer definition by far, and a more delicate picture, than anything that can be got on albumen paper. Several attempts have been made to prepare it commercially, by the Leptographic Company and by Obernetter. The writer has received from M. de Constant, of Lausanne, some excellent specimens of this work.

§ 4.—Photographic Enamelling.

Of all forms of picture making the enamel may be considered the most permanent. Even the carbon process is liable to the objection, that the paper on which the print is made is a very perishable substance, and positives on glass by the collodion process are liable at best to many injurious influences from which an enamel, burnt in upon glass or porcelain, is evidently free.

For reproducing photographs in enamel, several ingenious processes have been proposed. Two at least have been worked commercially upon a large scale: that of Lafon de Camarsac, in Paris, and that of Grüne, in Berlin. Lafon has maintained his a close secret, whilst Grüne, with commendable liberality, has given his to the public. It is his that will be here first given.

There exists no difficulty whatever in transferring a collodion film to any other support. For this purpose it is best to diminish the adhesion of the collodion, by rubbing the glass beforehand with a little wax dissolved in ether; or, as proposed by Mr. Woodbury, add to the collodion two or three drops to the ounce of a saturated solution of beeswax in ether, which renders the film easily transferred without affecting the photographic properties of the collodion.

The operator prepares a glass collodion positive, which must, of course, be a positive by transparency and not an ambrotype. This may be done in several ways (for which see the previous sections of this chapter).

The next step will be to tone with weak solution of bichloride of platinum instead of chloride of gold; wash and dry. Run a penknife round the edges, plunge the negative in water, and float off the film. It will be advisable to add a little acetic acid to the water; acids tend to loosen films from their supports, alkalies to increase the attachment. Receive the film on the porcelain surface, and after allowing it to dry, dissolve out the collodion film with mixed alcohol and ether. The image in platinum will remain upon the porcelain. It then only remains to apply a suitable flux, and burn in the picture in a muffle. Grüne has not given the composition of the flux that he uses, but it is probable that Leth's flux will be found satisfactory. It is made as follows:—

Red lead	6 ounces.
Fine quartz sand, or pounded quartz	2 "
Borax	1 ounce.

Melt in a crucible, and after cooling, reduce the glass formed to a fine powder. Strew this over the plate, place in a muffle, and raise the heat just high enough to fuse the coat of flux into a transparent glass over the picture.

This process can also be used for producing designs in gold upon glass or porcelain. To effect this, the positive is toned with gold, thoroughly, and the rest of the treatment remains the same, except that a reducing flux must be used. No half-tone can be obtained in this way, because the gold, no matter how thin, exhibits its full metallic color. It easily acquires a brilliant surface by polishing. Beautiful designs in gold of the most complicated figures, have been burnt into porcelain by Grüne by this process.

Leth's Process differs wholly from the above. He first prepares "enamel color" by heating together—

Sulphate of cobalt	1 part.
Sulphate of manganese	1 "
Sulphate of zinc	½ "
Sulphate of iron	1 "
Saltpetre	6 parts.

These are heated red-hot, and, after cooling, are finely pulverized. One part of this powder is mixed with two to three parts of lead glass, made by fusing together six parts of red lead, two of quartz sand, and one of borax, and constitutes the enamel color. Of best gum-arabic eighty grains are dissolved in five ounces of water, to which is added an ounce of saturated solution of bichromate of potash, and a drachm of honey. This mixture is carefully and thoroughly made, and is filtered clear; then poured on a sheet of plate glass, and off at the corner; like collodion, is kept level, and dried over a spirit-lamp, without too much heat. It is exposed in a copying frame under a transparent positive; if in the sun, about two minutes. Next the enamel color is dusted over; it adheres only in the parts not exposed, and the excess is removed with a soft brush. Plain collodion is next poured over. The chromate is removed with a mixture of one part nitric acid to sixteen of alcohol, after which the film is detached (best under water) and transferred to the porcelain, dried, and is ready to be burned in the muffle.

Joubert and Obernetter, in their respective processes, proceed in precisely the same way as the above, except that nothing is said about removing the chromates by nitric acid and alcohol, which is probably unnecessary, and their formulæ are somewhat different. Obernetter's is—

Gum-arabic	5 parts.
Sugar	15 "
Glycerine	5 "
Bichromate of ammonia	6 "
Water	100 "

In applying the porcelain color and flux (see *ante*), he adds to each ounce of the mixture five grains of soap.

Joubert uses—

Saturated solution of bichromate of ammonia	5 parts.
Albumen and honey, each	3 "
Water	20 to 30 parts.

The transparencies for printing by the bichromate processes must not be too dense. The density usually given to transparencies to be viewed by the eye is considerably too great; the right strength is that of transparencies for the lantern. For reducing such as may have been made too strong, a solution of iodine in cyanide of potassium, made very dilute with water, has been highly recommended.

It has been endeavored here to give briefly the most valuable of published information on this interesting branch of photography. Those desiring further details may consult the *Photographisches Archiv*, Band VI., 346; *Photog. News*, IX., 457; or Martin's *Handbuch der Email-photographie*, Weimar, 1867.

§ 5.—**Photolithography.**

To be able to transfer a photograph to stone or metal, and to print a large number of copies therefrom, is evidently a most valuable application of the science; and this is now accomplished in a very admirable manner.

It is evident that the production of half tone is more difficult than the simple obtaining of black and white, and that different means must be employed. I shall therefore classify the processes under these two different heads:—

A.—PROCESSES GIVING ONLY WHITE AND BLACK.

Liesegang's Process.—Liesegang floats ordinary albumenized paper (the salting is not objectionable) upon a solution of chromate of ammonium. Then exposes under a strong, clear negative, till a strong image is got. Next lays it against a zinc plate, and passes through a press. Next lays it, face up, on cold water, till the image becomes visible. Takes a clean sponge, previously cleaned well with chlorhydric acid to get rid of grit, and removes the excess of ink. Then transfers in the usual way of lithographic transfers.

Liesegang attaches importance to the nature of the ink used for inking in the zinc as above mentioned. He takes—

Venice turpentine	8¼ ounces.
Wax	1 ounce.
Palm oil	1 "

These are to be heated in an iron pot until they take fire. Then stir in—

Lithographic transfer varnish	33 ounces.
Linseed oil varnish, No. 2	16½ "

B.—PROCESSES GIVING HALF-TONES.

Asser's Process.—Negatives of a light-brown color should be made for this process, those of dark and more non-actinic shades do not give sufficient detail in the lights, though they are well suited for rendering black and white work. From the negative an image is made on paper, and this image is transferred to stone. The following are the details:—

Very fine, even, *unsized* paper is floated on boiled starch paste until it becomes well penetrated, which may be judged of on the back; the starch of the ordinary quality, not the so-called patent starch. After draining it a little, it is laid horizontally to dry. The starch must be very liquid, without being too thin.

To sensitize float (in the dark room) on a cold saturated solution of bichromate of potash for a brief time and hang up by one corner to dry. Print with the starch side next the negative till the image is reddish brown, wash out, and dry it in daylight. When quite dry, hold it a short time before a fire or over a gas-burner, so as to give the picture a slight scorching, which produces a green coloration. Immerse again in cold water till the starch swells, spread the paper, picture side up, on a flat stone or glass, and blot off with bibulous paper.

Mix equal parts of stearine tallow and printing ink of best quality, as furnished by the makers, and without addition of the so-called printer's varnish (boiled linseed oil).

This transferring ink is placed upon a stone, mixed with a little turpentine, and evenly rolled with a clean roller covered with cloth or fine felt. The roller is now applied to the damp starch-print and rolled backwards and forwards over it until the picture comes out in black with all its half-tones. When sufficiently developed, it is cleaned off with a sponge well moistened with water. The transferring to stone is done in the usual way. The best stones are the light yellow, and for half tints must be grained—for blacks and whites only, polishing with pumice is sufficient.

It will be seen from the above that Mr. Asser does not direct his transfers to be etched with acid, as most commonly done with lithographic transfers, and he remarks that this is a great advantage, inasmuch as where etching is required the application of the acid frequently takes the whole transfer off the stone. I am inclined to agree with him in this, for in some of my own experiments I have seen very beautiful transfers upon stones disappear totally when the acid was applied, even when done with great care and by an experienced workman.

Macquier's Process.—Equal parts of cold saturated solution of bichromate of potash and finely-powdered gum arabic are rubbed gently and evenly into a finely-grained lithographic stone, using a rag free from fuzziness, and the rubbing is continued till the surface is quite dry. A positive (glass or paper) is attached with a little wax and exposed to light—sunlight for vigorous, and diffused light for thin positives—for ten or fifteen minutes.

Next, wash off with a solution of caustic potash, marking 3° Baumé, using plenty. Wash off well and then wash again with solution of castile soap and a soft sponge. Wipe dry with soft rags, gum it twice, ink it, and pass through the press.

§ 6.—**Photogalvanography.**

It has been known for a period of years that when a mixture of gelatine and bichromate was extended on glass and exposed under a negative; all those parts protected from the light could be made to swell up by soaking the film in water. Consequently the image is produced in relief.

The possibility of obtaining metallic plates from such relief was immediately apparent, and the details have been worked out by several experimenters. Pretzch was the first to use it commercially, and, although he produced very good work, the enterprise was not financially successful and was abandoned. Pretzch's process was kept secret.

The writer of this manual worked out the details of a process himself, and was the first to publish any practicable method, which will be found in full detail in the *British Journal of Photography* for February 10th, 1865. Briefly, the process consists in coating glass with a film of—

Gelatine	200 grains.
Water	4 ounces.
Cold saturated solution bichromate of potash	5 drachms.

When dry expose under an average negative to direct sunlight for two to three minutes. Then leave in water for about two hours, changing frequently, then let dry.

The surface may receive a conductor in several ways. Brush over with an ethereal solution of chloride of gold, let dry, place in sunshine, and apply a solution of protosulphate of iron. This is the writer's method of gilding the film, which takes a brilliant gold surface, and is then ready to be plunged into the electrotype bath.

But, on the whole, the writer preferred to treat the dry gelatine film (after the bichromate, of course, had been thoroughly removed) with alcoholic solution of nitrate of silver, and then to fog it with pyrogallic acid.

By means of the electrotype bath, a copper reproduction of the relief is obtained from which to print.

Woodbury's Relievo Process.—The above method is evidently applicable only to the reproduction of engravings and woodcuts; negatives of natural objects, made up of half-tones, cannot be used for it. Woodbury ingeniously avoids this difficulty by a very valuable process, which has been patented.

It is easy enough by the process just above described, to obtain a reproduction in copper of a gelatine relief of objects containing half-tones. This reproduction will not, of course, have lines like a copperplate, but will consist of undulating depressions and elevations. The difficulty lay in making this to print. Mr. Woodbury's idea was to mix a little black pigment with gelatine, to spread this over the plate, and then with a flat surface to remove the excess. A piece of paper being then pressed against the plate, receives the remaining gelatine. In the portions but little sunk, there will have been but little pigment, and these will print light, and just in proportion to the depth of the sunk portion will be the blackness of the print.

Work of remarkable beauty has been executed by this process, which is applicable to printing on paper, glass, wood, or any other surface.

§ 7.—Willis's Aniline Process.

This process has likewise been patented. The work produced by it is of rather a common order; its recommendation is its extreme facility and cheapness.

Paper is impregnated with solution of bichromate of potash, to which a little phosphoric acid has been added. After exposure under a transparent positive, it is exposed to vapors of aniline, which develop a grayish image. The print is then merely fixed by simple washing. As a positive affords a positive, plates, drawings, &c., can be copied without the intervention of a negative or the use of a camera.

§ 8.—Printing Processes with Salts of Iron.

Most of the salts of the peroxide of iron are reduced by light to the corresponding salts of the protoxide, with a loss of one-third of their oxygen. By applying reagents which act differently on the two oxides of iron, this reduction is made apparent, and a colored picture is produced. Thus, if red prussiate of potash be applied, all the part acted upon by the sun becomes blue; with gallic acid the unexposed part becomes black, and so on.

Chloride of Iron.—Take

Perchloride of iron	50 grains.
Tartaric acid	15 "
Water	1 ounce.

Expose under the object itself or under a transparent positive. Plunge for an instant in distilled water, and then in a saturated solution of gallic acid, a decoction of nutgalls, or a mixture of gallic and pyrogallic acids, according to the time allowed. The impression is here in ordinary ink, gallo-tannate of peroxide of iron.

Oxalate of Iron and Ammonia.—Exactly saturate one ounce of oxalic acid with ammonia, add another ounce, and digest the mixture with freshly-precipitated and still moist peroxide of iron. The filtrate, after the liquid is fully saturated with peroxide, gives by evaporation in the dark, large and splendid green crystals of the double salt.

Paper is sensitized by floating in a minute or two upon a tolerably strong solution of these crystals, seventy to one hundred grains to the ounce, and dried, in which state it will keep for a long time. Exposed under a negative, an almost invisible image is obtained after a brief exposure, which by ferridcyanide of potassium, becomes a blue picture. This process is due to Herschel. It has the disadvantage that it does not give clean whites.

The writer imagined a remedy for this, which has been very successful; it consists in adding a little oxalic acid to the solution of ferridcyanide, the whites thus remain brilliantly clear. It is necessary, however, to be careful about putting the fingers into the bath. The free ferriprussic acid liberated by the oxalic acid continually decomposes, with production of prussic acid, in a very dilute form, it is true, but still active enough to render care advisable.

CHAPTER XXII.

CARBON PRINTING.

§ 1.—Introductory Remarks.

CARBON printing, in the form now in use, has been the result of the action of many minds, and the honor of its discovery cannot be ascribed to the ingenuity of any one person. It may be traced back as follows:—

The first step was the remark that paper imbued with solution of bichromate of potash, darkened when exposed to light. This was made in 1839 by Mr. Mungo Ponton.

The next was the discovery that gelatine, gum, and some other bodies, were rendered wholly insoluble when exposed to light in presence of bichromate of potash. This observation was first made by M. Becquerel; subsequently Mr. Fox Talbot patented a method of photo-engraving based on it.

The next idea evolved was, that the gelatine, made insoluble by light, might be made to imprison particles of coloring matter. Thus, where light acted these would remain; where it did not act, they would wash out by reason of the solubility of the portion of the film in which they were contained. This was an important step, and was made by M. Poitevin in 1855.

This was, in fact, a carbon process; but in this, and in all the efforts made for some time subsequently, the half tone was extremely defective.

M. Laborde seems to have been the first to perceive that the action of the sun was at first superficial, and only by degrees penetrating through the layer of gelatine. Thus those portions under the transparent parts of the negative became deep black, because the sun rendered the layer of gelatine insoluble through and through, and so attached it fully to the paper. But, in the half-tones, this penetration did not take place; the action was comparatively superficial; the lower part of the film remained soluble, so that the impressed portion above it was undermined in developing, and broken away. The only indications of half tone obtained seem to have been due to inequalities in the paper. M. Laborde, though he perceived the evil, did not find a remedy for it except to suggest exposing from the back.

The honor of devising the method of transferring is due to Mr. Swan. He showed that the true plan of developing lay in attaching the exposed surface to paper or other support, removing the original paper support, and so *developing on the under side.* Thus all the half tone was excellently preserved, and the picture was re-transferred to another and final sheet of paper.

§ 2.—**Details of Swan's Process.**

Preparing the Sensitive Tissue.—Swan prepares his tissue by forming an endless band of paper, which is stretched over rollers, and passes several times over a surface of melted gelatine, to which has been added sugar and Indian-ink or other pigment, until it has received a different coating.

This paper keeps indefinitely. When wanted, it is drawn, face up, through a solution of one pound of bichromate of potash in twelve of water, several times; and any bubbles that form on the back are removed by a camel's hair pencil. It should remain in till quite flexible, which will require from one to three minutes. Too short an immersion gives an insensitive paper; too long an immersion causes the paper to dry too slowly.

The drying is a matter of great importance. It must be complete, and quick, but not sudden; for gelatine, saturated with water, readily melts with a slight increase of temperature—consequently the temperature of the room must not exceed seventy degrees until the drying has pretty well advanced, afterwards it will be well to raise it to eighty degrees. If the paper is long (ten or twelve hours) in drying, pure whites cannot be expected.

If thoroughly dry, the paper will keep several days, but it is best to use it on the first or second. The paper should not, however, be so dried as to be horny. On the other hand, if the least dampness is present, the gelatine may be expected to stick fast to the negative; a danger which Mr. Swan endeavors to lessen by dusting over the negative with ground French chalk or soapstone.

A correct idea of exposure cannot be got by examining the print, which does not change in appearance. The operator must either rely on experience or must use an actinometer, of which Dr. Vogel's seems the most practical, though not very new in principle. A slip of bichromated paper in the actinometer is allowed to darken up to a certain point, which indicates that the action of light has been sufficient. The print is then withdrawn from the frame.

Transferring.—The print is now to be transferred to good Saxe paper. The method of preparing India-rubber varnish has been already explained (p. 262); a ten-grain solution in benzene will be proper. This is poured out into a pan, and paper is drawn over it, and hung up to dry.

Others soak the rubber in ten times its weight of ether for a day, then add benzene in quantity equal to the ether, and gum elemi or dammar in quantity equal to that of the rubber, obtaining a syrupy liquid, to be brushed over the paper.

Any adhering French chalk is wiped away from the print which is drawn over, not through the same rubber varnish, and is hung up for an hour. The print is then laid on the coated transfer paper, the two varnished surfaces together, and the two are passed through a powerful press, which produces a complete adhesion.

Some care is necessary in bringing the two coated surfaces together. Taking the two ends of the print in the two hands, these are approached till the print curves downwards, the middle is then brought into contact with the coated transfer paper, and by carefully covering the hands the whole surface is brought into contact with exclusion of air-bubbles. Once in contact the papers should not be slid over each other or altered in position.

So long as the print is undeveloped, access of light must be carefully avoided, though it is less dangerous after the surface of tissue has been protected by the transfer paper, therefore the operation of rolling may be performed in a room moderately lighted. The pressure should be very powerful, but care should be taken that it be not so applied as to allow the prints to slide or slip on the transfer paper.

Development.—Plunge into cold water for half an hour or more. Remove all bubbles that the moistening may be uniform. Next remove to tepid water (80° to 100° F.).

The paper which formed the original backing of the tissue becomes almost immediately loosened, and may be peeled off.

The soluble portions of the gelatine soon follow. The print should remain face down, and in from five to fifteen minutes it will be pretty well cleansed. A little motion through the water, or pouring water gently over it, or allowing a gentle stream to fall upon it, will get rid of the last portions and leave the whites pure, providing the exposure has been right.

Under and Over-exposure.—It is of course very desirable that the right exposure should be hit, but a certain latitude of error can be compensated for in the development. If the print clear itself with difficulty, hotter water may be cautiously applied, not, however, until its necessity has become apparent.

On the contrary, under-exposure will show itself by a tendency to clear rapidly as soon as the temperature of the water has been a little raised and when it is barely tepid. This will indicate the necessity of keeping down the temperature and finishing the print in water as cool as will clean the lights, which, however, by reason of the India rubber substratum, will at this stage look less clear than they really are.

Evidently it will be prudent to keep down the temperature in the early stages of the operation, and to raise it only as far as becomes manifestly necessary.

Retransferring.—This is done with gelatine solution.

Water	40 ounces.
Glycerine	1 ounce.
Gelatine	4 ounces.

Heat this long enough to expel all air-bubbles, but do not keep unnecessarily long in fusion, as by such treatment gelatine loses to some extent its power of setting.

Cover the surface of the print very carefully and evenly with solution, either by floating or brushing, then hang up to dry. Dampen carefully the mount, whether this be paper or cardboard, avoiding to dampen too much, lay the print on face down and pass at once through the rolling press.

The print is now left for a day to dry thoroughly before undertaking the last operation, that of removing the Saxe paper which has acted as a support during development. This is done by vigorously rubbing with tufts of cotton dipped in benzene. Then raise a corner, selecting one of the deep shadows where the film is thick, with a blunt knife, bend it well back and peel it gently off. In mounting on paper, Mr. Swan is in the habit of subsequently laying the print for an hour in a five per cent. solution of alum, a step which the writer believes he was the first to suggest.

Such is the very beautiful process which we owe to Mr. Swan, and which has already afforded thousands of admirable prints. It will be seen that the novelty ascribable to him is simply the system of transferring; this, however, is the keystone of the arch, the gradual construction of which has occupied so many ingenious minds. Sensitive tissue is also prepared in this country by Mr. Rowell, of Boston.

For many of the details of this method I am indebted to a useful little book, published by Mr. Simpson, entitled *On the Production of Photographs in Pigments*, to which and to Mr. Edward L. Wilson's treatise on the same subject those desiring further information are referred. It is believed, however, that the details given above are all that are essential to working this very interesting process.

§ 3.—Other Methods.

Carbon Direct Printing.—In the case of objects devoid of half tone and consisting altogether of white and black, the transferring is unnecessary. If gelatine or gum be mixed up with solution of bichromate of potash and a pigment be incorporated with it, this mixture may be spread evenly on sized paper, and if exposed under a negative a positive copy is obtained.

The writer has shown elsewhere that gum is preferable to gelatine for this purpose, inasmuch as it may be spread evenly over the paper with a brush; gelatine mixtures cannot, as they congeal in the operation. He also showed that the perfectly pure whites could be obtained by adding albumen to the mixture, and not without it.

Printing through the Supports.—Many experimenters have tried their hands at this: Mr. Blair perhaps more than any other. The writer has found the same result in his trials as got by others; that the grain of the paper prevents the result being thoroughly satisfactory. Despaquis has proposed to substitute mica, which by reason of its regularity and thinness should afford good prints by through printing. The writer has shown that very sharp positives could be got by printing through glass if only parallel rays be used: this he effected by using *reflected* sunshine. A glass plate coated with gelatine, pigment, and bichromate, was placed under a negative, *glass side next to the negative.* It was set against a wall next a window, and sunlight was thrown on it with a mirror. Four or five minutes gave a picture which proved clean and sharp.

Another process devised by the author consisted in covering paper with a coating of gelatine and bichromate *without* pigment. This was exposed for a minute or two under a negative, and was thrown into water for from twenty-four to forty-eight hours. In this time the image disappears so wholly that it is difficult to know which is the printed side of the paper. Dust of graphite is then rubbed over the still wet paper with a tuft of wet cotton, the color adheres to the unexposed parts only, so that a positive gives a positive. The process is a matter of curiosity only.

Pouncy's Process.—Excellent prints, better than any others except Swan's, have been obtained by Mr. Pouncy, an early and unwearied laborer in the field of carbon printing. In this process the sensitive pigment is composed of asphaltum, printer's ink, and a fatty matter, with or without bichromate of potash. The matters are incorporated with the aid of heat, and strained. All the information given by Mr. Pouncy is that there must be more ink than asphaltum, that it should be as thick as cream, and give an opaque coating when applied to glass. Only some sorts of asphaltum give good results.

The sensitive pigment is to be applied to paper with a broad camel's hair brush, leaving the brush in the pigment when not in use. The paper dries in a few minutes and keeps for months.

The paper to be used should be a very transparent tracing paper, or bank post rendered transparent with poppy oil. Expose with the paper side next to the negative, and develop by immersion in turpentine.

These prints are advantageously transferred to white paper. After the print has become thoroughly hard by exposure to light and air, after development, varnish the surface with a broad camel's hair brush, and lay the picture face down on the surface to which it is to be transferred, and press in a copying press; when dry, moisten the transparent paper, and it will come off leaving the print behind.

The exposures in this process are long; from three to five times those of chloride paper. The prints are very beautiful, and probably have the highest claim to permanence of any photographic work on paper, without exception.

PART IV.

THEORETICAL CONSIDERATIONS.

CHAPTER I.

GENERAL OBSERVATIONS.

WHEN we attempt to study the functions of light, we find ourselves face to face with questions which continually extend and expand as we consider them until we are lost in the immensity of the subject.

For all life, such as we know it on this planet, has been ordained by its Creator to exist only under the influence of light. By that agency, carbon is separated from the carbonic acid of the atmosphere, and is combined into all those organic forms of nutriment upon which we rely to support life, either directly as food, or indirectly to nourish those animals which are eventually to constitute our food. Thus, everything that lives upon the face of our planet owes its existence to light.

Light is so powerful in its influence upon organic bodies, that there exists scarcely one which is not directly affected by it. If an organic body be formed by the affinities of its component parts acting in the absence of light, then when that body so formed is submitted to the action of light, the affinities of its elements are in a vast number of cases so altered that decomposition results, at least if moisture be present. As familiar examples may be mentioned that almost all colors are bleached by exposure to sunlight, almost all organic substances are essentially altered in their nature by long action of sunlight. Perhaps no more striking instances can be adduced than those of the whole vegetable world. Plants of every description undergo incessant changes under the action of light; these changes take one course so long as the plant lives; with its death a new order of changes sets in. During its life it not only forms cellular and woody tissues and chlorophyll, &c., characteristic of vegetable life generally, but also vast numbers of complex organic bodies, such as the vegetable alkaloids, the gums, the resins, the sugars, the vegetable oils, the essential oils, &c. &c. After the death of the plant, an inverse action is set up, and these substances tend to resolve themselves, under the influence of light, heat, and moisture, more or less completely into carbonic acid and water.

Inorganic bodies as a class are less sensitive to light, but there are, nevertheless, very many even of these in which a change of affinities is brought about by its agency.

Most commonly the action of light is a *reducing* one, that is, there is a tendency to part with oxygen (similarly with other chlorous bodies, as iodine, bromine, and chlorine). This is analogical with the action of light in producing vegetation by which the carbonic acid of the atmosphere is made to part with oxygen, and enter into new forms of combination. So that the regular and normal action of light may be said to be the reducing one.

Occasionally, however, the action is contrary, and a combination with the oxygen of the atmosphere is promoted. *Phosphorus* is an example of this exceptional action, its union with oxygen is accelerated by light. Another prominent exception may be cited in the action of light upon a mixture of hydrogen and chlorine, bodies which, when mixed together, show no tendency to unite in the dark, but do so with explosion when light is allowed to fall upon the glass vessel in which these gases are mixed in proper proportions.

An examination into the action of light in those processes which the photographer employs, shows that so far as it is chemical, it is invariably reducing. Thus when a bichromate is exposed to light in the presence of organic matter, the agency of the light enables the organic matter to oxidize itself at the expense of a part of the oxygen of the chromic acid. When a persalt of iron is exposed to light, it tends to lose one-third of its oxygen, and to pass to the condition of a proto-salt. The same thing takes place in the salts of uranium, which principle forms the basis of the so called *Wothlytype process*. Some other metals are acted upon similarly: the salts of mercury tend to lose half their oxygen, chloride of gold may lose the whole of its chlorine, and the gold may be revived in metallic form.

It is, however, the action of light upon *silver compounds* that is at once the most interesting to the photographer and most difficult to interpret. It will form the subject of the following chapter.

CHAPTER II.

ACTION OF LIGHT ON COMPOUNDS OF SILVER.

§ 1.—Chloride of Silver.

LIGHT exerts a distinct chemical action upon chloride silver, of a reducing nature, that is, the chloride passes into sub-chloride with elimination of free chlorine, or of hypochlorous acid. If pure precipitated chloride of silver, well washed and freed from all organic matter, be exposed to light in a sealed glass tube, it gradually assumes a violet color, and loses chlorine. In the dark it regains its whiteness by recovering the chlorine lost. If free nitrate of silver be present, that is, if the chloride of silver be moistened by solution of nitrate of silver, the coloration proceeds much more rapidly.

If organic matter be present, the decomposition is more rapid still, and in many cases the sub-chloride of silver appears to unite with the organic matter, giving rise to the production of compounds much more deeply colored than the simple sub-chloride. Of these is the dark chocolate-colored substance, passing almost to black, which constitutes the body of an albumenized paper print before toning.

§ 2.—Iodide of Silver.

The study of the action of light upon iodide of silver presents very great difficulties, and considerable difference of views exists upon the subject.

In studying this subject, it becomes necessary, as the writer of this manual has more particularly pointed out elsewhere, to consider the question in two different forms, and distinguish between the action of light upon iodide of silver in the presence, and also in the absence of organic or other bodies capable of exerting special influences on it.

To be ably fully to eliminate the effect of these latter, the writer devised the method of precipitating metallic silver upon films of glass and then iodizing these films with iodine dissolved in solution of iodide of potassium. It had been held, indeed, that iodide of silver formed in presence of excess of iodide of potassium was insensitive to light; this view, however, the writer disproved by decisive experiments, and it is now abandoned.

As the film of iodide of silver upon glass was very liable to slip about, an expedient was found to fix it, by substituting ground glass, and this method of experimenting is now the only one capable of affording reliable results.

By these experiments, which cannot be detailed here, the writer was enbled to show—

1. That pure iodide of silver isolated undergoes no chemical decomposition even by very prolonged action of light. Thus a film exposed for many hours to brilliant sunshine was placed aside for a day or two in the dark. It was exposed for a second or two under a negative, and the image of that negative was then developed upon it without difficulty.

2. But if an organic substance be present, then chemical decomposition does take place. Thus, if a film of iodide of silver upon ground glass be washed over with a solution of tannin, and then be exposed for a sufficient time under a negative, a visible image of the negative is obtained.

Development on Iodide of Silver.—Very erroneous notions of the nature of development on iodide of silver have often been entertained, and the writer himself was at one time under the conviction that iodide of silver might undergo such a physical impression as to predispose it to decomposition when brought into contact with certain substances. Careful and extended experiment has led him to return to his older opinion, that the physical impression of light upon iodide of silver is such as merely to predispose it to receive a falling precipitate. This conception should be fully mastered by the student, and may be explained as follows:—

If we take a saline solution which is just ready to let fall a precipitate, and stir it well in a glass vessel, allowing the end of the glass rod to touch the sides of the vessel in stirring, we shall find that (in many cases) the precipitate will form first and in preference on all those parts of the glass which have been touched by the rod. Thus it may be said that the previously invisible path of the rod over the glass has been *developed* by the precipitate. The surface of the glass was only physically, not chemically altered by the passage of the rod over it; and yet it attracted, more powerfully than the rest, the descending precipitate. Just so the part of the iodide film which has been touched by light, exerts a more powerful attraction upon the descending precipitate of metallic silver from the developer than those portions which have not been touched.

It appeared to the writer that although the similarity of these phenomena was sufficiently obvious, yet the two might be brought closer together if he could show that an iodide film could receive a species of latent image by mere pressure, independently of light, capable of being developed by an ordinary developer. Experiment realized this without difficulty. Sensitive collodion films were pressed with various surfaces having raised or sunk devices. Then a developer poured over them brought out these devices with great distinctness, *the silver being attracted always in preference to those parts which had received the pressure.* The writer does not, however, mean to affirm that the action of light is necessarily mechanical, as in the foregoing illustration and experiment-

It is very remarkable that although invisible images may be developed on both chloride and bromide of silver, yet the phenomena are of quite a different nature. Development on pure iodide of silver results simply from a power in the film to attract to itself a descending precipitate, and is independent of any decomposition of the iodide in the film, either under the action of light, as may take place in the case of chloride of silver and bromide of silver, or under that of developer, as may happen in the case of bromide of silver.

That the development in the case of iodide of silver is perfectly independent of any decomposition of the iodide film, is shown by experiments published by the writer, together with Dr. Shepard, of Providence, in which after an image had been developed on an iodide film, it was dissolved away with solution of acid pernitrate of mercury, and was then, after washing, *reproduced by a second application of a developer.* This exhibits in a striking light what the writer holds to be the peculiar and characteristic action of iodide of silver, viz., that it is so modified by the action of light as to be capable of forming an image out of the silver in the developer, without itself having undergone decomposition either during exposure or under development. In this way only does it seem possible to explain the fact that a developed image may be dissolved away, and the power nevertheless be left in the film to reproduce the image by a second development.

It has been already explained that in the presence of certain organic and other bodies, iodide of silver undergoes chemical decomposition, and the same seems to be true when nitrate of silver is present. When, therefore, instead of experimenting upon a film of iodide of silver, isolated on glass, we take a common sensitized plate in which both nitrate of silver and an organic body (collodion) are present, the conditions are essentially changed, and chemical decomposition undoubtedly takes place. Consequently, in the ordinary wet collodion process, there appear to be two invisible images simultaneously present in the film—one a latent physical image due to the action of light upon the iodide, the other a chemical image, invisible simply by reason of its tenuity. Both of these may serve as bases of development.

The above are the views which the writer has entertained and supported. In the opinion of some photo-chemists, however, the action of light upon iodide of silver is always chemical, and no impression is formed except by actual decomposition. But this opinion seems to be at variance with observed facts, and the reactions of iodide of silver cannot be satisfactorily explained by it.

It will be interesting to note that in the case of iodide of silver the *chemical* latent image always offers a stronger basis of development than the *physical.* Now it has been already explained that, according to the view entertained by the writer, the chemical image is never produced upon isolated iodide of silver, but only when some suitable body is present to give rise to its production, consequently it follows that the presence of that body capable of giving rise to the production of a chemical image, may greatly exalt the sensibility of the iodide. It is for this reason that the presence of the bath solution (containing free nitrate of silver) in wet plates, and certain bodies, such as tannin, gum, gallic acid, etc., in dry plates, greatly diminishes the exposure needed. These latter substances have been called *preservatives*, though it is evident that they are sensitizers precisely as nitrate of silver is a sensitizer.

A theory was proposed by Poitevin, and afterwards independently by Vogel, and by the latter photochemist ably supported, that the action of these sensitizers lay in their capacity to take up iodine, and by so doing to aid in the conversion of the iodide of the film into subiodide. Vogel has affirmed that it is characteristic of all sensitizers that they will decolorize the blue solution of iodide of starch. The writer has found this always confirmed in a number of experiments made by him, though sometimes a powerful sensitizer would require twenty-four hours to effect this decoloration, a fact that seems to need explanation.

§ 3.—**Bromide of Silver.**

The action of light upon bromide of silver has been less studied than that of iodide, because the difficulties which it presents have been less evident than those in the case of the iodide. For it was easily shown in the case of bromide of silver that a chemical decomposition does take place by continued action of light.[1] Hence it was supposed that no physical action of light took place, inasmuch as none was apparently needed to explain the phenomena observed.

But the writer has pointed out elsewhere *that the mere fact of the possibility of development by pyrogallic aid in the absence of any free soluble silver compound*, is in itself an unanswerable argument for the existence of such a physical image.

Upon a dry collodio-bromide plate perfectly washed and having present no trace of the nitrate of silver, the application of pyrogallic acid will develop a visible image. Whence does this come? The image is evidently a sub-bromide of silver, perhaps combined with organic matter, but that the bromide of silver in the film afforded the sub-bromide by decomposition is sufficiently clear.

[1] This fact the writer has carefully verified upon films of bromide of silver isolated upon surfaces of ground glass.

Now although this image may be developed where there was no image visible upon the plate after its exposure, let us even suppose for argument that there was a faint visible image. If the development were conducted with nitrate of silver present, this faint visible image might certainly act as a foundation upon which the strong image was built up. But nothing of the sort can take place where the development is conducted in the absence of all silver compounds except those in the plate.

It, therefore, appears clear that a latent physical image may exist on bromide as well as on iodide of silver.

But the difference between these compounds in respect of the action of light upon them is very striking.

On iodide of silver the latent *physical* image is produced where the iodide is isolated.

But on bromide only where a "sensitizer" is present.

On bromide isolated, the action of the light can only produce a chemical image; on iodide isolated, it can produce a physical image only.

The action of the light upon bromide of silver, isolated, must be enormously long to produce an impression capable of being developed; the sensitizer abridges this period vastly more than in the case of iodide.

But on bromide isolated, the long-continued action of light may produce a strong, visible image (in an experiment by the writer this was attained by four hours' exposure to strong sun under a negative), which cannot take place in the case of iodide.

Development on Bromide of Silver.—In the case of iodide of silver, we have seen that development is essentially the attraction to the film of a descending precipitate, the film itself remaining (chemically) unaltered. But in the case of bromide of silver (acted on by light in the presence of tannin, or other sensitizer) development consists essentially in a reduction of the bromide in the film, and the production thereby of a more or less complex deeply-colored substance forming the image.

The remarkable distinctions between these two developments as respects their essential characters, corresponds to equally great differences in the practical operations based upon them. So that in the wet processes, in which iodide of silver is the altogether essential body, we see those forms succeed best in which a descending precipitate is applied to the invisible image.

But in the dry bromide processes we find only one thing essential: that to the exposed plate there shall be presented a substance like pyrogallic acid, which has a natural tendency to provoke reduction. This substance at once starts a decomposition in those parts that have been exposed to light. We may enhance its decomposing action by alkalies, and so exalt that decomposing agency until it is alone sufficient to produce such an image as we want; or, we take the image so produced, and by adding silver and acetic acid, we may *build upon it* a denser image for our purpose. So far as this building up is concerned, we proceed upon the same principles as in the wet process, but this second step does not in the least affect the character of the first, and that first step differs absolutely and essentially from anything that belongs to the wet development.

It is then (and this is what, if the writer is not mistaken, has not before been correctly presented) by a careful consideration of the essential characters of these two developments, that we arrive at the essential differences between the invisible image as formed on iodide, and on bromide of silver. Each in its absolute essence and freed from such accidental phenomena as may accompany it (and may lead to the production of a chemical image), is physical and not chemical in its nature. But in the iodide the physical impression is one tending to cause the attraction of a descending precipitate, in the bromide it is one predisposing to decomposition when a reducing agent of a proper character is presented.

CHAPTER III.

ACTION OF VARIOUS PORTIONS OF THE SPECTRUM.

WHEN, instead of exposing sensitive bodies to ordinary light, we let fall upon them a solar spectrum, we find that its different portions exercise widely different influences.

We find, also, that the *nature of the prism* used singularly affects the influences exerted by the different portions into which it separates white light. Thus, for example, with a flint glass prism, the most powerful actinic force is exerted by the invisible rays just beyond the violet. But if a prism filled with sulphide of carbon be used, a spectrum is formed devoid, or nearly so, of invisible ultra violet rays, capable of acting upon sensitive paper. A series of very interesting experiments, chiefly made by Herschel, on the action of different portions of the spectrum, have been tabulated, and will be found in Hunt's valuable *Researches on Light.*

As respects the silver haloids, the action of light commences far beyond the visible rays, and extends some distance into the visible spectrum. Bromide of silver is slightly affected by green rays, which do not act upon iodide. It has, therefore, a slightly wider range of sensitiveness than iodide.

Below the green come those brighter rays which form the principal illuminating part of white light. These are without effect upon sensitive films of the silver haloids that have never been exposed to light. But Ed. Becquerel has shown that these less refrangible rays have a "continuing" power, that is, that although incapable of themselves to *commence* an impression upon a sensitive surface, even by a very prolonged action, yet if that action be set up by the more refrangible rays, these less refrangible ones can continue and increase it. Thus, if paper prepared with iodide of silver be exposed to the spectrum, the impression ends with the blue rays. But if it be but exposed for a second or two to light, and then to the spectrum, and if a developer be applied, an impression is found to have been made extending to the very end of the visible spectrum.

What is also remarkable in this very interesting investigation is, that the bodies which act as a support to the silver compound, may control very remarkably the effects produced. Thus the iodide and chloride of silver in collodion or paper, or on a metallic film, are subject to this "continuing" power. Bromide of silver, when formed on a daguerreotype plate, is *not;* formed on collodion or on paper, it is. The image of the spectrum, when formed on bromide of silver *on a plate*, is much longer than the image upon chloride or iodide also on a plate, whereas bromide in collodion or on paper gives a spectrum no longer than iodide or chloride.[1]

These results are as important in their relations to photography, as they are interesting in themselves; and their bearing on the negative process is too evident to need that the writer should dwell on it. Only it may be remarked that they explain in part some of Mr. Rutherfurd's results in photographing spectra on collodion; they seem, however, to indicate that in his experiments the spectrum was not wholly purified from white light, for in these experiments impressions of many of the less refrangible portions of the spectrum were obtained in collodions containing the silver haloids.

[1] Becquerel, La Lumière, II. pp. 89–92.

PART V.

CHAPTER I.

PHOTOGRAPHY IN ITS RELATIONS TO HEALTH.

§ 1.—Poisons.

In adopting a pursuit, whether simply with a view to interest and amusement, or with the design of serious study and investigation, or as a business enterprise, every one should attentively consider its relations to his health. Permanent injury to bodily health is an evil so serious that its full magnitude is appreciated by none who have not learned by their own bitter experience. The writer, therefore, appeals to the good sense of every one who may adopt this manual as his guide through the study of photography, in the first place to neglect none of the general precautions which will be here recommended; and in the second, should he find his health in any way suffer, to ascertain at once to what that injury is ascribable, and to lose no time in taking such special action as the case may need. Speaking from personal experience, and having witnessed evil results in others, the writer earnestly desires to induce the habitual adoption of effective precautions.

It is not that photography is necessarily a hurtful art, but its practice brings its votaries into contact with several very strong poisons, which, if used without great care, and still more if used with the heedlessness that is only too common, are liable to produce the very worst effects. These substances are principally *ether, collodion, cyanide of potassium, corrosive sublimate, chloride of gold, nitric acid, acetic acid, and ammonia.*

Ether has a powerfully depressing effect upon the nervous system, and is used for that purpose in medicine. Continued exposures to ethereal vapor produces languor, depression of spirits, and bodily prostration.

Collodion, from the large quantity of ether which it contains, produces the specific effects characteristic of that substance, but also other effects, the precise source of which is not well understood. When collodion becomes much ripened, and especially when it takes on a deep color, it is found to give off a very irritating vapor, which attacks the face and especially the eyelids, producing severe inflammation. Cases have been cited in which photographers have been in this way obliged to interrupt their pursuit for times varying from a few days to many months. When the photographer perceives a disposition to irritation and inflammation in the face, he may at once suspect his collodion of being the cause.

Cyanide of potassium is, of course, the most dangerous chemical with which the photographer comes into contact. For clearing both positives and negatives, especially the former, it keeps its hold upon photographers, particularly amongst careless manipulators, through two causes. First, if by mismanagement the negative is a little fogged, cyanide, which has a stronger solvent action than hyposulphite, tends to clear it up. Second, the transfer of small portions of cyanide to other solutions by dirty fingers, has not the absolutely disastrous results that follow such transfers of hyposulphite. These advantages are not in the least creditable to the photographer who is influenced by them.

Cyanide of potassium is a compound of prussic acid with potash. In this compound it retains all the dangerous properties that characterize it in the free state. In fact, a solution of cyanide slowly but continually decomposes, absorbing carbonic acid from the air and giving off prussic acid in the form of gas.

This poison may act in three ways. Leaning over a bath of it, or even remaining in a room containing a solution of it exposed on a considerable surface to the air, a small quantity of prussic acid is continually inhaled.

In manipulating with its solutions, the hands come into contact with it. How far chemical solutions are taken up by a perfectly sound skin, has been a matter of considerable discussion among physicians, but recent careful experiments made in Paris, leave no doubt that the skin continually absorbs liquids which remain in contact with it.

If, however, the continuity of the skin be broken by a scratch, cut, pimple, or otherwise, cyanide is readily absorbed at such places, and a considerable amount of local inflammation may be produced. In some cases paralysis of the limbs has been affirmed to have resulted, and even paralysis of the whole side.

For several years past the photographic journals have published numbers of letters from photographers who have had their health injured, or, in many cases, ruined by the action of their chemicals, and especially by cyanide. *Paralysis* is the most common result, attacking most frequently an arm, but sometimes the entire side. One describes his hands as for months continually exuding some anomalous secretion, sticking them fast to his gloves, and interfering with their use. Another complains of intense pains in the fingers, only to be rendered endurable by keeping them for hours in cold water. Others find the whole bodily health broken down, and no help to be obtained from medicine. One photographer (M. Davanne), after having had his hands wet with cyanide solution, moistened them with acetic acid, and was almost instantly struck down insensible with symptoms of violent poisoning. His friends barely saved him by long-continued pouring of cold water on the head.

A very painful class of casualties is that resulting from *carelessness* with cyanide. Solutions are left about; sometimes the incredible carelessness of leaving them in drinking tumblers is committed. For all lives lost in this way (and there have been many), he who left the solution about is morally responsible. Once for all, the use of this chemical should be abandoned totally by photographers. If any insist on using it, the least such can do is to keep it exclusively in vessels marked conspicuously, POISON.

Corrosive sublimate is another dangerous chemical, but not capable of acting by inspiration through the lungs. Accidents with sublimate arise either from absorption or internal administration.

Absorption through the skin takes place slowly, and the fingers may be occasionally wetted with sublimate solution without any noticeable bad results; the danger lies in this, that there is no safe line that can be drawn, and that the photographer can form no conception as to the point to which he may go with impunity. Evil must be done before its danger can be recognized.

Administered internally, sublimate is a powerful corrosive poison.

Chloride of gold acts as a poison by causing deep and severe ulcerations upon the fingers of those who are continually working in toning baths. Such manipulation should be managed by means of spatulas and forceps of glass or whalebone.

Nitric acid acts toxically through the lungs. It stains the skin a deep yellow, which lasts until the epidermis is worn off, but no other evil seems to result from contact. It is possible that it is not absorbed, but that it kills the skin too quickly for such an effect. Nitric acid diffused through the atmosphere and inhaled, acts as a direct poison. Some years since Mr. Stevens, together with an assistant, undertook to sop up a quantity of nitric acid spilt by the breaking of a large vessel, an act which resulted fatally to the one and nearly so to the other.

In less quantities, and inhaled over a longer time, it may produce irritation of the lungs and chest diseases.

Acetic acid acts similarly to nitric, but in a less degree. Its fumes are very irritating to the lungs, especially to weak ones. The quantity of acetic acid used in photographic operations is often very large, so that in many professional establishments there is always a strong smell of this acid. Such a state of affairs must be hurtful to every one connected with the place, and ought to be done away with at any cost.

§ 2.—**Remedies.**

General.—It is evident that all poisons which are liable to be carried upon the atmosphere should, as far as possible, be kept in closed vessels. Cyanide should never be left in open pans or baths. Nitric acid baths used for cleaning (for which purpose bichromate and sulphuric acid is far preferable; see article on cleaning plates) should never be left exposed to the atmosphere, but the pans or baths should be protected, and be kept under a chimney or a draught of some sort.

Next to avoiding the production of fumes, the best thing is *ventilation.* In the case of ether and collodion, this is the only efficient means, as the fumes of collodion cannot be kept out of the air. For this reason plates should be collodionized, not in the open air of the dark room, but in a sort of closet partitioned off and provided with a vent above and below. The operator is outside of such a closet, and the fumes are not inhaled as the plate is coated. This is a very important precaution.

When acid fumes have got into the air, their removal can often be expedited by pouring out ammonia. This, though efficient, has the disadvantage of causing thick white clouds, which subside by degrees only. Still, its use is occasionally valuable.

Special.—Poisons taken internally must be treated with specific remedies; the object is always to bring the poisonous matter into some inert compound.

Cyanide of potassium has the remarkable property of taking up iron and forming a perfectly innocuous substance known as yellow prussiate of potash, ferrocyanide of potassium. *Proto*-sulphate of iron may, therefore, be taken internally in considerable quantity. Cyanide of potassium, in presence of a mixture of a protosalt and persalt of iron, is converted instantly into prussian blue, a substance not at all injurious to the system. Those who use cyanide habitually, will do well to keep the mixture of proto and persulphate of iron in readiness for accidents to others, if not to themselves. Common sulphate of iron in solution, by continued exposure to air, peroxidizes, and may be used for this purpose.

For *corrosive sublimate*, when taken internally, *white of egg* is usually administered. The quantity of the remedy must be considerable—one egg to each three or four grains swallowed.

Poisons in cuts and scratches should be immediately treated with the same remedies as those advised where the poison has been taken into the stomach. For injuries occasioned by the *continuous absorption* of poisons, no satisfactory remedies can be recommended, recourse must be had to the advice of an educated and intelligent physician.

The writer feels that he cannot leave this subject without again advising photographers to pay more attention to the conditions of health than is generally done. Those who have the direction and management of such establishments, should never forget that those whom they employ are often much more exposed to these dangers than themselves, without having the opportunity or the privilege of introducing better arrangements and precautions. And that, however employers may feel disposed to risk their own health, they are not justified in causing others, either ignorantly or knowingly, to share such dangers. Many a man, when he has found his nervous system permanently injured, or his lungs weakened, commences care-taking when it is too late. The needful precautions are neither many nor troublesome; they should be taken from the outset, and steadily persevered in.

CHAPTER II.

CHEMICAL MANIPULATIONS.

SOME of the simpler chemical manipulations are frequently needed in photography, and deserve a brief description here.

§ 1.—**Heating.**

The *alcohol lamp* was for a long time the favorite source of heat when needed on a small scale; its advantage lies in its high temperature and freedom from smoke. As alcohol both evaporates and absorbs water from the air, the wick should be covered. If the wick-tube is passed through a cork, this should always have a groove to permit escape of vapor, or it will be liable to be driven out with a dangerous explosion.

But whenever gas can be had, the *Bunsen burner* (see Fig. 82) conveniently and economically replaces alcohol.

The *sand-bath* is an excellent means of applying a gentle heat to large surfaces.

A very simple and convenient form of sand-bath is to have a circular rim on top of a stove, filled with clean building sand. The heat is thus applied much more evenly than if the vessel were set directly on the stove without the interposition of the sand, and the danger of breakage is greatly diminished.

A sand-bath may also be established over a Bunsen burner. Get a worker in sheet iron to make a cylinder of stout galvanized iron, about twelve inches in diameter, and ten high. The top and bottom are turned over heavy iron wire, and curved pieces are cut out at top and bottom, to serve as air passages. A circular piece of sheet iron is hammered into a basin thirteen inches across, and this, filled with sand, rests on the top of the cylinder. Such a cylinder will support a very heavy weight.

§ 2.—Evaporation.

In evaporation, two important points are to be borne in mind. First, the heat should not be contracted to a single point; and, second, it should not be so diffused as to be applied to that part of the vessel that is above the liquid. In either case fracture is apt to occur; in the latter case, almost certainly.

For large operations the sand-bath will be proper; that is, for evaporating negative baths, and such work. For small operations the following arrangement is capital. Procure a lampstand, with a strong ring about five inches in diameter. Take a piece of strong but fine and close-meshed brass wire gauze, six inches square, lay it on the ring and press the corners down under the ring, so as to fix it firmly to it. This wire gauze forms a support which will carry anything from a capsule an inch in diameter, to a basin of twelve or fifteen inches, provided the lampstand be strong and stout as it should be, as well as flasks, beakers, or, in fact, any utensil whatever. The Bunsen's burner stands under this, always ready for service at a moment's notice. The wire gauze stops the flame, and permits only the hot air to pass through, thus giving a great safeguard against accident, whilst scarcely interfering with the heating.

Fig. 82.

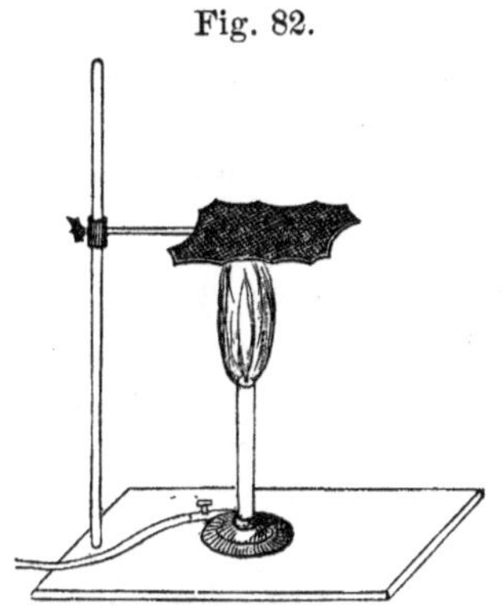

A *tripod* if made strong and stout, is also a good support, but far less convenient than the foregoing, inasmuch as it cannot be raised and lowered, and is never so strong as the lampstand. In this case, also, a piece of wire gauze should be interposed between the vessel and the source of heat.

Fig. 83.

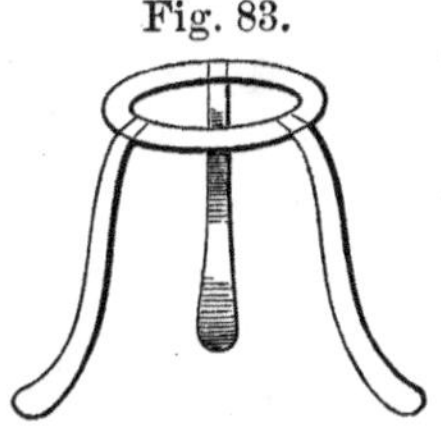

§ 3.—Filtration.

Of *filtration*, all that need be said is, make the filter always a little smaller than the funnel, and always wet it before pouring in the liquid to be filtered. Select a good paper, which filters clean and quickly, and when you find that which exactly suits, procure a good supply. Nothing is more vexatious than to wait for a slow filtration.

§ 4.—Pouring.

In transferring liquids from one vessel to another, there are two contrivances by which the clean performance of the operation without loss may be greatly facilitated. These are *greasing* and *rod-pouring.*

Greasing is the application of a little tallow on the finger under the lip over which the liquid is to be poured. For pouring valuable liquids out of large vessels, especially if nearly full, this mode is very useful.

In *rod-pouring*, the glass rod is first wetted with the liquid, and is then held to the lip of the vessel, which is so inclined as to pour slowly, the stream following the rod.

§ 5.—Fusing.

For reducing chloride of silver in the dry way, a Hessian crucible is the proper vessel. The chloride is intimately mixed with twice its weight of dry carbonate of sodium; this mixture is rammed tightly into the crucible, which is by degrees raised to a white heat.

For fusing nitrate of silver, a Berlin or Meissen porcelain basin will be required; none other can be depended upon. The Berlin are the best, and are stamped in blue; some with the letters K P M, some with a Prussian eagle inside of a circle. Both of these sorts are excellent. With care the operation is perfectly safe, and fracture need not be feared. The Bunsen burner will give the necessary heat for small quantities, or combined burners for large.

§ 6.—Neutralization.

Where the object is merely to render an alkaline liquid acid, or an acid one alkaline, it will be sufficient to add the appropriate reagent, until blue litmus paper, by turning red, indicates acidity; or red, by becoming blue, shows alkalinity, as the case may be.

But an exact neutralization, as where an acid or an alkaline liquid is to be rendered exactly neutral, is an operation requiring some circumspection. If, for example, an acid liquid is to be neutralized with ammonia, and the latter liquid is added a few drops at a time, the operation will be very tedious, and will be almost certain to fail, an excess of ammonia will almost certainly be at last introduced. The operator, therefore, feels his way. He pours off a part, say a third of the acid liquid, and adds boldly enough ammonia to make it quite alkaline. He then adds enough of the remainder of the original liquid to render the mixture decidedly acid. Repeating this several times, he gets a pretty clear idea of the proportion of ammonia, unknown at first, which is required. Towards the end, he diminishes the quantity of each successive addition, till with the last drops, with care, he obtains an exact neutralization.

There are some cases in which the neutralization is effected by the addition of a substance, which, even if added in excess, produces a precipitate, and so leaves the solution neutral, so that the addition of an excess of the precipitant is without much importance. An example of this is presented in the neutralization of an acid negative bath with carbonate of sodium. If an excess of carbonate of sodium be added beyond what is necessary to neutralize the free acid, carbonate of silver is formed, and this being but very sparingly soluble it water,[1] is precipitated. The addition, therefore, of a slight excess of carbonate of sodium does not render the liquid more than very faintly alkaline.

In other cases, the neutralization is effected by a substance insoluble in the solution after neutralization. This is the simplest case of all; it is sufficient to add the neutralizing substance in excess, and then to remove that excess by filtration. An example of this is afforded in the preparation of a neutral gold toning-bath. The acid solution of perchloride of gold is agitated with excess of precipitated chalk; as much chalk dissolves as is necessary to neutralize the excess of hydrochloric acid, and the rest is got rid of by filtration.

Negative baths requiring neutralization, must always be treated with bicarbonate of sodium, never with chalk.

[1] Soluble in 31,978 parts of water at 12° C. (Kremers.)

§ 7.—Decantation.

Fig. 84.

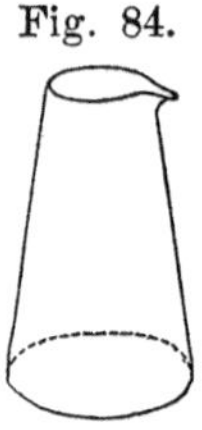

In all cases where a precipitate is to subside, that operation takes place best in vessels larger at the bottom than at the top, tolerably well in vessels with straight sides, and very badly in conical vessels, widening towards the top. Those of this last shape should, therefore, never be employed for decantation. The shape shown in the margin is the proper one.

§ 8.—Bending Glass.

An ordinary gas flame is sufficient for bending glass tubes up to half-inch diameter. No particular care is necessary except to apply the heat equally by slowly turning the tube round, and to avoid commencing to bend until the glass is quite soft, otherwise the tube will almost certainly break. The black from the flame will easily wipe off. Lay the bent tube on some non-conducting surface to cool slowly.

§ 9.—Piercing Holes in Corks.

This is best done with borers consisting of tubes of brass or tinned iron. The former are to be had of the instrument makers, in sets of different sizes sliding into each other. The tin tubes can be made by any tinsmith, and should have a cross-piece as a handle across one end.

§ 10.—Blackening Brass Surfaces.

Dissolve a drachm of bichloride of platinum in one ounce or one and a half ounce of water, and add a grain of nitrate of silver. Clean and polish the brass surface, warm it, and apply the solution with a small tuft of cotton. Rub till dry, and then finish off with a little dust of graphite, avoiding to put on any polish, which would convert the surface into a reflecting one, and enable it, though black, to send back white light.

Brass surfaces are cleaned for these purposes, either by rubbing with sand and polishing powder, or by applying nitric acid. The fumes that rise should be carefully avoided, and the acid be only left on till a bright surface is obtained.

INDEX.

M.

N.

O.

P.

R.

THE PHILADELPHIA PHOTOGRAPHER,

A Monthly Journal devoted to Photography.

Edited by EDWARD L. WILSON.

The SIXTH VOLUME of this MAGAZINE will begin with the January, 1869, issue.

Grateful for the many expressions of approval received from their subscribers in the past, and encouraged by their kind wishes for the future, the publishers respectfully beg you to give attention to the following

PROSPECTUS FOR 1869.

The Subscription Price will be, as heretofore, FIVE DOLLARS a year; $2 50 for six months, in advance. Postage payable at the office where received. SAMPLE COPIES mailed, postpaid, on receipt of Fifty Cents.

Mr. M. CAREY LEA will continue to contribute a monthly article, and his valuable summary. The interesting *German Correspondence* of Dr. HERMAN VOGEL will be continued. Prof. JOHN TOWLER will contribute to this Journal only. G. WHARTON SIMPSON, A. M., will contribute Practical Notes, monthly. Prof. HENRY MORTON, Ph. D., Rev. H. J. MORTON, D. D., Dr. E. LIESEGANG, the Editor, and other practical photographers contribute regularly.

The series of articles on *Art Principles applicable to Photography*, by the Editor, will be continued, amply illustrated by photographs, drawings, and lithographs, and prove a great help to photographers.

Still greater care will be exercised in future in the selection of the Photographic Studies that accompany each monthly issue. It is the hope and intention of the Editor *to make each picture teach a practical lesson.* Work by the best artists will be sought at home and abroad. Specimens may be expected during the year from M. ADAM SALOMON, Mr. H. P. ROBINSON, Mr. CHAS. REUTLINGER (the latter in January), the $50 prize negatives, and other superior pictures. No pains, no expense shall be spared to make the PHILADELPHIA PHOTOGRAPHER the cheapest and best Photographic Journal in the world for the live photographer to subscribe for.

The only journal in America in sympathy with the working photographer!

WHY YOU SHOULD TAKE IT.

1. No photographer can afford to do business without a journal to aid him in his work, and to inform him as to what is going on elsewhere.
2. *The Philadelphia Photographer* is the only *live, wide-awake* photographic newspaper in the country, and gives the freshest and best information pertaining to the art from all parts of the world.
3. Its editor and staff of contributors are practical workers in photography, and *it is devoted solely to the interests and wants of those who practise photography for a livelihood.* It independently takes sides against all who would impose upon its subscribers, its chief aim being to lighten their troubles and increase their skill and knowledge.
4. *Every number contains a large photographic specimen* by some leading home or foreign artist, giving its subscribers an opportunity of possessing and studying the work of their most skilful colaborers—*an advantage which cannot be overrated.*

In view of this promise, we look to our friends for their aid in increasing our circulation, and, as an additional inducement, offer to those disposed to raise clubs the following

PREMIUMS:

For five new subscribers for a year and $25, an additional copy to the getter-up of the club; $5 worth of Photographic books, or one of Braun's large panoramic Carbon prints, worth $5.

For five new subscribers for a half year and $12 50, an additional copy for the same time, $2 50 in books, or one of Braun's Carbon reproductions, worth $2 50.

For three new subscribers and $15, a copy of "Lea's Manual of Photography;" "The Silver Sunbeam," and "Photographic Mosaics" for 1866, 1867, 1868, or 1869; $3 worth of books, or one of Braun's smaller Carbon views, worth $3.

For two new subscribers and $10, "Leaf Prints," and "Mosaics" for 1866, 1867, or 1868; or $2 worth of books of any kind.

For one new subscriber, "Newman's Manual of Harmonious Coloring" (cloth), "Photographic Mosaics" for two years, or $1 worth of books.

Work hard and double our circulation. Parties desiring other Premiums, or special arrangements for agencies, will please address the publishers.

For advertising rates see 3d page of cover of each issue.

BENERMAN & WILSON, Publishers,

Office, Southwest corner Seventh and Cherry Streets (Sherman's Building),

PHILADELPHIA.

See further advertisements herein, in Wilson's American Carbon Manual, and the Photographic Journals of America.

Match it!! Give it a Trial.

MOUNTFORT'S
SELF-DRYING
CRYSTAL VARNISH.

Now used exclusively by the most eminent Photographers in this country. It contains ingredients never before used in Varnishes, and possesses the following merits over every other brand :—

This Varnish dries in a few seconds *without heat* almost as hard as glass.

It is perfectly transparent, and does not diminish the intensity of the negatives.

Negatives can be printed from, in a few seconds after having been varnished.

☞ ***It will not adhere to the paper or become soft in printing.***

It never chills if the plate is dry. It is equally good for positives or negatives.

It gives a beautiful gloss and brilliancy to Ambrotypes and Melaineotypes, and will not crack or peel. It is used without heat, thereby saving the cost of burning alcohol.

Read what Photographers and Stockholders say of Mountfort's Crystal Varnish.

ABRAHAM BOGARDUS, of 363 Broadway, New York, says: "I have used a great many kinds of Photographic Varnish since I have been in business (now over fifteen years), but never have I found anything to come up to Mountfort's Crystal Varnish. It is truly a big thing. It dries quickly without the use of heat, is as smooth and as hard as the glass itself. It improves rather than diminishes the intensity of a Negative, and it acts like a charm upon Porcelain, Iron Plates, and other small pictures. In fact, it is perfect in every respect, and I will use none other as long as I can get the true and genuine Mountfort's Crystal Varnish."

CHARLES H. WILLIAMSON, of No. 110 Fulton Street, Brooklyn, N. Y., says: "I do not know how we could well get along without Mountfort's Crystal Varnish. It has got to be as necessary to have it for preserving good Negatives, as it is to have good lights and chemicals to produce them; and it is so handy—requiring no heat in drying, it thereby does away with the old flaring Alcohol Lamp, and saves the cost of the Varnish by requiring no Alcohol. I consider it one of the greatest improvements, in the manufacturing departments of Photography, of the age."

JOSEPH THWAITES, of 687 Broadway, N. Y., says: "Please send me half a dozen bottles Crystal Varnish. I sent to a Stock House, as I had not time to send down to you, and they sent me a bottle of Varnish put up in some such style as Mountfort's Crystal Varnish. I paid no attention to it when it came in the Gallery, and my operator went on using it. It has ruined over five hundred dollars' worth of work. It is well that I saw the bottle as I did, or I would have been deeper into it.

"I have used your Crystal Varnish ever since you have made it, and I have never had the least trouble with it, and I never want any other but yours. The man that will sell an imitation is as mean as the man who manufactures it. Yours, truly, JOSEPH THWAITES."

A. S. ROBBINS, of Cleveland, Ohio, writes: "I am very sorry you did not send the Varnish along, as every man who has had any of it wants more for himself and friends. One man took all we had left before we wrote. Please send one gross along by U. S. Express as quick as possible,
And oblige, A. S. ROBBINS."

H. A. BALCH, of Memphis, Tennessee, writes: "I have used and sold a great many bottles of your very excellent Varnish. I consider it the best made, and shall recommend it to all my customers.
I remain, yours, respectfully, H. A. BALCH."

"June 5th, 1868.

"As I am only an amateur Photographer, my praise is worth little, compared with the opinions you so often receive from the 'trade,' but you may be glad to know that I have found your Varnish the *very best* of a dozen kinds I have tried, and the *only one* perfectly satisfactory.
"BEVERLY WRIGHT, Beverly, Mass."

"June 10th, 1868.

"I cannot use any other Varnish but yours. I would rather put my negatives away unvarnished than to use any other. I cannot depend upon any but your Crystal Varnish. My negatives are too valuable to be trifled with. CHARLES WORINS, 186 Bowery, N. Y."

"June 20th, 1868.

"Your Varnish is all you claim for it. It gives my customers better satisfaction than any other varnish made. FRED. F. HALE, Portland, Maine."

"August 5th, 1868.

"There is no use, I cannot use any other varnish but Mountfort's Crystal Varnish. Messrs. ——— on Broadway, N. Y., persuaded me to take a quart bottle of their varnish. I tried to use it, but it is impossible for me to make good work with it—in fact, I have tried all the different varnishes, and *there is none to compare with your Crystal Varnish.* You are at liberty to use my name at any and all times in commendation of your excellent varnish. I. P. DOREMUS, Paterson, N. J."

I have in my possession as many as fifty more testimonials from the most prominent Photographers and Stockdealers in the country. Had I the space to print them, I would do so. Any person who wishes can see them at my office.

CAUTION.

Ask for MOUNTFORT'S CRYSTAL VARNISH, and do not take it unless my SIGNATURE is upon the label. Imitators dare not counterfeit that. They have imitated my bottle as near as they dare. They have also copied the label as close as they dare. All that keeps them from counterfeiting my name is, they are afraid of the law.

All my Crystal Varnish is put up in bottles with my name blown in them, and my signature is upon every label. **TAKE NONE OTHER.** For sale by all Stockdealers. None genuine unless signed

WILLIAM H. MOUNTFORT,

1 Chambers Street, New York.

PHOTOGRAPHIC CHEMICALS.

The attention of Amateurs, Artists, and the Trade is called to

THE "SCALE" TRADE MARK CHEMICALS.

These Chemicals are manufactured especially for use in Photography, and in the hands of careful manipulators produce effects which cannot be excelled. They are equal in every respect to the finest imported chemicals, while they are much lower in price.

All goods of our manufacture bear our distinctive trade mark on every label.

In addition to our regular list of Photographic Chemicals, we offer our

CHALLENGE VARNISH,

which combines all the qualities of a good negative and positive varnish, and is invariably conceded by those who have given it a fair trial, to be "THE BEST."

MARDOCK'S COLLODION

is unsurpassed for rapidity, sensitiveness, clearness in working, and requisite detail.

Catalogues of our Chemicals sent to any address.

MARDOCK & WALLACE,

PHOTOGRAPHIC CHEMISTS,

417 Broome St., New York.

American Artists' Association,

FOR THE

Painting of Photographs,

MINIATURES ON PORCELAIN, ETC.

FOR THE TRADE.

A UNION OF THE BEST ARTISTS IN PHILADELPHIA.

It is well understood by persons familiar with art, that the proper painting of a Photograph can only be done by accomplished artists, who, being able to draw for themselves, can make those corrections in a picture which are demanded by the faults of expression, or other defects, which are often too prominent in a mere photograph.

The object of this Association is to enable Photographers all over the country to secure a talent in the finish of their pictures which they could not otherwise obtain, and which would surely increase their trade for fine work.

Satisfaction is guaranteed in every case, and parties may feel assured of the work being done as well as if under their own supervision.

PORCELAIN PICTURES, PHOTO MINIATURES, ETC.

Many refuse to make these beautiful pictures on account of the trouble they meet with in them, and having no one to color them. This Association pays especial attention to this class of work, both colored and uncolored. The plain work is made on an albumen surface by an unfading process peculiar to this Association.

DIRECTIONS.

For Porcelain Work, send a negative of proper character, with full directions as to dress, complexion, eyes, &c., and invariably a sample of the hair. Pack the negatives with great care in wooden boxes, and prepay express.

For other work, the paper prints must be sent, or in case of Solar Printing, the negatives. Also, explicit directions for coloring. When the prints are copies from other pictures, the original should in all cases be sent. The SCHEDULE OF PRICES has been arranged with a view to allow a liberal margin of profit to all in the trade, whose customers can appreciate the work of real artists. A copy will be mailed on application.

Address, American Artists' Association,

WILSON, HOOD & CO., Business Managers,

822 Arch Street, Philadelphia.

ZENTMAYER LENS,

For Views and Copying.

Although only the short period of two years has elapsed since this lens was first introduced it has already become widely popular, and its excellent qualifications well established, which are pre-eminently as follows :—

Width of visual angle, ranging from 80° to 90°; depth of focus; extreme sharpness over the whole field; true perspective; freedom from all distortion in copying; portability and cheapness.

Each mounting is provided with a revolving Diaphragm, containing the stops of the different combinations for which they are designed. The larger ones are provided with an internal shutter for making and closing the exposure.

No.	Focus		Plate		Price
No. 1,	2½	inch focus,	3 x 3	plate,	$20 00
" 2,	3½	"	4 x 5	"	25 00
" 3,	5½	"	6½ x 8½	"	30 00
" 4,	8	"	10 x 12	"	42 00
" 5,	12	"	14 x 17	"	60 00
" 6,	18	"	20 x 24	"	90 00

No. 1 and No. 2 combined,	$33 00
" 2 " " 3 "	40 00
" 3 " " 4 "	55 00
" 4 " " 5 "	75 00
" 5 " " 6 "	110 00
" 1, 2, and 3 "	48 00
" 3, 4, and 5 "	88 00

No. 3, with large mounting to combine with No. 4 and No. 5, $35.

No. 1 and No. 2, specially adapted for Stereoscopic Views, are furnished in matched pairs. No. 1, single, not to combine with other sizes, $36 a pair. This size is constructed for special cases where the largest possible angle is required.

Lenses and mountings to form all six combinations, from 2½ to 18 inches, $173.

Zentmayer's Stereoscopic Outfits.

Knowing that many Photographers are retarded from making stereoscopic views on account of the high prices heretofore charged for lenses, thus depriving them of what might be a source of considerable revenue, I take pleasure in announcing that in order to obviate this, I offer a **Stereoscopic Outfit**, consisting of

1 pair 3½ Focus Lenses, best quality, in mounting not to combine with other sizes.
1 American Optical Co.'s Stereoscopic Box, 4 x 7, made especially for these lenses.
1 Folding Tripod for box.
1 7 x 10 Tight Covered India Rubber Bath and Dipper.
2 4 x 7 American Optical Co.'s Printing Frames.

The whole, except the tripod and printing frames, contained in a neat box, with handle, convenient for carriage, and weighing only 11 pounds.

PRICE, COMPLETE, $60.

Nothing ever offered can compete with this outfit either in *price*, *quality*, or *convenience*.
This should enable every photographer to make first-class stereoscopic work.
Orders by mail will receive prompt attention. For further particulars, please address

JOSEPH ZENTMAYER,
147 South Fourth Street, Philadelphia.

THE DALLMEYER LENSES.

For Price List and full Description of the various Styles and Sizes of these Valuable Lenses, apply to

E. & H. T. ANTHONY & CO.,

501 BROADWAY, NEW YORK,

SOLE AGENTS FOR THE UNITED STATES.

☞ The splendid Stereoscopic Views of Wm. England and G. W. Wilson are made with Dallmeyer Lenses. All Stereoscopic Photographers should have them.

☞ The beautiful Cabinet Card Pictures of the White Fawn, by Gurney & Son, are made by a 3 B Patent Quick-Acting Dallmeyer.

We subjoin a few extracts from the numerous unsolicited testimonials we have received from our customers.

Mr. A. D. Deming, Oil City, Penn., writes:—"The Dallmeyer Tube continues to give entire satisfaction. Scarcely a customer that has Cartes de Visite taken with it but what duplicates the order at once on receiving the first lot. The standard of my work has been improved very much by having such a good instrument to operate with, which of course in due time will increase my business in the same proportion."

From S. B. Russell, Navasota, Texas, July 17, 1868.—"My work is increasing double since I received the Dallmeyer Lens. It is the cheapest of all instruments. One artist has tried mine (No. 2 B), and is determined to have one at once."

From J. F. Ryder, Cleveland, O., May 14, 1868.—"I have to say in favor of the Dallmeyer Lens that it improves on acquaintance. The longer I have it, the more I prize it."

From G. D. Wakely, Washington, D. C., April 28, 1868.—"The pair of Dallmeyer Lenses you sent me are very fine. They are the most useful instruments I have."

From H. Rocher, Chicago, February 5, 1868.—"I have used since July, '66, a Dallmeyer No. 2 B, and am perfectly delighted with the beauty of work made with it. Nothing satisfies me but the very best. I find this to be the best principle, for I command here the highest prices for my work."

From J. S. Broadway, Charlotte, N. C., Sept. 8, 1868.—"I like the Dallmeyer Lenses very much. They are increasing my business considerably. I think by their use I can increase my business double."

From Franklin White, Lancaster, N. H., Sept. 8, 1868.—"The 3 D Dallmeyer which you sent me is a splendid one. It is a pleasure to use it."

The truest ECONOMY is to use the best lenses.

www.ingramcontent.com/pod-product-compliance
Lightning Source LLC
LaVergne TN
LVHW010201110826
845151LV00002B/575
9781425535322